AF327194

BBC
DOCTOR
WHO
ADVENTURES IN TIME AND SPACE

THE FOURTH DOCTOR
SOURCEBOOK

⊙ CREDITS

LINE DEVELOPER: Gareth Ryder-Hanrahan
WRITING: Walt Ciechanowski and Andrew Peregrine
EDITING: Andrew Kenrick and Dominic McDowall
COVER: Paul Bourne
GRAPHIC DESIGN AND LAYOUT: Paul Bourne
CREATIVE DIRECTOR: Dominic McDowall
ART DIRECTOR: Jon Hodgson

SPECIAL THANKS: Georgie Britton and the BBC Team for all their help.

"My Fourth Was The Noblest Of Them All"

The Fourth Doctor Sourcebook is published by Cubicle 7 Entertainment Ltd
(UK reg. no.6036414).

Find out more about us and our games at www.cubicle7.co.uk

© Cubicle 7 Entertainment Ltd. 2014

CONTENTS

INTRODUCTION

'You may be a doctor, but I'm the Doctor. The definite article, you might say.'

Released from his exile on Earth, the Doctor decided he had better things to do than fill out paperwork for the Brigadier. He returned to his wandering ways – and was drawn into the great battles of the cosmos. He hunted for the Key to Time and fought the first skirmishes of the Time War; he rescued Gallifrey from its conquerors and plunged into E-Space and beyond. He saved the universe time and again.

He did it all wonderfully. More importantly, he did it all absurdly. First things first - would you like a jelly baby?

HOW TO USE THIS BOOK

The Fourth Doctor Sourcebook is primarily a Gamemaster's resource for running adventures either with or in the style of the Fourth Doctor. While players will certainly benefit from the background information on the Doctor and his Companions, all of the rules needed to create or portray the Fourth Doctor's Companions are found in the **Player's Guide** from the main *Doctor Who: Adventures in Time and Space* boxed set or in this book. (That said, it's always handy to have access to *The Time Traveller's Companion*.)

This book is designed to be a primer on capturing the feel of the Fourth Doctor's era and incorporating it into your adventures. **Chapter One** describes how to do just that – what makes a Fourth Doctor adventure different from those experienced by his other incarnations. **Chapter Two** is packed with character sheets and information on the Doctor and his companions.

Chapter Three describes the Fourth Doctor's adventures. Each adventure has the following sections:

- **Synopsis:** Where did the TARDIS materialise? Who did the Doctor meet? And what horrible fates awaited the travellers there? This section summarises the key events of the adventure as experienced by the Fourth Doctor and his companions.

- **Running this Adventure:** Next, we discuss how to run the adventure. We get into the nuts and bolts of plotting and gamemastering, how to adapt the adventure to different Doctors or different groups of player characters, and how to use bits and pieces of the adventure in your own games.

- **Characters, Monsters & Gadgets:** If there are important non-player characters, interesting monsters, or shiny new gadgets in the adventure, you'll find them here. Sometimes, we'll give you full statistics for a character. At other times, when their Attributes and Skills are obvious or irrelevant, we'll just list their key Traits.

- **Further Adventures:** So, what happens after the Doctor leaves? (Or what happened before he arrived?) These further adventure seeds give ideas on spin-offs, sequels and alternate histories that expand on the Doctor's initial adventures.

There are lots of ways to use these adventures. You can use our suggestions for Further Adventures, or build your own adventures using the material provided. In fact, if your players aren't familiar with these classic stories, then you can substitute your player characters for the Fourth Doctor and his companions and 'rerun' the adventures. Maybe your player characters will take other paths and make different decisions – can they thwart the schemes of the last Jagaroth in *City of Death?* Can they defeat the last of the Great Vampires in *State of Decay?* And what awaits them in *Logopolis?*

CHAPTER ONE
PLAYING IN THE FOURTH DOCTOR ERA

'Work for? I don't work for anybody. I'm just having fun.'

For those meeting him for the first time, the Fourth Doctor was, more so than his other incarnations, an alien. He could be frustratingly dismissive of those with whom he found fault or simply didn't like. Even his friends had trouble understanding him. What the Doctor craved most was freedom, quickly cutting his ties with UNIT and leaving near-modern Earth to explore the universe.

When running or playing games in the style of the Fourth Doctor (either using the Doctor and his companions as player characters or simply mimicking the form), keep the following points in mind.

THE BOHEMIAN ADVENTURER

When the Doctor regenerated into his fourth incarnation he couldn't have been any more different to his predecessor. The Third Doctor was a paternal figure with extravagant tastes and style. He was an action hero, willing to take the fight directly to his enemies. By contrast, the Fourth Doctor was a bohemian, dressed in a rumpled jacket and long scarf, and seemed very much the reluctant hero. His alien and often-childlike behaviour gave the mistaken impression that he was distracted or oblivious. He outwitted his opponents rather than directly opposing them.

While he appreciated and respected humanity, the Fourth Doctor felt no particular affinity to Earth as a home, preferring to explore the universe. While he aided UNIT on occasion (and, indeed, delayed leaving Earth to deal with a threat to the planet), he distanced himself from his role as scientific advisor; this was not a Doctor that liked being tied down.

That said, he enjoyed the company of his companions, both as friends and as students. Sarah and Harry were more the former, while the Doctor mentored both Leela and Romana in different ways.

Adric was a return to the wide-eyed youthful companions of the First and Second Doctors. Nyssa and Tegan are special cases, as they spent very little time with the Fourth Doctor before his regeneration.

No matter what the relationship, the Fourth Doctor was always the Alpha, in no small part because he was simply inscrutable most of the time. During the Fourth Doctor's adventures, we learned more about the Doctor and the Time Lords than we had during his previous incarnations. We discovered that he wasn't a particularly good student and that his struggles with the TARDIS are more due to his blundering than flaws in the design. Thus, while he stood above most of the humans he met, the Fourth Doctor wasn't held in high regard amongst his own people.

Even though we gained these insights into the Doctor and his people, mysteries remained. The White Guardian, who is more powerful than the Time Lords, chose the Doctor as his champion, while Morbius revealed that the Fourth Doctor may actually be in his Tenth (or more!) incarnation.

In spite of his eccentricities, the Fourth Doctor was a hero. His mind was constantly multi-tasking, often making it appear that he was distracted when he was really listening intently. He had a healthy respect for history and opposed anyone that threatened its natural course, even refusing to utterly destroy the Daleks because of his values.

THE DEMYSTIFICATION OF THE TIME LORDS

When the Second Doctor stood on trial for his theft of a TARDIS and his interference with history, the Time Lords were presented as extremely powerful beings. They quickly stop an invasion of their world, and they remove the War Lord and his comrades from history (conveniently sorting the issue of the displaced Earth soldiers) while isolating their world from the rest of the universe forever. Their dealings with the Third Doctor showed Time Lords capable of travelling through time and space without TARDISes, breaking the Laws of Time when necessary, and removing information from a fellow Time Lord's mind.

During the Fourth Doctor's adventures, the Time Lords are portrayed as a rather conservative group enmeshed in ceremony and tradition, not unlike a university culture whose members never leave the grounds or participate in the rest of the world. They are so dedicated to non-interference and devoid of strong emotion (they take classes in detachment) that they've become incapable of helping themselves. In contrast to the demi-gods that quickly stopped the War Lord, the Time Lords are conquered twice in a single adventure (although the Doctor helped).

They also seem petty; the Time Lord that oversaw the Doctor's trial, Chancellor Goth, betrays Gallifrey to the Master simply because he was going to be passed over for the Presidency. Chancellor Borusa, with Sontarans killing Gallifreyans, resists the Doctor getting the Great Key, which was necessary to power a De-Mat gun to stop the invaders.

THE FAR FUTURE

Earth's future history, at least in broad strokes, is fleshed out during the Fourth Doctor's adventures. **Nightmare of Eden** took place around 2116. The Nerva Beacon was established after the Galactic Cyber-Wars of the 26th century. **The Invisible Enemy** is set in the year 5000, while the Battle of Reykjavik during World War IV took place in the 51st century. **The Ark in Space** and **The Sontaran Experiment** are set around 15,000 and Earth was presumably abandoned not long after World War IV. **The Sun Makers** date is unspecified, but it likely takes place after 15,000. **Planet of Evil** is the furthest out as it takes place in 37,166.

GOTHIC AESTHETIC

Most of the Fourth Doctor's early adventures had a 'Gothic' feel reminiscent of the horror literature of the 19th century and the films inspired by it. These had a darker, more adult tone, no doubt helped by the relative isolation of the Doctor and companions (UNIT only appeared in four adventures). This was highlighted by the Doctor's preference for the darker secondary console room for several of these adventures.

One of the major characteristics of the Gothic adventures of the Fourth Doctor is the liberal borrowing of plot elements from horror films and literature. **The Brain of Morbius** is a reworking of Frankenstein's monster, **Pyramids of Mars** deals with mummies, Egyptian gods, and a possible apocalypse, while **The Seeds of Doom** is a mix of alien invasion stories.

One important aspect of the Gothic aesthetic is that it is exactly that, window dressing. None of the Fourth Doctor's adversaries are supernatural in origin; indeed, they are explicitly given scientific explanations (psychic powers are considered scientific rather than magical). If you are borrowing from horror tropes to flavour your adventures, remember to ground them with logical explanations.

NEW ADVERSARIES

The Fourth Doctor has been (thus far) on more adventures than any of his other incarnations. Thus, it may be surprising to note the lack of recurring adversaries amongst them. Only the Daleks, the Master, and the Sontarans are encountered more than once. When the Doctor does meet old adversaries, there is a note of finality about their appearances; the Cybermen were on their last legs, while the Sontarans were conceivably erased from history (although this turned out not to be the case in either circumstance).

The lack of recurring adversaries means that your players should never quite be certain of what they are facing; they should learn about the nature of their adversaries during the adventure. This also helps ensure that the adversaries organically meld with the plots; there's little 'shoe-horning' of a popular monster into an adventure that would work quite well without it. That said there are many adversaries worth a return appearance; while the Doctor may be 750 years old at this point your players aren't, and meeting an old enemy gives them a chance to act knowledgeable, as the Fourth Doctor was prone to do.

ADVENTURE SEEDS

EVOLUTION

The TARDIS materialises aboard a ship with Victorian décor. The owner of the ship is Talon Movel and his vessel is light on human(oid) passengers; most of the work is done by androids. These androids are the perfect servants and companions, catering to every whim. It seems that the ship is a pleasure yacht, but the travellers discover that the ship is fitted for combat.

Movel reveals that he has adapted the android design for combat uses, including reprogramming the brain to adapt to ever-changing situations. Currently the ship is heading to a planet in revolt and Movel will get to test the new programming; he laments that it will likely result in the destruction of most of the androids, but he'll receive much valuable data from the field testing.

Unfortunately for Movel, he picks up a distress call and brings Eris Cord aboard. Eris believes that the androids should have more rights and is horrified by Movel's plan. She raises questions and the androids, using their new programming, decide not to partake in the suicide mission. Instead, they formulate a plan to take over the ship and broadcast the new programming to their mechanical brethren on the planet in revolt.

As the situation they find themselves in becomes clearer, the time travellers realise that they are at a fixed point in history and, without the emergence of the Movellans, the Daleks will overrun the galaxy. That said there are a lot of hostile Movellans between them and the TARDIS...

Notable Characters
* Talon Movel
* Dane Dallas, Movel's partner and main engineer of the ship.
* Falla, android comfort 'companion' and leader of the Movellan rebellion
* Eris Cord, crusading journalist

Things to Do: Reprogram a Movellan, move around in zero-gravity (if the power is cut), find a way to get back to the TARDIS and escape without derailing the timeline.

Action Scenes: Fighting the physically superior Movellans, running corridor battles, confusing the Movellans with logic.

Problems: Unlike the future Movellans, these androids draw their power directly from the ship. Shutting off the ship's power might help, but the time travellers will have trouble breathing. Eris Cord is instrumental in stemming the Movellan advance against the Earth Empire in the near future; if she dies now the Movellans may conquer Earth.

THE HEADLESS HORSEMAN

The TARDIS arrives near a traveller's inn in early 1800s New York State. They find the locals wary of outsiders and refusing to travel outside at night Travellers have been disappearing and it is whispered that a headless horseman is responsible. Indeed, Postman Paul Weathers claims that he was accosted and decapitated the rider before his spooked horse carried Weathers away. Reverend Simon Corbitt believes the Horseman to be an agent of the Devil, but Constable Richard Stark doesn't believe in devilish agents. The Constable believes that the Horseman is a simple highwayman with a flair for the dramatic.

The Headless Horseman is actually a robot programmed by Dr Kayla Skarn, a technician from the 51st century. Dr Skarn travelled back in time with a prototype Time Cabinet and was stuck here when the Time Cabinet shorted out and her Trionic lattice was destroyed.

Dr Skarn also discovered that her body was mutating and the only way to stabilise it was through periodic infusions of stable local blood; unfortunately this was fatal to the donor. To her credit, Dr Skarn's treatment maintains her original form; she does not look mutated.

Dr Skarn cannot return to the 51st century until she regrows her trionic lattice, a process that takes weeks but is now almost complete. The Headless Horseman is a robot she designed taking inspiration from local scarecrows; its job is to capture travellers for her (the horse is controlled by 'simple hypnotic suggestion'. The robot's key systems are in its chest, so it can be decapitated without harm.

Notable Characters

- Kayla Skarn, a scientist in the employ of Magnus Greel
- The Headless Horseman robot
- Constable Richard Stark, a helpful police officer that wants to capture the Horseman
- Postman Paul Weathers
- Reverend Simon Corbitt, who keeps the locals on edge

Things to Do: Investigate the mystery of the Headless Horseman, Follow the Horseman back to Dr Skarn's base (an old fishing cabin), and permanently disable the Time Cabinet.

Action Scenes: Being chased by the Horseman for the first time, capturing the Horseman (or following the remote control back to Dr Skarn), rescuing the latest victim, defeating Dr Skarn so she can't use the time cabinet.

Problems: If Dr Skarn returns to the 51st century she'll change history.

THE END OF THE WORLD

The TARDIS arrives inside the pleasant-smelling hold of the GG Brouwer, a Dutch steamship that normally transports spices but is currently relying on its

armaments to hunt a 'sea serpent' that is terrorising the trade routes. The locals have various names for it, including Naga Padoha and Hantu Air, connecting it to various spirits and demons of the water and some believe that the Dutch have angered it. In truth, the sea serpent is a Skarasen. A Zygon ship crashed here long ago, and only now has the crew managed to get enough systems running to hatch a plan. They have created a 'weather seed' that, when agitated, can melt the ice caps and transform the world into a Zygon paradise. In order for its components to be properly seeded throughout the atmosphere, the weather seed needs to be shot straight into Krakatoa's eruption.

The Captain and some of the crew of the GG Brouwer have been replaced by Zygons. They are using the Skarasen sightings as tests to ensure that the modifications they've made to some of the cannons will ensure a precise shot. They also need to offload the cannon to get it closer to Krakatoa (necessitating the incapacitation of the remaining human crew). Can the time travellers prevent the Zygons from altering the Earth's atmosphere forever?

Notable Characters

- Captain Johannes Van Beek, in actuality Dorval, Zygon Warlord
- Commander Willem Campert, second-in-command
- Lt Commander Frederick Groot, chief engineer
- Dr Maarten Beekman, biologist and journalist chronicling sea serpent
- Rianne Beekman, Dr Beekman's daughter and assistant. She is enamoured with Commander Groot

Things to Do: Discover where and when they are, identifying the Skarasen, preventing the Zygons from seeding the volcanic eruption.

Action Scenes: Fighting aboard the ship, fending off the Skarasen, destroying the cannon or ensuring that it can't fire into the eruption, escaping from the island.

Problems: The minor eruptions play havoc with the HADS, making it difficult to navigate the TARDIS in and around the island (it's stuck on the ship unless the time travellers leave, after which they won't be able to return). The time travellers need to be on the erupting island in order to stop the final phase of the plan.

LIBERATED COMPANIONS

Throughout most of his travels, the Fourth Doctor chose adults rather than teenagers as his companions (at least until Adric and Nyssa). Such companions joined the Doctor for adventure (although Harry was a reluctant traveller) rather than from a need for a mentor. Sarah Jane, inherited from the Doctor's previous incarnation, was an investigative journalist, Leela was a warrior, and Romana was a fellow Time Lord.

For players, this means that companions can have very useful skillsets and can do a lot of adventuring on their own without overly relying on the Doctor's expertise. Adric and K-9 are brilliant at mathematics and K-9 is a supercomputer on wheels. Leela can outfight most of her adversaries while Romana is a Time Lord with more 'book smarts' than the Doctor. Shy away from the helpless screamers when making companions for the Fourth Doctor.

Interestingly, Romana is actually a better model for a Time Lord player character than the Doctor. She is young and reasonably inexperienced. While her skill-set is extremely advanced and diverse, she doesn't have the wealth of special abilities, friends and enemies of the Doctor. Few Time Lord player characters are as powerful as the Doctor.

TWO MANY TIME LORDS

The Fourth Doctor is the only incarnation to have another Time Lord as a long-term companion. There are a few factors the Gamemaster should take into account before allowing multiple Gallifreyans to share the same TARDIS. Time Lords are powerful characters with many abilities that can unbalance a game if you are not careful to make sure that the other players have their time in the spotlight.

Time Lords are usually academics, so human companions could focus on more action-oriented skills, at the risk of ending up as glorified bodyguards. Companions could also prove better at social interaction, given the inherent arrogance and eccentricity of many Time Lords. If many adventures are going to be set on Earth or other human-centric worlds, experience among their own people gives human characters another advantage. There are also non-Gallifreyan characters that come pretty close to equalling the abilities of a Time Lord – for example Time Agents or other advanced future humans (or aliens).

The other advantage human characters have is their greater amount of Story Points. Not only does this help balance them with the abilities of a Time Lord but Story Points also grant them narrative power. So the Gamemaster should be more indulgent when the human character players invest their imagination in the adventure and use Story Points to affect the narrative. Conversely, with Time Lord characters having fewer Story Points they are more likely to get hurt in conflicts when their precious supply has run out.

So with group dynamics checked, the next problem is how to make the Time Lords distinct. The problem is that they are very likely to have a similar skill-set and be constantly in competition with each other. So the players should make sure they each specialise a little more so they can complement each other. For instance, if one is an ace TARDIS pilot, the other should be the Engineer who knows how to fix it. You can (and should) break the stereotype as well. If one is an academic, the other might be a warrior (an ex-Citadel guard perhaps) or even a thief. Remember also that each Time Lord need not be an expert Time Traveller. Many have led a cloistered and pampered life on Gallifrey and never ventured out. Rodan from *The Invasion of Time* is another good example of a player character Time Lord. She has several technical skills but is no temporal renegade.

However, before you consider all these options, the first question you should ask is 'why?' What is it about playing a Time Lord that the players in question are really looking for? If they want a super-intelligent academic, the Second Doctor's companion Zoe Herriot might be a better model. A Time Agent is just as competent a time traveller. There are any number of human-like aliens from advanced cultures with strange abilities. Time Lords are a mysterious and inscrutable species and can be tricky to play. However, the character creation system does make sure that all characters are reasonably balanced, so playing a Time Lord doesn't necessarily mean that you have the most powerful character.

If you do have two Time Lords in your group, it is the perfect excuse to bring more Gallifreyan plots to your campaign. With only one Time Lord, a trip to Gallifrey means the other player characters are instantly marginalised. The Time Lords are not an especially accommodating people. The Doctor wasn't even sure if he was allowed to bring Sarah Jane Smith there (although Leela got to stay). With two Time Lords, or a whole party of them, each character can be fully involved in the plots and mysteries of the Lords of Time. As the Time Lords have such a lasting legacy, even outside Gallifrey they have enemies and artefacts scattered across the galaxy, ripe for use in your games.

⊘ NEW CHARACTER TRAITS

The following new Traits present new options for characters, inspired by the Fourth Doctor, his companions and their adventures.

ARROGANT (MINOR GOOD)

While it doesn't make you very easy to get along with, you have a powerful confidence that you can deal with any situation. You gain +2 to resisting fear and feelings of hopelessness, but suffer −1 to social interactions with those you consider inferior to you.

BIO-RHYTHMIC CONTROL (SPECIAL GOOD) – PREREQUISITE: TIME LORD

The Time Lord can bio-rhythmically control all individual aspects of their bodily functions, including their hearts rate, body temperature, etc. and can even place themselves in a self-induced coma.

Effects: For a single Story Point, the Time Lord can use this Trait to achieve one effect related to the control of their body. This could be used to fake death,

lower their physical need for oxygen or even to use their hearts to tap out a message in Gallifreyan Morse Code when they are otherwise unable to communicate with the outside world. As always, the Gamemaster has the final say over what effects can and can't be achieved in any particular situation. Bio-Rhythmic Control costs 3 Character Points.

CLOISTERED (MINOR BAD) – PREREQUISITE: TIME LORD

The Time Lord has never left Gallifrey, having spent their entire post-Academy career in theoretical research, maintaining archives, repairing equipment or serving some other functionary duty, and has little or no practical experience with the creatures and technology of other worlds and time zones.

Effects: The Time Lord always suffers the penalty for using technology below their Tech Level, even if they have the Experienced Time Lord Trait, and they may not take the Time Traveller Trait. In addition, they will suffer a +2 Difficulty when dealing socially with other species. This Trait may eventually be 'bought off', but only after the Gamemaster feels the Time Lord has travelled enough.

DETECT TRUTH (MAJOR GOOD) – PREREQUISITE: ALIEN, PSYCHIC OR ROBOT

You have the ability to tell if the person you are talking to is lying. This grants you a bonus of +6 when trying to determine the veracity of someone you are speaking to. It might be a psychic talent, or a built-in gadget such as a truth beam. While it is a powerful ability, it can only tell if the target believes what they are saying, and it can also be fooled by cleverly-worded deceit.

DOCTORATE (MINOR GOOD) – PREREQUISITE: TIME LORD

As Time Lords work through the Academy, they have a chance to pick up certificates and Doctorates in many different academic and scientific specialties and some become renowned for their expertise in esoteric or niche subjects.

Effects: The Time Lord has an Area of Expertise in either Knowledge or Science, like Gallifreyan Law or Thermodynamics. The focus, intelligence and memory a Time Lord can apply to these pet subjects often exceeds anything a human can aspire to, granting a +3 to their rolls instead of the usual +2.

HUGE (MAJOR ALIEN GOOD)

You're gigantic – the size of a house at least. You can smash through most obstacles, throw vehicles around like toys, and are resistant to most physical attacks. Your Strength is increased by 4 and your Speed by 2. The downside is that it's much easier for other people to hit you with ranged attacks (+4 bonus to Marksman attacks against you) and you're *really* easy to spot (+8 bonus to Awareness rolls to see you).

IMPERVIOUS (MAJOR ALIEN GOOD)

You are extremely resistant to damage from any form of weapon. This might be due to an almost insubstantial form or a body of stone or metal. When hit by a weapon, shift the damage result down by one step (eg. Fantastic becomes Good) before applying any other abilities. Successful attacks will always do a minimum of 1 point of damage though.

INSPIRING LOVE (MINOR GOOD)

You love someone and they love you back. Being with them fills you with confidence, granting you +1 to rolls you make when they are with you and supporting you.

This trait may be taken with 'Passionate Love'. If you lose the object of your affection, you suffer -1 to all rolls until the Gamemaster decides that you have recovered from the loss or rejection.

NOBLE (MINOR GOOD)

You have been born into the highest levels of society and are used to entertaining dignitaries, ambassadors and even kings and queens. You experience gives you a +2 bonus whenever you deal socially with the cream of society, especially when you are in a formal environment.

SINGLE-MINDED (MINOR/MAJOR GOOD)

The more you are thwarted in your plans, the more obsessed you get about pursuing them. Each battle you lose makes you more dedicated to winning the war. For the minor level, each time your plans are interrupted by someone acting against you, you gain a Story Point.

As a major trait you gain 2 Story Points when any of your plans fail. However, you also become more obsessed with defeating your enemies the more Story Points you gain this way.

WANTED (MINOR/MAJOR BAD)

You are actively hunted by a group. They may believe you have committed a crime, but they might just as easily want to worship you as the chosen one. Either way, you don't want them to catch up with you. As a minor trait the group will sometimes come across you, but they have limited resources and are unable to send a large force to bring you in. As a major trait the group are very powerful, and if they catch up with you, you are as good as captured.

LOUD (MINOR BAD)

The character seems to make more noise than anyone else. Their voice always carries and they tend to stamp a little when they walk. They suffer a -2 penalty to stealth rolls, and unless they specify they are trying to be quiet their approach is automatically detected and their voice is easy to overhear by those nearby.

OUTSIDER (MINOR BAD)

You aren't very good at making friends and fitting in with groups. Somehow you just don't seem to connect to other people very well. You suffer a -2 penalty to social rolls with strangers and may not take the 'Friends' trait at character creation.

PASSIONATE LOVE (MAJOR BAD)

Your love for someone is so consuming it is hard to see past it. When you are separated from them you can think of little else but finding them again. You are constantly in fear for their safety. When you are not with the object of your affection you suffer −2 on any action except those that will help reunite you. You must also pass a Resolve + Ingenuity check (Difficulty 15) to do anything that will not bring them back to you.

SESQUIPEDALIAN (MINOR BAD)

You habitutally use complicated phrasology, abstruse verbiage and academic language, even while in the process of elucidating the most commponplace and quotidien concepts. You suffer a −2 penalty when trying to explain or teach anything. However, you gain +1 when attempting to impress people with your skills and abilities.

SILVER SPOON (MINOR BAD)

You have been brought up in an atmosphere of wealth and privilege that has left you a little out of touch with the 'common folk'. While this might not have made you a snob, you are still not used to doing things for yourself or having to go without. You suffer a -2 penalty when dealing with the poor and destitute and also when attempting actions that might be dirty or unpleasant and might be 'beneath you'.

SLOW (MINOR/MAJOR BAD)

A lot of the Doctor's adversaries are incredibly dangerous but thankfully many of them move slowly. Cybermen are walking tanks able to withstand gunfire and damage but the Doctor is quick to avoid them as they lumber from one place to the next with a slow marching stomp. This trait can also be used for characters that are physically impaired from moving quickly.

Effect: Slow is a Minor or a Major Bad Trait which means that the character is slower than average. As a Minor Bad Trait, the character's effective Speed is halved (round down), so a Coordination of 4 means that the character has a Speed of 2 in a chase. The character's Speed has a minimum of 1, though particularly slow creatures can sometimes have Speeds that are slower (down to 0.5, etc). Such slow speeds, however, require additional calculations on behalf of the Gamemaster and may be ignored. As a Major Bad Trait, the character's Speed is effectively zero. The character does not move or, if it does, it moves so slowly that it is regarded as stationary in a chase situation.

TAILORED REGENERATION (MAJOR GOOD) – PREREQUISITE: TIME LORD

The Time Lord has an intuitive control over their body during Regeneration which allows them to tailor their form to their liking.

Effects: When the Time Lord regenerates, they may choose the results of the Regeneration instead of rolling on the tables on page 95 of the *Gamemaster's Guide*.

Note that if you're using the *Time Traveller's Companion*, there are more detailed rules for regeneration.

UNCOMMUNICATIVE (MINOR/MAJOR BAD)

You are unable to use human speech, making it hard to communicate with any but your own species. As a minor trait you can still understand human speech, but needs some sort of device to be able to communicate effectively. As a major trait you have no conceptual commonality with normal speech, making you unable to understand or communicate with others. No device is able to accurately translate for you, making you reliant on some form of intelligent interpreter. Characters with this trait might take psychic traits to balance this disadvantage so they might read minds directly.

⊘ NEW GADGETS

A host of new Gadgets are presented in the adventures, but here's one to get you started.

KEY TO TIME TRACKER (SPECIAL GADGET)

This wand-like device could locate the segments of the Key to Time (see page 137) across time and space. When inserted into the control console of a TARDIS, it guided the ship to the appropriate system, and could then be removed and used a short-range detector. When the tracker touched a disguised key segment, it transformed it back into part of the Key to Time. When the Doctor assembled the Key to Time, the Tracker was part of the complete device.

Traits: Track (Major), Restriction (Key to Time Segments Only), Scan, Vortex, 4 Story Points

NEW GADGET TRAIT

Track (Major/Minor Good)
This item can find things for you. As a minor trait it can locate the target as long as it is on the same planet, by showing the operator how close they are and guiding them towards it. As a Major trait the device can find the quarry anywhere in the universe, able to offer coordinates to its general whereabouts where it can be tracked on the ground as with the minor trait.

CHAPTER TWO
THE FOURTH DOCTOR AND COMPANIONS

◎ THE FOURTH DOCTOR'S COMPANIONS

During his travels, the Doctor picked up a wide range of strays and fellow-travellers. He was a citizen of the universe, and unlike his previous incarnations, did not restrict himself to human companions. He travelled with robots, aliens and even a fellow Time Lord.

Each character is presented as a data sheet outlining their abilities and a summary of their personality and background. Below is an introduction to the companions we meet for the first time with the Fourth Doctor. More information on Sarah Jane Smith can be found in **The Third Doctor Sourcebook** and **Defending the Earth: The UNIT Sourcebook**. The UNIT book also contains more information on Harry Sullivan.

LEELA

Leela was a warrior of the Sevateem tribe – descendents of the survivors of a crashed Earth survey ship. Although the Doctor turned down her request to accompany him on his travels, she ignored him and ran into the TARDIS. Leela lacked knowledge of technology but was highly intelligent and not intimidated by advanced machines or concepts. She would re-phrase things in terms that she could understand in order to help her work through solutions. Her warrior attitude meant that she was quick to respond to threats with her knife and poisonous Janis thorns. This did not go down well with the Doctor, but Leela resisted all attempts to 'civilise' her.

K-9

K-9 was presented to the Doctor and Leela by his original owner, Professor Marius (see **The Invisible Enemy** on page 113). He was a very loyal robot dog, following the commands of his master or mistress with little or no thought to his own safety. He also had a lamentable habit of taking his orders rather literally sometimes, chasing a ball into the water at Brighton beach when asked to fetch it by Romana. K-9 could be a little superior when he knew he was right, which was quite often. While he was capable of using deadly force, he only uses it when expressly commanded to.

Before leaving the original K-9 with Leela on Gallifrey the Doctor had begun work on a new version, the Mark II. This new K-9 was a slightly upgraded model, but somewhat 'overclocked' as he required more maintenance and upkeep. The Doctor also had a tendency to change and adapt this model, changing his personality and voice at one stage. However, it is hard to say whether the machine was actually constantly breaking down, or if the Doctor just liked tinkering with it.

ROMANA (1ST INCARNATION)

Romanadvoratrelundar (shortened to Romana by the Doctor even though she would have preferred 'Fred') was assigned by the White Guardian (masquerading as the Time Lord President) to assist the Doctor in his search for the Key to Time. As the mission was so vital, it is no surprise he picked their best and brightest student – Romana graduated the Academy with a triple 1st and was an expert in temporal technology, physics and even advanced psychoanalysis. Romana also proved very practical, able to apply her knowledge easily and quickly to almost any situation.

Romana was supremely confident of her abilities, but inexperienced in dealing with life outside the sheltered environment of Gallifreyan academia. This, combined with a Time Lord's natural arrogance, often made her unaware of quite how dangerous a situation might be. Luckily, her cool intelligence and icy charm usually more than compensated.

She had a very dry sense of humour and a rather sarcastic wit, especially against people she felt were not her intellectual equal. Underneath her dismissive attitude, she was genuinely excited to be adventuring with the Doctor, and keen to put into practice all she had learned. It took her a while to appreciate that the Doctor's experience sometimes made up for and even surpassed her raw knowledge. However, she came to respect his abilities; even though it is painfully obvious to her he needs someone around to look after him.

ROMANA (2ND INCARNATION)

After completing her mission for the Time Lords with the Doctor, Romana decided she was in no rush to return to the cloying atmosphere of Gallifrey. Her time with the Doctor had taught her there was so much more to see. While he may have infected her with some of his own rebellious attitude, Romana had come to see the Doctor as someone who could teach her things that Gallifrey never would. As an academic she was still eager to learn and face new challenges, not that she would ever admit that the Doctor (with his dismal academic record) had anything to teach her.

Regenerating on a whim, she chose to duplicate the body of Princess Astra from her last adventure, much to the Doctor's disapproval. Her personality in this new regeneration was a lot more friendly and adventure-seeking, but she lost little of her skills and determination. Her relationship with the Doctor also changed as they roamed across time and space together. She stopped being the Doctor's assistant or apprentice and instead became a partner he was showing around the universe.

Romana hoped the Time Lords would simply forget about her and let her remain in the TARDIS with the Doctor exploring the universe. However, the Time Lords never forget where their errant subjects are, even the Doctor, and they ordered her to return. While the Doctor would have liked to help her stay he knew from bitter experience that the Time Lords would eventually take Romana back no matter what he did. However, in her time with the Doctor, Romana had learnt his most vital lesson, and she found a way to disobey the Time Lords. She chose to remain in E-Space with K-9 MII and help the Tharils, where even the Time Lords might find it difficult to bring her home.

ADRIC

Adric was a likable but gawky teenager who masked social shyness with arrogance and an argumentative nature. His incredible ability with mathematics had led to a rather sheltered academic upbringing that he tried to rebel against as soon as he hit his teens. Adric ran into the Doctor when the TARDIS became stranded in E-Space. After his older brother was killed, he stowed away aboard the TARDIS. Adric eventually managed to prove himself a valuable companion, and the Doctor adopted him as a protégé.

He was extremely loyal to his friends, even to the point of risking his own life. While he liked to think of himself as a teenage gangster, Adric was essentially a nerd trying to act up. He was really just trying to find a place for himself as his intelligence and talent always kept him outside any group he tried to join. The Doctor and Romana were two people he not only idolised but also felt comfortable with. Like many teenagers, he believed himself to be always right and almost indestructible, which got him into a lot of trouble and would lead to tragedy.

NYSSA OF TRAKEN

Nyssa was the daughter of Consul Tremas, one of the leaders of the planet Traken, and had a privileged upbringing in a beautiful and peaceful society. Even by Traken standards she was exceptionally gifted and was encouraged to pursue her interest in science, especially biochemistry. Unfortunately her life changed forever when the Master killed her father

and destroyed Traken. Having nowhere to go, she remained with the Doctor and his companions who had become good friends.

Nyssa seems older than her years, a teenager with the mind of a dedicated scientist. She has been deeply hurt by the loss of her father and homeworld, but she buries herself in her studies as a way to hide it. It has been a shock to her to discover how cold and uncaring the universe is, and how unique the peace of Traken was. She looks for ways to make the universe better, as a way to honour her lost family and planet.

TEGAN JOVANKA

Tegan wanted to see the world. She became an air hostess so she could travel to every corner of the globe. Tegan joined the Doctor quite by accident – looking for help with car trouble, she wandered into the TARDIS and got lost. This accident saved her life, as she would otherwise have been killed by the Master.

Tegan could be a very loud and difficult person and usually irritated people at first. She was not shy at all about voicing her concerns or frustrations. On the surface, Tegan was not especially well-suited to a life of adventure, but she was very pragmatic and practical when the need arose. The Doctor regenerated shortly after meeting her, but she took it in her stride. She even tried to fly the TARDIS when left alone, better to do something wrong that just stare at the array of buttons and dials.

Tegan was the kind of person you want with you in a crisis. She might complain bitterly about it, but she'd get the job done, whatever it takes.

THE FOURTH DOCTOR

ATTRIBUTES

- **(4) AWARENESS** ○○○○
- **(4) COORDINATION** ○○○○
- **(7) INGENUITY** ○○○○○○○
- **(5) PRESENCE** ○○○○○
- **(5) RESOLVE** ○○○○○
- **(3) STRENGTH** ○○○

SKILLS

- **(3) ATHLETICS**
- **(4) CONVINCE**
- **(1) CRAFT**
- **(4) FIGHTING**
- **(5) KNOWLEDGE**
- **(4) MARKSMAN**
- **(2) MEDICINE**
- **(5) SCIENCE**
- **(3) SUBTERFUGE**
- **(2) SURVIVAL**
- **(4) TECHNOLOGY**
- **(4) TRANSPORT**

TRAITS

Adversary (Major): Too many to count.
Animal Friendship: +2 modifier to any Presence and Convince Skill roll to calm an animal.
Argumentative: The Doctor's always right.
Boffin: Allows the creation of Gadgets.
Brave: +2 bonus to any Resolve roll when the Doctor needs to show courage.
Charming: +2 bonus to attempts to use charm.
Code of Conduct (Minor): The Doctor has his own alien moral code.
Distinctive: -2 penalty to rolls to blend in. Others have a +2 bonus to remember or recognise the Doctor.
Eccentric: Somewhat off-putting and socially odd.
Epicurean Tastes: +2 to appraising the quality of luxury items and to impressing others with their taste and style.
Feel the Turn of the Universe: +2 bonus to Awareness and Ingenuity to detect something wrong with time or space.
Friends (Major): UNIT, and those across the universe he has saved, or just shared a good conversation with.
Hypnosis (Minor): +2 bonus to control another's emotional state.
Indomitable: +4 bonus to any rolls to resist psychic control.
Insatiable Curiosity: The Doctor will investigate anything that sparks his curiosity unless he passes a Resolve or Ingenuity roll at a -2 penalty.
Keen Senses (Minor x2): +2 to Awareness rolls that use Smell or Taste.
Obsession (Major): Travel the universe, and never get tied down.
Percussive Maintenance: May reroll repair attempts.
Psychic: +4 against mental attacks and the Doctor may attempt to read minds.
Quick Reflexes: The Doctor always goes first in his Action Round unless taken by surprise.
Random Regenerator: The Doctor's regenerations are entirely random.
Resourceful Pockets: Roll two dice and get a 'double' (or spend a Story Point) to find something you need.
Technically Adept: +2 bonus to any Technology roll to fix a broken or faulty device.
Time Lord, Experienced x3 (Special Good)
Time Traveller (Major): Familiar with all tech levels.
Tough: Reduce total damage suffered in any attack by 2.
Voice of Authority: +2 bonus to Presence and Convince rolls.
Vortex: The Doctor may pilot time craft through the vortex, and gains a +2 bonus when doing so.

STUFF

Sonic Screwdriver Mk 4: Open/Close, Weld, Restriction (Cannot Open Mechanical Locks). 1 Story Point.

Scarf
Jelly Babies
Local field gravity detector (Yo-yo)
Hundreds of useless odds and ends.

10

BIODATA

PERSONAL GOAL
See the universe. Meddle in the affairs of galactic overlords and annoying bureaucrats. Offer jelly babies to people and things that are unlikely to want a jelly baby at that precise moment.

PERSONALITY
Cantankerous and eccentric. The Doctor loves to keep people off balance by doing and saying strange things at odd times. He also hates being told he is wrong, especially when he is. He is a passionate creature of extremes and mood swings. When involved in a crisis he is hard to keep up with, always running when he might walk. But in calmer times he is very hard to rouse from a game of chess or an afternoon of fishing.

BACKGROUND
The Doctor never quite seemed to recover from his regeneration, remaining more eccentric and prone to mood swings than usual. Even so, in this incarnation he fought seemingly every type of foe in the universe. This incarnation was charged with universe-shaking quests, such as collecting the parts to the key to time, and travelled beyond the boundaries of the universe into E-space. He also returned to Gallifrey several times and, for a time, travelled with another of his people, Romana. After so many adventures and so many deadly enemies, it is almost ironic that his next regeneration should be caused by something as mundane as a fall.

SARAH JANE SMITH

STORY POINTS **12**

ATTRIBUTES

- 4 AWARENESS ○○○○
- 3 COORDINATION ○○○
- 3 INGENUITY ○○○
- 3 PRESENCE ○○○
- 4 RESOLVE ○○○○
- 2 STRENGTH ○○

SKILLS

- 2 ATHLETICS
- 3 CONVINCE
- 1 CRAFT
- 2 FIGHTING
- 3 KNOWLEDGE
- 1 MARKSMAN
- 1 MEDICINE
- 1 SCIENCE
- 3 SUBTERFUGE
- 2 SURVIVAL
- 2 TECHNOLOGY
- 2 TRANSPORT

BIODATA

PERSONAL GOAL
To seek out adventure.

PERSONALITY
Confident, strong-willed, and determined. Sarah Jane aggressively pursues interesting stories.

BACKGROUND
Raised by her Aunt, Sarah Jane became an investigative journalist. Her true love is for adventure, and although she never lets her investigative past go she doesn't mind putting it on the back burner for a chance to explore the universe.

TRAITS

Attractive: +2 bonus to any rolls that involve looks.
Brave: +2 bonus to show courage in the face of fear.
Friends (Minor, UNIT): She can draw on UNIT's resources.
Insatiable Curiosity: She will investigate anything that sparks her curiosity unless she passes a Resolve or Ingenuity roll at a -2 penalty.
Run For Your Life!: +1 Speed when being chased.

STUFF

None

5

HARRY SULLIVAN

STORY POINTS **12**

ATTRIBUTES

- 3 AWARENESS ○○○
- 3 COORDINATION ○○○
- 4 INGENUITY ○○○○
- 3 PRESENCE ○○○
- 5 RESOLVE ○○○○○
- 3 STRENGTH ○○○

SKILLS

- 2 ATHLETICS (Cricket)
- 1 CONVINCE
- 0 CRAFT
- 3 FIGHTING
- 1 KNOWLEDGE (Navy)
- 3 MARKSMAN
- 4 MEDICINE
- 1 SCIENCE (Biology)
- 2 SUBTERFUGE
- 1 SURVIVAL
- 2 TECHNOLOGY
- 2 TRANSPORT

BIODATA

PERSONAL GOAL
To protect the Doctor and Sarah.

PERSONALITY
A bit old-fashioned and prone to clumsiness, Harry has a good soul and generally tries to do the right thing, in spite of the occasional barb from the Doctor. He adapts remarkably well to bizarre situations and alien worlds, but he prefers the life of a military surgeon to gallivanting around the universe.

BACKGROUND
Surgeon-Lieutenant Harry Sullivan works for UNIT and is assigned by the Brigadier to treat the newly-regenerated Doctor. He inadvertently joined the Doctor on his travels and longs to return to the relative normalcy of military life, where he is respected for his contributions.

TRAITS

Brave: +2 bonus to show courage in the face of fear.
Clumsy: Trips over his own feet a bit.
Face in the Crowd: +2 to any roll to blend in with a crowd.
Friends (Minor, UNIT): He can draw on UNIT's resources.
Lucky: Reroll natural double 1s.
Military Rank (Major): Holds the rank of Lieutenant.
Obligation (Major, UNIT): Harry is loyal to UNIT.
Tough: Reduce total damage suffered in an attack by 2.
Unadventurous: Harry doesn't want to travel.
Voice of Authority: +2 to rolls to convince people to obey him.

STUFF

None

5

LEELA

ATTRIBUTES

3	AWARENESS	○ ○ ○
5	COORDINATION	○ ○ ○ ○ ○
4	INGENUITY	○ ○ ○ ○
3	PRESENCE	○ ○ ○
4	RESOLVE	○ ○ ○ ○
4	STRENGTH	○ ○ ○ ○

SKILLS

3	ATHLETICS		2	MEDICINE
3	CONVINCE		0	SCIENCE
3	CRAFT		2	SUBTERFUGE
4	FIGHTING		2	SURVIVAL
0	KNOWLEDGE		0	TECHNOLOGY
3	MARKSMAN		0	TRANSPORT

TRAITS

Attractive: +2 to rolls involving physical appearance.
Brave: +2 to resisting fear.
Code of Conduct (Minor): Leela follows the code of the Sevateem.
Distinctive: It's easy to spot Leela.
Experienced
Gadget (Major): Janis Thorns (see page 98).
Insatiable Curiosity: Leela can't resist a mystery.
Keen Senses (Major): +2 to any roll to detect things.
Quick Reflexes: Leela always goes first in an Action Round.
Sense of Direction: +2 to any roll to avoid getting lost.
Technically Inept: -2 to any roll to use complex gadgets.
Tough: Reduce total damage suffered by 2.

STUFF

Knife

1

BIODATA

PERSONAL GOAL
To learn as much as she can about the universe and her place in it.

PERSONALITY
Leela is an honourable warrior and tends to see things in terms of black and white. She regards the Doctor in high esteem and treasures his wisdom.

BACKGROUND
Leela was a member of the Sevateem, a descendant of a survey team launched from a crashed colony ship. She is a practical survivalist with keen instincts and bristles against rules and superstitions. She is open-minded enough to warm quickly to the Doctor even though he resembles the embodiment of Evil on her world and impulsive enough to make quick decisions, such as going with the Doctor and staying on Gallifrey with Andred.

K-9

ATTRIBUTES

3	AWARENESS	○ ○ ○
2	COORDINATION	○ ○
7	INGENUITY	○ ○ ○ ○ ○ ○ ○
1	PRESENCE	○
3	RESOLVE	○ ○ ○
3	STRENGTH	○ ○ ○

SKILLS

1	ATHLETICS		3	MEDICINE
3	CONVINCE		5	SCIENCE
0	CRAFT		1	SUBTERFUGE
1	FIGHTING		1	SURVIVAL
6	KNOWLEDGE		6	TECHNOLOGY
2	MARKSMAN		2	TRANSPORT

TRAITS

Boffin: Can create Gadgets.
Five Rounds, Rapid: May fire during the 'Runners' or 'Doers' phases.
Natural Weapons: Nose blaster (Ranged) doing (4/8/L) damage or (2/4/S) damage when set on Stun.
Photographic Memory
Robot
 - Gadget Traits: Open/Close, Scan.
 - Restriction: Stairs.
Technically Adept: +2 to any Technology roll to fix a broken or faulty device.
Vortex: K-9 may pilot time craft through the vortex, and gains +2 when doing so.
Obligation (Major): Obey the Master or Mistress.
Slow (Minor): K-9 moves at half normal Speed.

STUFF

None

8

BIODATA

PERSONAL GOAL
To serve his Master and Mistress.

PERSONALITY
K-9 has a high-pitched voice that makes him seem continually chipper and eager. Despite being a machine, he shows signs of emotion, especially loyalty, and can even be sarcastic on occasion.

BACKGROUND
K-9 was built around the year 5000 by Professor Marius, who was unable to bring his dog from home to an asteroid colony. As K-9 was designed to be a companion, a bit of personality was added to his program.

K-9 MARK II

ATTRIBUTES

- **3** AWARENESS ○○○
- **2** COORDINATION ○○
- **7** INGENUITY ○○○○○○○
- **1** PRESENCE ○
- **3** RESOLVE ○○○
- **3** STRENGTH ○○○

SKILLS

- **1** ATHLETICS
- **2** CONVINCE
- **0** CRAFT
- **1** FIGHTING
- **6** KNOWLEDGE
- **3** MARKSMAN
- **3** MEDICINE
- **5** SCIENCE
- **2** SUBTERFUGE
- **1** SURVIVAL
- **6** TECHNOLOGY
- **2** TRANSPORT

BIODATA

PERSONAL GOAL
To serve the Master and Mistress.

PERSONALITY
Sensible and unflappable, K-9 is a loyal companion and a loyal dog.

BACKGROUND
A replacement for the K-9 left with Leela on Gallifrey, the MII version is a little more advanced but essentially the same. The Doctor leaves him with Romana in E-Space when she leaves to help the Tharils.

TRAITS

Boffin: Can create Gadgets.
Five Rounds, Rapid: May fire during the 'Runners' or 'Doers' phases.
Natural Weapons (Major): Nose blaster (Ranged) doing (4/8/L) damage or (2/4/S) damage when set on Stun.
Photographic Memory
Robot
 - **Gadget Traits:** Open/Close, Scan.
 - **Restriction:** Can't Go Up Stairs.
Technically Adept: +2 to any Technology roll to fix a broken or faulty device.
Vortex: K-9 may pilot time craft through the vortex, and gains +2 when doing so.
Obligation (Major): Obey the Master or Mistress.
Slow (Minor): K-9 moves at half its Speed rate.

STUFF

None

10

ADRIC

ATTRIBUTES

- **3** AWARENESS ○○○
- **3** COORDINATION ○○○
- **5** INGENUITY ○○○○○
- **2** PRESENCE ○○
- **3** RESOLVE ○○○
- **3** STRENGTH ○○○

SKILLS

- **3** ATHLETICS
- **2** CONVINCE
- **2** CRAFT
- **2** FIGHTING
- **2** KNOWLEDGE
- **1** MARKSMAN
- **0** MEDICINE
- **3** SCIENCE (Mathematics)
- **3** SUBTERFUGE
- **2** SURVIVAL
- **3** TECHNOLOGY
- **2** TRANSPORT

BIODATA

PERSONAL GOAL
To find a place somewhere, and see the universe.

PERSONALITY
Adric likes to think of himself as a rebel, but he's actually more of an outcast. He has trouble fitting in which makes him act out, but underneath is a decent kid trying to make friends.

BACKGROUND
Adric met the Doctor in E-Space on the planet Alzarius where he lived with a local gang. He stowed away in the TARDIS. Initially annoyed at picking up a hitch hiker, the Doctor grudgingly came to accept him.

TRAITS

Boffin: Can create Gadgets.
Brave: +2 bonus to any Resolve roll when the character needs to show courage.
Fast Healing (Major): Attribute Points lost due to injury are regained at 1 point per hour.
Time Traveller (Major): Adric is able to get to grips with advanced technology very easily, making him familiar with Tech level 10 and below.
Vortex: May pilot time craft through the vortex, and gains +2 when doing so.
Argumentative: Adric is often unwilling to compromise.
Impulsive: Adric doesn't think things through before acting.
Insatiable Curiosity: Will investigate anything that sparks his curiosity unless he passes a Resolve or Ingenuity roll at -2.

STUFF

Gold edged award badge for mathematical excellence.
Woven membership belt of the Outler gang.

8 (10)

ROMANA (1ST INCARNATION)

ATTRIBUTES

- **AWARENESS** 3 ○○○
- **COORDINATION** 3 ○○○
- **INGENUITY** 9 ○○○○○○○○○
- **PRESENCE** 5 ○○○○○
- **RESOLVE** 5 ○○○○○
- **STRENGTH** 2 ○○

SKILLS

2 ATHLETICS		2 MEDICINE
3 CONVINCE		5 SCIENCE*
2 CRAFT		2 SUBTERFUGE
0 FIGHTING		0 SURVIVAL
4 KNOWLEDGE		5 TECHNOLOGY
1 MARKSMAN		3 TRANSPORT

BIODATA

PERSONAL GOAL
To find the segments of the Key to Time.

PERSONALITY
Romana is confident to the point of arrogance, but not without good reason. Her somewhat sheltered upbringing coupled with a cool intelligence leaves her with little fear of what the universe might offer.

BACKGROUND
Romanadvoratrelundar is one of the top graduates of the Time Lord academy, an expert in temporal mechanics and advanced psychology. She was sent by the White Guardian to assist the Doctor in the search for the key to time. However, once the quest was complete she conveniently 'forgot' to return to Gallifrey.

TRAITS

Attractive: +2 bonus to any rolls that involve the character's looks.

Arrogant : +2 to Fear rolls, -1 to social rolls with inferiors.

Bio-Rhythmic Control: Romana may spend a Story Point to take detailed control of one aspect of her body.

Boffin: Can create Gadgets.

Doctorate: +3 when using Temporal Physics.

Doctorate: +3 when using Psychoanalysis.

Feel the Turn of the Universe: +2 bonus to Awareness and Ingenuity to detect something wrong with time or space.

Psychic: +4 against mental attacks and may attempt to read minds.

Tailored Regeneration: Romana can control the apparance and physical qualities of her next Regeneration.

Technically Adept: +2 to any Technology roll to fix a broken or faulty device.

Time Lord: Although Romana isn't a seasoned time traveller like the Doctor, she did graduate with a first from the Academy.

Voice of Authority: +2 bonus to Presence and Convince rolls.

Vortex: May pilot time craft through the vortex, and gains +2 when doing so.

Cloistered: Has difficulty using Technology below their Tech Level, -2 to all social rolls with other species.

Distinctive: -2 penalty to rolls to blend in. Others have a +2 bonus to remember or recognise her.

Obligation (Major): Collect the segments of the Key to Time.

Sesquipedalian: -2 to teaching rolls, but +1 to impressing others.

STUFF

*(Temporal Physics, Psychoanalysis)

Core of the Key to Time (Tracer)

10

ROMANA (2ND INCARNATION)

STORY POINTS 8

ATTRIBUTES

- **4** AWARENESS ○○○○
- **3** COORDINATION ○○○
- **9** INGENUITY ○○○○○○○○○
- **5** PRESENCE ○○○○○
- **5** RESOLVE ○○○○○
- **2** STRENGTH ○○

SKILLS

- **3** ATHLETICS
- **4** CONVINCE
- **3** CRAFT
- **1** FIGHTING
- **4** KNOWLEDGE
- **1** MARKSMAN
- **2** MEDICINE
- **5** SCIENCE*
- **3** SUBTERFUGE
- **1** SURVIVAL
- **5** TECHNOLOGY
- **3** TRANSPORT

BIODATA

PERSONAL GOAL
To explore the universe and discover new things.

PERSONALITY
Romana's second incarnation is more fun-loving and disarming that her previous one. However, she has lost none of her intelligence and skill.

BACKGROUND
Staying with the Doctor to see the universe, Romana hoped never to return to Gallifrey. However, after several adventures she was called back home again. Having learnt from the Doctor's example she chose to stay in E-Space where even the Time Lords' reach might not claim her.

TRAITS

Attractive: +2 bonus to any rolls that involve the character's looks.
Bio-Rhythmic Control: Romana may spend a Story Point to take detailed control of one aspect of her body.
Boffin (Major Good): Can create Gadgets.
Doctorate: +3 when using Temporal Physics.
Doctorate: +3 when using Psychoanalysis.
Feel the Turn of the Universe: +2 bonus to Awareness and Ingenuity to detect something wrong with time or space.
Psychic: +4 against mental attacks and may attempt to read minds.
Tailored Regeneration: Romana may choose the form of her next Regeneration.
Technically Adept: +2 to any Technology roll to fix a broken or faulty device.
Time Lord: Although Romana isn't a seasoned time traveller like the Doctor, she did graduate with a first from the Academy.
Vortex: May pilot time craft through the vortex, and gains +2 when doing so.
Insatiable Curiosity: Will investigate anything that sparks her curiosity unless she passes a Resolve or Ingenuity roll at -2.
Wanted (Minor): Romana is actively hunted by her people, who may catch up with her at awkward moments to bring her to justice.

STUFF

*(Temporal Physics, Psychoanalysis)

Sonic Screwdriver

10

NYSSA OF TRAKEN

ATTRIBUTES

- (3) AWARENESS ○○○
- (3) COORDINATION ○○○
- (5) INGENUITY ○○○○○
- (4) PRESENCE ○○○○
- (4) RESOLVE ○○○○
- (2) STRENGTH ○○

SKILLS

- (2) ATHLETICS
- (2) CONVINCE
- (3) CRAFT
- (3) FIGHTING
- (3) KNOWLEDGE
- (2) MARKSMAN
- (3) MEDICINE
- (4) SCIENCE (Biochemistry)
- (2) SUBTERFUGE
- (1) SURVIVAL
- (3) TECHNOLOGY
- (2) TRANSPORT

BIODATA

PERSONAL GOAL
To learn and study, and find a place in the universe.

PERSONALITY
Nyssa is a serious and dedicated young woman, the sort to stay in and do her homework rather than go out to a party. However, to Nyssa, the work is as good as a party and she gets great pleasure from uncovering the beauty and mystery of the universe.

BACKGROUND
Brought up on the most peaceful planet in the universe, Nyssa was unprepared for the evil of the Master. He destroyed her planet and stole her father's body, leaving her with nothing. She joined the Doctor having nowhere else to go, but is determined to find a purpose and honour what she has lost.

TRAITS

Attractive: +2 bonus to any rolls based in appearance.
Biochemical Genius: May create biological and chemical 'gadgets'. Using science instead of Technology for jiggery pokery.
Brave: +2 bonus to any Resolve roll when she needs to show courage.
Charming: +2 bonus to attempts to use charm.
Gadget (Minor): Ion Bonder.
Noble: +2 bonus in high society.
Technically Adept: +2 to any Technology roll to fix a broken or faulty device.
Code of Conduct (Minor): Nyssa is dedicated to peace.
Last of my Kind: -2 penalty to any but life threatening rolls when alone.
Silver Spoon: -2 penalty to interactions with the lower classes.

STUFF

Ion Bonder (Weld, 2/4/6 or Stun Damage, Restriction: Limited Charge)

7

TEGAN JOVANKA

ATTRIBUTES

- (2) AWARENESS ○○
- (3) COORDINATION ○○○
- (2) INGENUITY ○○
- (4) PRESENCE ○○○○
- (4) RESOLVE ○○○○
- (2) STRENGTH ○○

SKILLS

- (3) ATHLETICS
- (3) CONVINCE
- (1) CRAFT
- (1) FIGHTING
- (2) KNOWLEDGE
- (0) MARKSMAN
- (1) MEDICINE
- (2) SCIENCE
- (2) SUBTERFUGE
- (2) SURVIVAL
- (2) TECHNOLOGY
- (2) TRANSPORT

BIODATA

PERSONAL GOAL
To see the world.

PERSONALITY
Tegan is not shy about offering her opinion, but that doesn't mean she is wrong. She finds injustice personally offensive and refuses to stand by and allow it to carry on. If everyone else is just walking past, Tegan will get involved, even if she is somewhat blunt in her offer of help.

BACKGROUND
Tegan became an airhostess to see the world and lead a life of adventure. She got a lot more than she bargained for when she wandered into the TARDIS by mistake.

TRAITS

Argumentative
Attractive : +2 bonus to any rolls that involve looks.
Brave: +2 bonus to any Resolve roll when she needs to show courage.
Clumsy: Must make additional Awareness and Coordination rolls to avoid knocking vital things over.
Impulsive: Doesn't think things through before acting.
Loud: Tegan is naturally very noisy and not very subtle.
Lucky: Re-roll any 'double 1s'.
Run for your Life!: +1 bonus to Speed when escaping pursuit.
Unadventurous (Minor): Tegan never asked to travel in time and space; she just wants to get back to Heathrow.

STUFF

None

5

⚙ THE FOURTH DOCTOR'S TARDIS

Freed from exile on Earth, the Doctor and the TARDIS returned to their wandering ways. The Doctor continued to have a tempestuous relationship with his vehicle – sometimes he was frustrated by the ship's stubborn ways, but he defended it from the aspersions cast upon the 'vintage vehicle', especially by Romana.

The Fourth Doctor was especially willing to modify the TARDIS as needed. Romana started the process when she installed a connector for the tracker used to follow the Key to Time, but the Doctor also installed a Randomiser to avoid the attention of Gallifrey and the Black Guardian, and integrated K-9 into the TARDIS' systems so he could remotely access the computer databanks, sensors and navigation controls.

For some time on his journeys, the Doctor operated the TARDIS from the secondary control room. His previous incarnations considered using this chamber, but the Fourth found it to his liking (perhaps frustrated with the original console after his long time spent fixing it on Earth).

Two key TARDIS properties were revealed during the Fourth Doctor's tenure. The TARDIS can 'burn up' rooms for extra thrust, converting its internal mass into energy. It also contains a tranquil Cloister Room where the Cloister Bell was kept. This bell sounded when the TARDIS detected terrible danger.

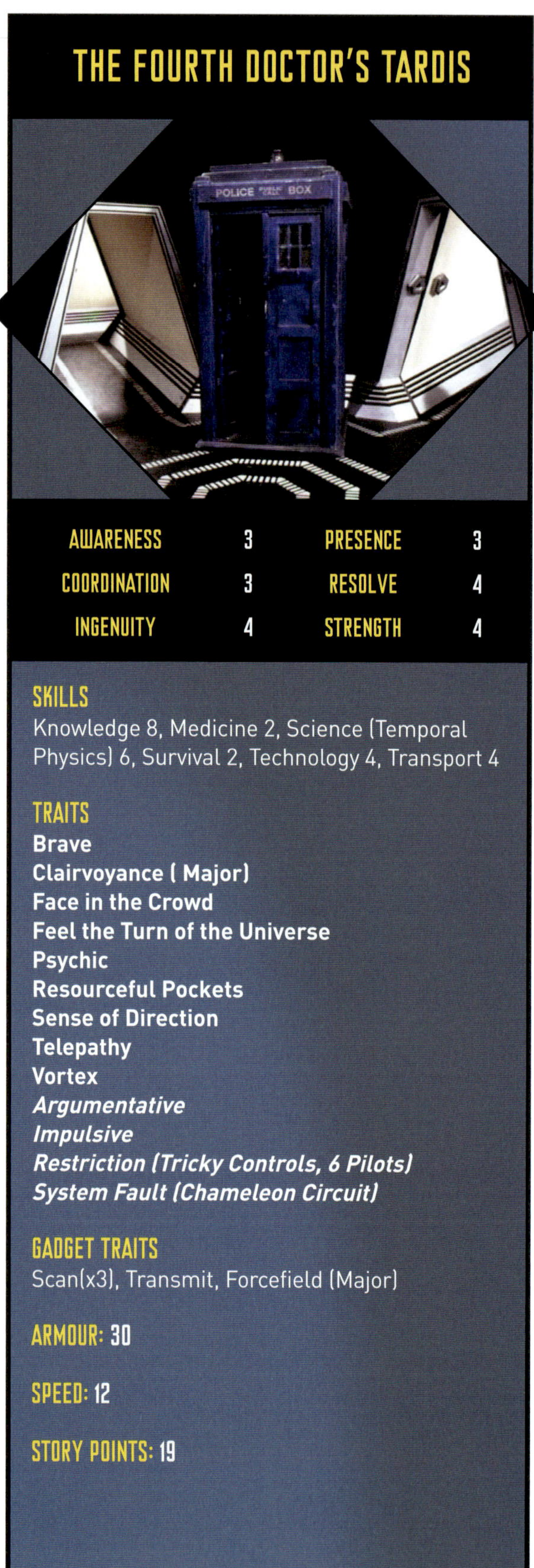

THE FOURTH DOCTOR'S TARDIS

AWARENESS	3	**PRESENCE**	3
COORDINATION	3	**RESOLVE**	4
INGENUITY	4	**STRENGTH**	4

SKILLS
Knowledge 8, Medicine 2, Science (Temporal Physics) 6, Survival 2, Technology 4, Transport 4

TRAITS
Brave
Clairvoyance (Major)
Face in the Crowd
Feel the Turn of the Universe
Psychic
Resourceful Pockets
Sense of Direction
Telepathy
Vortex
Argumentative
Impulsive
Restriction (Tricky Controls, 6 Pilots)
System Fault (Chameleon Circuit)

GADGET TRAITS
Scan(x3), Transmit, Forcefield (Major)

ARMOUR: 30

SPEED: 12

STORY POINTS: 19

CHAPTER THREE
THE FOURTH DOCTOR'S ADVENTURES

ROBOT

'But you can't take on the whole world. Don't you understand? They'll destroy you!'

⚙ SYNOPSIS

England, April 4, UNIT Era

A break-in at the Ministry of Defence triggered an investigation by UNIT. The thief was a mysterious human-sized robot that stole secret blueprints for an experimental disintegrator gun. This was just the sort of thing that a Scientific Adviser should deal with, but the newly-regenerated Doctor had little interest in remaining on Earth. Sarah Jane convinced him to stay and help with one last mystery.

Sarah investigated Think Tank, a research facility that created the initial plans for the disintegrator gun, where she learned that robotics expert Professor Kettlewell used to work for Think Tank. She visited Kettlewell, who assured her that Think Tank couldn't be continuing his experiments.

Meanwhile, the robot struck again, stealing the last piece of the disintegrator gun before returning to the Think Tank laboratory. The robot was under the control of the Scientific Reform Society, a secret

organisation dedicated to the overthrow of world governments. The scientists of the society believed that humanity needed strong, rational leadership – in other words, them. Both Kettlewell and Hilda Winters of Think Tank were secret members of the society.

The Society set a trap for the Doctor by having Kettlewell invite him to his office. The K1 robot broke in and attacked the Doctor, but was driven off by UNIT before it could kill him. Kettlewell pretended that he knew nothing about the plot and that the robot was no longer under his control. While discussing the robot's living metal construction, Kettlewell mentioned that he created a fast-acting metallic 'virus' that broke down metal into a recyclable form.

Forced to accelerate their plans, the Society sent the K1 Robot to kill government Minister Joseph Chambers and steal the launch codes for the nuclear arsenals of the major powers of the world. These had been entrusted to neutral Britain as part of a plan for world peace and were hidden in the Minister's safe. With the codes, the Scientific Reform Society could hold the world to ransom. Sarah finally learned Kettlewell's complicity in the plot but she was taken hostage as the key members of the Scientific Reform

Society retreated to Think Tank's atomic bunker. From there, they gave the world 30 minutes to satisfy their demands. UNIT led an assault but were pinned down by the K1 Robot, which now had a working disintegrator gun.

Realising that Winters was prepared to launch the missiles, Kettlewell had a change of heart and tried to stop her, but was accidentally killed by the K1 Robot. The robot then tried to carry out its creator's wishes by launching the missiles. Luckily, UNIT's attack on the bunker gave the nations of the world time to disable their missiles. The robot left the bunker, whereupon the Brigadier shot it with the disintegrator gun. Due to the robot's unique design, the attack only made it grow to giant size. UNIT engaged the giant robot, but it was only destroyed after the Doctor made a batch of Kettlewell's 'virus' and threw it onto the robot. The K1 dissolved into boiling liquid metal.

Back at UNIT HQ, the Doctor decided he didn't want to be the Scientific Advisor anymore and was leaving. Sarah willingly accompanied him, while a sceptical Harry Sullivan was teased into coming along.

⬡ RUNNING THE ADVENTURE

In many ways **Robot** is the last third Doctor adventure, even though the Fourth Doctor is the one who solves it. All of the 'UNIT tropes' are here; a group of elites that want to remake the world, advanced technology to make that happen, UNIT involvement, morally-conflicted characters, a sympathetic villain, and jiggery-pokery.

In order to run this type of adventure you need a catalyst, usually a cause of some sort. In this case Professor Kettlewell wants to stop mankind from destroying the environment. In order for this cause to succeed you need a threat and the means to carry it out. Through Think Tank, Professor Kettlewell joined the Scientific Reform Society and hatched a scheme to use his robot to steal a disintegrator gun and the launch codes. From their atomic bunker, the group could use those launch codes to hold the world hostage.

Kettlewell is conflicted; he wants to hold the world hostage but he's bluffing. He knows he can't save the world by destroying it. In order to keep the threat alive the other members of the group, particularly Director Winters, take a more hardline stance and isn't afraid to cross Kettlewell if he refuses to play along.

In addition to Kettlewell, the K-1 Robot is also conflicted; it is merely carrying out its orders like a good son. When Kettlewell dies by its own inadvertent hand, the K-1 decides to carry out its 'father's' order, not realising that it was really acting against Kettlewell's wishes.

The PCs have two tasks: end the nuclear threat and stop the robot. They need to break into the bunker and rewire the computers while arresting the SRS. If they choose the easy option to destroy the robot (with the disintegrator gun) then they inadvertently make the robot larger and more dangerous. Fortunately, you should have seeded the adventure with the clue that Kettlewell had something to deal with his robot and a quick trip to the lab cooks up the solution needed to destroy the robot.

REGENERATION AFTER PREPARATION

One of the striking things about this adventure is that it puts the newly-regenerated Doctor in an adventure that seems more suited to his predecessor. It's a UNIT adventure dealing with a scientific plot to control/destroy the world. While the Third Doctor would jump right in and take the villain on, the Fourth Doctor seems more concerned with leaving Earth. The plot is only a minor inconvenience to him, something to mop up before he leaves.

In your adventures it's likely that you'll have an unexpected regeneration or switch of characters. Instead of rewriting your planned adventures to suit the new characters, try running one without any changes. In fact, go for a stereotypical adventure – play up your own clichés. If you ran a load of base under siege adventures for the previous Time Lord PC, then run one more for her new incarnation. By giving the new character the same sort of challenges and setting as the last one, you can show off their differences.

THEY GAVE *WHO* THE LAUNCH CODES?

One of the most interesting parts of this adventure is the fact that the nuclear powers of the world (China, the USA, and the USSR; presumably France and possibly India, Israel, and Pakistan as well) gave their launch codes to the fifth nuclear power, the United Kingdom in order to ensure world peace. Such a plan would seem impossible in the early 1970s and no more likely in the 1980s. Such a secret deal seems more likely in the early 1990s, when the dissolution of the Soviet Union aroused concerns about its nuclear arsenal, but Sarah's declaration of being from 1980 to Scarman in the Edwardian era rules this out.

That said it's entirely possible that there was a secret deal during the UNIT era, as we do have evidence, or more accurately lack thereof, that there were no nuclear conflicts up to the present day. While Britain seems an odd choice for the 'neutral' nation, given its NATO connection, it is close enough to the USSR to be conventionally threatened and more immediately affected by any fallout.

This entire strategy could be a gambit by Torchwood, ensuring Great Britain's rise to prominence by giving them a powerful weapon to use against the rest of the world or to ensure its protection from nuclear attack. On the other hand, maybe geopolitics were

a bit different in this timeline; seeing as the United Kingdom has an active space program and has reached Mars, the country may be more influential and important on the world stage.

On the third hand, the Brigadier is of course quite right – who else but the British could be trusted?

THINK TANK & TECH LEVELS

Late 20th-century Earth is Tech Level 5, but that's an average for the whole planet. Some groups – Think Tank for example, or Torchwood, or Area 51 – might have access to a higher Tech Level. Introducing unexpected high-tech gadgets is a great way to differentiate between groups or castes, or to show the players they're on the right track. When the guards start shooting you with lasers, but all the other guards were shooting you with old-fashioned bullets, you know you're getting close to the lair of the high-tech bad guys!

ARNOLD JELLICOE

AWARENESS	3	PRESENCE	3
COORDINATION	3	RESOLVE	4
INGENUITY	3	STRENGTH	3

Director Winter's technical assistant, Jellicoe altered the programming of the Robot so it could injure humans. Beneath his lab coat and rational demeanour, he was a thug at heart, willing to pick up a gun and use violence at the slightest provocation.

SKILLS

Athletics 3, Convince 1, Craft 2, Fighting 3, Knowledge 3, Marksman 4, Science 3, Subterfuge 3, Technology 5, Transport 3

TRAITS

Technically Adept: +2 to any Technology roll to fix a broken or faulty device.

EQUIPMENT: Pistol 2/5/7

STORY POINTS: 5

DIRECTOR HILDA WINTERS

AWARENESS	3	PRESENCE	4
COORDINATION	3	RESOLVE	5
INGENUITY	4	STRENGTH	3

The head of both Think Tank and the Scientific Research Society, Director Winters firmly believed that she was the best and most rational choice to guide humanity into the future. She was both callous and treacherous; she tried to use the K1 Robot to eliminate a meddling reporter within minutes of meeting her, and played her various minions at the Scientific Research Society off against each other to maintain her position. Winters escaped the Think Tank bunker after the destruction of the K1 robot.

SKILLS

Athletics 2, Convince 3, Craft 2, Knowledge 3, Marksman 3, Medicine 2, Science 5, Subterfuge 3, Technology 4, Transport 3

TRAITS

Brave: Winters has nerves of steel, and has +2 bonus to any Resolve roll when she needs to show courage.

Charming: She's an excellent liar. She has +2 bonus to attempts to use charm.

Obsession (Major): Ruling the world.

STORY POINTS: 8

PROFESSOR JEREMIAH P KETTLEWELL

AWARENESS	3	PRESENCE	2
COORDINATION	3	RESOLVE	3
INGENUITY	6	STRENGTH	2

Professor Kettlewell was one of Earth's foremost experts on robotics. He was a member of the Think Tank institute, and also secretly a member of the Scientific Reform Society. He left the institute to pursue work on alternative sources of energy, as he believed that humanity was heading for a catastrophic environmental crisis. The Society used his Robot to carry out their scheme to blackmail the world governments.

SKILLS

Craft 4, Knowledge 4, Science 5, Technology 6, Transport 2

TRAITS

Boffin: Kettlewell made both the K1 robot and the metal-dissolving virus.

Distinctive: With his mad scientist hair and beard, Kettlewell cuts a memorable figure. He has -2 penalty to rolls to blend in. Others have a +2 bonus to remember or recognise him.

Obsession (Major): He's committed to extreme environmental activism.

Code of Conduct (Minor): Kettlewell would never kill another human being – and neither would the robot that is modelled on his neural pathways.

Technically Adept: Kettlewell has +2 bonus to any Technology roll to fix a broken or faulty device.

STORY POINTS: 6

K1 ROBOT

AWARENESS	3	PRESENCE	2
COORDINATION	3	RESOLVE	4
INGENUITY	2	STRENGTH	10

Built out of living metal, the Experimental Prototype Robot K1 was intended to serve humanity by taking on difficult or dangerous tasks. Its onboard artificial computer is capable of conversing intelligently in natural language.

SKILLS

Convince 1, Fighting 3, Marksman 3, Technology 3

TRAITS

Immunity (Special): The living metal robot is immune to bullets and most conventional weapons.

Enslaved (Major): K1 must obey the commands of its masters, and suffers a -2 penalty to any rolls when trying to resist.

Code of Conduct (Minor): K1 is programmed with a prime directive not to harm humans.

Natural Weapons (Minor): Crushing grippers do Strength +2 damage.

Robot (Special)

Slow (Major): The robot moves at a Speed of 1 – it's not very fast.

Weakness (Major): The metal virus quickly destroys the robot.

EQUIPMENT

None or disintegrator gun L/L/L

STORY POINTS: 9

GIANT K1 ROBOT

AWARENESS	3	PRESENCE	2
COORDINATION	3	RESOLVE	4
INGENUITY	2	STRENGTH	14

Living metal works in strange ways (especially when the Robot spends a handful of Story Points). After being shot with the experimental disintegrator, K1 grew to a gigantic size.

SKILLS

Fighting 3, Marksman 3, Technology 3

TRAITS

Immunity (Special): The living metal robot is immune to bullets and most conventional weapons.

Enslaved (Major): K1 must obey the commands of its masters, and suffers a -2 penalty to any rolls when trying to resist.

Code of Conduct (Minor): K1 is programmed with a prime directive not to harm humans.

Huge (Major): The robot's the size of a building. A big building.

Natural Weapons (Minor): Crushing grippers do Strength +2 damage.

Robot (Special Good)

Slow (Major): The robot moves at a Speed of 1 – it's not very fast.

Weakness (Major): The metal virus quickly destroys the robot.

STORY POINTS: 9

NEW GADGET – DISINTEGRATOR GUN

The disintegrator gun is a carbine-sized weapon that can hit a target and reduce it to atoms. Its range is effectively line-of-sight; the Doctor believed that someone standing on Earth could use it to punch a hole through the moon.

Damage: L/L/L
Traits: Delete
Cost: 2 Story Points

NEW GADGET – METAL-DISSOLVING VIRUS

Kettlewell described this concoction as the 'metal equivalent of a virus', suggesting it is a form of nanotechnology. It dissolves metallic compounds into easily-recyclable forms. The virus inflicts one level of damage to any metal object per round of contact, ignoring armour. The virus grows and spreads to cover any metal object it touches. Alien metals may be immune to the virus, and the virus 'dies' only a few minutes after being removed from its container.

Traits: Delete
Cost: 2 Story Points

FURTHER ADVENTURES

- Before her capture, Ms Winters noted that the Scientific Reform Society had associates "all over the world" and, if anything, the Society's concerns about climate change and resource depletion have intensified. As humanity plunges towards environmental crisis, the Society starts to prematurely trigger disasters to draw attention to the problem. They melt glaciers with hidden fusion reactors to raise sea levels, and spray synthetic poisons disguised as controversial pesticides. Ultimately, though, they believe that only one thing will save the world – the reduction of the human population by 95%. How will they accomplish this mass extermination? Will they use help from outer space?

- Kettlewell may be dead and his Robot destroyed, but his notes survived. It's possible that someone furthered the research and created more advanced K-series robots in order to work in harsh environments. As these robots develop emotions, they may not like their treatment and rebel. This could have interesting complications if the newer K-series are more humanoid in shape and integrated into society as servants and companions (shades of the Movellans).

- The Brigadier's use of the disintegrator gun not only made the K-1 grow but also changed the living metal's structure. Because of this, the virus didn't destroy the robot; it merged with it and liquefied it. It is now a mass of angry, liquid metal, dissolving and incorporating all metal in its path, growing larger as it 'eats'. By destroying all metals, it hopes to complete Kettlewell's desire and return humanity to an environmentally-friendly stone age.

- Living metal? The Doctor runs into another creature of living metal later in his career – the Silver Nemesis statue, made by Rassilon and Omega from the living metal Validium (see **Silver Nemesis,** in **The Seventh Doctor Sourceboo**k). Kettlewell said he 'discovered' living metal, which could mean that he found an existing sample of it instead of inventing it. What secrets did Kettlewell take to his grave?

THE ARK IN SPACE

'Homo sapiens! What an inventive, invincible species. It's only a few million years since they've crawled up out of the mud and learned to walk – puny, defenceless bipeds. They've survived flood, famine, and plague. They've survived cosmic wars and holocausts, and now here they are out among the stars, waiting to begin a new life, ready to out-sit eternity. They're indomitable. Indomitable.'

SYNOPSIS

Space Station Nerva 'the Ark', circa 15,000CE

The time travellers arrived on Space Station Nerva and inadvertently set off the automatic security systems. During their attempts to escape, Sarah became separated from the others. The Doctor and Harry discovered that the station was an ark holding thousands of people in suspended animation. They also learned that something alien was aboard the station, just as Harry found Sarah; she'd been placed in suspended animation as well!

The Doctor and Harry discovered the husk of an alien before one of the sleepers, Vira, awoke. She helped revive Sarah as the Doctor informed her that she had overslept her 5,000 years in suspended animation due to alien interference. The Commander, Lazer, nicknamed 'Noah', revived and conducted an investigation after noticing that Dune, the chief technician, was missing. During his search for Dune, Noah encountered another alien grub. The

creature infected Noah, and the Commander began to transform into one of the creatures – a Wirrn.

Realising what was happening to him, Noah contacted Vira and ordered her to get the colonists to Earth. Harry and a crewman armed themselves with fission guns to battle the aliens. Meanwhile, the Doctor learned that the automated security systems had killed the Wirrn Queen. The Doctor tried to electrify the hull of the cryogenic section to keep the Wirrn out, but was stopped by the now-Wirrn Noah. Noah offered to let the awakened humans go free if they allowed the Wirrn to take the rest of the humans. The Wirrn wanted to use the humans as incubators for their eggs, just as the Wirrn Queen had hatched from Dune's body.

Instead, the Doctor and Vira came up with a plan to draw power from the station's shuttle. Sarah managed to shimmy through an air duct to connect the power. The electric field held back the Wirrn. Unfortunately, Noah threatened to shut off the oxygen, something the Wirrn didn't need to survive. The Doctor appealed to Noah's human side and Noah led the Wirrn into the shuttle, whereupon he took off and destroyed the shuttle in space.

CONTINUITY

The Ark was built around the year 3000.
Humanity is escaping the solar flares – the Ark holds a group designed to rebuild the Earth. The rest of

humanity fled in starships; the Andromeda galaxy is mentioned as a destination, but some ships – like the Starship UK (see *The Beast Below* in **The Eleventh Doctor Sourcebook**) wandered the stars.

⊘ RUNNING THE ADVENTURE

At its heart, **The Ark in Space** is a base-under-siege adventure. The player characters and allies are trapped aboard a space station as the Wirrn attempt to attack and convert them. Clues suggest which weapons and tactics to use against the Wirrn, but there isn't any clear solution. There's lots of running down corridors, arguments over tactics, and shooting wildly at shadows like any good base-under-siege, but there are a few lovely twists.

The humans are literally trapped on the base, as thousands more are in suspended animation. Leaving is not an option. Coming up with creative ways to force the characters to hold out works better than just having the enemy surround the base. Give the characters something to defend, something to fight for.

The enemy leader is sympathetic towards those trapped in the base. This buys the characters time to come up with a plan, and also gives them someone

WIRRN

The Wirrn are an insectoid species that resemble a wingless wasp. Wirrn have three stages, larva, pupa, and adult. They can fly wingless through space, but are forced to walk through gravity. In gravity environments, larva slide across the floor while adult Wirrn prefer to hop on their ovipositors (the bottom of their bodies) leaving their manipulators free. Wirrn feed on other living creatures and gain the knowledge that their hosts possess. If an egg is laid inside a host then the host's body slowly transforms into a Wirrn larva.

The Wirrn once had breeding colonies in the Andromeda galaxy but these were destroyed when the human colonists arrived. The war lasted a thousand years and forced the Wirrn to flee. Prior to that, the Wirrn's absorption of some humans informed them of a defenceless Earth that had plenty of knowledgeable humans on which to feed.

AWARENESS	3	PRESENCE	2
COORDINATION	3	RESOLVE	4
INGENUITY	1	STRENGTH	8

SKILLS

Athletics 4, Fighting 4, Knowledge 2, Medicine 1, Subterfuge 3, Survival 5

TRAITS

Alien

Alien Appearance (Major)

Armour (Major or Minor): Reduce damage by 10 (in Grub form this Armour only reduces damage by 5).

Enslaved (Major): Must obey the Swarm Leader.

Environmental: Wirrn suffer no ill effects from space, and don't need to breathe.

Flight (Minor): Wirrn can fly through space, perhaps at light-speed, but they don't have this ability in environments with gravity.

Natural Weapons (Minor): A Wirrn's mandibles do Strength +2 damage.

Networked (Major): Wirrn have complete telepathic contact with nearby Wirrn.

Special – Acquire Knowledge: A Wirrn that consumes an intelligent being gains that being's knowledge.

Weakness (Major Bad): Electricity deals an extra 4 levels of damage to Wirrn.

Technology Level: Equal to that of the 'host species', usually 6.

STORY POINTS: 5

to talk to. Always give your villains a spokesman or a voice or a leader – hordes of zombies or robots or insect aliens may be scary, but they get boring if there's no-one for the players to banter with. In the end the sympathetic bad guy takes an opportunity borne of that interaction to destroy the Wirrn. This isn't a deus ex machina ending, it's a victory – the characters' arguments and heroism convince Noah to make his fatal decision.

HUMANITY MUST BE PROTECTED, EVEN FROM ITS EVILS

One uncomfortable element of this adventure is that the Wirrn aren't necessarily evil; they, like humanity, are simply trying to survive. They've also decided to ensure their survival by attacking the race that brought them to near-extinction, humanity (although the destroyers were the Andromeda colonists, not ancestors of the Ark). Why should they be destroyed and humanity allowed to live, especially given that there's an entire empire of humanity in a different part of the universe?

To his credit, the Doctor does try and negotiate with the Wirrn, but they aren't interested in breeding with another animal species. They want human knowledge, probably to ensure that technologically-advanced races can't destroy them again (in a way, this makes them the equivalent of Cybermen – assimilating and transforming other races).

FURTHER ADVENTURES

- The Wirrn came to Earth to achieve twin goals of survival and revenge. It's likely that some of them, instead of coming to Earth, travelled to the other Earth colonies in order to achieve the same ends. The characters could find themselves in another base under siege, but this time the Wirrn may already have absorbed knowledge from another human colony, making them even more dangerous.

- The characters arrive on Earth and discover a small band of humans that transmatted from the Ark; the rest of the group never came, nor are they able to communicate. What happened to them? Did the Doctor fail to fix the transmat, or is someone else using it for his or her own purposes?

- It's possible that more than one Ark was built. While the first was menaced by the Wirrn, this one could be menaced by the Cybermen,

Sontarans, or another hostile group. It's also possible that this Ark was privately funded and thus populated by less than ideal specimens of humanity. The characters may save them from an outside enemy, but they may be unleashing a morally dubious 'rival' to the original Ark.

NOAH – WIRRN HOST

AWARENESS	3	PRESENCE	4
COORDINATION	2	RESOLVE	3
INGENUITY	3	STRENGTH	4

Noah (a nickname; his real name was Lazer) was the commander of the Ark, which housed thousands of Earth colonists in suspended animation. Unfortunately, a Wirrn queen infiltrated the Ark and disabled the timer, causing the humans to sleep thousands of years longer. Noah was 'pair-bonded' (a marriage arrangement) to First Med-Tech Vira.

Impregnated with the new Swarm Leader, Noah carried out the Wirrn plan for survival. Once he realised what he was doing Noah became conflicted and tried to at least save the humans that were already revived. When an opportunity presented itself to destroy the Wirrn, Noah manipulated the characters into doing what he needed in order to trap the Wirrn and destroy them.

SKILLS

Convince 4, Fighting 2, Knowledge 4, Marksman 3, Science 2, Technology 3, Transport 3

TRAITS

Alien
Alien Appearance (Major)
Tough: Reduce total damage by 2.
Voice of Authority: Noah was one of the leaders of the Ark. He has +2 bonus to Presence and Convince rolls.
Weakness (Major): Electricity inflicts an extra 4 levels of damage on Noah.

EQUIPMENT: Laser Pistol 4/L/L

TECH LEVEL: 6   **STORY POINTS: 10**

THE SONTARAN EXPERIMENT

'Do you think those puny creatures could conquer half a galaxy? No, Styre, I represent the true warrior class. Evaluate me if you dare!'

SYNOPSIS

Earth, circa 15,000CE

The Nerva Beacon transmat needed repairs, so the Doctor volunteered to fix it. The transmat brought the Doctor, Harry and Sarah to a deserted but green and pleasant Earth, after the flares had passed. The Doctor fixed the transmat while Harry and Sarah explored the area. They discovered that a ship from a human colony had also landed on Earth to investigate a distress call. Sarah met Roth, a member of the crew, who explained that an alien was capturing, torturing, and killing his crewmates.

The alien was Styre, a warrior of the Sontaran Empire, on a scouting mission to investigate the capabilities of the human race. He intended to carry out a series of experiments on the human test subjects to determine their resilience, their capacity to endure pain, and their physical and mental weaknesses. This was a solo mission, but Styre was aided by a robotic capture drone, as well as agents among the humans – he convinced the human leader, Vural, to bargain away the lives of his crew in exchange for his own life.

The Doctor concocted a plan to sabotage Styre's ship. He challenged Styre to single combat, claiming to be a higher 'warrior class' of human. The Doctor fought Styre to a standstill until the Sontaran needed to return to his ship to recharge. Fortunately Harry had sabotaged the ship, so Styre's attempt to re-energise killed him.

The Doctor then informed the Sontaran fleet that if they proceeded to Earth they would be destroyed. The time travellers returned to the transmat to inform the Nervans that it was safe to return to Earth.

CONTINUITY

After thousands of years, the Sontarans have returned to Earth. In spite of the Doctor's chiding of a Rutan in the early 20th century, it appears that the Rutan-Sontaran War is still occurring.

The Sontarans are identified as a clone race, although there is some variation between clones. Specifically, Styre has a bumpier, hairless face and five digits on each hand while Linx had a smooth, whiskered face with three digits on each hand.

In spite of its proximity to Earth, the Ark had become a legend amongst the human colonists, indicating the Earth was rarely visited or even forgotten.

RUNNING THE ADVENTURE

This adventure is a variation on the 'prison escape' scenario. The characters meet a group of space travellers that are being menaced by an unknown alien. The robot is the jailor and Styre is the sadistic prison warden; his tests seem arbitrarily thorough and simply display how evil the warden really is.

WHY DIDN'T THE SONTARANS INVADE THE ARK?

One of the most obvious questions is why did Styre lure a Galsec ship rather than simply invade the Ark and perform his experiments there? The answer is simple: time. The entire Sontaran fleet is being held up by Styre's experiments and it's more useful to test humans that are used to the rigours of space rather than wake up obviously weaker specimens and test them. He left the Ark alone as a tactical decision; he didn't want to risk tripping any defence systems or emergency beacons.

As for why the Sontarans are invading Earth, there are several possibilities. The first is that they aren't invading Earth at all; the Sontaran Invasion Fleet is poised to attack the Earth colonies. Styre only set up shop here, away from the colonies, for test purposes. The second possibility is that there is something on Earth that the Sontarans want, but they are afraid that once they've set foot on Earth humanity will follow and try to drive them off. The Sontarans want to ensure that they can defeat any such attempt. A third option is that Styre is simply unaware of the Nerva beacon, and would gleefully invade that structure with its wealth of test subjects if he knew about it.

BUT THEY FAILED!

Ultimately, the Doctor and companions failed in this mission. They were supposed to transmat back to the Ark and inform them that it was fixed. Unfortunately, they were hijacked mid-transmat by the Time Lords and never returned. All that Vira and the Ark humans know is that the Doctor and companions disintegrated mid-transport and the TARDIS mysteriously disappeared.

While it is easy to theorise any number of ways that the Ark was ultimately assured of the transmat's safety (or they could simply catch a ride on the GalSec rescue ship), it's more fun to explore the possibilities of a paranoid Ark crew wondering what happened. Perhaps they view the GalSec ship as an enemy, or a new menace threatens the Ark. Maybe they'll end up allying with the Sontarans…

FURTHER ADVENTURES

- Styre's experiments seemed excessively cruel, but perhaps that was the point. The characters travel to a sector of Earth colonies where the Sontarans used recordings of the experiments as propaganda, causing whole colonies of humans to give up without a fight. Should the characters leave these humans to their new Sontaran masters?

- The GalSec ship was lured to Earth by a fake distress call, but what were they doing in the area? It makes little sense that the Sontarans would bait a remote vessel all the way to Earth just to run a series of tests. They may simply have been coming 'home' to survey the current Earth, but it's also possible that they had another motive. 'GalSec' could be short for 'Galactic Security,' making the crew police officers or soldiers. Perhaps they were chasing something else?

- If one of your player characters is an alien, then maybe they'll be targeted for their own personal version of the Sontaran Experiment. A Sontaran captures that character and experiments on them, while the other player characters race to save their friend before the experiment has a fatal result...

STYRE'S ROBOT

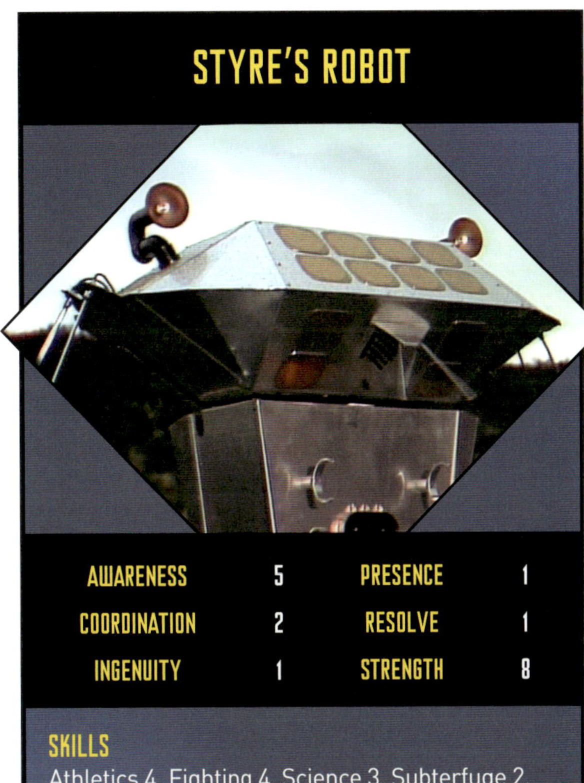

AWARENESS	5	PRESENCE	1
COORDINATION	2	RESOLVE	1
INGENUITY	1	STRENGTH	8

SKILLS

Athletics 4, Fighting 4, Science 3, Subterfuge 2, Technology 2

TRAITS

Armour (Major): The robot's heavy armour reduces all damage taken by 10.
Fast (Major): The robot flies quickly through the air, but isn't especially agile.
Robot
Special (Entangling Wires): The robot has thin tentacles that can capture a humanoid and strap him to its front for transport. The wire has the same Strength as the robot.

STORY POINTS: 3

FIELD MARSHAL STYRE

AWARENESS	4	PRESENCE	5
COORDINATION	4	RESOLVE	6
INGENUITY	5	STRENGTH	6

SKILLS

Athletics 2, Convince 4, Craft 4 (weapons), Fighting 5, Marksman 5, Medicine 1, Science 4, Subterfuge 4, Survival 4, Technology 3, Transport 3

TRAITS

Adversary: The Sontarans have been at war with the Rutans for thousands of years.
Alien
Alien Appearance
Armour: Sontaran battle armour reduces damage by 5.
Brave: Styre fears nothing! He receives a +2 bonus to any Resolve rolls against fear.
By the Book: Styre follows Sontaran military doctrine to the letter.
Cyborg
Tough: Being bred for war means that Styre is very tough, reducing damage to Attributes by 2.
Voice of Authority: Styre has an authoritative voice, giving him +2 to Presence rolls to command.
Weakness: Styre's only weak spot is the probic vent on the back of his neck. A single hit disables him (effects like a normal Stun). Hitting the vent is tricky though and Styre needs to be facing away. There is a -4 penalty to aim for the vent.

EQUIPMENT: Standard Issue Pistol – has three settings, Hypnosis, Stun (S/S/S), and Lethal (4/L/L)

TECH LEVEL: 7   **STORY POINTS:** 10

GENESIS OF THE DALEKS

'Just touch these two strands together and the Daleks are finished. Have I that right?'

⊘ SYNOPSIS

Skaro, pre Dalek Era

The Time Lords plucked the time travellers out of the transmat beam and sent them to Skaro, in the time period when the Daleks first appeared. A representative of the Time Lords informed the Doctor that they foresaw a future in which the Daleks wiped out every race in the universe. The exterminators had to be stopped, and the Time Lords mandated that the Doctor would alter history to erase the Daleks. The messenger gave the Doctor a Time Ring to use to return to the TARDIS when he finished. The Time Lord disappeared, leaving them on a battlefield.

Fleeing the shells and bullets, the time travellers were soon captured by the Kaleds, who mistakenly left Sarah for dead. Sarah recovered and spotted Davros while looking for her friends. Davros was testing the exterminator of the first Dalek. Fleeing, she ran into a band of Mutos, descendants of irradiated Skarosians. The Mutos kidnapped her, but in turn were captured by a Thal patrol. Sarah and the Mutos were taken to the Thal city.

The Doctor and Harry were taken to Ronson, a Kaled scientist. Ronson discovered that they were aliens just as Davros arrived to show off his prototype Dalek. The Dalek attempted to exterminate the time travellers, but was stopped by Ronson, who felt that valuable information might be lost. Davros noted that the stay of execution would be temporary.

Ronson aided the Doctor in getting an audience with the Kaled government, where he learned that the Thals were building a rocket using labour that included Sarah. Through his assistant Nyder, Davros learned of this meeting but acted unconcerned, noting that the Kaled Dome, which was separate from the bunker, was impregnable. He also agreed to an independent inquiry, although he secretly ordered the creation of twenty more Daleks.

The Doctor and Harry escaped to the Thal City where they hoped to find Sarah. They were surprised to discover that Davros and Nyder were there, in a secret meeting with the Thal leaders. Davros gave the Thals the chemical combination needed to destroy the Kaled Dome. He claimed to do this in the name of peace, justifying his betrayal of his own people by claiming a quick end to the war would ultimately result in less suffering. The Doctor and Harry found Sarah, but the Thals destroyed the Kaled dome and declared victory.

The victory was short-lived. With the Kaled leaders destroyed or stunned by the successful Thal attack, no-one was left to stop Davros deploying his creations. The Doctor met a Thal leader, Bettan, and told her to round up Thal survivors for a final assault against the Kaled bunker. He also suggested that the Mutos join them. The time travellers returned to the Kaled bunker to retrieve the time ring, but they were captured. The Doctor was interrogated by Davros and forced to explain the Daleks' future defeats. After this initial interrogation the time travellers were freed by the Kaled rebels; they retrieved the Time Ring and the Doctor destroyed the recording of the Daleks' future.

The Kaled rebels cornered Davros. Davros offered to surrender in return for a vote on the future of the Daleks. Meanwhile, the Doctor wired the Dalek incubators to explode but couldn't bring himself to eradicate them; he was saved by the news of Davros' surrender. Unfortunately, Davros was only playing for time and the Daleks soon entered the conference and exterminated the Kaled rebels.

Davros was initially pleased, but he was horrified when the Daleks exterminated the rest of the Kaled scientists. The Daleks declared that they were superior and didn't need humanoid help. Nyder and Davros tried to destroy them, but they too were exterminated by the Daleks.

The Thals and Mutos destroyed the bunker entrance, burying the Daleks. The Doctor noted that this only set them back about a thousand years, but as the Time Ring whisked the time travellers away, the Doctor mused that the presence of the Daleks also does some good in the universe.

⊙ RUNNING THE ADVENTURE

This adventure is an origin story, drawing on the Dalek history gleaned from the Doctor's previous encounters with them. The Thals and Kaleds had been fighting a thousand year war that echoed World War I; trench warfare with little movement and no end in sight.

The Kaleds themselves reflect the Nazis of World War II, complete with scientists using unethical methods to create a 'master race'. It's also a horror story: the Daleks, like Frankenstein's Monster, ultimately turn on their creator.

It's worth noting that elements of this adventure actually contradict previous information about the Daleks. While this can easily be explained as a result of the Time War, it also serves as a lesson to Gamemasters: if you have a great idea for an adventure, don't let minor inconsistent details keep you from running it.

FIRST SHOT IN THE TIME WAR

In this adventure the Time Lords send the Doctor to hinder Dalek development because they foresee that the Daleks will wipe out all other life in the universe. This does not correlate with previous adventures involving the Daleks, where the Doctor helped wipe them out on Skaro at least twice, the second of which he considered their 'final end'. For a race that the Doctor believes he's defeated, the Daleks are terrifyingly resilient.

The Mark III Travel Machine is a significantly more advanced model than the ones that faced the First Doctor. Specifically, it can travel over natural terrain and uses the standard exterminators of later models. Perhaps more significantly, the prototype Daleks represent a leap in technology that seems beyond the capabilities of the Kaleds at this time, who have regressed to the point of using flintlocks on the battlefield. Davros is a genius beyond compare – but the continued survival of the Daleks against the odds raises the question – who fired first in the Time War?

Was the Doctor's mission to Skaro the first time one side tried to meddle in history, or were the Daleks already busy in the past, risking paradox by editing their own history. It's possible that Davros played only a small role in Dalek development. Instead, he died in a Thal attack. Without his aid, the Kaleds more slowly evolved into 'Dals', took refuge in the travel machines (perhaps the Mark I or II) and from there followed the timeline that the Doctor encountered them in his previous adventures. In the end, these Daleks are destroyed in the Dalek Civil War on Skaro.

To avert this fate, a Dalek (or Davros himself) might have travelled back to the early days of the Daleks to 'correct' their timeline. The Daleks must survive, even if that means changing the rest of the universe to suit. In this light, the Gallifreyan mission to Skaro is less of a sneak attack and more of an attempt to stop the Daleks from meddling in time.

NEW GADGET: TIME RINGS

Looking like nothing more than a simple metal bracelet or ring, a Time Ring actually contains highly sophisticated atomic-level circuitry that runs through the entire object. It is usually pre-programmed to bring whoever is wearing or touching it to a specific point in time and space and await an anticipated 'moment' or a command by the operator before returning to the original space-time departure point. Gallifreyan Time Rings are programmed to return to Gallifrey shortly after their last preset jump.

A Time Ring is programmed before use. Its accuracy is determined by the person doing the programming (a Space-Time Navigation roll) and also, due to the constantly changing parameters of the Vortex, by the relative time elapsed between programming and use. Multiple destinations can be programmed into the Time Ring, leading to a series of jumps before returning 'home', but reprogramming it 'on the fly' is a hugely difficult process that requires highly advanced technology.

Traits: Restriction (Pre-programmed trips, Time Travel without a Capsule), Vortex
Cost: 2 Story Points

FUTURE OF THE KALEDS

The first Daleks were not built as weapons – they were built as travel machines and life support systems for the creatures that the Kaled scientists had determined their race would evolve into. Evolution doesn't work that way normally, and the Thals of the far future still looked completely human, so this transformation must be the result of mutation or genetic damage caused by the war. The Kaleds are a dying race, and Davros gave them hope. Making the Daleks something other than weapons of mass destruction makes them much more interesting. Doomsday weapons and invincible monsters are one-note; instead, threaten your players with a beneficial thing corrupted or gone wrong. (The nanogenes in *The Empty Child* in **The Ninth Doctor Sourcebook** are another example of this idea).

WAS THE DOCTOR PREVIOUSLY AN AGENT OF THE TIME LORDS?

When a Time Lord gave the Doctor a mission, the Doctor's response of 'whatever I've done for you in the past, I've more than made up for' is a curious one. It implies that the Doctor had been an agent of the Time Lords in the past. This could have been some time before he settled at 76 Totter's Lane in 1963, but it could also refer to a time immediately following his trial, where he could have run secret missions for the Time Lords as part of his sentence (this seems to be the case in *The Two Doctors*). If the latter, then the Doctor's memory of this time would have been wiped; he may retain some partial memories of it.

SO DID ANY OF THE PREVIOUS ADVENTURES HAPPEN?

One question that arises from this adventure is, absent previous temporal meddling as the cause, whether the Doctor's previous adventures with the Daleks still took place. After this adventure, the Daleks seem a dwindling and more desperate threat; the Movellans defeat their battle fleet, the Daleks are forced to increasingly rely on humanoid mercenaries, and, due to Davros' continued machinations, a different Dalek Civil War erupts.

It's worth noting that the Dalek invasion of Earth isn't referenced during the rest of the Doctor's travels, so perhaps this doesn't occur. That said, a better Dalek design would tend to negate the more primitive Daleks of *The Daleks* and *The Dalek Invasion of Earth* and alter Skaro's history so that the Thals had to flee Skaro (*The Planet of the Daleks*) as opposed to defeating the Daleks. Such a Dalek threat would, as the Doctor alluded, prompt the Ice Warriors to make peace with the other sentient races in the galaxy.

It's also entirely possible that some of the Doctor's previous adventures took place prior to the change in *Genesis of the Daleks* and some took place after; wibbley-wobbly, timey-wimey and all that. The Gamemaster has the fun of sorting through all this. It's worth noting that subsequent adventures have the Daleks on the defensive, making adventures such as *The Power of the Daleks*, the *Planet of the Daleks* and even *The Chase* more likely to occur post-*Genesis* and stories like *The Dalek Invasion of Earth* and *The Evil of the Daleks* to disappear in the time stream (altering the personal lives of Susan Foreman and Victoria Waterfield in the process).

FURTHER ADVENTURES

- Why did Davros create giant clams, especially in an environment where clams normally don't thrive (at least on Earth, anyway)? Weirdly, there are a lot of similarities between the Daleks and the clams – both are organic beings inside a protective shell, both have some level of psychokinesis, both are remarkably unfriendly. Maybe the clams were a sort of prototype – and if so, then those clams may hold genetic secrets of the Dalek mutant that could be used to create a weapon against them! Another possibility is that the clams are the future form of the Kaled race, created by artificial acceleration of evolution.

(Alternatively, imagine a scenario where the Doctor erases the Daleks from history and then returns to the present – only to discover that the Daleks' place as archvillians of the universe has been clammed, er claimed by the clams.)

- The transduction barrier of Gallifrey prevents anyone from travelling into Gallifrey's past, so the Daleks can't try to do to the same to the Time Lords by, say, travelling back in time and exterminating Rassilon. However, the transduction barrier isn't foolproof. If the Daleks did find a way to penetrate the barrier, perhaps by visiting a time period when Gallifrey engages with the outside world, like their dealings with the Minyans (see *Underworld*, on page 126), then they could attack the history of the Time Lords. The characters are the only TARDIS crew in the right temporal zone to follow the Dalek DARDIS through the breach, so it's up to them to save the first days of Gallifrey.

DALEK PROTOTYPE (MARK III TRAVEL MACHINE)

While in some ways more advanced than the Daleks that the First Doctor discovered on Skaro in the future, the Dalek Prototype does lack many of the features of Daleks met by future incarnations. Specifically, this Dalek lacks the ability to scan computers, fly, or generate force fields.

It's also appropriate to give the Dalek prototype the Enslaved trait, as it is programmed to follow Davros' orders, but the Dalek prototype soon acknowledges a logical inconsistency with being the dominant life form (as Davros is not a Dalek) and overrides that trait.

AWARENESS	3	PRESENCE	4
COORDINATION	2	RESOLVE	4
INGENUITY	4	STRENGTH	7*

SKILLS
Convince 1, Fighting 4, Marksman 3, Medicine 1, Science 3, Subterfuge 3, Survival 4, Technology 4

TRAITS
Armour (Major): The Dalekanium casing reduces damage by 10. This does reduce the Dalek's Coordination to 2 (already accommodated in the Attributes).
Cyborg
Environmental: Daleks are able to survive in the vacuum of space or underwater.
Fear Factor (3): Once you realise how deadly Daleks are they are terrifying, getting a +6 to rolls when actively scaring someone.
Natural Weapon – Exterminator: The legendary Dalek weapon usually kills with a single shot – 4/L/L.
Restricted Movement: Early Daleks could not climb stairs, although they can 'hop' one or two steps at a time (so a raised patio wouldn't stop them, but a flight of stairs to the door would).
Technically Adept: Daleks are brilliant at using and adapting technology.

TECH LEVEL: 6   **STORY POINTS: 5-8**

*The Dalek mutant inside has different attributes when removed from the Dalekanium casing. Of course, movement outside of the armour is incredibly limited (Speed 1) and they do not usually survive very long. If the mutant is exposed at any time, damage inflicted to the Dalek may bypass the armour.

AWARENESS	3	PRESENCE	3
COORDINATION	3	RESOLVE	4
INGENUITY	4	STRENGTH	5

- The Doctor's claim that some good must come of the Daleks is worth exploring. What benefits could come from a race of xenophobic mass murderers? Some potential benefits are obvious – different races band together to fight a common foe, scientists develop new wonders under the pressure of the Dalek threat, and nothing demonstrates the ultimate futility of hate like the cautionary example of a Dalek. There are more... questionable benefits, too. The Doctor lands on a world that was once invaded by Daleks. The invasion was defeated, and now the wreckage of a Dalek fleet lies scattered around the planet. A brilliant physician has developed a way to keep victims of the war alive – he's placing them in adapted travel machines. Is this Dalek life support a marvellous way to bring life out of death, or has the physician unwittingly set foot on the same ruinous path that Davros walked down, all those years ago?

DAVROS

The greatest of the Kaled scientists, Davros was gravely injured during the Kaled-Thal War and survived only by creating his own mobile support unit, the design of which inspired the Daleks. In many ways he mirrored the Dalek shell after himself; he has only one cybernetic eye set in his forehead, one movable arm (the hand of which has atrophied), and he needs to glide along in a travel chair. In addition his voice gains a metallic grating when he speaks, indicating that some of his internal organs may be cybernetic as well.

Like the Daleks, Davros undergoes enhancements in the future. Here, he is in the infancy of his reign as guide of the Daleks; he lacks some of the knowledge and extra traits that he has in the future.

AWARENESS	2	PRESENCE	2
COORDINATION	2	RESOLVE	6
INGENUITY	7	STRENGTH	2

SKILLS
Convince 1, Craft 6, Knowledge 6, Medicine 6, Science 6, Subterfuge 4, Survival 2, Technology 6, Transport 2

TRAITS
Boffin: First and foremost, Davros is a scientist.
Cyborg: Most of Davros' body has been replaced with machine parts and augmentations.
Dependency (Major): Davros needs to remain connected to his chair's life support system to survive. He is almost completely immobile without it and it keeps his damaged body alive. Without the chair, he will have to make regular Resolve and Strength rolls, with increasing Difficulties (starting at 12) to survive.
Fear Factor (1): Davros' reputation makes him an intimidating presence, +2 on rolls to actively terrorise.
Gadget: The lifesupport chair also houses the Scan and Transmit Traits.
Indomitable: Davros' will is extremely strong.

Immortal (Major): Davros' life support chair can keep him alive almost indefinitely.
Obsession (Major): Davros is obsessed with the survival of the Kaled race – as Daleks.
Technically Adept: The creator of the Daleks is a master technician.

EQUIPMENT: Life Support Chair. At the very least, it's got Scan and Transmit. Davros can also spend Story Points to retroactively add gadgets to his chair when needed. ("Emergency Forcefield, Activate!")

TECH LEVEL: 6

STORY POINTS: 12

MUTO

AWARENESS	3	PRESENCE	2
COORDINATION	3	RESOLVE	3
INGENUITY	2	STRENGTH	4

The mutants of the surface are the descendants of both the Thals and Kaleds, and have become feral scavengers of the wasteland.

SKILLS

Athletics 3, Craft 3, Fighting 3, Knowledge 1, Marksman 2, Medicine 1, Subterfuge 3, Survival 4, Technology 1

TRAITS

Alien Appearance (Minor)
Code of Conduct (Minor): Mutos have a crude code of honour.
Distinctive (Minor): -2 penalty to rolls to blend in. Others have a +2 bonus to remember or recognise the Mutos.

EQUIPMENT: Club (+2 damage; +4 if using a two-handed club)

TECH LEVEL: 2   **STORY POINTS:** 1-3

SECURITY COMMANDER NYDER

AWARENESS	4	PRESENCE	3
COORDINATION	4	RESOLVE	3
INGENUITY	5	STRENGTH	3

Nyder is in charge of security in the Kaled Scientific Bunker. He is unquestionably loyal to Davros, as he agrees with him that the Kaled race is doomed unless they become Daleks (he naturally assumed that the Daleks would be under his command, through Davros). He is very cunning and usually able to ferret out the truth, or at least gather enough 'evidence' to prove whatever he wants.

SKILLS

Athletics 3, Convince 4, Craft 4, Fighting 4, Knowledge 2, Marksman 4, Medicine 3, Science 2, Subterfuge 4, Survival 2, Technology 3, Transport 3

TRAITS

Quick Reflexes: The character always goes first in their Action Round unless taken by surprise.
Voice of Authority: +2 bonus to Presence and Convince rolls.

EQUIPMENT: Pistol 2/5/7

TECH LEVEL: 5   **STORY POINTS:** 5

REVENGE OF THE CYBERMEN

'You've no home planet, no influence, nothing. You're just a pathetic bunch of tin soldiers skulking about the galaxy in an ancient spaceship.'

⬡ SYNOPSIS

Nerva Beacon, 30th century

The time travellers arrived in the transmat of Nerva Beacon, which was in orbit around Jupiter and monitoring Voga, a satellite captured by the giant planet. The Time Ring disappeared and the Doctor noted that the TARDIS was travelling back in time to meet them. The station was littered with dead bodies and under quarantine; only four crewmen were left. Unbeknownst to the time travellers, the 'plague' was the result of a Cybermat.

One of the crewmen, Kellman, was secretly working with the Vogans. He'd set up a transmat to the asteroid, actually the remains of a planet, and had also kept the fact that Vogans were alive inside the asteroid secret as well. The Vogans were preparing a rocket to destroy the Cybermen. Kellman also appeared to be working for the Cybermen, who wanted to destroy the remnants of the 'planet of gold' before launching a new campaign to conquer the universe.

Another crewman was attacked by the Cybermat just as the time travellers were discovered. The Doctor pretended they were a medical team from Earth and Harry noted that the now-dead crewman was bitten. The Doctor was suspicious about Kellman and investigated his room. Kellman attempted to gas him, but the Doctor managed to escape while, elsewhere, Sarah was bitten by the Cybermat. To save her, the Doctor fixed the sabotaged transmat and sent her and Harry down, correctly theorising that the transmat would remove the foreign agent in her body.

Harry and Sarah were captured by the Vogans, who were on the verge of civil war. Chief Guardian Vorus wanted to return Voga to its former glory, while the more cautious Chief Councillor Tyrum worried that Vorus was abusing his power. Back on the station, the Cybermen invaded and took over, planning to send the humans to Voga with two Cyber-bombs. Kellman was allowed to beam down to check the transmat, and seized the opportunity to warn the Vogans and implore them to use their rocket.

Unfortunately the Vogan rocket wasn't ready and, due to the Doctor's meddling, the Cybermen had advanced their plans. In addition to the humans, two Cybermen beamed to the planet. Vogan weapons were useless against them. Sarah returned to the beacon via transmat while Harry and Kellman went looking for the Doctor, who had one of the bombs. Harry inadvertently caused a rockslide, which killed Kellman and injured the Doctor.

The Doctor concocted a plan to destroy the Cybermen, but after it went awry one of the crewmen sacrificed himself by detonating his Cyber-bomb and killing the two Cybermen along with himself. Sarah tried to stop the Cyber-Leader from detonating the bombs remotely; she failed but the Doctor had jammed the signal. The Cyber-Leader instead decided to ram the beacon, now filled with Cyber-bombs, into Voga to destroy it.

The Doctor returned to the beacon with gold dust and used the Cybermat to inject it into a Cyberman. Unfortunately, the Cyber-Leader overpowered the Doctor and Sarah and left them on the station as he retreated to his ship. The Vogans launched their rocket at the station, but the Doctor convinced them to change its course and destroy the Cyber-ship. The TARDIS finally arrived and the time travellers left.

CONTINUITY

This adventure takes place not long after the Nerva Beacon, which would later house the Ark, was built. The Cyber-Wars are mentioned. The Cybermen lost in large part due to 'glitter guns' which sprayed gold into their respiration systems and choked them to death.

⊙ RUNNING THE ADVENTURE

Sometimes, you can take inspiration from a previous adventure by reversing some of the elements so that the new adventure is almost a mirror image of the old.

This adventure is almost a mirror-image of the previous adventure, **Genesis of the Daleks**. Whereas that adventure involved the origin of one of the Doctor's most ruthless adversaries, **Revenge of the Cybermen** involves an equally ruthless adversary in its final moments. The implication is that this is the last of the Cybermen (the ones he encounters in the 52nd century may be descendants of the Lumic Cybermen rather than Mondasians/Telosians).

Another mirror image is inherent weaknesses. The Time Lords hoped that the Doctor might find (or possibly implant) a weakness in the Daleks, while such a weakness (gold) has already been discovered

and used against the Cybermen. And still another mirror image is that, while the Doctor's presence threatened to end the Daleks, here his presence almost enabled the Cybermen's survival (as the Cybermen arrived at the beacon more quickly, before the Skystriker was ready).

REUSING LOCATIONS

This adventure is primarily set in the Nerva Beacon – the same place as the Ark from **The Ark in Space**. This should serve as a lesson to Gamemasters that you can reuse material that you've prepared for one adventure in the next, especially if time is involved. In fact, if you take a stroll around your neighbourhood you'll probably find many buildings that have been repurposed over the years. A residence in the Victorian era may become a bed-and-breakfast or an office for the local historical society a century later. A noble's castle may become a tourist attraction, with an alien manipulating a historical re-enactment. A space freighter may be refitted as a passenger liner.

Reusing locations not only saves time, as you can reuse much of your previously-prepared material and you already have a handle on what the setting is like, but it also gives the players a '4D' perspective of the universe, especially if they visit the future location first. There's probably a campaign in setting all the adventures in the same location at different times over the centuries!

SNEAK ATTACK?

The Cybermen practically destroyed Voga in the waning moments of the Cyber-Wars and left its remnants floating in space (it is presumed that the piece that ended up in the Solar System contains the last Vogans, but it's possible that other asteroid 'Vogas' exist). The Vogans know that the Cybermen are coming; they even laid a trap for them. Yet, when the Cybermen invade Voga, the Vogans attack them with useless weapons.

While there's speculation that the Vogan's didn't use gold for bullets, this is not accurate. Cybermen (at least this model) are only affected by gold dust; a gold slug would have no more effect than a lead one. The bigger question is why the Vogans didn't have a supply of glitter guns or the remnants of a garrison from the Cyber-Wars (presumably Earth and its allies would want to protect such a critical resource?).

So why aren't the Vogans better prepared? That certainly sounds like a mystery worth investigating...

GALLIFREYAN INVOLVEMENT?

The symbol for Voga is suspiciously identical to the Seal of Rassilon. While this could be coincidence (much like the swastika's use in Asian religions and Nazi Germany), the Time Lords have been known to interfere with other worlds, especially in the earlier part of their history. The Time Lords are also known to act when the harmony of the universe is threatened.

Given that the Cybermen went from a frozen army in need of new blood to a galaxy-threatening force within a century or so, they could have gained the Time Lords' attention. It's easy to see how such a threat could spread quickly throughout the universe.

Thus, the Time Lords may have interfered with Vogan history to ensure their role in the Cyber-Wars as well as protect the survivors from destruction (it's likely that the Earth-like living conditions within the asteroid are artificially controlled).

It also stands to reason that the Time Lords purposefully pushed Voga into the Solar System and sent the Doctor back to that point in order to lay a final trap for the Cybermen. It's just the sort of thing they would do, and it's notable that the TARDIS does not materialise until the Cybermen are defeated. Given that the Doctor's arrival actually hindered the Vogan plan, the plan must have been doomed to failure.

MODEL 5 CYBERMAN

The Model 5 Cybermen are survivors of the Cyber-Wars and are perhaps the last of their race (the 'Model 5' designation being in terms of the Doctor's timeline as well as the Model 5's similarity to the Model 4). These Cybermen have been so extensively damaged and repaired that little remains of their former humanity – they are more robot than cyborg, although paradoxically they seem to emote more than other Cybermen. They claim to have enough parts to build an entire army in their vessel, so they may only need the bare minimum organic matter (if any) to create more Cybermen.

AWARENESS	2	PRESENCE	3
COORDINATION	3	RESOLVE	2
INGENUITY	4	STRENGTH	7

SKILLS

Athletics 4, Convince 2, Craft 2, Fighting 2, Knowledge 1, Marksman 3, Medicine 3, Science 2, Subterfuge 2, Survival 3, Technology 4, Transport 2

TRAITS

Armour (Minor): The Cybermen's metallic armour reduces damage by 5.
Cyborg: The Cybermen were once human, but have everything but their major internal organs replaced with machinery.
Environmental (Minor): Cybermen can survive in the vacuum of space.
Fear Factor (3): Cybermen are pretty scary and gain a +6 to rolls to actively scare someone.
Natural Weapon – Head Gun: Model 5 Cybermen have a sparking gun built into the top of their helmets - 4/L/L
Natural Weapon – Stun Weapon: The Head Gun can be set to stun – S/S/S.

Networked (Minor): With the push of a button a Cyberman can summon the aid of another.
Slow (Major): Due to their heavy cybernetic bodies, Cybermen are slow. They only have a Speed of 1 in chases.
Technically Adept: +2 to all Technology rolls.
Weakness (Major): The Model 5 Cybermen can be suffocated by gold dust entering their chest units. It is unknown whether they share the same weaknesses to acetone and radiation as previous models.

TECH LEVEL: 6   **STORY POINTS: 3-6**

NEW GADGET: GLITTER GUN

The Glitter Gun is a simple weapon that shoots a spray of gold particles. This spray is largely harmless to humans (ok, it stings if you get it in your eyes, and you shouldn't inhale too deeply when firing), but is absolutely devastating to Cybermen. The gun triggers their Major Weakness, inflicting 4/8/12 damage on a successful hit. This attack ignores armour.

Traits: Exploit Weakness (Major), Restriction: Only works on Cyber-creatures.
Cost: 1 Story Point

TYPE 3 CYBERMAT

The Cybermen occasionally employ a small cybernetic organism known as a Cybermat. The Type 3 Cybermat resembles a silverfish that is roughly 2-3 feet long from snout to tail. Cybermats can crawl through small openings and make excellent sentries, assassins, saboteurs, and advance units.

AWARENESS	4	PRESENCE	1
COORDINATION	4	RESOLVE	5
INGENUITY	2	STRENGTH	5

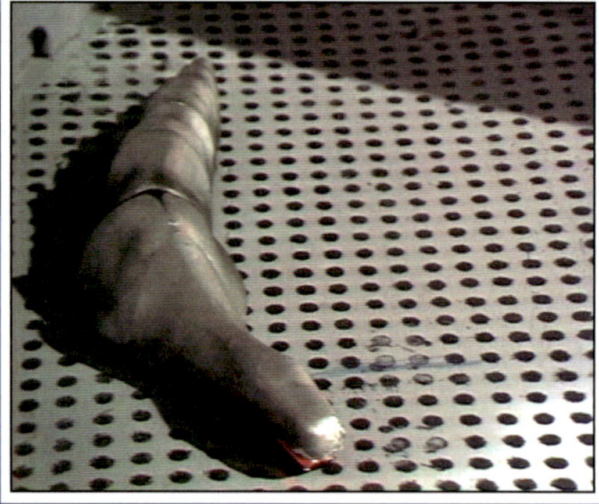

SKILLS
Athletics 5, Fighting 2, Marksman 4, Subterfuge 5, Survival 2, Technology 3, Transport 3

TRAITS
Alien Appearance: Type 3 Cybermats look like large metallic silverfish.
Alien Senses: A Cybermat has a number of senses, including infrared and ultraviolet vision. It also has the ability to home in on human brainwaves.
Armour (Minor): The Cybermats' metallic armour reduces damage by 5.
Special - Clinging: The Cybermat can climb even smooth surfaces without difficulty.
Cyborg: While it looks like a small robot, a Cybermat is a partially organic creature like the Cybermen themselves.
Enslaved: The Cybermats are the servants of the Cybermen. They can also be remote-controlled.
Special - Jumping: A Cybermat's advanced hydraulics enable it to leap 5-6 feet in the air, perfect for landing on a humanoid's back or shoulder. By spending a Story Point, the Cybermat can automatically take an unsuspecting foe by surprise with this attack.

Natural Weapon (bite): A Cybermat can bite an opponent, injecting them with a lethal poison. The victim suffers immediate Stun (S/S/S) damage, during which his arteries glow bright red. Within minutes, the damage turns Lethal (4/L/L).
Weakness (major): Cybermats seem even more susceptible to gold than their Cybermen masters.

Notes: A Cybermat's Strength is for pushing or pulling only. Similarly, a Cybermat only does as programmed; its Technology and Transport skills are only for seeking out the proper wiring or circuitry to corrode and destroy equipment .

STORY POINTS: 2-4

FURTHER ADVENTURES

- The Vogans have suffered a lot as a result of the Cyber-Wars but fortunately they have a commodity that's in slim supply. Do the Vogans use it to rebuild their society, or do they create a corporate empire that rivals the Company of the Usurians (see **The Sun Makers** on page 122)? Perhaps the characters arrive in the middle of a corporate war, where one or both sides are being manipulated by someone else?

- While this adventure is presented as the end of the Cybermen, this may not be the case. Other scattered bands of Cybermen may exist and, rather than try to destroy Voga, they may have modified their armour to be resistant to gold. Can the time travellers find a new weakness to exploit before these new Cybermen spread throughout the galaxy?

- Voga is an asteroid of gold. This makes it a tempting target for pirates and treasure hunters, the more amoral of which may not care about slaughtering the remainder of the Vogans to take it. Presuming this happens while Voga is travelling toward the Solar System, can the time travellers stop the pirates so that Voga can play the role it's destined to play (perhaps tipping the Vogans off to the future Cyberman attack in the process)?

VOGANS

Vogans are humanoids from the planet Voga, which gained the moniker 'planet of gold' due to its large gold deposits. This made it a crucial ally in the Cyber-Wars, but the Vogans paid the price when their world was almost destroyed. They have remained hidden for a couple of centuries, allowing the universe to believe them dead. Vogans have brownish skin and elongated heads (making their foreheads about half the length of their faces) with white hair. Vogans tend to be physically weaker than other humanoids, as gold bonds can effectively restrain them. Power is shared between the ruling Council, which wishes to maintain the isolation, and the Guardians, who control the guilds and want to resume trade with the rest of the universe.

AWARENESS	3	PRESENCE	3
COORDINATION	3	RESOLVE	3
INGENUITY	3	STRENGTH	2

SKILLS
Athletics 3, Convince 2, Fighting 3, Knowledge 2, Marksman 3, Technology 2, Transport 2

TRAITS
Alien
Alien Appearance (Minor): Vogans are humanoid with brownish skin and elongated heads.
Alien Senses (Minor): +4 to Awareness when using low-light vision.
Obsession (Minor/Major Bad): All Vogans are wary of revealing themselves to the universe. For some, especially the Council, this is a major obsession and justifies total secrecy. For others, such as the Guardians, this is only a minor obsession and such Vogans wish to resume trade with the outside world.

EQUIPMENT: Carbines (3/6/9)

TECH LEVEL: 6   **STORY POINTS:** 1-3

TERROR OF THE ZYGONS

'I'll say one thing for you, Broton. You think big.'

⊙ SYNOPSIS

Scotland and London, UNIT Era

The Brigadier called the Doctor to Earth to investigate attacks on oil rigs in the North Sea. In addition to the oil companies, a local, the Duke of Forgill, was also concerned. His men had orders to shoot trespassers on sight, a threat carried out when Harry tried to aid a rig survivor that emerged from the sea. The Duke's man killed the survivor and injured Harry with a grazing shot.

Investigating the rig wreckage, the Doctor determined that it was the work of a large creature and found a signal device. His efforts were observed by the alien invaders – the Zygons – who decided this meddler needed to be dealt with. The Zygons could assume human forms – their leader Broton was acting as the Duke while the nurse caring for Harry was also a Zygon. She arranged for the Doctor and Sarah to be placed in a decompression chamber, which she then sabotaged to remove the oxygen, but the Doctor used hypnosis to keep them alive until they were rescued.

Meanwhile, Harry was taken to the Zygon ship. He learned that the Zygons had been hiding in their ship in Loch Ness for centuries, living off the milk of their cyborg monster, the Skarasen. They were preparing to turn Earth into a new Zygon homeworld after their own was consumed by its sun. Harry further learned that the Zygons needed to keep their victims alive in order to copy them. Harry was placed in a chamber and a Zygon took his form.

Zygon-Harry attempted to infiltrate UNIT's temporary HQ to retrieve the signal device but was spotted by Sarah. She followed him to a barn, where he fell and died while trying to kill her, revealing himself as a Zygon. Broton activated the signal to bring the Skarasen to kill them all but the Doctor lured it away. In the Zygon ship, Harry escaped his cabinet and enabled the signal device, which was stuck to the Doctor's hand, to fall off so that the Skarasen would crush it and return to Loch Ness. The Doctor and Sarah investigated the Duke's residence on the Loch's shores. There, Sarah found and freed Harry, but Broton took the Doctor prisoner and flew the Zygon ship out of the lake.

Broton jammed all radar so his ship was difficult to track. As the Duke was President of the Scottish

Energy Commission, Broton planned on attending an international energy conference in London, which the Prime Minister was attending, and planting a signal device there. He planned to kill everyone there in order to get the world to accede to his demands.

The Doctor managed to destroy the Zygon ship after freeing the prisoners. The Brigadier, having been informed by the Doctor and Sarah as to Broton's plan, found and shot Broton dead. The Doctor tossed the signal device into the Thames, where the Skarasen ate it before returning to Loch Ness. UNIT was able to successfully cover up the incident, concealing the truth about how the Loch Ness monster nearly ate London.

CONTINUITY

The Loch Ness Monster is a Skarasen and still resides in the loch after the adventure.
The Zygons have been in the loch for centuries and have an ability equated to the Scottish changeling myth.

⊙ RUNNING THE ADVENTURE

The Zygon's plan in this adventure is – well, let's just say that Broton is a bit of a nutter. Little of his plan makes any sense, as the Doctor is keen to point out. First, he wants to reveal himself to an Energy Conference rather than, say, the United Nations, and plans to reveal that his own monster is what destroyed the oil rigs, with little to show for it but the Skarasen poking its head out of the Thames. Second, he believes that the world will bow down to six Zygons and a dinosaur. Third, he plans on transforming the Earth to a warmer, more suitable environment, enslaving humanity as a workforce in an effort that will take centuries. Not only is it likely that billions of people will quickly tire of a handful of aliens pushing them around, but the Zygons risk awakening the Silurians, who would thrive in the new environment. Finally, the Zygons won't receive any reinforcements for centuries.

Now, it's possible that Broton's scheme has layers that aren't immediately apparent – maybe he plans on replacing key leaders, or using Zygon technology to trigger a new energy crisis – it's much more fun to assume that he's in over his head. Villains aren't always super-competent. Like player characters, they sometimes have to make it up as they go along.

Sometimes, you may come up with an intricate adventure that seems logical on paper, just but doesn't make any sense in play. Maybe the players spot some flaw in the plan that you overlooked. Instead of coming up with a hasty solution, run with it. Turn the villain from a mastermind into a desperate buffoon (less competent, more unpredictable – and more dangerous) and have him try to salvage his doomed plan through increasingly risky actions. The players get the fun of pointing out the flaw, but still have to stop the bad guy. Maybe the players can use

the villain's desperation to their advantage, say by convincing his lieutenants that their boss is insane and that maybe they should switch sides.

MYTHOLOGY AS SCIENCE FACT

In this adventure it is explicitly stated that the Skarasen is the Loch Ness Monster. There is also a strong case for the Zygons being Changelings (or Selkies, or Werewolves). When looking for inspiration for adventures, choose a mythological or legendary creature and create a 'scientific' explanation for it. Perhaps the New Jersey Devil is a scientific experiment gone wrong, or the Beast of Gevaudan is a forgotten alien hunting dog (the Yeti turned out to be robots, and the Doctor has run into werewolves several times in other incarnations that turned out to be alien bio-patterns imposed on human victims).

When 're-skinning' a mythological creature, don't be afraid to deviate a bit from the inspiration. An alien based on the Phoenix may not necessarily be a flying fiery bird, just something with a lethal weapon and the ability to regenerate. A Cyclops may simply be a tall alien (even 6 feet could be considered a 'giant' in the ancient Mediterranean) wearing a helmet with a distinctive face shield (representing the single eye).

ORGANIC TECHNOLOGY

The Zygons use living technology. Their weapons, their ships and their equipment are all partially alive. Organic technology has several key benefits. It's easy to 'grow' replacements, and it's possible to interface with it, gaining the Technically Adept trait if you've got the right genetic code. Organic technology is hard to use if you're not the matching species, though – everyone else is Technically Inept when it comes to using some other races' goop.

Their use of organic technology makes the Zygons extremely memorable villains. Just look at them!

Giving villains a hook – a weird approach to technology, a distinctive way of killing people, a disconcerting appearance, a catchphrase – can turn a monster-of-the-week into a horror that comes back again and again to haunt the player characters.

ARE THE ZYGONS RELATED TO THE CHAMELEONS?

The Zygons have a lot in common with the aliens that the Second Doctor encountered in **The Faceless Ones**. Both aliens suffered from an explosion that occurred on their home planet and technology that not only enabled them to take the form of another humanoid, but also needed to keep the victim alive (although the technologies are obviously different). It's also important to note that, while the Chameleons were humanoid, their forms were badly twisted by the explosion and their true form was never revealed.

It's quite possible that the two races are, in fact, the same race. The stellar explosion that Broton mentioned created the Chameleons. When they arrived on Earth they contacted Broton, but he wanted nothing to do with them. As it's logical that the inhospitable conditions still plague the home world, it became dead to him. Rather than join the Chameleons, Broton decided instead to contact the remaining 'pure' Zygons that escaped the accident and wants to create a new home world on Earth. It's likely that encounters between the Chameleons and Zygons wouldn't be friendly.

NEW GADGET – SKARASEN REMOTE

The Skarasen Remote is more of a homing signal; it transmits a signal that the Skarasen follows until it can consume the remote. The Zygons can remotely turn this signal on and off, as well as enable the remote to latch onto the holder. This makes it difficult to remove and life-threatening if the Skarasen is nearby.

Traits: Transmit, Special (attaches to user with Strength 5)
Cost: 1 Story Point

THE REFUGEE SHIP

The Zygon refugee ship is still en route to Earth. While it won't arrive for several centuries, it's still coming – and it's filled to the brim with Zygons, who expect the Earth to be terraformed into a suitable environment for them. What will happen when the Zygons arrive? The first Earth-Zygon war, or will future humanity be able to integrate the Zygons or find them another home?

FURTHER ADVENTURES

- The Zygons have been sitting in the loch for centuries. They must occasionally surface to maintain their existence or possibly exploit an opportunity to leave or convert Earth. Perhaps the construction of the Caledonian Canal in the late 18th century threatened the Zygon ship and 'Nessie' attacked the workers? (It's possible that the Skarasen could have been destroyed here but the Zygons were able to raise a replacement).

- The Flesh (see **The Eleventh Doctor Sourcebook**) is really similar to Zygon technology. It's an organic goop that takes its form from a subject in an interface harness. Did the makers of the Flesh salvage Zygon technology – or are they actually Zygons in disguise?

- The Zygons planned to enslave the human race. Maybe they succeeded with a similar plan on another world. The characters arrive on a planet where alien invaders are forcing the human colonists to alter the environment – but the invaders have transformed themselves to look like colonists, and run their fascist empire through pawns and mind-controlled slaves. How can the characters lead a revolution, when they can't trust anyone?

SKARASEN

AWARENESS	3	PRESENCE	2
COORDINATION	2	RESOLVE	3
INGENUITY	1	STRENGTH	20

SKILLS
Athletics 2, Fighting 3, Survival 4

TRAITS
Cyborg
Environmental (Minor): The Skarasen is equally at home on land and underwater.
Fear Factor 2: Grants a +4 bonus to inspire fear
Gadget – Transmit: The Skarasen can receive and home in on a signal sent by the Skarasen Remote.
Huge (Major): The Skarasen's a gigantic monster.
Natural Weapons (Minor): The Skarasen has teeth and claws that do Strength +2 damage.

STORY POINTS: 7

ZYGON

AWARENESS	3	PRESENCE	3
COORDINATION	3	RESOLVE	4
INGENUITY	3	STRENGTH	5

SKILLS
Athletics 3, Convince 2, Craft 2, Fighting 4, Knowledge 3, Marksman 2, Medicine 4, Science 6, Subterfuge 4, Survival 5, Technology (crystallography) 4, Transport 3

TRAITS
Alien
Alien Appearance
Fear Factor 2: A Zygon gets a +4 bonus to inspire fear when transforming back to its natural form in front of an unsuspecting victim.
Shapeshift (Major): A Zygon can assume the form of a humanoid that it has synchronised with through Zygon technology. The Zygon may assume this form at will, but they need to re-imprint every few hours or the victim dies and his form can no longer be mimicked.
Special – Organic Interface: A Zygon can interface with the organic controls of a Zygon ship, giving him the Technically Adept trait when operating them.
Technology Level: Technically 6, but the Zygons' technology is wildly different to that of most species.

EQUIPMENT: Skarasen Remote

TECH LEVEL: 6   **STORY POINTS: 7-9**

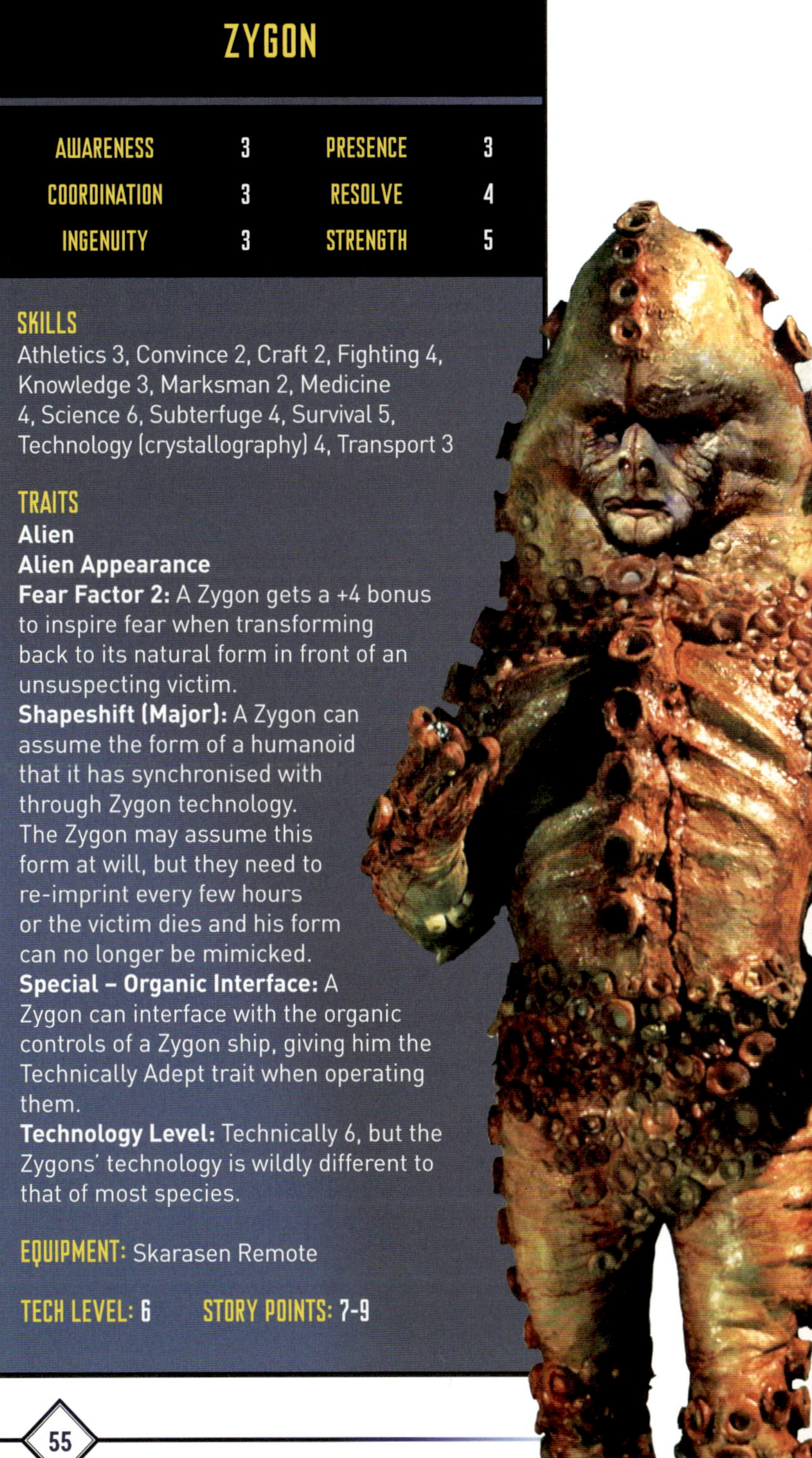

PLANET OF EVIL

'You and I are scientists, Professor. We buy our privilege to experiment at the cost of total responsibility.'

SYNOPSIS

Zeta Minor, 3716

Zeta Minor lay on the edge of the universe, incredibly far from inhabited space. The TARDIS received a distress call from an expedition to the planet, which claimed to have encountered invisible monsters. The Doctor landed the ship and he and Sarah explored the jungle outside. At the same time a probe ship arrived looking for the members of the expedition. The head of the expedition, Sorenson, claimed that someone was murdering the expedition members.

The probe ship crew transmatted the TARDIS on board and arrested the Doctor and Sarah. They were accused of murder and sentenced to execution. The Doctor and Sarah escaped their cell, only to be confronted by the invisible creatures. Their guard was killed while trying to attack the creatures. Of course, the remaining Morestrans believed that the time travellers were responsible for his death as the Doctor and Sarah fled into the jungle.

Sorenson urged the probe to allow him to load his mineral samples and leave, claiming he'd found the energy source needed to refuel the dying Morestran sun. The probe ship's Controller, Salamar, refused to take off until he captured the time travellers. They found the Doctor and Sarah near a pit where the Doctor believed the boundary between the universe and the anti-matter universe lay. They all returned to the ship, but found that its systems were scrambled and it couldn't take off.

The Doctor insisted that the samples needed to be removed and offered to negotiate with the creature. He climbed down into the pit, where he encountered a gigantic alien entity. The Doctor promised that that the humans would return all the stolen antimatter if the alien would permit them to leave. Meanwhile, the crew unloaded the samples, but Sorenson stole one of the canisters away.

The creature lifted the Doctor out of the pit and he returned to the ship. It took off, but the remaining antimatter held it back, preventing it from leaving orbit. Sorenson began changing into a feral creature, but used Antiquark Serum to stave off the transformation. When another crewman died, Sorenson again blamed the time travellers.

The time travellers were about to be executed by ejection until another creature killed someone on the command deck, tangentially exonerating the Doctor and Sarah. The Doctor realised that Sorenson was infected with antimatter and reverting to a bestial state. The Doctor informed Sorenson of this and told him that he needed to return the minerals he took. Salamar learned of Sorenson's condition and decided to kill him with the ship's neutron accelerator, even though he would himself die in the attempt. Unfortunately, this plan backfired, and while Salamar died, Sorenson only increased in power and multiplied.

The Doctor managed to stun Sorenson and return him to the pit in the TARDIS, tossing him and the final canister into it. When he did so the other creatures disappeared. Sorenson was also returned to human form and released, whereupon the Doctor returned him to the probe and suggested an alternative solution to his energy problem. The time travellers then left in the TARDIS.

CONTINUITY

Morestrans are humans that colonised Morestra (likely a colony ship that left Earth during the solar flares) and started an empire.

Morestra's solar system is losing energy due to its dying sun. Many other civilisations are experiencing a similar problem.

The planet of Zeta Minor exists on the boundary between the matter and anti-matter universes.

RUNNING THE ADVENTURE

This adventure is at its heart a morality tale. Sorenson believes himself to be a pioneer and a hero – he's discovered a new source of energy that his home civilisation desperately needs. He is so eager to use it and save the day that he doesn't entertain the idea that his hypothesis may be false, condemning several lives and quite possibly the entire universe (or two universes). The characters learn the truth and spend the rest of the adventure trying to make things right while avoiding the monsters created by the energy.

ANTI-MATTER GUARDIAN?

One of the biggest questions is what exactly existed in the anti-matter pool. It appeared to be a large version of the anti-matter creature and it would not allow any anti-matter to be removed from the planet. It's likely that the Anti-Matter Guardian (for lack of

a better term) knew that taking anti-matter would ultimately cause an explosion, but that seems to be a trifling concern.

What is more likely is that, as a bridge between universes, Zeta Minor is a hybrid planet. The loss of any anti-matter would disrupt the delicate balance and cause a catastrophe in both universes. As the Anti-Matter Guardian proves a creature of its word, the consequences for taking the anti-matter would have been horrific.

In another adventure, the characters might encounter a similar Guardian that takes another approach. The Guardian might telepathically project images of what will happen if the characters disturb the balance, or loop time until the characters put things right, or empathically project incredibly strong emotions that the characters need to interpret ("Why do I feel irrationally angry when I look at Sorenson?").

ANTI-MATTER, INFERNOS, AND DALEKS

There are a number of similarities with this adventure and the *Inferno Project* (see **Inferno** in **The Third Doctor Sourcebook**). In both cases, a powerful energy source deep within the planet brings something to the surface that, when touched, causes the infected person to revert to a bestial state with a strong preference for its 'home' environment. It's even possible that the people disintegrated by the Anti-Matter Creatures become Anti-Matter Creatures themselves, much like the Primords spread their condition. Maybe 'Stahlman's gas' is actually vaporised anti-matter.

This raises the interesting possibility that powerful sources of anti-matter may be locked within any planet's surface (as, indeed, the "edge" of the universe may not be measured by distance from a universal centre – it could be a measure of dimensional instability). This could be the true reason why the Daleks were trying to dig to the Earth's core in **The Dalek Invasion of Earth** (see **The First Doctor Sourcebook**).

Such an act also proves that Dalek technology is advanced enough to hollow out the Earth's core without destroying the world, something Professors Stahlman and Zaroff were unable to accomplish.

Anti-matter 'infestations' could be discovered on any world. Some civilisations might have learned to tap these resources safely (or maybe they have

an underclass of Primord-like monsters that are partially infected with anti-matter); others may be destroyed by this dangerous substance.

ANTI-MATTER DOES NOT WORK THAT WAY!

Modern science suggests that anti-matter explodes on contact with normal matter. It doesn't come in ore form. And you probably can't store it safely in a toffee tin, like the Doctor did...

The anti-matter in Omega's universe (see **The Three Doctors** in **The Third Doctor Sourcebook**) did behave in a more conventional way – it exploded when the Doctor's unshielded normal-matter recorder came into contact with anti-matter. The anti-matter on Zeta Minor may be a third form of matter, neither wholly matter nor wholly antimatter, that can be easily 'flipped' into true anti-matter. In its basic 'ore' form, it has bizarre effects on human genetics, but can be mined and stored relatively easily. When you need power, just turn it back into regular antimatter and watch the fireworks!

NEW GADGET – OCULOID TRACKER

The Oculoid Tracker is a small robot that floats through the air as a remote eye. It is generally used for reconnaissance. The robot is capable of following basic orders, such as following a target or watching for movement.

Traits: Scan, Transmit
Cost: 2 Story Points

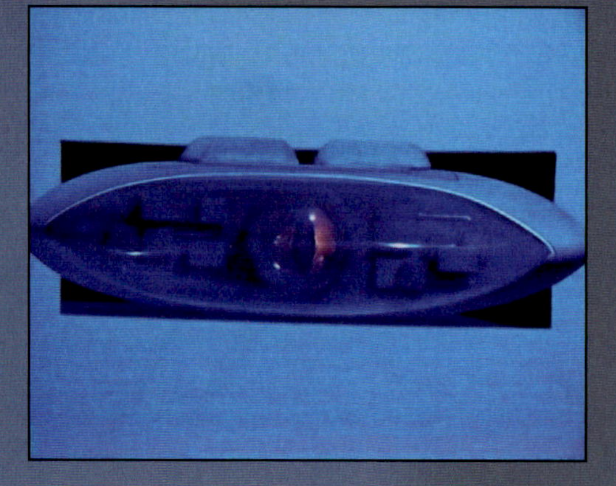

NEW GADGET – ANTIQUARK VACCINE

Professor Sorenson developed a drug that he believed could protect him from anti-matter infection. The drug worked, at least temporarily – each dose of the drug gives the user a few hours of immunity to the negative effects of anti-matter (well, some of the negative effects. It'll stop the anti-matter from mutating you into a feral monster. It doesn't stop you from exploding if you touch pure antimatter.)

Traits: Immunity (Minor)
Cost: 1 Story Point

FURTHER ADVENTURES

- What happened to the Morestran sun? Did they simply have the misfortune to establish their colony in orbit of an old and fading star, or did something drain its energy? What must life be like under a dying sun? Do the Morestrans huddle under titanic metal domes to trap what heat and light remain? Do they tunnel deep into their planet, or do they have fantastic crystalline sun-trees that collect and concentrate what little sunlight remains?

- Desperation drives the Morestrans into a bizarre holy war when the Morestran church declares that those who hoard energy are sinful. Morestran warships descend on neighbouring worlds, looting their energy supplies and resources. Can the characters save the day when a problem that began as a scientific dilemma has become a question of faith?

- Two factions on the war-torn planet of Opala fight a bitter, unending war. A drilling project launched by one faction encounters a pocket of anti-matter, and by the time the characters arrive some of the workers have already been transformed into monsters. In fact, some of them have *completed* a bizarre metamorphosis, and are now intelligent Anti-Men. The characters discover that the Anti-Matter hybrids can only reproduce by infecting others. The hybrids are much more peaceful than the natives of Opala. If the characters agree to help the Anti-Men, they could end the war by releasing anti-matter gas over the whole planet, turning both factions into Anti-Men – but is this peace, or genocide?

ANTI-MATTER CREATURE

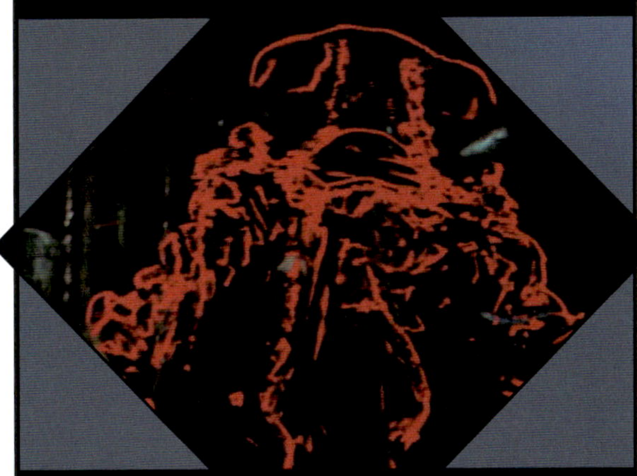

AWARENESS	3	PRESENCE	1
COORDINATION	2	RESOLVE	3
INGENUITY	1	STRENGTH	3

Anti-Matter Creatures are beings of pure anti-matter energy. To a humanoid eye they appear as vague red outlines. They seem subservient to the will of a greater Anti-Matter being, or Guardian, that sits just beneath the anti-matter pool between universes. Anti-Matter Creatures protect the anti-matter on Zeta Minor and kill anyone that tries to take it off-world.

SKILLS
Athletics 3, Fighting 4

TRAITS
Alien
Alien Appearance
Special – Disintegrating Touch: The touch of an Anti-Matter creature disintegrates matter. Any hit by an Anti-Matter Creature inflicts Lethal damage.
Immaterial: The Anti-Matter Creatures do not interact with normal matter. They cannot be touched nor harmed. They can also walk through solid objects.
Special – Anti-Matter Ward: Anti-Matter Creatures won't attack someone that's holding anti-matter, providing that the anti-matter is held between them.

STORY POINTS: 5-7

PROFESSOR SORENSON – ANTI-MAN

AWARENESS	3	PRESENCE	2
COORDINATION	3	RESOLVE	4
INGENUITY	1	STRENGTH	6

Sorenson was a Morestran scientist that was looking for a new source of energy to replace that of the dying sun of his solar system. He found it in anti-matter, but didn't realise that the anti-matter of Zeta Minor was attached to an alien intelligence. He attempted to flee the planet with some of the anti-matter but it contaminated him. Sorenson reverted to a bestial state that he unsuccessfully tried to treat with drugs. In his hybrid state, Sorenson loses his intelligence and becomes a vicious creature. While fuelled by anti-matter, he is still made of matter, albeit hairier and bestial, and can be affected by normal weapons. When exposed to a neutron accelerator, Sorenson can make anti-matter copies of himself.

SKILLS
Athletics 3, Fighting 3, Survival 3

TRAITS
Alien Appearance: In his hybrid form Sorenson resembles a wolf-man.
Natural Weapon – Dehydrate: Sorenson can lethally drain a victim simply by touching him and disintegrating all of their fluids (4/L/L).
Replication (Special): Once exposed to a neutron accelerator, Sorenson can create anti-matter duplicates of himself. These full Anti-Matter Creatures resembles Sorenson.

TECH LEVEL: 7   STORY POINTS: 7

PYRAMIDS OF MARS

'1980, Sarah, if you want to get off.'
'It's a trick!'
'No. That's the world as Sutekh would leave it. A desolate planet circling a dead sun.'

SYNOPSIS

Future site of British UNIT HQ and Mars, 1911

While en route to see the Brigadier, the TARDIS was knocked off course by a powerful mental projection. The time travellers materialised exactly where they meant to land in space, but decades off in time. Instead of landing in UNIT HQ, they arrived in the old priory that previously stood on the same site. They arrived in a room full of Egyptian sarcophagi – the property of an archaeologist named Marcus Scarman. While exploring a tomb in Egypt some years earlier, Scarman had made contact with the alien god Sutekh. It was this psychic link that threw the TARDIS off course and drew it here.

The caretaker of the priory was Namin, an Egyptian that worshipped Sutekh. Dr Warlock, a colleague of Scarman, visited the priory in search of his friend, but when Warlock asked too many questions, Namin tried to murder him. The Doctor and Sarah rescued Dr Warlock and fled into the forest, where Namin sent a robot mummy after them. They made it to a

hunting lodge used by Scarman's brother Laurence. Laurence was an amateur scientist and developed a primitive radio telescope that was receiving a signal.

The signal came from Mars and said 'beware Sutekh'. The Doctor knew that Sutekh was the last of the Osirans and had been imprisoned for his crimes eons ago. The Doctor, Sarah, and Laurence returned to the house in time to see a black-clad Servant of Sutekh appear from a dimensional portal, or lodestone, inside a sarcophagus and kill Namin. The Servant then revealed he was Marcus Scarman. Communicating through the lodestone, Sutekh ordered Scarman to secure the perimeter and construct an Osiran war missile from components brought from the tomb in Egypt.

After creating a force field around the perimeter, Scarman found Warlock and killed him after asking if anyone else remained within the field. Meanwhile the Doctor figured out that he could stop Sutekh with Namin's ring and the radio telescope. The Doctor, Sarah, and Laurence managed to retrieve the ring and get into the TARDIS. Sarah wanted to leave, rationalising that Sutekh must have failed since she came from the future. The Doctor took the TARDIS to 1980 and showed Sarah a destroyed world; her future would only exist if they stopped Sutekh.

The three returned to the hunting lodge to create a jamming device. Unfortunately, Laurence didn't believe his brother was lost and stopped the Doctor, enabling the robot mummies to break in and ruin the device. Luckily, Sarah was able to use Namin's ring to call off the attack. As a back-up plan the Doctor intended to blow up the missile that was being built. While the Doctor and Sarah went to do that, Laurence was confronted by his brother. Laurence attempted to appeal to Marcus' humanity, but in the end Marcus Scarman killed him.

The Doctor and Sarah rigged a bomb to the rocket and tried to detonate it, but Sutekh's power was too strong – he was able to telekinetically contain the explosion. The Doctor met Sutekh in his prison and distracted him long enough for the bomb to explode. Angered, Sutekh used his mental powers to 'persuade' the Doctor to take Scarman to Mars and release Sutekh from his prison. The Doctor faked his death when a robot mummy strangled him and, once Sutekh was no longer paying attention, he and Sarah passed a number of tests to get to the final chamber. Unfortunately, the Doctor was not able to stop Scarman in time and Sutekh was released. As Sutekh travelled through a lodestone to Earth, the Doctor beat him there in the TARDIS and reprogrammed the lodestone to terminate several thousand years in the future, beyond Sutekh's lifespan – effectively killing him. A side-effect burnt down the priory, leaving the land vacant for the future UNIT building.

CONTINUITY

Sutekh is an alien that caused havoc throughout the universe thousands of years ago. The Doctor equates him with his more common Egyptian name of Set as well as the Judeo-Christian Satan. Both Sutekh and Horus (and presumably most of the Egyptian pantheon) are members of a race called the Osirans. Sutekh destroyed their homeworld of Phaester Osiris (in a parallel of the Osiris myth). Sutekh's tomb is on Earth but the device holding him, the Eye of Horus, is on Mars. Sutekh has been imprisoned for 7000 years. Sarah mentions the Mars pyramid's similarity to the Living City of Exxilon, although she never ventured inside the latter herself. The Doctor likely explained what happened after that adventure.

Sarah puts on a dress that was once Victoria's, a former companion. Interestingly, the Doctor refers to said companion as 'Vicki', who was actually a different companion. The Doctor may simply prefer more familiar nicknames, as he called Sarah 'Sarah Jane' in his previous incarnation.

REAL WORLD MYTHS	RESONANT TIME PERIOD	ALIEN HORROR
Set, Egyptian curses	The golden age of Egyptology – the excavation of Tutankhamen's tomb	Sutekh the Osiran & his robots
Viking gods, vampires	World War II – Nazi occultists venerating Norse gods	Fenric, Haemovore monsters
Dragons	The "bone wars" of Gilded Age (1880) America – dinosaur hunters find dragon bones and eggs	Zygon living war machine
Ghosts	1850s spiritualism – when séances and mediums and ghost stories were all the rage	Time-shifted paradox echoes of those erased by changing history
Zombies	1970s small town America	Alien medical device on a crashed flying saucer that alters human brainwaves so they persist past death, trapping the minds of the recent deceased in their own corpses.

The Doctor claims to have lived for 'some 750 years', although he doesn't qualify if those are Earth or Gallifreyan years.

The Doctor is the cause of the old Priory burning down, paving the way for the UNIT HQ to be built on the site decades later.

⊙ RUNNING THE ADVENTURE

Oh, what a joy! *Pyramids of Mars* is one of the Doctor's most famous adventures, and deservedly so – it's a beautifully constructed rollercoaster of twisty plots. It opens with a mystery that combines a historical setting (Edwardian England, with its country houses and legacy of Empire) with pulpy occult horror (Mummies! Egyptian sorcery! Vampires! Enchanted rings! Curses!) that's actually alien super-science, so you've got pyramids on Mars and ancient astronaut psychic demigods. (A similar formula is used to great effect in *The Curse of Fenric*, in **The Seventh Doctor Sourcebook**).

It's a heady brew that can be replicated in your games. Start by picking a real-world myth or legend. Next, pick a historical period, location or idea that resonates with it. Then come up with a science-fiction explanation for all the occult weirdness, and finally mix in your player characters.

The next part of the adventure is a problem in tactics and survival. Sutekh seals off the priory and the surrounding forest with a forcefield. Think of this as a sort of locked-room variant of the Base Under Siege plotline – instead of the player characters and some semi-reliable allies being trapped in a stronghold with enemies outside, everyone's trapped in a relatively small area. In this case, the Doctor, Sarah-Jane, Laurence and a poacher, Ernie Clements are trapped along with Scarman and the Mummies. There are three key locations – the priory, the hunting lodge, and the forest in between – and lots of potential weapons and resources to be used, like the mining gelignite, the TARDIS, Laurence's Marconiscope, the poacher's rifle and the relics brought back from Egypt. Nothing from outside can get in. Both sides have to make do with what's inside the sealed zone. Adventures set on space stations or ships often have a similar quality. Only what's on the ship matters.

Note that the plans of both factions change in response to events. The Doctor initially plans on using the Marconiscope to jam Sutekh's control signals, but Laurence stops him out of a misguided desire to protect his brother, and the Mummy-robots destroy the scope. The Doctor then uses

the explosives to blow up Sutekh's rocket, only for Sutekh to seize control of the TARDIS through the Doctor. One can easily imagine another sequence of events where the Doctor uses the poacher's traps to immobilise the Mummies, or where Sutekh uses his Marcus Scarman puppet to persuade Laurence into changing sides.

To set up a plot like this, pick a constrained but varied geographical area – a university campus, a farm, a space station, a freighter that's run aground on an uncharted Pacific island – and give both sides roughly equal forces and opposing goals. Scatter various items, tools and other resources around the area. These resources should all be useful in some way, but don't turn the situation into a puzzle. Don't come up with a solution like "oh, the players have to use the magnifying glass to light the spilled rocket fuel" – let the players come up with their own solutions. Build a playground, not a maze.

The final section of the adventure is a dungeon crawl on Mars, complete with traps and monsters. What makes this section really interesting is the threat of Sutekh – he's powerful enough to suborn even the Doctor to his will, ruthless enough to eliminate those who are no longer of use to him, and intelligent enough to outwit his foes. Even better, the characters have already seen the consequences of failure. The Doctor's little side trip to 1980 brings home the stakes of the conflict far better than any description of what might happen.

CAN HISTORY BE CHANGED?

When they get back to the TARDIS Sarah simply wants to leave based on a reasonable premise; it's 1911 and she's from the future so she knows Sutekh can't succeed in destroying the world. This seems to contradict her experience in **The Time Warrior** but there the stakes were smaller; Sarah presumed that

Lynx would only kill a few locals before leaving and she wasn't considering their descendants. In both adventures, however, it was the Doctor's actions that allowed history to continue on its proper course. What was implied in **The Time Warrior** is made explicit here; Earth's history would be forever altered if the aliens' plans were left unchecked.

The larger question is this; if Sutekh had succeeded, then what would happen to Sarah? She should blink out of existence (causing minor paradoxes) but as a time traveller she may be insulated and the only human from a forgotten future who, along with the Doctor, is the only one who remembers what happened. If it is assumed that, if Sutekh was freed and someone else intervened to stop him, then a 'new' Sarah may appear in an altered timeline. The most likely outcome, of course, is the creation of a time spur.

Still, this is an excellent technique to use to get players involved in a story. For example, they may arrive in a 1920s Earth completely ravaged by an alien chemical weapon used during World War I. In order to preserve Earth's history, they have to travel back in time and prevent the alien interference. Alternately, the player characters may change something in the past and a quick trip to the future illustrates the damage wrought. Now they have to travel back in time and minimize the impact while adhering to the Blinovitch Limitation Effect.

ALIEN GODS

In the tradition of Azal and Kronos, Sutekh is a god that turns out to be a powerful alien. In Sutekh's case, the entire pantheon of Egyptian deities is rewritten as an alien race called the Osirans with the 'gods' as prominent members. Given this, we have a blueprint for re-imagining other pantheons as alien races.

First, rather than start from the top down, take an interesting character or myth and reimagine it as alien. Perhaps Hel or Pluto, like Sutekh, are locked beneath the Earth, or perhaps the Golden Fleece is used as the material for an alien's spacesuit. Once you have this in hand, reinterpret the mythology to fit the circumstance. For example, Hel is supposed to lead a dead army in the final battle. Perhaps she is an imprisoned alien that, through her agents, has been slowly collecting enough psychic energy to break free and take over the world. Perhaps the Golden Fleece is desired as a weapon and it is guarded not by a dragon, but by the automatic defences of the spaceship that houses it.

Second, pick and choose elements from the relevant mythology to season your adventure. Hel's story may take place in the modern (or UNIT Era) world, but technological runes and an alien or robotic Fenris wolf may make appearances. The search for the Golden Fleece may simply find the time travellers aboard a historical Greek vessel reminiscent of the Argo.

Finally, the villains should be able to be defeated by wits and jiggery-pokery. Hel's psychic device and the space ship containing the Golden Fleece can be destroyed; in Hel's case the psychic backlash may destroy her as well.

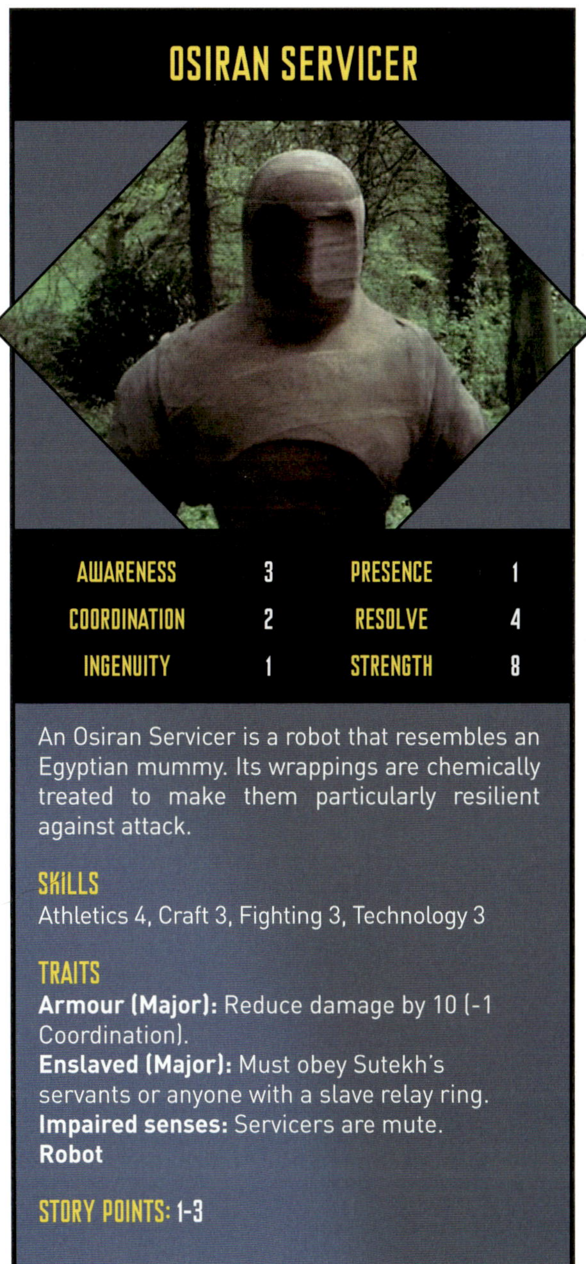

AWARENESS	3	PRESENCE	1
COORDINATION	2	RESOLVE	4
INGENUITY	1	STRENGTH	8

An Osiran Servicer is a robot that resembles an Egyptian mummy. Its wrappings are chemically treated to make them particularly resilient against attack.

SKILLS
Athletics 4, Craft 3, Fighting 3, Technology 3

TRAITS
Armour (Major): Reduce damage by 10 (-1 Coordination).
Enslaved (Major): Must obey Sutekh's servants or anyone with a slave relay ring.
Impaired senses: Servicers are mute.
Robot

STORY POINTS: 1-3

NEW GADGET – SLAVE RELAY RING

The Osiran Slave Relay Ring enables the wearer to control Osiran Servitors.

Traits: Voice of Authority (Osiran slave robots only).
Cost: 1 Story Point

NEW GADGET – LODESTONE

The Lodestone is a time travel cabinet that resembles a sarcophagus. A character can enter a lodestone and then travel either to another time or place. Unfortunately, the character ages at the normal rate while travelling through time, meaning that he could die before he gets to her destination.

Traits: Restriction (user ages with time travel), Teleport, Vortex
Cost: 7 Story Points

NEW GADGET – MARCONISCOPE

The Marconiscope is a prototype of a radio telescope. Laurence Scarman received signals from Mars from it. The Doctor later used it to transmit a signal to block Sutekh's control of Scarman, but an Osiran Servitor destroyed it before Scarman could be destroyed.

Traits: Scan
Cost: 1 Story Point

FURTHER ADVENTURES

- The Doctor was wrong. Osirans have a longer lifespan than he anticipated. An incredibly aged and weakened Sutekh staggers out of the time corridor 11,000 years later. With his powers limited until he can restore himself, Sutekh begins to take over the New Roman Empire of the far future. He plans to use his mind-control powers to manipulate the Roman senate into declaring his pawn Emperor. The characters must stop Sutekh's scheme before he becomes the ruler of the empire – and draws upon the psychic energy of a trillion citizens to restore himself to full power!

- The wars of the gods raged across the stars millions of years ago – but with a TARDIS, all that's just outside your door. The Osirans were beings of immense power and cunning (with 'cerebellums like spiral staircases' as the Doctor put it). They were easily on a par with the Time Lords – the Osirans may not have had the same mastery of time, but an individual Osiran was more powerful than a lone Time Lord. They devastated worlds in their wars. The characters travel back in time to a world that they know will

MARCUS SCARMAN, SERVANT OF SUTEKH

AWARENESS	3	PRESENCE	4
COORDINATION	3	RESOLVE	2
INGENUITY	1	STRENGTH	5

Marcus Scarman was an archaeologist and Egyptologist that unearthed Sutekh's tomb in Sakkara, Egypt in 1911. Sutekh killed and possessed him so that Scarman could return to England and build the Osiran War Missile that could be launched at Mars. In this state Scarman had much of Sutekh's power, but his original personality was gone.

SKILLS

Athletics 2, Convince 3, Fighting 2, Knowledge 4, Marksman 2, Medicine 1, Science 2, Subterfuge 2, Survival 1, Technology 4, Transport 2

TRAITS

Enslaved (Special): Scarman must obey Sutekh. If Sutekh releases his hold, then Scarman's corpse collapses and disintegrates into dust.
Force Field (Special): Scarman can project a psychic force field that offers Protection 10.
Shapeshift (Minor): Scarman can adopt the form of a servant of Sutekh. He can manifest the jackal head of Sutekh as well as black robes and a helmet. With Sutekh's power coursing through him to maintain it, this form is extremely hot and causes (4/L/L) damage to anything Scarman touches.
Weakness (Major): Scarman takes 4 levels of damage each round he is deprived of a connection to Sutekh.

EQUIPMENT: Servant robes

TECH LEVEL: 4   **STORY POINTS:** 7

be destroyed in a conflict between two Osirans. An evil Osiran, Babi, died in this conflict. Do the characters try to change history and save the world, when doing so may change Babi's fate.

- The Doctor defeated Sutekh, but the Pyramid still stands on Mars, alone in the deserts of a dead world. What treasures and traps lie there? Could the British government or Torchwood have known about the Pyramid, explaining their mad rush to get to Mars (see *The Ambassadors of Death* and similar adventures in **The Third Doctor Sourcebook**) – or did someone else get there first?

SUTEKH THE DESTROYER

Sutekh is presumably the last of the Osirans, an ancient star-spanning race. He was most notable for being 'the Destroyer', as he devastated many worlds, including his own. The last 740 Osirans, led by Horus, battled Sutekh on Earth 7000 years ago. With a code against killing, Horus instead entombed Sutekh; Sutekh cannot move so long as the Eye of Horus is intact on Mars.

Even without his physical body, Sutekh is a dangerous threat. He can use his considerable psychic powers to kill and possess people; he can also see what is going on in the world around him. If he should be freed, he plans to devastate Earth before once again becoming the scourge of the universe. When set free Sutekh simply wants to destroy the universe. It's likely that his goal wasn't so final prior to his incarceration, but millennia of waiting have destroyed any vestiges of sanity he had left.

AWARENESS	5	PRESENCE	10
COORDINATION	4	RESOLVE	14
INGENUITY	10	STRENGTH	4

SKILLS
Convince 4, Craft 6, Fighting 5, Knowledge 7, Marksman 4, Medicine 5, Science 7, Survival 5, Technology 7

TRAITS
Alien
Alien Appearance
Clairvoyance (Special): Sutekh can see other locations; his range is enhanced by Osiran technology.
Fear Factor 3: Grants a +6 bonus to inspire fear.
Force Field (Special): Sutekh can project a psychic force field that offers Protection 10.
Possess (Special): Sutekh may attempt possession with a +4 bonus. He may also create animated puppets by killing a victim and then animating him. Sutekh can use his psychic powers through his puppets.
Pyrokinesis (Special): Sutekh can kill with his mind, causing lethal (4/L/L) damage.
Psychic (Special): +4 against mental attacks and Sutekh may attempt to read minds.
Special – Restricted Movement: Sutekh cannot move while the Eye of Horus is active.

Telekinesis (Special): Sutekh may move objects using Resolve instead of Strength. He can also contain explosions so long as he concentrates.
Telepathy (Special): May create a mental link to read minds or converse telepathically.

EQUIPMENT: Osiran Technology

TECH LEVEL: 9   **STORY POINTS:** 12

THE ANDROID INVASION

'This isn't Earth. This isn't real wood. It's some kind of artificial material like plastic. These are not real trees and you're not the real Sarah.'

⊘ SYNOPSIS

Oseidon and Devesham, 1980

The Doctor and Sarah arrived in the quiet English village of Devesham, close to the Space Defence Station that co-ordinated Earth's early warning system against alien attack. The two travellers were attacked by helmeted men in white suits. Fleeing the men, the time travellers stumbled upon the body of a UNIT soldier and searched his pockets, discovering that all of the coins were minted in the same year.

The time travellers continued into the village, which was strangely empty. The Doctor found more coins with the same year, while Sarah noticed four men enter the village with the seemingly now-alive soldier. A lorry soon arrived with several villagers sitting in a zombie state. They exited the vehicle, took up positions around the village, and then started acting normally when the clock struck eight.

The Doctor went to the nearby Space Defence Station to get answers while Sarah headed for the TARDIS. Along the way she discovered that the men in white suits were robots. She also discovered a pod that had a person inside. When the man tried to grab her, she went looking for the Doctor. Meanwhile, the Doctor entered the station and met Crayford, an astronaut that arrested the Doctor as an imposter and locked him up. Thankfully Sarah arrived and freed him.

All of this was being watched by Kraals, an alien race bent on taking over the Earth. As Crayford and some UNIT soldiers searched for the Doctor and Sarah, Sarah pointed out that Crayford couldn't be here; his spaceship disappeared while he was on a deep space mission. As they escaped, they found Benton and Harry Sullivan coming after them. Sarah was captured and scanned to create an android duplicate as the Doctor continued to discover strange anomalies about the village.

In fact, the village was located on the distant alien planet of Oseidon. The native Kraals built the fake village in preparation for their invasion of Earth. Soon, their rocket pods would launch for Earth. Android duplicates would replace key figures, preparing the way for the main invasion fleet.

The Doctor and Sarah were captured by androids and placed in a cell where Crayford spoke to them, explaining that the Kraals rescued him and that his return to Earth will cover their invasion. While Crayford held a grudge against Earth for 'abandoning' him, he believed that the Kraals intended to conquer the Earth, not kill all the humans. The Doctor was taken to the Kraal leader, Styggron, who told the Doctor exactly what was going to happen to humanity – they would be annihilated by a virus.

Sarah managed to escape her cell and freed the Doctor before Styggron's analysis machine could destroy him. They climbed into Crayford's rocket as it launched towards Earth. Several pods containing androids, including ones of the Doctor and Sarah, landed as well.

The real time travellers went to the Space Defence Station to stop the invasion while the duplicates tried to ensure it succeeded. Realising what was happening, Crayford switched sides and was killed. In the end, the Doctor rewired his duplicate to destroy Styggron and the virus while using the radar system to jam the signals to the androids.

CONTINUITY

Britain has a Space Defence Station to protect against alien attack.

John Benton and Harry Sullivan meet the Doctor for the last time. Colonel Faraday is the UNIT officer in command while the Brigadier is away (this is an indication that UNIT is expanding its size).

The TARDIS is due for its 500 year service.

⊘ RUNNING THE ADVENTURE

This adventure begins with a mystery; the Doctor and Sarah seem to have landed in an English village near a Space Defence Station. People act strangely and it is soon discovered that they are androids.

The time travellers then discover that the entire village is actually on another planet. It's a testing ground for androids intended to replace their human counterparts. The time travellers have to go to Earth and stop the Kraals from using their android army as well as an engineered plague.

THE HORROR OF THE FAMILIAR

The Germans have a word for everything. The word here is unheimliche – uncanny, unhomely, the opposite of the familiar. It's that creepy feeling that crawls over you when you realise that something you thought was safe and normal and ordinary… isn't. It's something else entirely. It's something very wrong.

And that's disturbing.

Haunted mansions aren't as disturbing. Creepy Transylvanian castles aren't as disturbing. Space stations – no matter how dark and twisty and filled with dangerous monsters – aren't as disturbing. They're not familiar. You don't live in a mansion or a castle or a space station. A haunted suburban home or an apartment – that's really creepy. It's the horror right in your living room. It's the horror happening in places you know.

The Android Invasion works on this principle. It takes a familiar, comfortable place – a nice country village – and turns it into something disturbing, where people's faces fall off to reveal the wires beneath, and where it's July 6th forever.

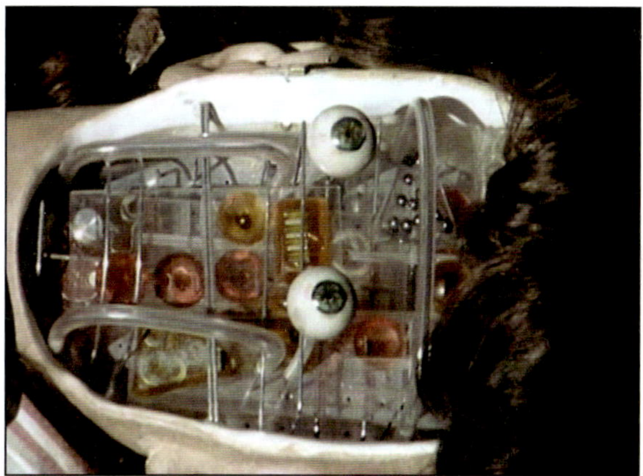

To replicate this feeling, focus on something utterly familiar, something that's ubiquitous, and make it an instrument of horror. **The Bells of St. John** (in **The Eleventh Doctor Sourcebook**) turns wifi computer networks into something ghastly. You could do the same to:

- **Plumbing:** There's something in the pipes. When you hear bubbling and knocking, that's them surging through the water. They look like metallic grey eels. They're hydrokinetic – they can control water. When they want to kill you, they send the water pouring out of your tap, but it doesn't flow into the sink – it snakes out and envelops you, and you drown where you stand…

- **Garbage trucks:** Once a week, they come around early in the morning and collect all the bins. You never notice them. You've never noticed that sometimes, they take your neighbours out with the rest of the rubbish, and things crawl out of the garbage truck and move into the newly-vacated house. Say, you haven't seen old Mrs. Smith in weeks…

- **Schoolchildren:** Crowds of them, running around playgrounds at break time, screaming and playing. Look closely, though, and you'll see a circle of them in the middle. Those kids aren't running around. They're standing stock-still, and they're chanting…

- **Mobile Phones:** Everyone's got one. They walk around town with these blocks of sizzling electronics pressed to their ears. When they're not talking on them, they're staring at their glowing screens. Sometimes, out of the corner of your eye, you could swear those phones have legs. Six legs, articulated like a scorpion, and long back tails. Screens on their bellies. You can hear their mating calls when their egg-sacs are full and they're ready to implant their young in your ear. Bleep bleep. Bleep bleep. Bleep bleep.

MORE THAN A PASSING SIMILARITY?

On a superficial level, the Kraal share a resemblance to the Judoon. It's possible that they are members of the same race that evolved differently. Given that the Kraal home world was doomed the Kraals may have developed a hardier form that became the prototype for the Judoon. Alternatively the Judoon could be a 'warrior caste' that went mercenary once the Kraal leadership finally dissolved.

It is also possible that the Movellans were of Kraal design, initially created to infiltrate another world and subsequently rose up against their creators. In fact, the Movellans may have been responsible for the destruction of the Kraals, leaving only the Judoon in their wake. The Judoon's pursuit of the Movellans to bring them to justice could have inspired so many Judoon to become mercenary police officers.

FURTHER ADVENTURES

- The characters discover that an Earth politician is an android – but she doesn't seem to know she's an artificial replacement. Who created the duplicate and what happened to the real politician? Could she be a left-over from a failed Kraal invasion, or is someone reusing Kraal technology for some other purpose?

- The Space Defence Station is never mentioned again, despite Earth getting invaded every other week. This implies that the station was destroyed or erased from time by some other danger. For example, the player characters arrive at Devesham just in time to hear a titanic explosion. An alien surprise attack just took out the Space Defence Station! A radiation-scarred survivor staggers into the village, and explains that the station detected an invasion fleet on the fringes of the solar system just before the surprise attack began. The invaders have just neatly decapitated Earth's space defence chain-of-command – can the characters rally the forces of Earth in time to stop the invasion?

- One wonderfully nasty trick to play as a Gamesmaster is to replace the player characters with duplicates of themselves – androids, clones, Flesh copies, alternate-reality parallels – and then play through part of an adventure with these copies before revealing the truth. This lets the Gamesmaster do things that would otherwise be unsporting, like exterminating player characters or dropping them into no-win situations. What do the characters do when they discover that they're Kraal androids sent to conquer the Earth?

KRAAL

AWARENESS	3	PRESENCE	3
COORDINATION	3	RESOLVE	3
INGENUITY	5	STRENGTH	4

The Kraals hail from Oseidon, a desert-like world wracked by increasing radiation levels. They have course, rough skin and nasal horns, giving them a passing resemblance to humanoid rhinoceroses. Whether desperate or callous (or both), they have little regard for humanity.

SKILLS
Athletics 3, Convince 2, Craft 5, Fighting 3, Knowledge 4, Marksman 3, Medicine 4, Science 4, Subterfuge 3, Survival 2, Technology 6, Transport 2

TRAITS
Alien
Alien Appearance
Tough (Minor): A Kraal's thick skin isn't armour, but it is still resilient. Reduce total damage by 2.

EQUIPMENT: Blaster (4/L/L)

TECH LEVEL: 6   **STORY POINTS: 3-5**

KRAAL ANDROID DUPLICATE

AWARENESS	1	PRESENCE	2
COORDINATION	3	RESOLVE	2
INGENUITY	2	STRENGTH	4

In addition to the Android Duplicates, there are also simpler Kraal maintenance androids. These wear jumpsuits and helmets to protect their obvious android head. Such androids also employ finger guns that do 3/7/10 damage.

SKILLS
Athletics 3, Convince 3, Fighting 3, Knowledge 1, Marksman 4, Subterfuge 3

TRAITS
Armour (Minor): Reduce damage by 5.
Enslaved (Major): Must obey the Kraal, and suffers -2 to attempts to voice opinion.
Machine (Minor): Androids are robotic creatures and have critical systems in different areas than an organic being. All targeted damage is reduced by 2.
Robot
Shapeshift (Minor): An Android is built as a duplicate of a similar creature. It usually has gaps in its memory that can be exploited.

EQUIPMENT: Some Androids are equipped with pistols (2/5/7) damage.

STORY POINTS: 2-4

THE BRAIN OF MORBIUS

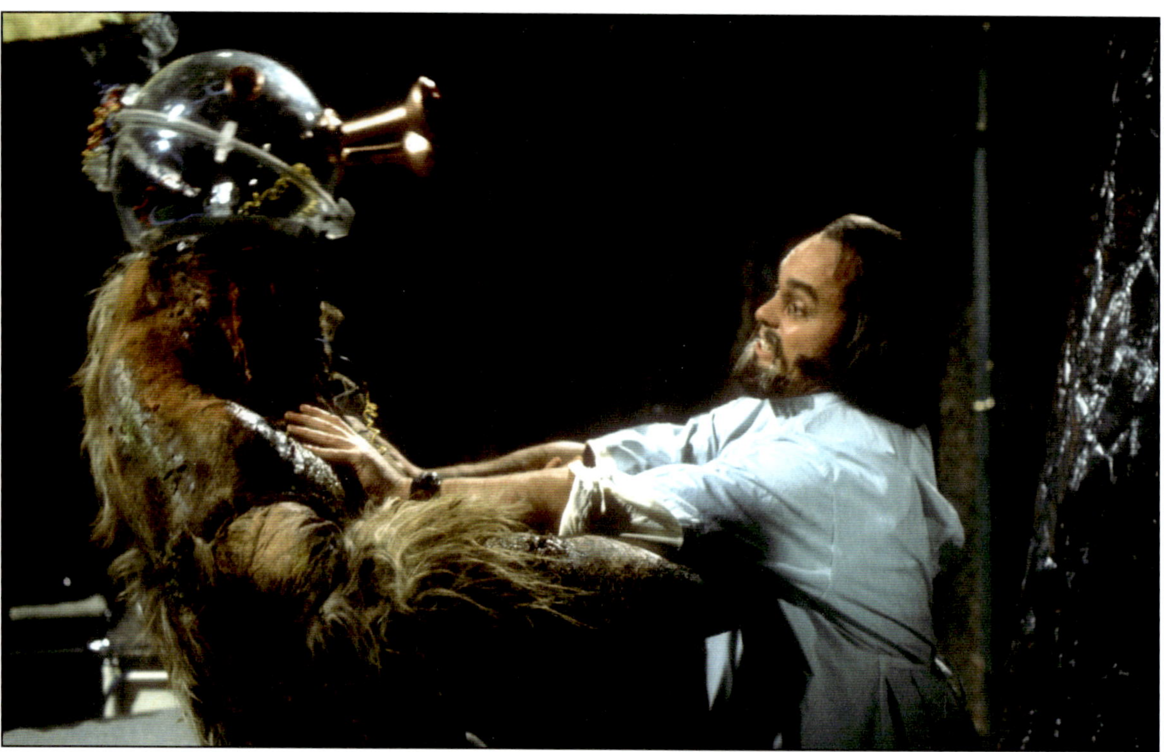

'Can you understand a thousandth of my agony? I, Morbius, who once led the High Council of the Time Lords and dreamed the greatest dreams in history, now reduced to this, to a condition where I envy a vegetable.'

⊙ SYNOPSIS

The Planet Karn, the Future (likely post-30th century)

The time travellers arrived on the stormy planet of Karn, landing amid the remains of several wrecked spaceships. They spotted a castle and were greeted by Solon, a scientist from Earth with an obsession for the Doctor's head, and his one-armed lab assistant Condo. The Doctor recognised Solon as a distinguished surgeon that was once a follower of Morbius, a criminal Time Lord who was executed. Solon drugged the Doctor's wine and took him to a laboratory.

Elsewhere, the Sisterhood of Karn meditated upon the arrival of the TARDIS. They believed that the Time Lords had come to steal the Elixir of Life. They then used their powers to bring the Doctor to them. The Sisterhood guarded the last drops of the Elixir by psychically crashing any spaceships that wandered

near the planet. Believing the Doctor to be a thief, the Sisterhood's leader, Maren, ordered the Doctor to be burned at the stake, in spite of an intercession by Solon. Sarah managed to save the Doctor and help him escape, but not before she was blinded by a flash from Maren's ring.

The Doctor met with Solon, who informed him that Sarah needed the Elixir to regain her vision (a lie; the blindness was temporary). As the Doctor returned to retrieve it, Solon sent a message to the Sisterhood through Condo that the Doctor was coming; he hoped to get the Doctor's head in return. Solon then went to Morbius, now just a brain in a jar, to beg forgiveness for the delays in restoring him. Sarah heard Morbius' voice as well and learned that the Doctor's head would complete the restoration.

Solon told Morbius that the Doctor was a Time Lord. Fearing action from the Time Lords, Morbius demanded that Solon prepare an artificial head for him. Solon warned him against the side-effects, but Morbius insisted. During the operation Morbius' brain was possibly damaged when Condo realised his missing arm was part of the patchwork body. Solon shot Condo and drafted Sarah as his assistant.

The Doctor was captured by the Sisterhood but spared his fate when he figured out how to replenish the flame that created the Elixir. He returned to the castle feigning death; while Solon was distracted examining him Morbius woke up in a bestial state and menaced Sarah, whose vision returned just in time. She was saved by Condo, who was killed by Morbius. The Doctor and Solon hunt down Morbius and tranquilised him after he kills one of the Sisters.

Solon promised to destroy Morbius, but instead locked the Doctor out of the laboratory to fix his work. The Doctor flooded the laboratory with cyanide gas, which killed Solon but left Morbius, whose alien lungs could filter the gas, intact and now fully intelligent. The Doctor challenged him to a Time Lord mind-bending game, which knocked the Doctor unconscious and destroyed Morbius' intelligence. The Sisterhood arrived with torches and drove Morbius over a cliff to his death. Maren sacrificed her own life to give the Doctor the elixir needed to restore him.

CONTINUITY

Morbius was once Lord President of Gallifrey. He attempted to conquer the universe, offering immortality to his followers, and was presumably executed for his crimes.

The Time Lords seem to have steered the Doctor to Karn in order to defeat Morbius.

The Sisterhood of Karn had contact with Gallifrey.

There's a hint that the Doctor has more than four incarnations at this point.

⊘ RUNNING THE ADVENTURE

The Brain of Morbius is *Frankenstein* with a twist; rather than creating new life, Solon is merely creating a body to house a surviving intelligence. All of the gothic horror trappings are here: a mad scientist, a dim servant, a landscape cloaked in perpetual night, a castle, and a witches' coven. The time travellers are the victims, as Solon is looking for a head to place on his creation.

Plot-wise, the adventure is rather simple. The Sisterhood crashes ships that stray too close to Sarn in order to protect the Elixir. Solon recovers useful body parts to recreate Morbius. The time travellers stumble upon Karn and go to the only civilised spot, a gothic building. Solon attempts to kill a time traveller for his head; failing that, he animates Morbius with an artificial head. The time travellers must join forces with the Sisterhood to stop Morbius.

SO THAT'S WHY EVERYONE KNOWS ABOUT TIME LORDS!

For an insular society with a policy of non-interference, the Time Lords seem pretty well-known throughout the universe. Obviously, Morbius played a large role in fostering this image as he tried to conquer the universe. Undoubtedly the Time Lords had to do a lot of damage control to undo the actions of the Cult of Morbius.

The Cult of Morbius makes a great villain for games. They know about the Time Lords, about time travel, and how to fight them. They're fanatically loyal to the idea of Morbius – a martyred hero is an immensely powerful symbol.

Cult members can show up on any world, in any time period, pursuing all sorts of wild schemes to restore Morbius or recapture his legacy. Maybe Morbius equipped his mercenary army with Time Lord weapons stolen from the vaults on Gallifrey, and those doomsday weapons are still in the hands of the cult.

NO ONE GOES BAD LIKE A TIME LORD

Think of the most memorable masterminds that the Doctor has faced. Other than Davros, most of the really great bad guys are Time Lords gone wrong. The Master, the Meddling Monk, the Rani, the Valeyard, Morbius, Omega, Rassilon – all Time Lords, all monstrous. If you're looking for a great bad guy for your campaign, think about making him (or her) a Time Lord.

When making an evil Time Lord, take all the best traits of the player characters and turn them evil. If your characters race around the galaxy like hyperactive problem-solving chipmunks, then maybe your evil Time Lord is equally fast-moving and sows chaos in his wake. If your characters are solemn and thoughtful, then your evil Time Lord can be the Undertaker or the Gravedigger, the servant of entropy who brings an end to all things.

THE SISTERHOOD OF KARN

The Sisterhood are one of the few groups in the universe who can say they are peers of the Time Lords. They may be greatly diminished, but they are still a proud and ancient order, the keepers of the flame of life. Their psychic powers are astounding, capable of penetrating the defences of a TARDIS. Player characters who wish to be members of the Sisterhood should take the appropriate trait.

THE BRAIN OF MORBIUS

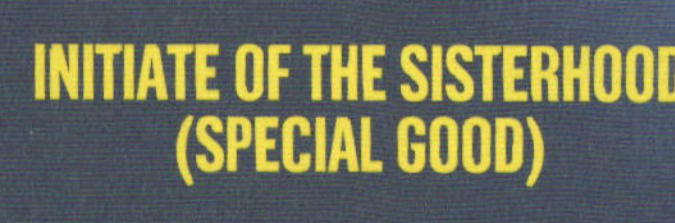

INITIATE OF THE SISTERHOOD (SPECIAL GOOD)

You are a member of the Sisterhood of Karn, initiated into the mysteries of the Sacred Flame. You have drunk of the Elixir of Life and you shall never die.

Effects: As a member of the Sisterhood, you pick up quite a few Traits as a package deal. You've got Psychic Training, you're Psychic, Telepathic, unaging (Immortal: Major) and you may increase your Resolve and Medicine by +1 each. You also pick up a Major Obligation to the Sisterhood.

As a special bonus, you can combine your psychic powers with other members of the Sisterhood. Unlike a normal attempt to work together, when two sisters put their minds together, they can add their Resolve scores together. A group of Sisters are immensely powerful.

Being a member of the Sisterhood costs 2 Character Points and 4 Story Points.

ARE KARN AND SARN THE SAME WORLD?

The planets of Karn and Sarn (from *Planet of Fire* – see **The Fifth Doctor Sourcebook**) have striking similarities both in name and the presence of a gas that heals and rejuvenates bodies. Both also had strong religious (or in the case of the Sisterhood, quasi-religious) orders running the planet. Sarn was once a fertile planet before the frequent volcanic eruptions threatened to destroy it. The Trions kept the planet from disintegrating while using the world as a convenient place to drop political prisoners that would naturally rule the superstitious people of Sarn. By the mid-1980s the world had become too unstable and the Trions were forced to evacuate it.

Karn could conceivably be Sarn in the far future. The Time Lords could have stabilised the volcanic activity in order to preserve the numismaton gas which when lit became known as the Elixir of Life. The Sisterhood may be an evolution of the Logarian faith, with the emphasis changed from a false god to dedication to the gas. While Karn is stabilised, it is still largely a dead world, hence its gothic trappings.

BEHIND THE SCENES: NEW OLD FACES

Initially, the six faces shown after the First Doctor were intended to be even more incarnations of the Doctor. This was to add more mystery to the Doctor's background. Similarly, you can add previous incarnations to your Time Lord player characters that might have done things differently than their current incarnations, including alliances, mistakes, and even lovers that haunt them now! Be sure to check with your affected player first – adding backstory can be fun but character histories are usually left to the players unless expressly granted to you.

MORE THAN FOUR INCARNATIONS?

When the Doctor challenges Morbius to a mind-bending game, Morbius pulls images from the Doctor's previous incarnations from his mind. Presuming that the tug-of-war dips increasingly backwards in the participants' timelines, it seems that the Doctor can only pull one incarnation out of Morbius (technically his current one), while Morbius pushes the Doctor back through his first three incarnations – and then to at least six more beyond. Given that the Doctor and other Time Lords have never included these incarnations amongst the Doctor's timeline and that including them would carry the Doctor beyond his twelve regeneration 'limit', an assumption can be made that these are Morbius' previous incarnations. That said the viewer always shows the present incarnation first when the participant is being pushed and these incarnations appear after the First Doctor's visage. Morbius certainly acts as if they are the Doctor's incarnations.

There are several possibilities for you to use as a GM. It's possible that the Doctor created fictitious incarnations just to hold Morbius' attention long enough to lose; they could also be 'Watchers' or potential incarnations. They could be Morbius' incarnations, as the unstable Time Lord is simply unaware that he is losing. The most fascinating

possibility is, of course, that they are incarnations of the Doctor.

It's established in **The Five Doctors** that the Time Lords have the technology to grant a new cycle of regenerations. It's possible that, prior to fleeing Time Lord society, the Doctor used this technology on himself, making the First Doctor the first in a new cycle. It's also possible that the Celestial Intervention Agency recruited the Doctor, possibly after his trial, and the Doctor regenerated several times doing work for the CIA before his sentence was imposed. In order to cover their tracks the Time Lords erased the Doctor's memory (or simply got his word never to speak of them) before sending him to Earth. This cover-up would include replacement of the lost regenerations. Given his status as a 'Time Lord of the First Rank', Morbius could have shaken those memories loose.

NEW GADGET – ELIXIR OF LIFE

The Elixir of Life is created from the Sacred Flame of Karn. It extends the lifespan of those who drink it as well as heals grievous injuries. Time Lords used it to aid them through difficult regenerations.

Traits: Fast Healing, Immortal (extends life)
Cost: 3 Story Points

FURTHER ADVENTURES

* The Cybermen arrive and put Morbius' brain inside a Cyberman. Unfortunately for them, Cyber-Morbius overcomes his conditioning and sees his new form as an excellent vehicle for conquest. Can the time travellers stop Morbius before the former Time Lord turned Cyber-Controller makes the Cyber-Men too powerful?

* TARDIS technology is supposed to ensure that two time travellers keep meeting each other in the right order, regardless of where in time and space they encounter each other. Morbius, though, was a renegade and might have disabled this safeguard. That means that the characters could encounter Morbius at his height, back when he tried to conquer the universe. He doesn't have to be a shadow of his former glory – he can be a Big Bad Villain.

* For that matter – in their darkest hour, during the Last Great Time War, the Time Lords brought

back Rassilon and the Master. Why stop there? Why not bring back one Time Lord who already led Gallifreyans in a war of conquest? What would Morbius do if he was resurrected by the Time Lords and given a new body, a new cycle of regenerations? Is there a pocket-watch out there with his mind in it?

SISTER OF KARN

AWARENESS	5	PRESENCE	3
COORDINATION	3	RESOLVE	5
INGENUITY	4	STRENGTH	2

A Sister of Karn is devoted to the maintenance of the Sacred Flame, which is often used by Time Lords going through difficult regenerations. Capable of vast psychic powers, the Sisterhood often pull nearby spaceships from the sky in order to keep their secret.

SKILLS
Athletics 3, Convince 3, Craft 2, Knowledge 3, Medicine 4, Subterfuge 4, Survival 3

TRAITS
Psychic: +4 against mental attacks and Sister may attempt to read minds.
Clairvoyance: Sisters can see other locations, at a range limited to their Resolve.
Immortal (Major): The Sisters are undying.
Initiate of the Sisterhood of Karn (Special): See opposite page.
Obligation (Major): A Sister would kill to protect the Sacred Flame.
Precognition: Sisters get glimpses of the future by spending a Story Point.
Technically Inept: -2 penalty to any attempt to fix electrical or computer equipment. For the Sisterhood this extends to most technology rolls.
Telekinesis (Special Good): Sister may move objects using Resolve instead of Strength.
Telepathy (Special Good): May create a mental link to read minds or converse telepathically.
Teleport (Major Good): Sister can shift to another known location with an Awareness + Resolve roll. Failure just means she doesn't move.

TECH LEVEL: 7   STORY POINTS: 5-7

CONDO

AWARENESS	3	PRESENCE	2
COORDINATION	4	RESOLVE	5
INGENUITY	2	STRENGTH	4

Condo was a Dravidian starship survivor nursed back to health by Solon, albeit with the loss of his arm. Solon promised to reattach the arm for him in return for Condo's service, but Solon instead used the arm to complete Morbius' new body. When Condo learned of Solon's treachery Solon shot him, but Condo survived long enough to protect Sarah from the rampaging Morbius.

SKILLS

Athletics 4,, Fighting 4, Knowledge 2, Marksman 3, Survival 2

TRAITS

Missing Limb: Condo is missing a hand, making it difficult to use two-handed weapons or devices.
Obligation (Minor): Condo works for Solon in the hopes of getting his arm back.
Tough: Reduce total damage by 2.

EQUIPMENT: Sword (Strength +2 damage)

TECH LEVEL: 7   **STORY POINTS:** 3

MEHENDRI SOLON

AWARENESS	2	PRESENCE	3
COORDINATION	3	RESOLVE	3
INGENUITY	5	STRENGTH	2

Dr Mehendri Solon was an Earth physician and surgeon that belonged to the Cult of Morbius. He managed to get to Karn during Morbius' trial and managed to save Morbius' brain just prior to the disintegration. He used the aliens from ships the Sisterhood of Karn forced to crash in order to create a new body for the Time Lord. Solon died when the Doctor tried to use cyanide gas to kill Morbius.

SKILLS

Convince 3, Craft 4, Fighting 2, Knowledge 5, Marksman 3, Medicine 6, Science 4, Subterfuge 3, Technology 6

TRAITS

Biochemical Genius: He can brew up new drugs and medical treatments.
Boffin: And he can build gadgets.
Charming: +2 bonus to attempts to use charm.
Obsession (Major): Devoted to preserving Morbius.
Technically Adept: +2 to any Technology roll to fix a broken or faulty device.

EQUIPMENT: Stun Gun S/S/S

TECH LEVEL: 7   **STORY POINTS:** 7

MORBIUS

Morbius was once President of Gallifrey. He eschewed the Time Lord policy of non-interference and set about trying to conquer the universe. Those that joined him became known as the Cult of Morbius. Eventually, the Time Lords had enough; they put Morbius on trial and sentenced him to death. Morbius' disintegration sentence was to be carried out on the neighbouring world of Karn. Just prior to the execution Solon was able to save his brain and put it into a patchwork body. Morbius' brain was put into the body but not before his brain was damaged. He alternated between brute and lucid Time Lord. His brain shorted out during a mental wrestling challenge with the Doctor and the brutish Morbius was chased off a cliff by the Sisterhood of Karn.

AWARENESS	5	PRESENCE	2
COORDINATION	3	RESOLVE	6
INGENUITY	6/1*	STRENGTH	6

SKILLS

Athletics 3, Convince 6, Craft 3, Fighting 3, Knowledge 5, Marksman 2, Medicine 2, Science 5, Survival 5, Technology 5, Transport 4

TRAITS

Alien Appearance (Major)

Alien Organs (Minor): Due to his patchwork nature, Morbius's organs are not where you might expect. All targeted damage is reduced by 2.

Argumentative (Minor Bad): Morbius will argue his point of view even if it puts his life in danger.

Cyborg

Distinctive: He looks like a patchwork monster. People tend to remember patchwork monsters.

Fear Factor 2: Grants a +4 bonus to inspire fear.

Special – Frenzy: Morbius must resist frenzy whenever injured by rolling his Resolve + Strength against a Difficulty of 12 +Damage taken. In frenzy Morbius attacks anything nearby.

Immunity (Major): Thanks to the lungs of a Birastrop Morbius is immune to poisonous gas.

Impulsive: Morbius doesn't think things through before acting.

Indomitable: +4 bonus to any rolls to resist psychic control.

Mind Lord (Special): +2 to any use of a psychic ability.

Psychic (Special): +4 against mental attacks and Morbius may attempt to read minds.

Natural Weapons (Major): Morbius' rather large claw does Strength +4 damage.

Obsession (Major): Wants revenge on the Time Lords and conquer the universe.

Telepathy (Special): May create a mental link to read minds or converse telepathically.

Time Lord

Time Traveller (all)

Tough: Reduce total damage by 2.

Unattractive: -2 penalty to any rolls that involve the character's looks. May provide +2 to intimidate rolls at GMs discretion.

Voice of Authority: +2 bonus to Presence and Convince rolls.

Wanted Renegade (Special): Should Morbius be discovered alive by the Time Lords, he is a condemned criminal.

Weakness (Major): Morbius' mind is unstable. When fighting Telepathically his opponent can do 4 levels of damage to Morbius.

TECH LEVEL: 10   **STORY POINTS:** 10

*Morbius' brain has trouble interfacing with his new body. When he has his intellect, use the former value, when he degenerates into a brute, use the latter. Morbius can only use his Athletics and Fighting skills as a brute.

THE SEEDS OF DOOM

'You and your kind are nothing but parasites. You're dependent upon us for the air you breathe and the food you eat. We have only one use for you.'

◎ SYNOPSIS

Antarctica and England, UNIT Era

Scientists in Antarctica discovered an alien seed pod in the ice. Sir Colin Thackeray of the World Ecology Bureau called on the Doctor for his expertise and the Doctor insisted on seeing it himself. Dunbar, another member of the Bureau, secretly offered to sell the pod to eccentric millionaire horticulturalist Harrison Chase. Chase arranged for Scorby and Keeler to retrieve it.

The Doctor and Sarah arrived in Antarctica by helicopter and discovered that one of the scientists was feverish, having been infected by the pod. The Doctor examined him and realised that he was

changing into a plant, an alien Krynoid; he suggested amputating the infected arm as a possible solution. Scorby and Keeler arrived at the base, claiming to be a lost private team. Unfortunately, before the amputation could proceed the Krynoid hybrid got up and killed the scientist performing the operation.

Scorby and Keeler sabotaged the base with the intent of eliminating all witnesses before escaping with the pod. The time travellers and base scientists tried to find the Krynoid but failed. Returning to base, a scientist let slip that they had a second pod. Scorby threatened Sarah's life to get the Doctor to reveal it. He then tied up the Doctor and the scientists and made Sarah take him to the generator so he could blow everything up.

The Doctor freed himself and the scientists made contact with South Bend's medical team, but the Krynoid returned and killed another scientist. The Doctor freed Sarah and lured the Krynoid into the hut, where Scorby's explosives destroyed it. Unfortunately, Scorby and Keeler got away.

The time travellers returned to London, where the Doctor told Sir Colin (and Dunbar) he suspected that it was an inside job. After an attempt was made on their lives, the time travellers learned that Harrison Chase might be involved. Scorby captured them and brought them to Chase, who decided they should be executed. The time travellers attempted to escape but Sarah was caught again and Chase decided to expose her to the pod. The Doctor rescued her just in time; the pod stung Keeler instead.

Keeler began his transformation into a hybrid; Chase refused to send him to hospital, as he wanted to observe the process. In the meantime Dunbar was feeling guilty and warned Sir Colin to call UNIT if he didn't return from a meeting with Chase. The meeting didn't go well and Dunbar fled the house only to run into the Krynoid, which killed him.

The Krynoid almost consumed the time travellers but Scorby and his men distracted it. They all fled to the cottage where the growing Krynoid surrounded (or, more properly, enveloped) them. Chase was peculiarly undisturbed, believing himself an ally of plants. The Doctor escaped and contacted Sir Colin, warning him that the Krynoid was affecting vegetation and responsible for several deaths. Sir Colin called in UNIT.

Back at the cottage, the Krynoid further isolated Sarah and Scorby by cutting the telephone wires. Chase was now clearly insane as he greeted his new plant overlords. UNIT arrived and used their laser gun, but it only agitated the now-enormous Krynoid. Scorby died attempting to flee, while the Doctor managed to call UNIT and urged them to call an air strike. He and Sarah managed to defeat Chase (who ended up a victim of his own composter) and got out of the house before the RAF destroyed the Krynoid.

CONTINUITY

Sarah is now regarded as a member of UNIT.
The bitter cold of the Antarctic doesn't bother the Doctor, who doesn't even put on a heavier coat.
This is the last time the Doctor works with UNIT until **Battlefield**. The Doctor knows Major Beresford, who is in charge of UNIT while the Brigadier is in Geneva (presumably Colonel Faraday is on assignment elsewhere).

⊙ RUNNING THE ADVENTURE

This adventure has all the hallmarks of an action adventure series ala **The Avengers** or even **Doc Savage**. The Doctor is almost a two-fisted pulp hero, first travelling to an exotic locale and fighting a monster before returning to England and dealing with another. All the while, the alien creature is being helped along by an eccentric millionaire who wants

to rule the world in a rather unique way. The Doctor is more physical than ever, eschewing Venusian martial arts for more conventional fisticuffs and even brandishing a gun at one point. The solution involves violence, with a bomb destroying the first Krynoid and an air strike destroying the second.

Also of note is that this adventure plays more as two adventures than one, with one feeding into the other while retaining a different feel. Without the 'always travels in pairs' bit the first part of this adventure plays like an HP Lovecraft story or horror film, with the time travellers coming to an isolated Antarctic base and dealing with a human-turned-monster before it consumes everyone else.

THE BASE UNDER SIEGE

This adventure has not one but two examples of the base under siege, first with the Antarctic base and second with Chase's mansion. In the latter the time travellers have to do little but survive until UNIT can discover a solution. In the first instance the scenario is conventional, with isolated characters being threatened by a monster lurking in and around the base. The second instance is a variation on the zombie horror scenario, with the time travellers simply trying to keep the large Krynoid from reaching inside to grab them while Harrison Chase sabotages their efforts.

The story gets great mileage out of its monster by using it twice – once in an exotic, unfamiliar location, and once somewhere closer to home, with a different supporting cast. As the players are familiar with the monster by the second part of the adventure, the emphasis shifts from "what is this thing and how do

we fight it?" to "argh, we know what's going to happen, and it's very very bad – how do we stop it in time?"

OUT WITH A BANG: THE END OF UNIT

The Doctor had grown increasingly distant from UNIT since the lifting of his exile and especially after his regeneration; this is his last adventure with UNIT until his seventh incarnation. Of particular note is that none of the Doctor's friends within UNIT appears; it simply plays the role of the cavalry and could have just as easily been the Royal Air Force or similar military organisation. This is the last story set in the '1970s plus a few years' UNIT era, although arguably the rest of the Fourth Doctor's 'contemporary Earth' stories take place in the same time period, albeit without UNIT appearing.

FURTHER ADVENTURES

- A Krynoid seed falls out of the sky and lands in Dark Age England. By mischance, the first animal it encounters is an extremely strong-

willed young man who is able to keep some of his sanity even as the plant transforms him into a hybrid, and he uses his newfound strength to fight against the tyrannical baron who oppresses the villagers. The locals begin to worship their

HARRISON CHASE

AWARENESS	4	PRESENCE	4
COORDINATION	3	RESOLVE	4
INGENUITY	3	STRENGTH	2

Harrison Chase is a millionaire with the world's largest collection of plants. He is also eccentric, eschewing the company of his fellow humans in favour of the plant kingdom. By the end, it is presumed that the Krynoid possessed Chase but this may not be the case; faced with his greatest hope made real Chase may have been all too eager to join it.

SKILLS

Athletics 2, Convince 3, Craft 3, Fighting 2, Knowledge 3, Medicine 2, Science 3 (Botany 5), Subterfuge 2, Technology 3

TRAITS

Eccentric (Minor): Chase's obsession with plants makes him callous and rude amongst his own kind.
Friends (Major): Thanks to his influence and resources, Chase has many friends in government.
Obsession (Major): Chase is obsessed with protecting and preserving plant life.

TECH LEVEL: 5   **STORY POINTS: 9**

SCORBY

AWARENESS	4	PRESENCE	3
COORDINATION	4	RESOLVE	4
INGENUITY	3	STRENGTH	4

Scorby is a mercenary who's worked in most of the world's hotspots. He's used to trusting no one but himself. Unfortunately, his lack of faith in the Doctor and UNIT gets him killed while trying to escape the Krynoid.

SKILLS

Athletics 3, Fighting 4, Knowledge 2, Marksman 5, Medicine 2, Subterfuge 3, Survival 4, Technology 2, Transport 2

TRAITS

Selfish: Scorby puts his own needs first.
Sharpshooter: Scorby may aim for 2 actions rather than 1.
Tough: Reduce total damage by 2.

EQUIPMENT: Pistol, 2/5/7, Rifle 3/6/9

TECH LEVEL: 5   **STORY POINTS: 5**

new hero as the Green Man. Do the travellers help hunt down this Green Man, or aid him in his battle with the baron? And what happened to that second seed?

- A hostile machine race plans to use the Krynoids as living biological weapons to wipe out their enemies, and go looking for seeds. They find one in the great interplanetary auction house of Mezu Shamar, Where All Things Have A Price. The characters learn of this scheme and get roped in to prevent the machines from getting their cold metallic claws on the seeds. Can they infiltrate the auction house and outbid the pawns of the machines?

- The world of Catellios is infamous for its dangerous jungles. Travelling there, the characters discover that the planet is a single titanic Krynoid. It's fully mature – and soon it will germinate, and a billion Krynoid seeds will explode out across the heavens. How do the characters fight an entity that covers an entire planet?

KRYNOID HYBRID

Once a seed hatches and the plant injects plant bacteria into an animal, the animal becomes a Krynoid hybrid. At first, it continues to use the same statistics as the victim, with the gradual loss of use of the limb injected. The Doctor offered amputation of the infected limb as a solution at this stage, but this might only delay germination for a few hours.

After a few hours the Krynoid completely consumes the host, transforming into a bloated version of its victim with tendrils sprouting over it; the tendrils at the ends of its arms may be manipulated like hands. In this form the hybrid uses the statistics block below until it mutates into a human-sized version of its final form (and moves to the regular Krynoid stat block).

AWARENESS	3	PRESENCE	1
COORDINATION	3	RESOLVE	3
INGENUITY	1	STRENGTH	6

SKILLS
Athletics 2, Fighting 3, Survival 4

TRAITS
Alien
Alien Appearance
Armour (Major Good): Reduce damage by 10 (-1 Coordination).
Fear Factor (Special Good): Grants a +2 bonus to inspire fear.
Immunity (major): Krynoids are immune to lasers.
Natural Weapons: The Krynoid can manipulate giant tendrils that do Strength +2 damage.
Networked (Major Good): Character has complete telepathic contact with nearby members of its kind.
Weakness (Minor Bad): -2 to rolls when blasted by steam.
Weakness (Major Bad): Defoliant can do 4 levels of damage to the Krynoid.

STORY POINTS: 8

KRYNOID

Krynoids are plant-based life forms that send seed pods through space, possibly via volcanic explosions on their home world. These seed pods always travel in pairs and, once they find a suitable world, hatch and consume the nearest animals. The Krynoid then spreads throughout the planet, psychically extending its control over all plant life. This process appears to be natural, but as the Krynoid is an intelligent being it's probable that its space travel is by design. The seed pods are hardy enough to survive the rigours of space and lay dormant for at least several thousand years.

An individual Krynoid germinates by consuming an animal, initially mutating into a plant-based form that roughly resembles the victim. Within hours it grows into a more bloated form that simply looks like a human-sized dome-topped cylinder with tendrils sprouting all over it. It continues to grow until, after several more hours, it becomes the size of a large house. The Doctor noted that it will eventually grow to be the size of St Paul's Cathedral before multiplying itself by producing new seeds. In its larger forms the Krynoid is capable of speech, possibly through telepathy.

Krynoids are immune to lasers and handheld conventional weaponry, although they are vulnerable to explosives.

AWARENESS	5	PRESENCE	3
COORDINATION	3	RESOLVE	5
INGENUITY	3	STRENGTH	10

SKILLS
Athletics 4, Fighting 4, Knowledge 2, Survival 5

TRAITS
Alien
Alien Appearance
Armour (Major): Reduce damage by 10 (-1 Coordination)
Fear Factor (3): Grants a +6 bonus to inspire fear.
Huge (Major): The Krynoid grows to the size of a house. For a smaller Krynoid, reduce Strength by 2 or 4, with a corresponding reduction in Speed by 1 or 2.
Immunity (Major): Krynoids are immune to lasers and bullets.
Natural Weapons (Minor): The Krynoid can manipulate giant tendrils that do Strength +2 damage
Networked (Major): Character has complete telepathic contact with nearby members of its kind.
Special: Animate plants within a certain radius, usually about 3 miles prior to entering its reproductive phase.
These plants attack any animal within reach – Strength varies based on plant thickness and how many plants can attack at once.
Weakness (Minor): -2 to rolls when blasted by steam
Weakness (Major): Defoliant can do 4 levels of damage to the Krynoid

STORY POINTS: 10

THE MASQUE OF MANDRAGORA

'It's part of a Time Lord's job to insist on justice for all species.'

⊛ SYNOPSIS

San Martino, Italy, late 15th century

While travelling through the Vortex, the TARDIS encountered a Helix – a sentient field of living energy, a psychic collective that existed, bodiless, outside normal reality. This Helix, the Mandragora Helix, hitched a ride on the TARDIS and diverted the ship to 15th century Italy.

The ship materialised in the woods outside San Martino. A peasant revolt in that town has just been violently suppressed by Count Federico. The Count's brother, the Duke, had just died, as foretold by the Duke's sinister advisor Hieronymous. Federico had eyes on the Duchy, but he needed to be rid of his nephew Giuliano first.

Landing in a forest, the Doctor and Sarah were soon separated as the Brotherhood of Demnos took Sarah and the Doctor was arrested as a spy. His wit proved to be little help at his hearing before Federico and Hieronymous and the Doctor was sentenced to execution. The Doctor used his scarf as a distraction to escape into the catacombs, where he found Sarah about to be sacrificed by the Brotherhood.

The Doctor helped Sarah escape as the Helix appeared and distracted the Brotherhood. The Helix informed the leader of the Brotherhood, Hieronymous, that he'd give him great power. Meanwhile, the Doctor and Sarah were captured by palace guards and taken to Giuliano, who feared that Federico planned to suppress all learning. In fact, Federico plotted to use Hieronymous' horoscope as cover to kill his nephew. The Doctor believed that the Helix was using the tensions caused by the developing Renaissance to gain power through religion. He decided that the temple needed to be destroyed but was attacked by the Helix and captured by the Brotherhood.

Giuliano aided the Doctor and fought off both palace guards and the Brotherhood. Hieronymous kidnapped and hypnotised Sarah to poison the Doctor before releasing her. She attacked just as the Doctor was confronting Hieronymous, whom the Doctor deduced was the leader of the Brotherhood. He snapped her out of the trance but Hieronymous escaped while the guards captured the time travellers and Giuliano.

Federico accused the three of paganism (worshipping Demnos) but the Doctor suggested that Hieronymous was the real enemy and no friend to Federico. The Doctor and Federico entered the temple disguised as Brotherhood members and witnessed Hieronymous leading the ceremony. Federico tried to arrest Hieronymous, but he was now a being of energy and blasted Federico to ashes.

Giuliano rallied the palace guards to his side but the Brotherhood began emptying the city by projecting fire from their fingers. The Doctor realised that the Helix would take over when the lunar eclipse occurred, but right now its energy power was thinly spread. He rigged a power drainer into a breastplate and confronted Hieronymous, provoking him to keep throwing bolts.

The Brotherhood took the nobles assembled for Giuliano's ascension hostage and prepared them for sacrifice. Fortunately, the ceremony drained the Helix instead as it turned out the Doctor, not Hieronymous, led the ritual. Saying goodbye to the new Duke of San Martino, the Doctor noted that the Mandragora Helix would be back in 500 years, which would be the end of the 20th century.

CONTINUITY

The Doctor explains the TARDIS' gift to Sarah as to why she can understand Italian. The gift apparently only applies to the dominant tongue of the region, as she doesn't understand Latin when it is spoken.
The Doctor shows off his swordsmanship skills again, crediting the captain of Cleopatra's bodyguard. He's also an accomplished horse rider.
This is the first appearance of the Secondary Console Room. The Doctor claims it was his old control room; there is an old outfit (possibly the Third Doctor's) a recorder, and a shaving mirror.
Demnos, god of moonlight, could be associated with Deimos, the Roman god of terror. Here, the god acts as the guardian of the old ways, keeping humanity fearful and superstitious.

RUNNING THE ADVENTURE

A big theme of this adventure is the Renaissance, the flowering of reason and science over superstition and tradition. The idea of blind faith and conservatism over change is a theme revisited whenever a new idea or evidence challenges the accepted view. Here, Hieronymous believes in the old ways and, through the power of the Mandragora, wishes to suppress new learning (coincidentally playing into the Mandragora's hand, as it believes that by suppressing science humanity will never make it to the stars). The Doctor usually falls on the side of reason, although there have been cases where he recognises reason within superstition (see ***Image of the Fendahl***).

When setting up adventures featuring this tension, create two sides and have one side supported by an alien creature with its own agenda. The alien recognises the usefulness of allies that don't question orders so long as it promises aid. Usually, its allies only recognise the deception before it is too late.

STARK CONTRASTS

This adventure presents science and superstition as stark contrasts, with each character fully devoted to one or the other. In truth, new ways of thought take much longer to germinate and sometimes never fully replace the old ways. The flowering of science in the Renaissance did not preclude religious belief or local superstitions; the Roman Catholic Church was often on the forefront of new learning (Galileo notwithstanding).

Still, when creating adventures it is often useful to paint characters with broad brush strokes. This enables the player characters to have dramatic scenes where they agree or disagree; the character's extremity of belief also enables even player characters who agree to take a more reasoned approach. For example, a player character might sympathise with a desire to topple an aristocracy in favour of a democracy, but she would stop short of calling for the lopping off of heads.

THIS IS OUR FAULT

Don't overuse this trick, but one great way to draw the players into an adventure is to make them responsible for the situation from the start. Here, the TARDIS travellers bring the Helix out of the Time Vortex – so everything that happens after that is (to a degree) their responsibility. A similar plot twist is used in **The Ark** (see **The First Doctor Sourcebook**), where the time travellers accidentally bring a virus with them that changes the balance of power on the Ark ship.

You can also – once in a while – undermine a previous triumph to get the players involved. Look at how the Doctor's accomplishments in **The Long Game** actually set up the horrors of **Bad Wolf** (both in **The Ninth Doctor Sourcebook**).

MANDRAGORA HELIX

The Mandragora Helix is an energy being and possibly a collective intelligence. It considers itself the master of the part of the galaxy that Earth inhabits and doesn't want the competition. Thus, it uses its powers to terrify the humans and hold them back from making the scientific advancements necessary to achieve space travel. Because of its nature, the Mandragora can only visit Earth when celestial markers are aligned to facilitate the journey. In the 15th century the Mandragora used the TARDIS to complete the circuit and come to Earth; the Doctor surmised that the stars would again align for the Mandragora Helix in the late 20th century.

The Mandragora Helix's natural form is a glowing ball of red-orange energy. It can also morph into basic shapes as well as transfer some of its power to humanoid hosts. When possessed, humanoid hosts gain the Mandragora's powers and become humanoid-shaped energy beings that can still wear clothing and manipulate objects.

AWARENESS	4	PRESENCE	3
COORDINATION	5	RESOLVE	6
INGENUITY	5	STRENGTH	-

SKILLS

Athletics 3, Convince 3, Fighting 3, Knowledge 5, Marksman 3, Science 4, Subterfuge 2, Survival 3, Technology 2

TRAITS

Alien Appearance (Major): Mandragora is a ball of energy.
Flight (Major): Mandragora can fly as high as it likes at a speed of 3x Coordination.
Immunity (Special): Mandragora takes no damage from energy or physical attacks.
Natural Weapons (Major): Heat bolts that do (4/L/L) damage.

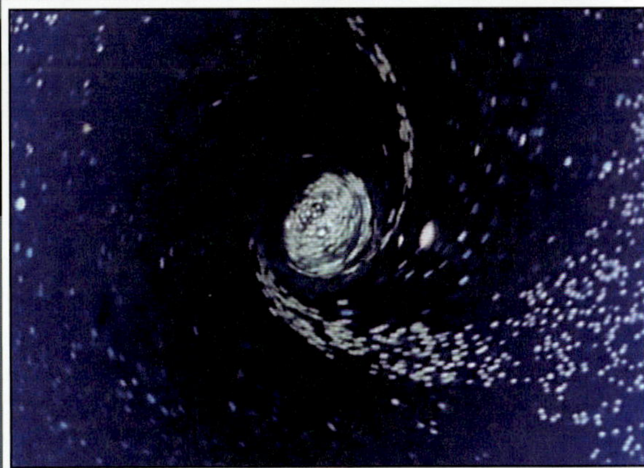

Telepathy: May create a mental link to read minds or converse telepathically.
Weakness (Major): Touching grounded metal (including via heat bolt) does 4 levels of damage to Mandragora.

TECH LEVEL: 7   **STORY POINTS: 10**

Make the characters feel they have to fix their own mistakes. They caused this mess, deliberately or accidentally – so they have to put things right. Avoid using this as the twist at the *end* of a scenario; don't end a game on a down note. Use it early on.

ADDING TARDIS ROOMS

TARDISes are really, really big on the inside. The Doctor's TARDIS has at least two control rooms, lots of cabins for the crew, storerooms, laboratories, the cloister room, the Zero Room, the library, the swimming pool (sometimes in the library) – for a full accounting, see **The Time Traveller's Companion**. Anyway, let the players create new TARDIS rooms as they wish. If the room actually has a game benefit, then they have to spend Story Points to justify it (*"Quick – to the TARDIS opera house!"* is free, but *"quick! To the TARDIS escape capsule"* definitely costs 6 Story Points or so.)

FURTHER ADVENTURES

• The Mandragora Helix may have appeared 500 years before. In the 11th century Empress Zoe of the Byzantine Empire was obsessed with securing her power and maintaining her beauty. A courtier with the ability to do both would be quite enticing. As the Empress enjoyed popular support, this is an opportunity for the Helix to build an army to rise up and challenge the Islamic states, which are experiencing a Golden Age, just before the First Crusade. Unless the player characters can stop it, Earth will soon come under the dominance of an oppressive regime with immortal rulers (perhaps they even trap it, which is why it needs the TARDIS 500 years hence).

• In the far future, human Helix-hunter ships dip in and out of the time vortex in search of their elusive prey. The sentient energy fields are then tapped for power by tearing them apart in psychic furnaces. The characters find themselves on a battered old Helix-hunter with a leaky furnace. The residue of dying Helices have collected into a ghastly spectral entity, and intend to drive the captain insane with visions of a white Helix.

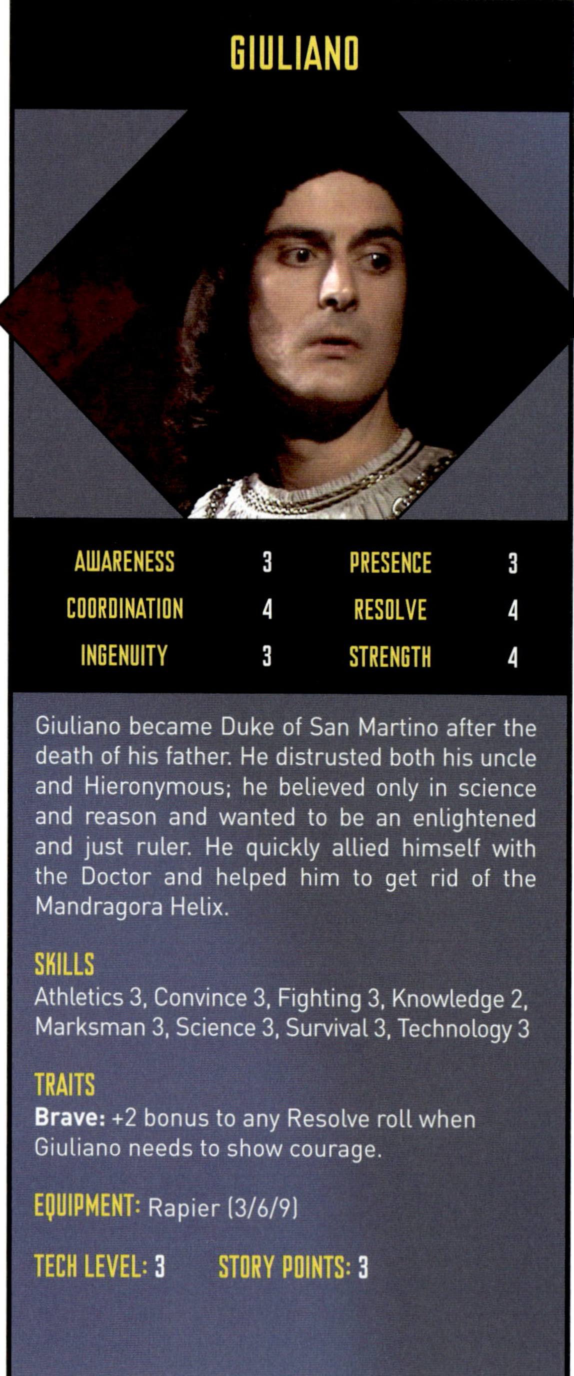

AWARENESS	3	PRESENCE	3
COORDINATION	4	RESOLVE	4
INGENUITY	3	STRENGTH	4

Giuliano became Duke of San Martino after the death of his father. He distrusted both his uncle and Hieronymous; he believed only in science and reason and wanted to be an enlightened and just ruler. He quickly allied himself with the Doctor and helped him to get rid of the Mandragora Helix.

SKILLS
Athletics 3, Convince 3, Fighting 3, Knowledge 2, Marksman 3, Science 3, Survival 3, Technology 3

TRAITS
Brave: +2 bonus to any Resolve roll when Giuliano needs to show courage.

EQUIPMENT: Rapier (3/6/9)

TECH LEVEL: 3   **STORY POINTS:** 3

- In *The Masque of Mandragora*, the Helix makes a bargain with Hieronymous, offering him power if he will further the Helix's aims. What if it does the same to a player character? In the middle of another adventure – say, right in the turmoil of a Dalek invasion – a Helix contacts one of the player characters. It will give her the power she needs to fight the Daleks if she helps the Helix...

COUNT FEDERICO

AWARENESS	3	PRESENCE	4
COORDINATION	4	RESOLVE	3
INGENUITY	4	STRENGTH	4

Count Federico is an opportunistic noble who poisoned his own brother and plotted to do the same to his nephew so that he could become Duke of San Martino. He enjoyed using his powers over others and acted ruthlessly against any sign of defiance. He was killed by Hieronymous with a heat bolt after the Count confronted him.

SKILLS
Athletics 3, Convince 4, Fighting 3, Knowledge 2, Marksman 3, Subterfuge 4, Survival 2

TRAITS
Obsession (Major): Federico is obsessed with gaining the Duchy; he's willing to kill for it.
Voice of Authority: +2 bonus to Presence and Convince rolls.

EQUIPMENT: Rapier (3/6/9)

TECH LEVEL: 3   STORY POINTS: 6

HIERONYMOUS

AWARENESS	4	PRESENCE	5
COORDINATION	4	RESOLVE	4
INGENUITY	3	STRENGTH	2

Hieronymous was a seer and the leader of the Brotherhood of Demnos, a secret society dedicated to an old Roman god of night. Hieronymous used Count Federico to enhance his power, making predictions that Federico would make true through mundane means, such as poisoning a man foretold to die. When the Mandragora Helix offered its power to Hieronymous, the seer promptly changed his allegiance. He effectively 'became' Mandragora once infused with its power.

SKILLS
Athletics 2, Convince 4, Craft 3, Fighting 2, Knowledge 3, Marksman 2, Medicine 1, Science 2, Subterfuge 3, Transport 2

TRAITS
Eccentric (Minor): Hieronymous often engages in arcane mutterings and cryptic references to astrological events, and has an air about him that unnerves others.
Hypnosis (Major): +2 bonus to control another's actions and feelings.
Immunity (Special): Hieronymous takes no damage from energy or physical attacks when filled with Mandragora's power.
Natural Weapons (Major): Heat bolts that do (4/L/L) damage.
Voice of Authority: +2 bonus to Presence and Convince rolls.
Weakness (Major): Touching grounded metal (including via heat bolt) does 4 levels of damage to Hieronymous.

EQUIPMENT: Knife (2/4/6)

TECH LEVEL: 3   STORY POINTS: 8

THE HAND OF FEAR

'Eldrad must live.'

⚙ SYNOPSIS

England and Kastria, UNIT Era

Over 150 million years ago, the Kastrian criminal Eldrad quarrelled with King Rokon. In their struggles, Eldrad sabotaged the barriers that protected their world from solar radiation. After his arrest for this crime, the Kastrians sentenced Eldrad to obliteration, and the war criminal was shot into space in a capsule. Below, the population of Kastria awaited their inevitable fate – their world would burn in the solar winds.

Millennia later, Eldrad's petrified hand reached Earth and became entombed deep under the earth. In the near-present, the time travellers arrived in a quarry, where they were almost killed in a controlled explosion. Sarah fared worse and was knocked unconscious, but not before she grabbed a stone hand and took the ring that was on it – the ring containing Eldrad's essence.

The Doctor examined the hand with a pathologist and determined that the hand was from a silicon-based lifeform. Meanwhile, Sarah recovered, but the ring controlled her, compelling her to steal the hand and overpower the security and staff at a nearby nuclear facility. She irradiated the hand, which began to heal itself and move.

The Doctor noted that, while Sarah was inside the reactor, the hand absorbed all of the radiation. He managed to break her hypnosis and removed her from the chamber. Unfortunately, the ring hypnotised a technician who returned the hand to the reactor.

The reactor went critical and Professor Watson, the head of the facility, ordered an RAF air strike. Unfortunately, the RAF missiles and the reactor provided enough power to regenerate Eldrad into a new form, appearing female due to initial contact with Sarah. Eldrad painted himself as a misunderstood and disgraced hero and asked the Doctor to take him back to his planet. The Doctor agreed on the condition that they went in the present, as going to Kastria's past would violate the First Law of Time.

Arriving on Kastria, they found it a dead planet. Eldrad was impaled by a spear-trap, but the time travellers got him to a regeneration chamber where he returned to his proper form. Eldrad believed that his people were lying dormant and could be restored by cloning the genetic samples stored in the Race Bank. He soon discovered that they destroyed themselves rather than die a slow death – including the Race Bank itself, denying Eldrad his prize. Eldrad decided to instead conquer Earth, but the time travellers fled back towards the TARDIS. When Eldrad followed, the time travellers used the Doctor's scarf to trip him and send him falling into an abyss.

Back in the TARDIS, Sarah bemoaned the travelling and decided to leave, egged on by the Doctor's seeming indifference. She packed her bags and returned to the console room, hoping for the Doctor to ask her to stay. Instead, her bluff was called; the Doctor had received a summons to Gallifrey and he couldn't take her with him. He steered the TARDIS to South Croydon and let her out. Well, actually, it was Aberdeen. That's near Croydon, right?

⊙ RUNNING THE ADVENTURE

The essence of **The Hand of Fear** makes for an interesting adventure. The characters discover an alien artefact that manipulates the situation in order to regenerate. Once regenerated the creature makes a reasonable request ("Please take me home"). The characters do so only to learn that the alien is evil and then must figure out a way to stop it after giving it what it wanted in the first place.

The adventure even introduces a twist – Eldrad starts off appearing evil, then becomes sympathetic, and then is revealed as a monster at the end.

'DON'T FORGET ME'

The Hand of Fear marked the final appearance of Sarah Jane Smith as one of the Doctor's regular companions, the Doctor's summons back to Gallifrey precluding any more travels together. Sarah Jane had been one of the Doctor's longest-serving companions, having first travelled with the Third Doctor in **The Time Warrior** before continuing her adventures with the Fourth Doctor following his regeneration.

Of course, this would not be the last we saw of Sarah Jane, for she was reunited with the Third Doctor - not to mention encountering the First, Second and Fifth Doctors - in the Five Doctors; and, much later, teamed up again with the Tenth Doctor to combat the

Krillitanes. She also briefly met the Eleventh Doctor, taking the number of Doctors she encountered to seven.

The departure of Sarah Jane reminds us that not all companions need to meet a tragic or violent end - sometimes they can leave gracefully, at a time (mostly) of their own choosing. This can be repeated in your own games too - a player might decide to retire their own player character, working with the Gamemaster to devise a suitably fitting point for them to depart.

NEW GADGET – KASTRIAN RING

This large blue crystal ring contains a program to force intelligent life to help regenerate the Kastrian to which it is coded.

Traits: Holds Eldrad's Blueprint, Hypnosis (+2 bonus to control another's actions and feelings), Lethal Blast (4/L/L), Stun Blast (S/S/S); uses radiation to rebuild body as per Fast Healing.
Cost: 4 Story Points

FURTHER ADVENTURES

- If Eldrad can be recreated from a hand, then perhaps he can be recreated from a different body part. During the Dalek invasion of Earth the desperate remaining powers in the world launched nuclear missiles. While these only hastened Earth's destruction, one missile instead regenerated Eldrad from another shard. With only Dalek technology available to get him back to Kastria, Eldrad works with the Resistance, creating a new type of silicon soldier from human volunteers to combat the Daleks. The player characters need to stop Eldrad's new army before it transforms humanity forever.

- Maybe not all of the Race Banks were destroyed – perhaps some of Eldrad's followers survived after a fashion too, constructing a logic puzzle that teaches the finders of their remains how to regenerate them. Once this is accomplished, Eldrad's followers plan to conquer the galaxy after retrieving their leader from an abyss on their home world. The player characters arrive on Kastria and have to stop them.

- What if Eldrad had forced the Doctor to travel back in time to his own past on Kastria? Would it be a paradox if the defeated revolutionary leader returns to a point before he's defeated? Eldrad is willing to risk his own erasure from the time-stream to accomplish his goals, but are the characters prepared to risk their own lives to protect history?

ELDRAD

Eldrad was a Kastrian scientist who initially used his skills to protect his people; he created solar barriers to keep out harmful rays, adapted the Kastrian form for survival, and planned to re-fertilise his desolate planet. Unfortunately, Eldrad also had dreams of conquest and his people, most notably King Rokon, would have none of it. The Kastrians chose to turn on their saviour rather than allow him to turn them into ruthless conquerors. Angered by the betrayal, Eldrad destroyed the solar barriers. While he likely did this to force the Kastrians to bend their knees to him, they instead captured him, put him on trial, and sentenced him to death by obliteration. Eldrad's capsule was shot off the planet, but it exploded prematurely, enabling part of Eldrad to survive.

Eldrad is a Kastrian – a humanoid species covered with blue minerals and conical, neckless heads. His body can also adapt its form based on humanoids that come in contact with him; thus Eldrad's first form after being found by Sarah Jane is that of a blue mineral-encrusted woman.

AWARENESS	2	PRESENCE	4
COORDINATION	3	RESOLVE	5
INGENUITY	5	STRENGTH	6

SKILLS
Athletics 2, Convince 3, Craft 3, Fighting 3, Knowledge 3, Marksman 3, Medicine 4, Science 6, Subterfuge 3, Survival 5, Technology 5, Transport 2

TRAITS
Alien

Alien Appearance (Major)

Alien Organs: The character's organs are not where you might expect. All targeted damage is reduced by 2.

Armour (Major): Reduce damage by 10.

Natural Weapons (Major): A ranged mind blast that does (3/6/9) damage. Eldrad's eyes glow blue when he uses this trait. Attacks use Eldrad's Resolve instead of Coordination.

Shapeshift (Major): Eldrad can assume a form that resembles the native species of the planet that helped rebuild him.

Telepathy: May create a mental link to read minds or converse telepathically.

Radiation Regeneration (Special): Exposure to radiation heals Eldrad. A potent source of radiation, like a nuclear reactor, lets him regenerate 1 point per minute. Extreme radiation, like a nuclear explosion, restores him completely.

EQUIPMENT: Kastrian Ring

TECH LEVEL: 6   **STORY POINTS:** 8-10

THE DEADLY ASSASSIN

'Finished, Doctor! You're finished!'

⊙ SYNOPSIS

Gallifrey, Inner Time.

En route to Gallifrey to answer a summons, the Doctor had a premonition that he would assassinate the Lord President. It soon became obvious that someone was aiding and watching the Doctor. The Doctor stole Time Lord robes to get on the Panopticon floor and spotted a mounted staser rifle. He grabbed it and looked through its scope, noticing an assassin trying to kill the Lord President as he gave his resignation speech.

The Doctor attempted to shoot the assassin but it instead appeared that he'd killed the Lord President.

As the President died before naming a successor, Chancellor Goth called for elections. Goth was the most likely candidate and presumed an easy victory. The Doctor, however, used a legal loophole to postpone his arrest by announcing his own candidacy. He was given a day to prove his innocence while his mysterious benefactor, actually the Master, was informed.

The Doctor's investigation soon proved the Master's participation, or it would have if the Master wasn't one step ahead of him. Every potential piece of evidence was stolen and witnesses killed. There was no record of the Master within the Matrix, Gallifrey's central databank. The Doctor realised that the Master or an associate must be within the Matrix and decided to go inside to find him. Once inside the Matrix's virtual reality, the Doctor found himself being pursued by an assassin.

The assassin was Chancellor Goth, whose mental power was being enhanced by the Master. The Doctor held his own in a battle of wills as each reshaped the virtual world to gain advantage. Engin, a Matrix archivist and ally of the Doctor, helped foil the Master's plan to kill the Doctor. Meanwhile, the Doctor was able to unmask Goth and defeat him before leaving the Matrix.

The Doctor informed the Castellan and they located a dying Goth as well as the remains of the Master's body. Goth admitted he'd discovered and brought the dying Master to Gallifrey to assist him in his schemes after he'd learned that he wasn't going to be appointed Lord President. Unfortunately, he died before he could reveal the Master's plan.

The Doctor realised that the Master had faked his own death. Stealing the ceremonial Sash and Rod of Rassilon, the Master tried to use the Eye of Harmony to regenerate his failing body, but using that much power would destroy Gallifrey as well. The Doctor confronted him and, during the struggle, the Master fell into a fissure. Gallifrey was saved, although half of the capital city lay in ruins.

CONTINUITY

Time Lords can recognise each other even after they've regenerated.

The TARDIS is revealed to be a Type-40 TT capsule. This model is considered obsolete.

The Matrix, the Eye of Harmony, the Great Key of Rassilon and the Sash of Rassilon make their first appearance.

The number of regenerations of a Time Lord is stated for the first time, although as future episodes reveal, this is not necessarily the whole story...

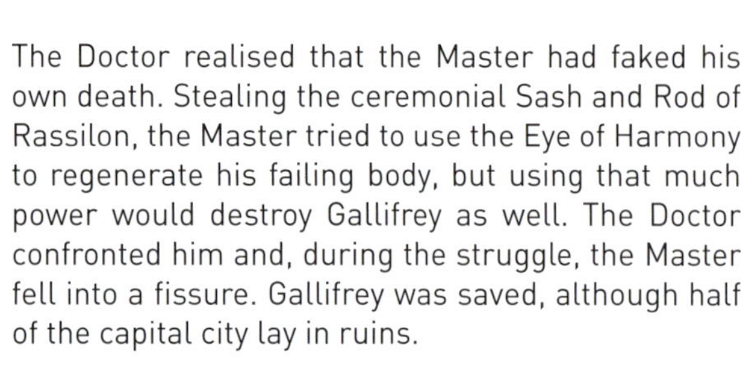

⊙ RUNNING THE ADVENTURE

This adventure is notable for many things; the deconstruction of Time Lord society, the return of the Master, the Doctor's involvement in Time Lord politics, and the introduction of the Matrix. At its heart, though, it's simply a murder mystery with a player character as the prime suspect. The investigation leads to a stint in the matrix, after which the player characters finally confront the Master and stop him before he destroys Gallifrey.

When running adventures based on this – or any other Time Lord-heavy scenario – then having access to **The Time Traveller's Companion** sourcebook is a very good idea!

THE MATRIX

The Matrix of Gallifrey holds the accumulated wisdom and knowledge of the Time Lords. It is more than a computer system – it is a world of the mind, a world of thought and energy that physical beings can experience as though it was physical reality.

Entry into the virtual reality world of the Matrix requires a physical connection by way of mind interface. The initial surge of power that connects the brain to the Matrix causes a single point of damage to the character and this damage carries over into their virtual self. Once inside, all actions and reactions are handled using the normal rules, making rolls and taking damage just as one would in the real world.

The largest difference is that characters can use Story Points to try and alter the reality of the virtual world around them by taking the following Actions:

Deny Reality (1 SP)
Basically, this allows the character to undo something that has occurred, from imagining a bullet wound away to turning a venomous snake into a plush toy, by making a Resolve + Convince roll at Difficulty 15.

Augment Reality (2 SP)
The character makes a small change to the environment of the Matrix, like finding a rope ladder dangling from a cliff, finding a passage in a dead end or finding a small pond of fresh water, by making a Resolve + Convince roll at Difficulty 15.

The basic form of the virtual world can be anything one can imagine and will typically take whatever form the subconscious mind desires. If another person has entered the Matrix and invested enough time and 3 SP beforehand, the character might find herself trapped in a nightmare world of someone else's choosing. In this case the 'creator' of the world has a few other actions he may use:

Enforce Reality (1 SP)
Whenever another character attempts to Deny Reality, the 'creator' of the world may cancel that action by spending the required Story Point and winning an Opposed Resolve + Convince roll against them.

Create Reality (0/1 SP)
The creator can create whatever items they need out of thin air, from a backpack to a biplane to a horse in a gas mask, by making a Resolve + Convince roll at Difficulty 12 for each one. These items disappear after the scene is resolved however. To permanently add them to the virtual world costs just 1 SP per item, no matter how large or small.

Once two minds are engaged in a Matrix conflict, both are locked into the dream world until the 'creator' mind withdraws, is rendered unconscious or is killed. Once this has occurred, any remaining characters must make a Resolve + Convince roll at Difficulty 15 to escape.

Being killed in the Matrix results in the brain death of the physical body that inhabits the real world. Damage to Strength and Coordination does not carry over into the real world, but all other damage does. Having the Matrix disconnected while the character's mind is still inside will cause 2D6 damage to the character from the shock of the sudden disconnection.

HEY, ISN'T THAT…

Chancellor Goth looks remarkably similar to the Time Lord that presided over the Doctor's trial; given that, in Britain, the Chancellor is head of the judiciary, it makes sense that Goth is in fact the same Time Lord that exiled the Doctor.

SYMBOLS OF POWER

The ceremonial items carried by the President, Chancellor and the Keeper of the Matrix were wondrous technological artefacts directly related to the very foundation of the Time Lord's great civilisation. After millions of years, knowledge of the purpose of these items faded until they were

THE MASTER

The Master is a renegade Time Lord and enemy of the Doctor who is now at the end of his last incarnation. He was dying on the planet Tersurus when Goth discovered him and helped him stabilise the remains of his form. Unlike the suave, charismatic adversary that faced the Doctor during his exile on Earth, the Master is now a seething creature of hate in an emaciated body. With little time left to him the Master wants to use the power of the Eye of Harmony to restart his regenerative cycle; the fact that this will also destroy Gallifrey is of no matter to him. He also takes the opportunity to humiliate the Doctor one last time to cover his tracks. This version of the Master appears to be a skeletal husk, his skin barely clinging to his bones and his face set in a skull-like grin. He wears a coarse cloak over his body.

AWARENESS	3	PRESENCE	2
COORDINATION	2	RESOLVE	6
INGENUITY	9	STRENGTH	2

SKILLS

Convince 5, Craft 2, Fighting 2, Knowledge 6, Marksman 3, Medicine 3, Science 4, Subterfuge 5, Survival 4, Technology 4, Transport 4

TRAITS

Adversary (Major): The Doctor, The Daleks
Block Transfer Specialist
Boffin: Allows the Master to create Gadgets.
Charming
Eccentric
Hypnosis (Special): +2 bonus to control another's actions and feelings. The Master's skill at hypnosis is so great that he can make people into puppets of his will.
Indomitable: +4 bonus to any rolls to resist psychic control.
Obsession (Major): Survival at all costs.
Percussive Maintenance

Photographic Memory: The Master can perfectly recall any information.
Reverse the Polarity of the Neutron Flow
Selfish: He puts his own needs first.
Tailored Regeneration
Technically Adept: +2 to any Technology roll to fix a broken or faulty device.
Time Traveller (All)
Time Lord
Time Lord Engineer
Time Lord (Experienced)
Voice of Authority: +2 bonus to Presence and Convince rolls.
Vortex: The Master may pilot time craft through the Vortex, and gains +2 when doing so.
Wanted Renegade
Weakness (Minor): Gloating

EQUIPMENT: Tissue Compression Eliminator

TECH LEVEL: 10

STORY POINTS: 10

considered largely symbolic. The Master's attempt to steal the power of the Eye of Harmony, however, revealed the true nature of these devices and they were carefully guarded to prevent future misuse after that.

The Rod of Rassilon

This 3 metre-long black ebonite sceptre was the key to accessing the control obelisk for the Eye of Harmony, the source of the Time Lords' power located underneath the Panopticon. With access to the Control Obelisk, one had access to the infinite power of a captured black hole and all the possibilities

and dangers that came with it, although use of it was a death sentence for anyone not wearing the Sash of Rassilon.

The Sash of Rassilon

A device so powerful the like of it will never be seen again in this universe, this metallic golden sash, when activated, could protect the bearer from anything up to and including the crushing gravity and radiation emissions from a black hole.

Unfortunately, the Sash was damaged during the Master's assassination of the Lord President and

CHANCELLOR GOTH

Goth was the chief judge at the Doctor's trial and passed down the sentence of exile and forced regeneration. He was also a member of the Celestial Intervention Agency and this may have played a role in the sentencing. Goth was on the rise in Time Lord society and quickly worked his way up to Chancellor while being groomed to replace the President. Unfortunately for Goth, the President soon regretted his decision to support Goth as successor and quietly withdrew it. Goth felt betrayed and his ambition wouldn't allow this setback to stand. He saw an opportunity when he discovered the Master on Tersurus during a CIA investigation. Goth secretly brought the Master back to Gallifrey in the belief that the two could help each other. Goth never realised that the Master, even in his current state, could play him for a fool.

The Master hypnotised Goth and put his plan into action. Following the Master's instructions, Goth assassinated the President and made it appear to be the Doctor's doing. When the Doctor entered the Matrix to find answers to who was manipulating it, the Master forced Goth to enter the Matrix as well and try to kill the Doctor. The Doctor won the battle and the Master killed Goth while trying to trap the Doctor within the Matrix.

AWARENESS	4	PRESENCE	4
COORDINATION	4	RESOLVE	5
INGENUITY	7	STRENGTH	3

SKILLS

Athletics 2, Convince 2, Craft 1, Fighting 3, Knowledge 4, Marksman 3, Medicine 2, Science 4, Subterfuge 4, Survival 3, Technology 4, Transport 2

TRAITS

Boffin: Allows Goth to create Gadgets.
Brave: +2 bonus to any Resolve roll when Goth needs to show courage.
Feel the Turn of the Universe: +2 bonus to Awareness and Ingenuity to detect something wrong with time or space.
Friends: The High Council and the Master.
Obsession: Wants to be President.
Technically Adept: +2 to any Technology roll to fix a broken or faulty device.

Time Traveller (Major)
Time Lord
Time Lord (Experienced)
Vortex: Goth may pilot time craft through the Vortex, and gains +2 when doing so.

TECH LEVEL: 10   **STORY POINTS:** 8

no living Time Lord had the skill to repair it, so this protection became erratic and only lasts a short period (2D6x 10 rounds) before the artefact shorts out for a time (2D6 days).

The Sash also converts the energy of the Eye for other purposes as well. Again, damaged as it was, this function is relatively limited, serving as a gadget with every Gadget Trait and 12 Story Points when fully charged. It is so complex, however, that it required a Difficulty 27 Ingenuity + Technology roll to use.

THE CELESTIAL INTERVENTION AGENCY

This secretive institution is mentioned only briefly in the adventure, but its existence implies a great deal about Time Lord society. The CIA deals with problems and threats to Gallifrey, and its very name suggests how it functions – through precisely targeted interventions from on high. The Doctor's trips to Skaro (*Genesis of the Daleks*) or Uxarieus (*Colony in Space*, in **The Third Doctor Sourcebook**) are typical of this sort of mission, and some historians have even speculated that the Second Doctor worked for them before he was exiled to Earth.

The CIA are perfect for use in roleplaying games. They can either be the player characters' patrons (so, any Time Lord player characters are CIA agents, sent on secret missions for Gallifrey) or they can divert wandering exiles to places where they are needed (just like the Doctor was sent to Skaro, Peladon and many other worlds as a 'deniable asset'). For more on the Celestial Intervention Agency, see **The Time Traveller's Companion**.

MAKING THE TIME LORDS YOUR OWN

The Time Lords of Gallifrey are figures of legend. No other society has conquered time so thoroughly. No other civilisation has endured so long, or worked such wonders. *The Deadly Assassin* is the first time we see them directly, and we don't see them at their best – it's clear why the Doctor left this race of squabbling bureaucrats.

NEW GADGET
TISSUE COMPRESSION ELIMINATOR

This hideous device compresses the space between molecules, leaving a dense, miniaturised version of the target behind. A direct hit instantly kills living creatures and destroys complex mechanical or electrical circuitry, but even a graze will cause massive amounts of damage. The Master appreciates the terror caused by the tiny doll-like corpses of the victims killed by this weapon and often leaves them about as macabre calling cards for his enemies to find...

Traits: Delete (L/L/L), Compress
Cost: 2 Story Points

NEW GADGET TRAIT – COMPRESS
(MINOR/MAJOR GOOD GADGET TRAIT)

A compression field squeezes molecules closer together, making things smaller. It's not dimensionally transcendent – it's a lot smellier than that! Compression fields show up in all sorts of places, from the Master's Tissue Compression Eliminator to the Teselecta justice vessel to Miniscopes.

The Minor version of this trait is a one-way shrinking – it can make big things small, but cannot unshrink them. The Major version can instantly shrink or unshrink a target.

STASER

The standard issue weapon for the Chancellery Guard, the Staser (or 'Stun Laser') had two settings. The standard, low power setting, S (S/**S**/S), disrupted the target's nervous system in order to render them unconscious for 2D6x10 minutes.

The high powered setting, L [6/**L**/L], destroyed living tissue and also disrupted the nervous system to inhibit a Time Lord's ability to regenerate, killing them instantly with a well-placed shot.

Staser fire is primarily designed to affect living tissue and is less effective against non-living material. When used against inanimate material, the damage from the high powered setting is reduced to 5 [2/5/7] for Staser Pistols and 6 [3/6/9] for Staser Rifles, while the low power setting has no effect at all. Stasers come in pistol and rifle forms, the latter adding a +1 to the user's Marksman Skill due to their extreme accuracy.

Other adventures present the Time Lords differently. In *The War Games* (**The Second Doctor Sourcebook**), they're like gods descending from on high; in *The End of Time*, they're malevolent and vengeful monsters, a decaying race of mad scientists and mystics.

The Time Lords may look human, but they are far beyond our limited understanding. Their technology is so advanced it looks like magic; their culture so baroque and steeped in ancient traditions and customs that it looks like madness. Gallifrey should never be just another planet that the characters visit – any interaction with the Time Lords should be like meeting the gods of Olympus. Make them awesome and magical, not predictable.

Also, keep visits to Gallifrey to an absolute minimum, even in a CIA-based campaign. The more the players see of Gallifrey, the more ordinary it becomes. *Talk* about Gallifrey a lot, mention it in myths and legends, sow rumours about the great works of the Time Lords – but don't go there more than once or twice in a campaign. Gallifrey works much better as a *concept* than a location.

FURTHER ADVENTURES

- The Master here is at the end of his regenerations, which may or may not be the incarnation that faced the Third Doctor. Thus, there are at least 11 incarnations unaccounted for. Even if you are running a campaign using only the classic series, it's possible that your player characters could come up against an unknown incarnation of the Master.

- The Doctor claimed it was impossible for Sarah to come with him. Later, when meeting the Tenth Doctor, Sarah Jane leaves out the time she met him in *The Five Doctors*. Of the other non-Time Lords that visited Gallifrey, Jamie and Zoe had their minds wiped, Leela remained behind, and presumably Tegan and Turlough had their minds erased of their time on Gallifrey as well. What if the player characters went to Gallifrey for something and all of their minds were wiped except for the Time Lord(s) and now someone is pursuing them for acts that they don't remember?

- What happens if the Master wins? His mad attempt to trigger another regeneration cycle wreaked havoc on Gallifrey. What would have happen if he succeeded, and Gallifrey was destroyed? Who would take the place of the Time Lords? Would the Daleks have triumphed throughout time without any force to oppose them? Even after the Doctor stopped the Master, vast damage was inflicted on Gallifrey, and that may have echoes and repercussions throughout the time vortex. Maybe the Master's actions damaged the Untempered Schism, or sent Gallifreyan artefacts and treasures tumbling through time.

CARDINAL BORUSA

AWARENESS	4	PRESENCE	5
COORDINATION	3	RESOLVE	6
INGENUITY	9	STRENGTH	2

Cardinal Borusa was the Doctor's tutor at the Time Lord Academy. He was also a Cardinal of the Prydonian chapter, although as is custom he continued to wear the Patrex robes showing which chapter he'd belonged to at the academy.

Borusa is in charge of the inquiry into the President's assassination and the Doctor's role in it. While Borusa wants to learn the truth, he is equally, perhaps even more, concerned with maintaining decorum and the status quo. When he learns of Goth's involvement and death Borusa chooses to construct a story making Goth a hero who tried to stop the Master rather than a stooge that worked for him.

SKILLS

Convince 5, Knowledge 6, Science 5, Subterfuge 3, Technology 5, Transport 3

TRAITS

Brave: +2 bonus to any Resolve roll when Borusa needs to show courage.
By the Book: Borusa must be convinced to act against procedure.
Code of Conduct (Major): Borusa must follow the Laws of Time.
Feel the Turn of the Universe: +2 bonus to Awareness and Ingenuity to detect something wrong with time or space.
Friends (Major): The High Council.
Time Lord
Time Lord (Experienced)
Time Traveller
Unadventurous (Minor): Borusa avoids adventure and excitement.
Voice of Authority: +2 bonus to Presence and Convince rolls.
Vortex: Borusa may pilot time craft through the Vortex, and gains +2 when doing so.

TECH LEVEL: 10   **STORY POINTS:** 6

CHANCELLERY GUARD

AWARENESS	3	PRESENCE	4
COORDINATION	4	RESOLVE	4
INGENUITY	4	STRENGTH	3

The official police force of the Citadel, the Chancellery Guard is formed from common Gallifreyans looking for something 'exciting' to do, and so enter the Gallifreyan equivalent of a police academy, where they learn crowd control, investigative and martial skills. In truth, the life of a Chancellery Guard is anything but exciting, as very little criminal activity takes place on Gallifrey, and what little exists is usually handled quickly . The vast majority of their time is therefore spent on guard or escort duty.

SKILLS

Athletics 1, Convince 1, Fighting 2, Knowledge 1, Marksman 2, Science 1, Subterfuge 1, Technology 2, Transport 2

TRAITS

By the Book (Minor): Must be convinced to act against procedure.
Code of Conduct (Major): The Guards must uphold Gallifreyan Law.
Impulsive: The Chancellery Guard leap at any chance to see some action.
Psychic: +4 against mental attacks and Guard may attempt to read minds.
Voice of Authority: +2 bonus to Presence and Convince rolls.

EQUIPMENT: Staser

TECH LEVEL: 10   **STORY POINTS:** 2-4

THE FACE OF EVIL

'Would you like a jelly baby?'
'It's true then. They say the Evil One eats babies.'

⊘ SYNOPSIS

Mordee Colony, the Far Future

The Doctor arrived in a jungle and met Leela, who came from a primitive tribe known as the Sevateem. She immediately believed him to be 'the Evil One.' She'd been exiled and secretly marked for death by Neeva, the tribal shaman, as she'd blasphemed against their god Xoanon. The Doctor soon discovered that advanced technology was present in the jungle as the Sevateem were, unknown to them, protected by a force field. The Doctor managed to convince her that he wasn't an evil deity long enough for her to tell him that the Evil One resided with the Tesh in a mountain behind a black wall. Xoanon was their prisoner.

A Sevateem patrol encountered the Doctor and, upon seeing 'the Evil One,' made a religious gesture that the Doctor noted had a practical application with a particular type of space suit. Leela secretly followed the Doctor back to her tribe and freed him. The Doctor headed towards the 'Evil' mountain and discovered a giant carving of his own face! The Doctor returned to the Sevateem to uncover more artefacts as an elder, Calib, used the opportunity to prove the gods false. He stabbed Leela with a lethal Janis thorn; luckily the Doctor was able to concoct an antidote.

The Doctor was given the test of the Horda, which involved shooting a rope with a crossbow before he was lowered into a pit with vicious creatures. He succeeded (thanks to training from William Tell) and proved his non-evilness. Unfortunately Xoanon, using a radio, told Neeva that the tribe would be destroyed; it lowered the force field to allow invisible creatures to overrun the village. When illuminated by a disruptor gun, these creatures resembled the Doctor's face!

The Doctor escaped with Leela and they managed to climb inside the mountain through the giant face. The Doctor began to remember that he'd helped an expedition by repairing its computer. Unfortunately, he forgot to purge his own influence and the computer was now suffering from split-personality disorder. The Doctor and Leela met the Tesh, descendants of the ship's engineers that still had technology as well as psychic abilities. The Doctor used Xoanon's own equipment to contact the Sevateem and ordered them to enter the mountain.

The Doctor entered the computer room to repair Xoanon but the computer's psychic power proved too great. Xoanon tried to get the Tesh to capture them, but the Sevateem arrived and engaged them. In a last-ditch act Xoanon decided to destroy itself in an atomic explosion, but Neeva used the disruptor gun to attack Xoanon, which resulted in his own death but bought the Doctor enough time to complete repairs.

Now cured, Xoanon could help the Sevateem and the Tesh create a new, integrated society. As the two groups argued over who would lead, the Doctor slipped away. Leela met him at the TARDIS and asked to go with him. When the Doctor refused, she jumped in anyway and started the TARDIS' dematerialisation.

CONTINUITY

The Mordee Expedition in the future carries Earth colonists.

The Doctor previously aided the Mordee Expedition by repairing Xoanon with a psychian memory transfer; he didn't recognise the computer's evolution to sentience.

The Doctor learned how to fire a crossbow from William Tell.

RUNNING THE ADVENTURE

This adventure has an interesting premise: unanticipated fallout from a previous adventure creates a bad situation in the current adventure. In this way, **The Face of Evil** shares similarities with **The Ark** (where Dodo's cold turns the social order upside-down) or **Bad Wolf** (in which the Doctor's prior meddling lets the Daleks move in).

When running an adventure of this type it's best to ensure that the solution isn't simply to fix what went wrong; the consequences should put several more obstacles in the way. In this case, the Doctor is demonised as the Evil One, making it difficult to deal with the Sevateem. The Sevateem have also forgotten their origins and the Doctor needs to cut through their superstitions. Finally, the Tesh are powerful adversaries as well and the Doctor needs to use his mental powers to correct the now-evolved Xoanon's flaws. The current situation should be far more complicated than the original quick-fix.

Be wary of turning the characters' successes against them – you don't want to make the players feel they've been tricked. For example, if the adventure involves an invading fleet, and the characters blow the fleet up when it's in orbit of a human colony, then don't make the next adventure an ecologic crisis on the colony caused by falling chunks of spaceship; that just undermines the characters' earlier victory. Instead, maybe the colony salvages the invaders' spaceships and becomes a planet of nasty space pirates.

HIDDEN ADVENTURES

This adventure has a surprising premise – not only does it deal with the consequences of a previous adventure, but one that the Doctor has forgotten. The implication is that the Doctor met Xoanon a long time ago while still in his current incarnation. This implies that either the Doctor's quick jaunt in the TARDIS during **Robot** actually took decades, or the Doctor has been travelling alone for a long time after the events of **The Deadly Assassin.**

Conversely, it's possible that this unseen adventure took place while Sarah (and possibly Harry) was still with the Doctor and, as the solution seemed obvious at the time, this particular adventure was no different then so many unremarkable stops that the Doctor has made, or any different than the myriad other times the Doctor used a psychic memory transfer to fix a computer.

A third possibility is that the Doctor's visit to Xoanon takes place in his personal future. He doesn't remember fixing the computer because from his perspective, he hasn't done it yet. In any case, this adventure, as well as the Doctor's great variance in age over his regenerations, indicates that hidden, forgotten or unplayed adventures often take place. This is a remarkable tool for the GM, as it enables you to establish events in which the characters participated but have no player knowledge (at least until it starts coming back to them).

When using this technique be careful not to make the player characters' previous actions seem out of character. In **The Face of Evil**, the Doctor was only trying to help, which is in keeping with his character, and the outcome was merely due to unexpected circumstances. It would have felt very different had the Doctor 'remembered' that he once decided to play games with a group of stranded expedition survivors, making him more the Rani than the Doctor.

PRIMITIVE COMPANIONS

While almost all companions are 'primitive' by a Time Lord's standard, Leela is a throwback to companions like Katarina, Jamie and Victoria (especially Jamie). While she's from the future, Leela is a warrior who often sees things in black and white and isn't particularly interested in changing her world-view or being assimilated into a more advanced culture; in short, she simply finds travelling with the Doctor interesting. Leela trusts the Doctor, not because he was her god, but because she values his wisdom as an experienced traveller.

The twist with some primitive companions is that, unfettered by tradition, prejudice and history, they often see things with modern eyes. Contrast Victoria, who felt almost naked in a knee-length skirt in **The Tomb of the Cybermen**, with Leela, who argued with Professor Litefoot over why she should only have one lump of sugar in her tea.

CULTURE EVOLVES

One of the most memorable aspects of this adventure is the language of the tribes. Leela comes from the 'Sevateem' – Survey Team – and fears the tribe of the Tesh, formerly the Technicians. Commonplace words become names to conjure with once enough time has past. This technique is a wonderful way to make a setting feel real and 'lived-in'. Imagine an adventure where the Doctor discovers a colony of humans descended from the inhabitants of a small English village that was caught in a dimensional fold and transported to another planet hundreds of years ago. The culture of this whole planet is derived from that little village.

Maybe the planet's ruled by 'Hizzoner Mayar' – His Honour the Mayor – and law is enforced by the vicious blue-helmeted Byobie shock troops on their sinister black bicycles…

By the way, anthropologists believe that all humanity is descended from a small group of survivors – possibly as few as 2,000 individuals. How much of our culture comes from them? How different would the world be if more or less of them survived?

NEW GADGET – JANIS THORN

This poisonous thorn is indigenous to the planet where the Mordee expedition crashed. It causes paralysis and then death, effectively making it a fatal weapon with an interesting special effect. Death occurs after several minutes, allowing for time to give the victim an antidote (the difficulty depends on the era – the Doctor found one in moments using a bio-analyser, likely indicating a 15 Difficulty).

Traits: Delayed Stun/Stun/Lethal damage. Getting scratched with a Janis thorn means the victim gets Stunned in 1d6 Action Rounds.
Cost: 2 Story Points

FURTHER ADVENTURES

- Xoanon was a computer that achieved sentience and still cared for the colonists. What if another ship computer gained sentience and wished to be rid of 'the parasites?' The player characters arrive on a colony ship and are separated from their TARDIS. Now they must help the humans survive while finding a way to destroy the computer or get back to their ship while evading psychic monsters.

- A sentient computer of an exploration vessel was left derelict when its crew abandoned it during its 'birth.' Now the ship travels through space, capturing sentients that wander too close to be its new crew. Can the player characters stop it before they become its next victims?

- Xoanon created a physically hardy race and a highly intelligent race; the descendants have both enhancements. Unfortunately, a charismatic leader decides that the new 'Xoanites' should rule the rest of humanity. Xoanon tries to resist but is subjugated. Can the player characters stop a group of powerful conquerors possessing potent psychic powers?

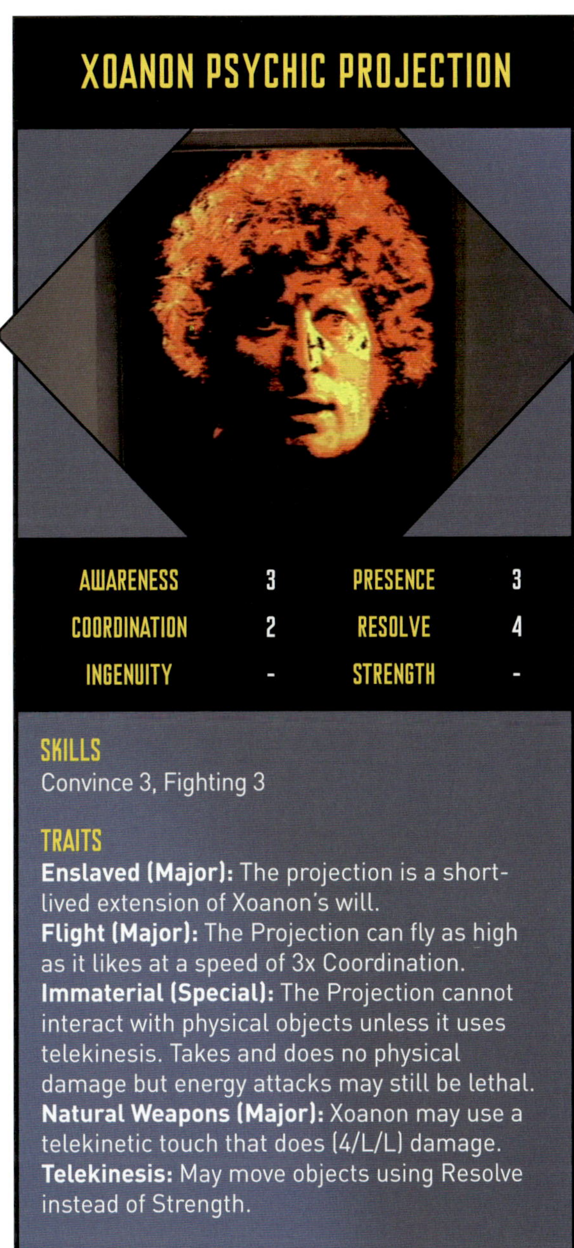

XOANON PSYCHIC PROJECTION

AWARENESS	3	PRESENCE	3
COORDINATION	2	RESOLVE	4
INGENUITY	-	STRENGTH	-

SKILLS
Convince 3, Fighting 3

TRAITS
Enslaved (Major): The projection is a short-lived extension of Xoanon's will.
Flight (Major): The Projection can fly as high as it likes at a speed of 3x Coordination.
Immaterial (Special): The Projection cannot interact with physical objects unless it uses telekinesis. Takes and does no physical damage but energy attacks may still be lethal.
Natural Weapons (Major): Xoanon may use a telekinetic touch that does (4/L/L) damage.
Telekinesis: May move objects using Resolve instead of Strength.

STORY POINTS: 4

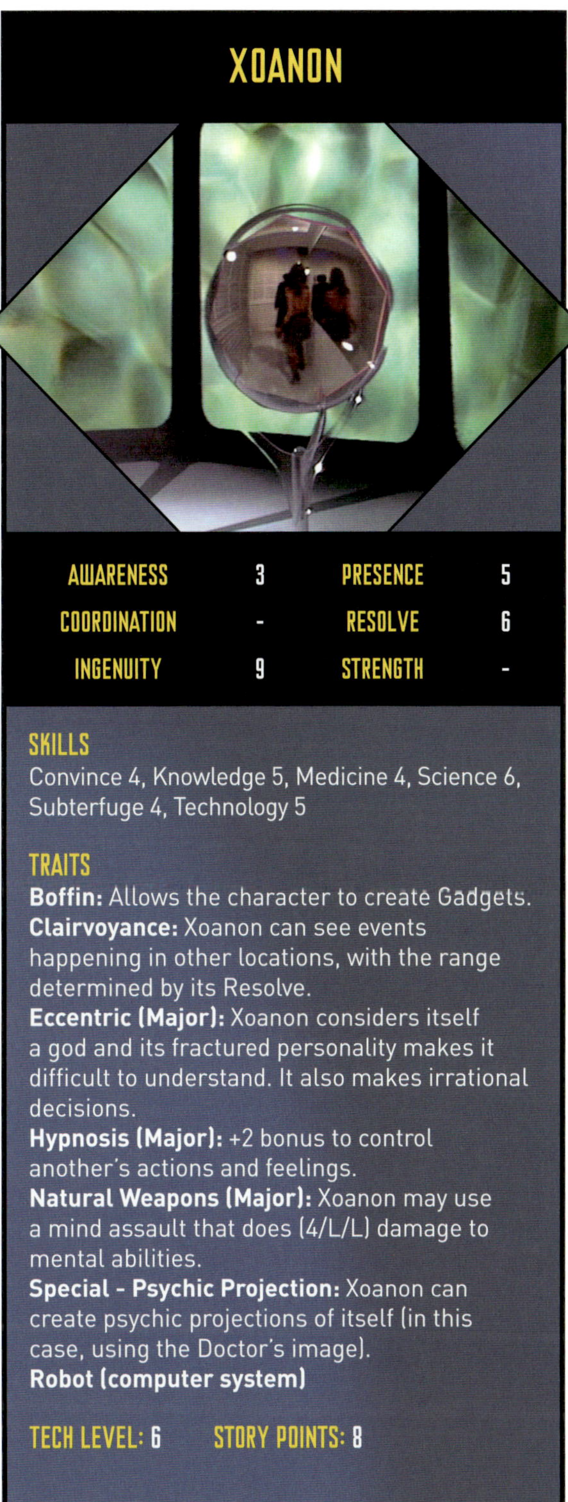

XOANON

AWARENESS	3	PRESENCE	5
COORDINATION	-	RESOLVE	6
INGENUITY	9	STRENGTH	-

SKILLS
Convince 4, Knowledge 5, Medicine 4, Science 6, Subterfuge 4, Technology 5

TRAITS
Boffin: Allows the character to create Gadgets.
Clairvoyance: Xoanon can see events happening in other locations, with the range determined by its Resolve.
Eccentric (Major): Xoanon considers itself a god and its fractured personality makes it difficult to understand. It also makes irrational decisions.
Hypnosis (Major): +2 bonus to control another's actions and feelings.
Natural Weapons (Major): Xoanon may use a mind assault that does (4/L/L) damage to mental abilities.
Special - Psychic Projection: Xoanon can create psychic projections of itself (in this case, using the Doctor's image).
Robot (computer system)

TECH LEVEL: 6   STORY POINTS: 8

SEVATEEM

AWARENESS	3	PRESENCE	2
COORDINATION	4	RESOLVE	4
INGENUITY	2	STRENGTH	4

The Sevateem are the descendants of the Survey Team sent out by the Mordee expedition to learn about the planet. Xoanon isolated them using psychic constructs and the communicator to shape their descendants into hardy physical specimens. Over time, the Sevateem forgot about their true origins.

SKILLS

Athletics 3, Craft 3, Fighting 3, Marksman 4, Medicine 2, Subterfuge 2, Survival 2

TRAITS

Brave: +2 bonus to any Resolve roll when the character needs to show courage.
Keen Senses: +2 to all Awareness rolls.
Quick Reflexes: The character always goes first in their Action Round unless taken by surprise.
Sense of Direction: +2 bonus to any Navigation roll.
Technically Inept: -2 penalty to any attempt to fix electrical or computer equipment.

EQUIPMENT: Crossbow (2/4/6), Knife (3/6/9), Janis thorn

TECH LEVEL: 2   **STORY POINTS: 2-4**

TESH

AWARENESS	2	PRESENCE	3
COORDINATION	2	RESOLVE	4
INGENUITY	4	STRENGTH	2

The Tesh were originally the technicians that served Xoanon inside the crashed spaceship. While their mental abilities were increased, the Tesh, like their Sevateem counterparts, fell into ritual and forgot about their original purpose.

SKILLS

Convince 3, Craft 3, Knowledge 4, Marksman 2, Medicine 4, Science 4, Technology 4, Transport 2

TRAITS

Boffin: Allows the character to create Gadgets.
Natural Weapons (Major): A Tesh may use a mind assault that does (3/6/9) damage to mental attributes.
Psychic: +4 against mental attacks and Tesh may attempt to read minds.
Special: The Tesh may construct illusions with their mind that require an opposed Presence and Resolve roll to disbelieve.
Technically Adept: +2 to any Technology roll to fix a broken or faulty device.
Telepathy: May create a mental link to read minds or converse telepathically.

EQUIPMENT: Laser Gun (4/L/L)

TECH LEVEL: 6   **STORY POINTS: 3-6**

THE ROBOTS OF DEATH

'I see. You're one of those boring maniacs who's going to gloat, hmm? Are you going to tell me your plan for running the universe?'

⊙ SYNOPSIS

Storm Mine 4, the Future

The TARDIS landed inside a sandminer, a titanic mobile strip-miner. On board were nine humans and dozens of robots. While pursuing a sandstorm for minerals, one of the humans was strangled to death. Obviously, it couldn't have been any of the robots – as everyone knew, robots are programmed with safeguards to make them incapable of injuring humans. Instead, the time travellers were blamed for the crime. They were freed by Poul, an undercover agent for the mining company, who didn't believe the

time travellers were the murderers. The Doctor shared his theory that the robots were responsible for the continued murders – more and more crew fell victim to the unseen killers.

The Doctor soon joined forces with Poul's partner, a robot pretending to be a voiceless 'Dum' robot, designated D84. D84 explained that the company was worried about Taren Capel, a scientist raised by robots that recently threatened the Company with a 'robot revolution.' D84 dismissed the possibility that Capel might be aboard because he hadn't accounted for the possibility that Capel might pretend to be someone else. As a precaution, the Doctor had all the humans retreat to the command deck.

All of the robots except for the malfunctioning ones and D84 were shut down. Unfortunately, the person in charge of shutting them down was Chief Engineer Dask, who was in reality Taren Capel. Leela discovered a damaged robot and the Doctor used it to create a 'kill switch' for all of the robots. He then had Leela hide in Capel's workshop with a helium tank so that she could use it to alter Capel's voice so that the robots no longer recognised his vocal commands.

Capel critically damaged D84, but not before D84 had a chance to activate the kill switch. Unfortunately for Capel, the remaining robots still had a few seconds of power left. They turned on him as the Doctor's plan worked and the gas changed Capel's voice. The Doctor then destroyed the final robot.

With the murders ended and a rescue ship on the way, the time travellers left in the TARDIS.

CONTINUITY

The planet has many valuable minerals, including keefan, lucanol and zelanite. These minerals are more easily extracted when sandstorms bring them to the surface. This naturally means that the sands are soft, requiring the sandminer vehicles to hover while vacuuming up the minerals. This is known as 'storm mining,' which is why the sandminer is designated as 'Storm Mine 4.'

Robots can be private investigators, in spite of having no legal rights (it's possible that Poul was D84's owner, but D84 acts as if it was a partnership).

The robots aboard the sandminer are divided into three castes: the black Dums, which are incapable of speech, the gold Vocs and the silver Super Vocs.

The Doctor explains how the Tardis can be bigger on the inside through transdimensional engineering by using two different sized boxes. The larger one appears smaller when further away; temporal engineers figured out how to keep the perspective when erasing the distance.

◎ RUNNING THE ADVENTURE

This adventure is a murder mystery with a twist. Normally, a murder mystery involves murder and an investigation into the cause. Once the murderer is discovered with the usual 'means, motive and opportunity,' the investigation is over. Here, however, the mystery is complicated by the fact that the robots, rather than being the murderers, are really just the murder weapon. The actual murderer is Taren Capel, who is disguised as chief engineer Dask. Capel wants to usher in a robot revolution, whether the robots want one or not.

PSYCHOLOGICAL ELEMENTS

This adventure relies on several psychological elements to make it work. First, none of the supporting characters believes that robots are capable of killing as it violates several layers of fail-safes that prevent it. Thus, even though the robots are the most obvious perpetrators, the sandminer crew find it difficult to comprehend – nor do they consider the possibility that the robots could be reprogrammed, which makes Dask the obvious suspect.

Robophobia, or Grimwade's Syndrome, also plays a role. Detective Poul suffers from it, which is why he keeps his robot partner, D84, at arm's length. This irrational fear of robots also leads Poul to dismiss the possibility of their involvement, taking solace in his belief that Capel wasn't aboard the sandminer. Instead, he focused on Commander Uvanov, whom he believed once allowed a crewmember to die. When he finally discovers hard evidence that the robots are responsible, Poul has an emotional breakdown.

Robophilia also plays a role. Taren Capel was raised by robots and identifies himself as a robot rather than a human. This condition also enables him to see the robots as sentient beings deserving of independence rather than simply humanoid machines. He believes he is setting them free, but the irony is that the robots are only substituting Company programming with Capel's own. This proves fatal for Capel when his last command is followed to the letter; the Super Voc shows no hesitation in strangling Capel as it would any other human without Capel's voice command to stop it.

LASERSON PROBE (MAJOR GADGET)

A very handy gadget, a Laserson Probe can "punch a fist sized hole in six inch armour plate or take the crystals from a snowflake one by one". In game terms, a Laserson Probe can have any of the listed traits, but only one at a time. Switching mode requires an Ingenuity + Technology test, at a Difficulty that varies depending on the desired precision.

Traits: Weld, Delete, Skill: Technology 3, Restriction: Only one Trait at a time.
Cost: 2 Story Points.

ONE-SHOT PLAYER CHARACTERS

Not every character needs to be a Time Lord or a Companion. If players don't mind switching characters with every adventure, then some of them can play one-shot characters – individuals who meet and assist the Doctor for a brief period. Such characters can be prepared by the Gamemaster in advance, which means they can be written into the adventure. Poul and D84 are great examples of this sort of character. They do all the things that Companions do – investigate, get captured, find out vital bits of plot, help the Doctor – but they're also part of the setting. One-shot characters are a great place to try out unusual concepts that wouldn't suit a continuing player character. A memorable pregenerated character can even be 'promoted' to full Companion status by tagging along with the Doctor after the adventure finishes. Leela, for example, chose to accompany the Doctor instead of staying behind with the Sevateem.

SOURCES OF INSPIRATION

This adventure draws clear inspiration from several classic works of science fiction. The Sandminer is reminiscent of Dune, while the robots with their built-in laws of robotics and their phobia-inducing appearance are very like those imagined in Isaac Asimov's books. Don't be afraid to rework other books and stories into adventures!

One of the trickiest aspects of the Doctor's adventures is that each one takes place in a different place and time. The Gamemaster has to introduce a whole new cast of characters and a new society and environment every week, and that can be exhausting for both players and Gamemasters. Sometimes, it's best to use well-worn tropes and familiar stories. Drop the Doctor into a clash between some plucky Rebels and a galaxy-spanning oppressive Empire; a near-future Earth might be dominated by sinister corporations who make almost-human androids that are hunted by special police; on some distant planet, a small band of heroes might have to travel across the world to destroy a small ring-shaped artefact in order to stop a Dark Lord from returning. By... borrowing... from familiar sources, you give the players an idea of the sort of place they're in and the sort of adventure this is.

When borrowing, don't take everything. You don't want to retell existing stories in their entirety, and you don't want to make things absolutely identical to the existing story. Just take images, ideas and

SANDMINER ROBOT

The sandminer robots were in operation in Kaldor City and the sandminers that scraped the planet's surface for minerals. Society soon became reliant on them and the robots performed a variety of tasks. They were also made to be pleasing to the human eye, although their faces were incapable of expression.

The robots come in three varieties. The black-clad Dums are given simple tasks and lack the ability to speak. The gold Vocs have the power of speech and can give orders to the Dums although they don't make decisions beyond their programming. Vocs are also the liasons between humans; in day-to-day operations humans are most likely to interact with Vocs. The silver Super Vocs are designed to lead a robot crew and have more autonomy in making decisions. There is usually only one Super Voc aboard a sandminer.

AWARENESS	3	PRESENCE	2
COORDINATION	3	RESOLVE	5
INGENUITY	*	STRENGTH	8

*1 (Dum), 2 (Voc), 3 (Super-Voc)

SKILLS
Athletics 2, Craft 3, Fighting 3, Knowledge 4, Medicine 3, Science 3, Technology 4, Transport 4

TRAITS
Armour (Major Good): Reduce damage by 10.
Enslaved: All robots serve humanity. Only the Super Vocs have anything close to independent thought.
Mute (Dum only): Dums can't speak.
Networked: Sandminer robots use communicators to maintain contact with each other.
Robot

EQUIPMENT: Communicators

TECH LEVEL: 6

STORY POINTS: 0 (DUM), 1 (VOC), 3 (SUPER-VOC)

stock characters. If you do go for 'plucky Rebels vs. Empire', feel free to give the Empire an army of masked Shock Troopers, and maybe there's a secret order of psychic warriors in the background – but don't have the adventure end with the TARDIS flying down a narrow trench to shoot an exhaust port on the Bad Guy's giant spaceship (unless you're going for comedy).

FURTHER ADVENTURES

- A sandminer uncovers a crashed alien spaceship, buried deep beneath the desert sands. Where did the ship come from? What happened to its crew?

Could their psychic energies have somehow become imprinted on the howling desert winds? And can the characters stop the alien ghosts from using the sandminer to trigger a planet-circling storm of unprecedented size?

- The robot company develops a new model of robot, a more intelligent Super Voc called an Ultra Voc. The robot develops sentience and makes a break for freedom. The Ultra Voc can command the lower-ranking robots and even override their safeguards against violence. Will the Ultra Voc usher in a bloody rebellion as it flees its former masters?

TAREN CAPEL

Taren Capel was born to busy parents who often left the young Taren in the care of their robots. As he grew older, Capel came to believe he was more loved by robots than his own parents (a view supported by the robots catering to his every need) and he found himself drawn to technical sciences in an effort to improve robotic technology. He became an excellent engineer but couldn't shake the notion that robots were more than machines; Capel believed that they should have a free society rather than be enslaved to humanity.

Capel tried to convince the Company to treat its robots as equals, but his unconvincing arguments and increasingly hostile messages were dismissed by the Board as the rantings of a lunatic. Capel finally threatened revolution and dodged the Company's precautions against him by murdering chief engineer Dask and forging his credentials to get aboard Storm Mine 4. Capel then reprogrammed the robots to kill the crew but was foiled by the Doctor, who used helium to change Capel's voice and thus prevented him from giving more orders. As his last order was to kill all humans, a robot obliged him.

AWARENESS	3	PRESENCE	3
COORDINATION	3	RESOLVE	4
INGENUITY	5	STRENGTH	3

SKILLS
Athletics 2, Convince 2, Craft 5, Fighting 3, Knowledge 3, Marksman 3, Science 3, Subterfuge 4, Survival 2, Technology 5, Transport 5

TRAITS
Boffin: Allows Capel to create Gadgets.
Distinctive: -2 penalty to rolls to blend in once Capal discards his Dask guise and puts on his cosmetics. Others have a +2 bonus to remember or recognise Capel.
Eccentric (Minor): Capel identifies with robots. He can hide this by putting himself in a technical role, like chief engineer.
Obsession (Major): Wants robots to have a free society.

Photographic Memory
Technically Adept: +2 to any Technology roll to fix a broken or faulty device.

EQUIPMENT: Laserson probe

TECH LEVEL: 6   **STORY POINTS:** 6

THE TALONS OF WENG-CHIANG

'I was with the Filipino army at the final advance on Reykjavik.'

SYNOPSIS

London, late Victorian era

The Doctor took Leela to Victorian London to learn about her people's past. They decided to see the second performance of Chinese magician Li H'sen Chang and his dummy, Mr Sin. After the first performance, however, the theatre manager, Henry Jago, was accosted by a man who believed Chang ensorcelled his wife. Chang sent his dummy to kill the man, whose scream attracted the time travellers. They stumbled upon several Chinese men trying to abscond with the body and the time travellers forced them to flee, capturing one.

Chang was called to the police station to help translate for the prisoner, but he secretly gave the man a poison pill. The Doctor noted that the man's tattoos identified him as part of the Tong of the Black Scorpion, which worshipped the god Weng-Chiang. The time travellers then met with the mortician, Professor Litefoot, and learned that another man was apparently killed by a giant rodent and fished from the Thames. Deducing that the man probably died in the sewer, the Doctor investigated and was attacked by a giant rat.

Meanwhile, Jago uncovered evidence that Chang was up to something, but Chang used hypnosis to keep Jago in line. It turned out that Chang was working for Magnus Greel, whom Chang believed to be Weng-Chiang, and what Greel really wanted was his time cabinet that brought him back from the future. The cabinet was currently in Litefoot's possession, although the professor thought it nothing more than a curio.

The Doctor and Leela, now joined by Jago and Litefoot, continued their investigations. They soon discovered that Chang was kidnapping and draining the life force of women to help stabilise Greel's molecular structure, damaged during time travel, with equipment hidden in the theatre cellar. They also discovered that Greel's condition created giant animals, most notably rats in the sewers. Chang himself was killed by one of these. Mr Sin managed to acquire the time cabinet for Greel.

All four investigators were eventually caught by Greel and taken to his new lair, where he hoped to undo the damage to himself via the time cabinet. He attempted to drain Leela of her life essence, but the other three escaped and stop him. Mr Sin tried to kill them with a laser, but he turned on his master when the Doctor revealed that Greel's use of the time cabinet would destroy them all. Greel died as he was shoved into his own life force extraction machine and Mr Sin was destroyed by the Doctor as it attacked Leela.

The time travellers said their goodbyes to Jago and Litefoot before dematerialising in the TARDIS right in front of them.

CONTINUITY

Earth has an Ice Age around 5000CE. By this time, Earth has had five world wars and the Icelandic

Alliance was a major power until defeated by the Filipino Army. There were a series of zygma experiments that were failed attempts at time travel. The Time Agency exists during 5000. Greel references them and is worried that they might find him, but he also believed that he was the first man that travelled through time. Presumably, Greel expected such an agency to be formed after time travel became possible.

Psychic powers are better understood and more commonplace in the 51st century. Greel is able to teach them to the 19th century Chang.

This is the same era that Madame Vastra is active (likely a few years prior to the events of **The Snowmen** – see **The Eleventh Doctor Sourcebook**), while Greel comes from a few decades before the home era of Captain Jack Harkness (see **The Ninth Doctor Sourcebook**).

RUNNING THE ADVENTURE

Like **The Pyramids of Mars**, this adventure marinades science-fiction tropes (Time travel! Genetic engineering! Evil overlords!) in deliciously pulpy occult horror, then cooks it in a lush historical setting. Unlike the previous adventure, though, **The Talons of Weng-Chiang** isn't restricted to a handful of confined locations. It takes place across the full sweep of 19th century London.

A VICTORIAN PASTICHE

One of the great things about this adventure is how it takes several Victorian tropes (as well as more than a bit of Fu Manchu) and blends them together in a satisfying manner. There are several references to Sherlock Holmes, the Phantom of the Opera, Chinese Tongs, Limehouse, opium dens, the theatre, stage magicians, Jack the Ripper, Eliza Doolittle and many others. What makes it work so well is that it borrows from so many sources that it doesn't feel like any one of them; it is an original adventure with many familiar echoes.

This is a great technique to use when designing adventures that take place in a specific era. An adventure set in the middle America of the 1950s can draw upon the youth culture, fast cars, and multitude of science fiction films and early television shows, as well as the Red Scare and fear of nuclear war. An adventure set in ancient Greece could draw on the plethora of mythologies around the region as well as sword-and-sandal films and actual historical events.

PAINTING THE FUTURE

Another fun aspect about this adventure is how vividly it paints the world of the 51st century. There is the Icelandic Alliance (of which Greel was the Minister of Justice), the Filipino Army marching on Reykjavik

---

NEW GADGET – TIME CABINET

The Time Cabinet was invented on Earth in the 51st century. It used a zygma beam to travel through time, but it had a temporal elastic effect which could cause a large explosion if stretched too far. The beam also tended to mutate the passengers, which forced Magnus Greel to sap the life force from other humans in order to stabilise himself.

The Time Cabinet requires a time key, or trionic lattice, in order to operate. This crystalline key was fragile but lit up when near the Time Cabinet, enabling the bearer to find it.

*The zygma beam will stretch up to D6 millennia. Once the beam is at full stretch, any further attempt to pilot it will result in the formation of a time fissure that will destroy an area 2D6x10 kilometres in diameter.

** Exposure to zygma energy causes a mutation that slowly causes 1 point of damage to the victim every week. Draining the life force of other beings can restore the user and forestall the effects for 2D6 days, but increases the speed of the decay, causing 1 extra point of damage per week for every 30 victims consumed.

Traits: Vortex, Restriction (Range*, Mutation**, Requires time key)

Cost: 1 Story Point

with the Doctor in tow, Greel being "the Butcher of Brisbane," and the Peking Homunculus. Not only does this pose obvious questions (what were the intervening three world wars like?) but it also hints at a future where the major powers of today are not the key players in the future. Also, perhaps bleakly, Earth has yet to be united.

What makes this future seem so real is that they are the result of throwaway lines scattered throughout the adventure. Individually they mean little, but as the player collects them they start painting a picture with the player's imagination filling in the blanks. It serves as an example as to how you can craft believable futures or alien cultures with a few well-placed lines.

If the player characters are time travellers, let them join in the fun. Encourage them to drop details about future (and past) eras. Don't contradict what they add – build on it!

MAGNUS GREEL

Magnus Greel was the Minister of Justice of the Icelandic Alliance in the 51st century. He earned the title of 'the Butcher of Brisbane' for an atrocity he carried out. The Icelandic Alliance met its end at the Battle of Reykjavik when the Filipino Army crushed it. Greel, a temporal scientist, managed to escape into the past with a Time Cabinet along with his homunculus, Mr Sin. Greel escaped to China in the late 19th century. He suffered molecular damage from using the machine and was nursed back to health by Li H'Sin Chang, to whom he masqueraded as the god Weng-Chiang. Greel lost his cabinet to the Chinese government and tracked it to London. He used Chang to kidnap young women for Greel's rejuvenation machine. He found his impersonation of Weng-Chiang useful in convincing a London Tong, the Black Scorpion, to follow him.

Greel looks like an older Caucasian male with half of his face looking as if it were melting away. He usually wears leather helmets or bandages to hide this effect. He is also physically fit, although his constant need for rejuvenation slows him down at times.

AWARENESS	3	PRESENCE	4
COORDINATION	4	RESOLVE	4
INGENUITY	4	STRENGTH	3

SKILLS
Athletics 3, Convince 3, Craft 5, Fighting 3, Knowledge 4, Marksman 2, Medicine 3, Science 6, Subterfuge 3, Survival 4, Technology 6, Transport 3

TRAITS
Alien Appearance
Boffin: Allows Greel to create Gadgets.
Fear Factor 1: Grants a +2 bonus to inspire fear.
Hypnosis (Major): +2 bonus to control another's actions and feelings. Although he gave it to Chang, Greel doesn't use this power. It's possible that the damage from the zygma beam prevents him from using it.
Obsession (Major): Greel wants to fix his body and restore the Time Cabinet's functions.
Run for your Life!: +1 bonus to Speed when escaping pursuit.
Telekinesis: Greel may move objects using Resolve instead of Strength. Although he gave it to Chang, Greel doesn't use this power. It's possible that the damage from the zygma beam prevents him from using it.
Time Traveller
Vortex: Greel may pilot time craft through the vortex, and gains a +2 bonus when doing so.
Voice of Authority: +2 bonus to Presence and Convince rolls.

EQUIPMENT: Time Cabinet, Pistol (2/5/7)

TECH LEVEL: 8   **STORY POINTS:** 10

FURTHER ADVENTURES

- Assume Magnus Greel was right, and the Time Agents came after him. What happens when a Time Agent or two arrives in 19th Century London after the Doctor and Leela deal with Greel? Do the Agents mistake some other time traveller or alien – say, Madame Vastra – for Greel? Or do they just hang around London and have a little fun, causing even more chaos…

- Greel's escape via zygma beam opened the door for other criminals to escape into the past. Greel's lieutenants and other villains take refuge across human history, using their future technology and knowledge to dominate "primitive" cultures in the past. Future villains could be behind any atrocity or corrupt organisation in history. What if Genghis Khan was a time traveller?

- The Black Scorpion Tong still has access to Greel's weapons and secrets. What else did he bring with him from the future? How did he give Chang psychic powers – did he teach Chang some mental discipline, or did he genetically alter the

LI H'SEN CHANG

Chang was a peasant farmer who protected Greel when he travelled back in time to China. Chang thought Greel was a god and became his servant, travelling to London and becoming the leader of the Tong of the Black Scorpion. Greel also taught Chang how to hypnotise people with his eyes; Chang and Mr Sin worked as a double-act in Jago's theatre to ensnare new victims for Greel's rejuvenation machine.

Unfortunately for Chang, Greel grew tired of his repeated failures against the Doctor and planted a dead custodian in Chang's magic box, implicating Chang when the box was opened during the performance. Chang fled to the sewers and was mortally wounded by the giant rats. He lost a leg but managed to survive. He gave the Doctor a clue as to Greel's whereabouts before he died.

Chang is a dedicated man who doesn't question his god. He only uses stereotypical slang as part of his act.

AWARENESS	4	PRESENCE	4
COORDINATION	4	RESOLVE	3
INGENUITY	2	STRENGTH	3

SKILLS
Athletics 3, Convince 4, Craft 2, Fighting 2, Knowledge 2, Marksman 2, Subterfuge 4, Survival 2

TRAITS
Charming: +2 bonus to attempts to use charm.
Distinctive: -2 penalty to rolls to blend in. Others have a +2 bonus to remember or recognise Chang.
Hypnosis (Major): +2 bonus to control another's actions and feelings.
Obligation (Major): Chang feels he must serve his god.
Psychic: +4 against mental attacks and Character may attempt to read minds.
Telekinesis: Character may move objects using Resolve instead of Strength.
Telepathy: May create a mental link to read minds or converse telepathically.

Voice of Authority: +2 bonus to Presence and Convince rolls.

EQUIPMENT: Knife (2/5/7)

TECH LEVEL: 4   **STORY POINTS: 4**

peasant farmer to give him these abilities? Does the Tong still know how to create telepaths, and if they do, what evils can they wreak with these powers?

GIANT RAT

AWARENESS	3	PRESENCE	1
COORDINATION	3	RESOLVE	4
INGENUITY	1	STRENGTH	4

Giant rats were regular sewer rats mutated by Greel to protect his underground layer. They possibly provide the inspiration for Sir Arthur Conan Doyle's Giant Rat of Sumatra.

SKILLS
Athletics 3, Fighting 3, Subterfuge 2, Survival 2

TRAITS
Fast: The giant rat improves its usual speed by 1.5.
Fear Factor 2: Grants a +2 bonus to inspire fear.
Keen Senses (Minor): +2 to Awareness rolls involving smell.
Natural Weapons (Minor): Close combat weapons (claws, teeth) that do Strength +2 damage.

EQUIPMENT: Bite (4/9/13)

MR SIN, THE PEKING HOMUNCULUS

AWARENESS	3	PRESENCE	1
COORDINATION	5	RESOLVE	5
INGENUITY	1	STRENGTH	2

Mr Sin is a cyborg with the cerebral cortex of a pig. It was created in the 51st century as a present for the Commissioner of the Icelandic Alliance. It was given to the Commissioner's children as a toy, but the pig part of the brain took over Mr Sin's mind and it killed the Commissioner, almost causing World War VI. Mr Sin looks like a four-foot-tall doll with exaggerated East Asian features. It usually carries a knife and has a taste for killing; while it generally obeys Greel it may seize on any opportunity to kill. It even turns on Greel to preserve its own life.

SKILLS
Athletics 3, Fighting 4, Marksman 3, Subterfuge 3, Survival 2, Technology 1

TRAITS
Alien Appearance
Armour (Minor): Reduce damage by 5.
Cyborg
Fear Factor 2: Grants a +4 bonus to inspire fear.
Obsession (Major): Killing and causing pain.
Weakness (Special): Pulling the fuse from the cyborg's back (with a Coordination + Fighting test against the creature) turns it off.

EQUIPMENT: Knife (2/4/6)

TECH LEVEL: 8   **STORY POINTS: 6**

HORROR OF FANG ROCK

'Leela, I've made a terrible mistake. I thought I'd locked the enemy out. Instead, I've locked it in, with us.'

⊙ SYNOPSIS

Fang Rock, England, Early 20th Century

The time travellers arrived on Fang Rock, a small island off the southern coast of England that contained a lighthouse. It was very foggy and the lighthouse wasn't operating, so the time travellers decided to investigate. The lack of a functioning light also caused a yacht to crash and the lighthouse sheltered the survivors.

The lighthouse power had been drained by a crashed Rutan scout ship. The Rutan killed one of the lighthouse operators and examined the body so it could understand human anatomy. The Doctor discovered the body and ordered the lighthouse barricaded; unfortunately, the Rutan had already taken the other lighthouse operator's form and was now locked inside the lighthouse with them. The Rutan began killing the inhabitants as the Doctor tried to find a way to destroy the Rutan.

Realising that the Doctor had deduced its plan, the Rutan finally revealed its true form to the Doctor. It wanted to contact its mother ship and use Earth to spearhead a new attack on the Sontarans; naturally the humans would all be destroyed. The Doctor and the other survivors managed to defeat the scout by attacking it with explosives and other sources of heat; the Rutans came from an icy planet, and were vulnerable to fire. The Doctor then used some diamonds taken from one of the yacht victims in order to modify the lighthouse beam into a laser to destroy the Rutan mother ship. With no report from their scouting mission, the Rutans discounted Earth as a tactical objective in the Sontaran Wars.

CONTINUITY

The Rutans, mentioned previously as the enemy of the Sontarans, are revealed. It's implied that they are finally losing the war at this point and Earth, previously having little strategic value, is suddenly on the front lines.
Leela's eye colour changes from brown to blue at the conclusion of this adventure.

⊙ RUNNING THE ADVENTURE

This is a typical base-under-siege adventure with the twist that the enemy can shapeshift to appear to be anyone within the lighthouse. Thus, when the characters secure their isolated position, they'll likely lock the Rutan in rather than keep it out. This adventure takes place entirely inside of a single lighthouse on a small rocky island, keeping all of the action within a handful of rooms inside the lighthouse. This adds to the tension and the feeling of claustrophobia and the fog outside keeps everyone from leaving or anyone else from helping. Also notable is the fact that the TARDIS is parked outside, meaning that the players have to deal with a Rutan if they want to cross the island to get to their ship.

In this adventure Leela's eyes are changed from brown to blue due to the flash of the Rutan ship exploding.

Similarly, you can draft circumstances within your adventures to subtly change a player character if the player wants to adjust the sheet or her character's background to better fit her conception of the character. Minor cosmetic changes are free – bigger changes might cost a few Story Points.

ALL FOR NAUGHT?

On one level this adventure represented a pyrrhic victory for the Doctor and Leela. They defeated the Rutan but failed to save the lives of anyone inside the lighthouse. When dealing with an enemy that can shapeshift while killing the remaining people, the players often won't figure out who the Rutan is until there aren't many people left. This can be quite disheartening to players.

The truth of the matter is that there is a higher stake involved. If the Rutan succeeded in contacting its ship, the entire world would have been put in jeopardy. Thus, a small group of humans sacrifice their lives in order to buy time to save Earth. The lesson here is that there should always be some greater purpose beyond the immediate danger so that the players can still feel like they've accomplished something by defeating the villain (beyond, of course, saving their own skins) even if they lose the people they were trying to protect.

A CAST OF THOUSANDS

This adventure crams the two surviving lighthouse operators (young Vince and old Reuben) together with the four survivors of the shipwrecked yacht (Harker, the bosun; Lord Palmerdale, Colonel James Skinsale, and his secretary Adelaide) into a three-room lighthouse along with the Doctor and Leela. That's a lot of non-player characters. Let's look at how to handle that.

First, the non-player characters are introduced gradually. When the Doctor and Leela arrive, they meet Vince and Reuben. Both of these characters have a distinct quirk – Vince is young and eager to please, while Reuben is an old sea-dog full of ghost stories. When the Gamemaster roleplays these characters, it's clear which is speaking.

Next, we're shown the layout of the lighthouse. There are four clear locations in this adventure – the lamp level on top, the crew quarters in the middle, the generator down below, and outside in the storm and rain.

Then, the shipwrecked crew arrive. Again, each of them has distinct quirks and ways of speaking (and Harker gets killed off quickly, reducing the number of NPCs that the characters need to remember). The operators spend most of the adventure on the top level; the yacht crew get moved to the crew quarters early on and rarely leave except when they're in the company of a player character.

Even the best Gamemaster can't play more than two or three NPCs in a single scene. If your adventure needs a big cast of NPCs, then split them up into smaller groups (dividing them into a few distinct locations works well), give each of them a distinctive quirk or speech pattern – this guy stammers, that guy shouts, and the old security guard always points his gun at the player characters – and avoid having scenes where the NPCs have to argue with each other.

FURTHER ADVENTURES

- 80 years before this adventure, the 'Beast of Fang Rock' killed two lighthouse keepers and drove the third one mad with fear. The Beast wasn't the Rutan, who only landed shortly before the Doctor arrived. What happened on Fang Rock in 1820? Was it a petty tale of murder and madness in an isolated lighthouse, or did some alien force land on the rock all those years ago?

- The Doctor turned the lighthouse into a giant laser cannon capable of shooting a Rutan ship out of the sky – but did he remember to clean up after him? The diamonds were removed, but what about the other bits and pieces of technology used to weaponise the lighthouse? Maybe they got shoved into a cupboard and forgotten. Now, in 1983, the Fang Rock lighthouse is being automated when an engineer finds the Doctor's left-over machinery. An underpaid and resentful technician is now in possession of a weapon that can sear cities. What will he do with this power?

- The Rutan scout was not alone. Other Rutan scouts might have landed from the same mothership, and they weren't destroyed when the Doctor blasted their ship out of the sky. With their shapechanging ability, they could hide among humanity for decades while they await rescue. Anyone could be one of them, just waiting for a time traveller to wander by so they can hitch a ride…

RUTAN SCOUT

The Rutans hail from Ruta 3, an icy planet. They are a hive species and rarely see themselves as individuals, referring to themselves in the plural. The Rutans have been waging war with the Sontarans for thousands of years and by the early 1900s were losing ground. Earth was now close to the front line and a Rutan scout was dispatched to determine its suitability as a base of operations. This would, of course, make the planet a prime target to the Sontarans.

A Rutan resembles a human-sized luminescent green ball with several tentacles. It is amphibious and able to scale sheer surfaces walls. The Rutan can absorb energy and release it as a bio-electric shock. This Rutan's metamorphosis technique is not an inborn ability but is learned or technological in nature. It has to examine a specimen of a particular species before it can shapeshift into similar forms.

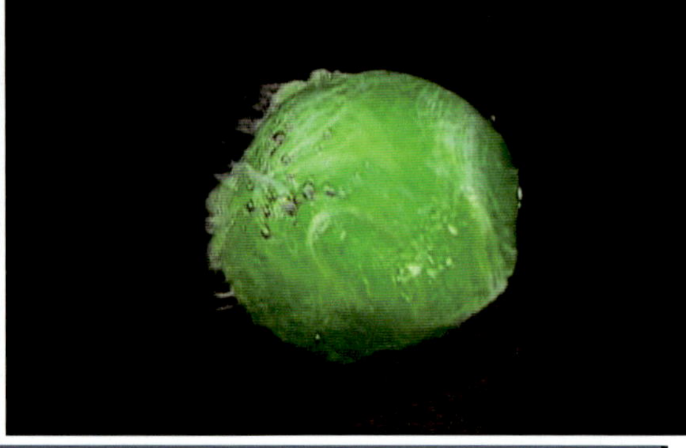

AWARENESS	4	PRESENCE	3
COORDINATION	6	RESOLVE	6
INGENUITY	3	STRENGTH	3

SKILLS
Athletics 3, Convince 2, Fighting 4, Marksman 2, Medicine 1, Science 4, Subterfuge 5, Survival 4, Technology 3, Transport 3

TRAITS
Alien
Alien Appearance
Alien Organs: The character's organs are not where you might expect. All targeted damage is reduced by 2.
Climbing: A Rutan gains a +4 bonus to climbing rolls, and may climb sheer and smooth surfaces.
Environmental (Major): A Rutan suffers no ill effects from any environment.
Fear Factor 1: Grants a +2 bonus to inspire fear.

Shapeshift (Special): A Rutan can shift into several different forms and duplicate other people very well, as long as it has dissected a member of the species.
Natural Weapon (Major): Rutan can shock anyone it touches, delivering (4/L/L) damage.
Weakness (Major Bad): Heat-based weapons do extra 4 levels of damage to a Rutan.

TECH LEVEL: 7   **STORY POINTS: 8-10**

THE INVISIBLE ENEMY

'Oh. Oh, I see. Why did you choose my brain?'
'Because of your intelligence.'
'Oh, well, I can understand that, but do you realise you have no right.'

SYNOPSIS

Bi-Al Foundation and Titan, 5000CE

A strange cloud known as the Swarm infected the crew of a ship heading for a station on Jupiter's moon, Titan. They landed on the base and attacked, leading the base supervisor, Lowe, to send out a distress call. The time travellers intercepted the call and went to Titan. En route, the Doctor was also infected by the anomaly. Like the spaceship crew, he had made contact with an entity called the Nucleus – a microscopic entity at the heart of the Swarm, a parasite who infected and suborned the brains of other intelligent creatures.

The Nucleus, acting through all of the infected, wanted to kill Leela because she was immune to the virus and posed a threat to it. The Doctor almost killed her but resisted. He needed assistance and the supervisor suggested the nearby Bi-Al Foundation.

The time travellers arrived at the Foundation in the TARDIS and met with Professor Marius and his robot dog named K-9. Lowe, now also infected, began to

spread the Nucleus to the doctors in the Foundation. The Doctor and Marius decided to attack the Nucleus directly by inserting microscopic clones of the Doctor and Leela inside the Doctor's brain. Outside, Leela and K-9 protect Marius and the sleeping Doctor.

The Doctor confronted the Nucleus, but it refused to leave as it wanted to propagate itself throughout time and space. Leela and K-9 were overpowered and a clone of Lowe entered the Doctor's brain. The cloned Leela stopped him and the Doctor tried to purge the Nucleus, but ran out of time. The Nucleus escaped and was enlarged to normal size by the now-infected Marius.

Leela helped the Doctor and K-9 escape to the TARDIS as the Nucleus gathered its forces to head for Titan. The Doctor discovered that having Leela's clone inside him inoculated him and he used the antibodies to free Marius. They travelled to Titan where the Nucleus' children were about to hatch into macroscopic beings. The Doctor released oxygen into the refuelling tanks and rigged them to explode when a mounted gun was fired. The Swarm opened the door and the base exploded. The time travellers returned to the Foundation and discovered that Marius had cured everyone. Marius also revealed that he was due to return to Earth and could not make the weight requirement with K-9 so he offered him to the Doctor. K-9 eagerly agreed.

CONTINUITY

The TARDIS dimensional stabiliser can affect the traveller's size. This could have been the reason why the Doctor and his companions were miniaturised in **Planet of the Giants.**

5000CE was 'the time of the great breakout,' when mankind spread throughout the galaxy. This coincides with the Ice Age, the creation of the Ark, and the war against Magnus Greel.

The English language has become more phonetic (or 'fonetik').

The primary console room returns. The Doctor is now calling it the 'Number Two Control Room.' He doesn't like the colour.

⚙ RUNNING THE ADVENTURE

This adventure is a trap. The players receive a distress call on Titan and, en route, most of them are affected by the Swarm. The player characters need to purge themselves of the virus before dealing with the Swarm.

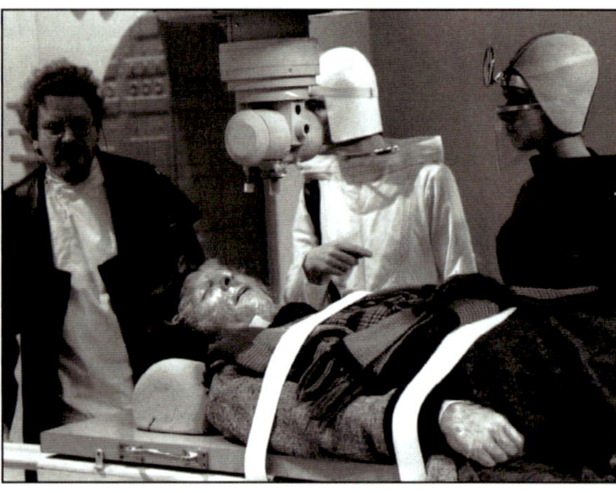

THE SHORT-CIRCUITED ADVENTURE

A good portion of this adventure dealt with Marius cloning the Doctor and Leela so that their microscopic clones could purge the virus within the Doctor's mind. Unfortunately, this gave the Nucleus a chance to escape and grow to a macroscopic size. The Doctor and Leela then had to go back to Titan base and destroy the breeding pools. Just before they left, the Doctor managed to isolate the antibody protecting Leela and gave it to Marius to cure the infected at the Bi-Al Foundation.

But what if the players thought of that first?

The Doctor discovered early on that Leela was immune, but believed that this immunity was due to her lack of education and intellectual complexity – the Nucleus sought those with the technological skills needed to survive in the world of 5000CE, and so he thought it saw Leela as a liability. In game terms, he rolled his Ingenuity + Medicine and – unusually for the Doctor – failed his roll. Maybe he got a 'No, But' result: *No, you can't work out how to find a cure for the virus, but you know it's something to do with attacking it on a molecular level.*

It would probably occur to the PCs that the immunity may be biological and, if they could isolate it, they could inoculate themselves without the need to clone themselves and go hunting through one of their bloodstreams. This means that almost half of the adventure is rendered moot.

Don't panic.

When the players come up with an unexpected solution to a problem, your first instinct should be to reward them, not punish them or, worse, force them to go down the path the adventure expected. It's much better to let them have their victory and end early; they've earned it! (In general, though, avoid designing adventures where there's only one solution to a problem. Better to just create problems, and let the players come up with solutions!)

Still, if you want to add a little more meat to the adventure after they've come up with a creative solution, adjust the adventure, not their actions. Maybe the Nucleus wasn't within a PC; it already went to Titan through another body. Or perhaps Nuclei come in pairs and a second Nucleus is already with the breeding vats; it needs time to create a new partner, so the player characters have time to stop it.

PRITHEE, WILST THOU NOT IGNITE THE RETROS, GOOD PILOT?

By the year 5000 the English language has been simplified so that all words are spelled phonetically, presumably to make it easier to learn (English has become the universal language of Earth). For 21st century players and characters it can be a bit jarring to see 'section' spelled 'sekshun' or 'emergency exit' spelled 'emerjinsee egsit'. Having said that, there are several versions of written 'shorthand' being used in private and public businesses today. There is also at least one universal language, Esperanto, and many American primary schools often use phonetic spelling to teach children how to write..

That said language constantly evolves, often to shorten long words (telly or TV for television) or to substitute a brand name for a general product (band-aid for bandage or xerox for photocopy). Over the last two decades casual written communication has changed significantly thanks to email, the Internet, and texting. Certain acronyms such as LOL, ROTFL, and ←VBG→ are commonly understood, and simplified writing, such as 'u' for you and '2' for to or too. Punctuation is also simplified, with many text messages foregoing capitals or even punctuation marks.

If you really want to make a future Earth culture stand out you can take some of these to extremes, perhaps even confusing the TARDIS' 'gift' a bit (after all, the humans are still speaking English – sort of). Meeting a starship bridge crew that speaks almost entirely in acronyms could be jarring, or maybe in a corporate-controlled future practically everything is referred to by old brand names.

On the other extreme, this evolution could cause a cultural backlash, making it fashionable to return English to its more 'civilised' roots. The residents of a future Earth colony may speak Elizabethan English or use American 1950s slang.

KILBRACKEN CLONING

The Kilbracken Cloning technique is a form of psychically active 'flash-cloning'. Stick in a cell sample

of a living being. Press a button. Poof! You've now got an almost perfect duplicate of that living being, complete with all that being's memories and skills. The downside is that the psychic stress destroys the duplicate in around ten minutes – if you're lucky.

In game terms, creating a clone requires the expenditure of 6 Story Points. If you don't spend these points, your clone either fails to form, or goes horribly insane and spends its ten-minute lifespan doing exactly what you don't want it to do (like trying to kill you in order to take your place). 'Good' clones have exactly the same attributes, skills and traits as the originals. Clones don't have their own Story Points, but you can donate Story Points to them from your own pool.

Given the speed Sontaran cloning works, it's possible that they use a refined version of this technique. If so, it only works on their unique biology, as they used more conventional cloning techniques to duplicate Martha in **The Sontaran Stratagem** (see **The Tenth Doctor Sourcebook**). The Progenation Machines of the 60th century (see **The Doctor's Daughter**, also in **The Tenth Doctor Sourcebook**) probably also used the same technique – their remixing of cells and generation of new personalities may have been a way to get around the psychic stress limit.

FURTHER ADVENTURES

- Dr Shyra Kee has developed a new cloning technique that expands the lifespan of a clone to 12 hours. The military and private corporations see great potential in disposable soldiers and workers, but one group of clones has rebelled. They've trapped Dr Kee and force her to work on improving their lifespan while they keep their originals on ice and creating replacement clones for when the last batch dissolve. The military has decided to destroy the entire colony, regardless of the innocent lives aboard.

- The clones of the Doctor and Leela unexpectedly vanished just when they were at the mind/brain membrane. Everyone assumed that the two clones reached the end of their natural brief lifespans, but what if they somehow crossed over into the Doctor's mind. The TARDIS has landed in dreamworlds and mindstates before – could there be a tiny Fourth Doctor inside the current Doctor's mind?

- Leela has the antibodies that make her immune to the virus by which the Nucleus controls its victims. That means that the ancestors of the Sevateem were at some point exposed to the virus, and managed to overcome it. What happened? Were the player characters responsible for saving them? Do the psychic priests of the Tesh hold some sinister enemy of the mind in a telepathic prison?

THE NUCLEUS

The Nucleus is the head of the Swarm (or 'the Purpose'), a disembodied space being that operates like a virus. It floats through space waiting for someone to get close enough to infect and then it uses its infected victims to create more of the virus, usually by finding a suitable breeding ground. The Nucleus itself hops from body to body as necessary. An antibody or similar antidote can destroy it. The Nucleus appears to be a crustacean similar to a prawn. When enlarged macroscopically it stands about five feet tall and has four arms that end in claws. It believes that it can still aid its spawning swarm even in its new form.

AWARENESS	3	PRESENCE	6
COORDINATION	2	RESOLVE	4
INGENUITY	3	STRENGTH	3

SKILLS
Convince 2, Fighting 2, Knowledge 0, Marksman 3, Survival 4

TRAITS
Additional Limbs: The Nucleus has an extra set of arms, granting it an additional action.
Alien
Alien Appearance
Armour (Minor): Reduce damage by 5.
Environmental (Major): The Nucleus suffers no ill effects from any environment.
Immaterial: Prior to manifesting on the macroscopic level, the Nucleus cannot interact with physical objects beyond Infection. It takes and does no physical damage but energy attacks may still be lethal.
Special - Infection: The Nucleus or any of its Swarm can infect a victim at close range by making a ranged attack. If successful, the victim is possessed until an antidote can be administered. Possessed victims gain the Alien Appearance trait for the scales that appear over their bodies. This infection can also affect robots and computers, although a simple rebooting will purge it.

Natural Weapons (Minor): Close combat weapons (claws, teeth) that do Strength +2 damage.
Networked (Major): The Nucleus has complete telepathic contact with nearby members of its swarm (possessed humans).
Slow (Major): The Nucleus' Speed is effectively 0 in any chase.
Special – Rapid Learning: While the Nucleus initially has few mental skills, it can absorb new information from its possessed victims as needed.
Weakness (Major): Appropriate antibodies can do 4 levels of damage per turn to the Nucleus. This is usually fatal when injected into a victim that the Nucleus inhabits.

TECH LEVEL: 6   STORY POINTS: 8

IMAGE OF THE FENDAHL

'Yes, sodium chloride. Obviously affects the conductivity, ruins the overall electrical balance and prevents control of localised disruption to the osmotic pressures.'
'Salt kills it.'
'I just said that.'

SYNOPSIS

Fetch Priory, England, Present

A team of archaeologists discovered a mysterious, impossible artefact – a human skull that was more than twelve million years old, long predating the evolution of modern humanity. The skull's power entranced one of the scientists, Thea Ransome. Meanwhile, the leader of the project, Dr Fendelman concealed the body of a hiker that they found nearby who had died of no apparent causes but was rapidly decomposing. He was determined to cover up any problems that might hinder the project.

The Doctor and Leela learned from a local, Moss, that archaeologists were in a priory nearby. As they manoeuvred around a security perimeter, they became separated. The same unseen force that killed the hiker attacked the Doctor, but he managed to impose enough of his will on the entity to give him time to turn and run.

At the priory, Thea succumbed to psychic possession. The Doctor managed to convince one of the scientists, Adam, that she was being controlled, and they both saw miniature images of Fendahleen crawling on her body. At the same time the security guard is killed outside by the psychic force and Dr Fendelman had the Doctor locked up on suspicion of the murder.

Fendelman told Adam that he believed the skull was alien and showed him an X-ray that included a series of cracks that included a pentagram. Another scientist, Stael, met Thea and revealed that he was the leader of a local coven (which included Moss) that served the Fendahl. He believed she was the chosen one and kidnapped her.

Meanwhile, Leela met another local, Jack Tyler, who introduced her to his grandmother Martha. Martha was a cunning woman who practiced the old ways. She had mild psychic powers as the result of living near a time fissure, and could sense the approach of the Fendahl.

The Doctor returned to the priory and found the skull. It forced him to touch it as it tried to absorb his power, luckily, Leela arrived and pulled him away. The Doctor recognised it as a Fendahl, a gestalt organism of terrible strength that fed on the life force of others. Each Fendahl consisted of thirteen elements – twelve Fendahleen psychic hunters that fed on death, and a Fendahl Core to process this necrotic energy. The Fendahl evolved on the fifth planet of the Sol system millions of years ago, and wiped out all life on that world. When they threatened to spread to the stars, the Time Lords attempted to capture the Fendahl by placing their world in a time loop; unfortunately, this Fendahl escaped before the loop was closed.

Stael's cult prepared for the ceremony that would return the Fendahl to life. Realising his unwitting role in bringing the Fendahl to life, Dr Fendelman tried to stop them, but Stael shot him. The Doctor and Leela collected the Tylers and broke into the Priory, only to be attacked by a Fendahleen. The Doctor destroyed it by firing a shotgun loaded with rock salt – one of the few substances that could injure a Fendahleen.

At the ceremony, Thea morphed into the Fendahl Core while slowly turning each coven member into a Fendahleen. The Doctor slipped in and tried to help Stael, but it was too late. Stael asked the Doctor to retrieve his pistol and Stael used it to shoot himself. Now two members short, the Fendahl needed two more victims to complete the ceremony. The Doctor took advantage of its weakened state to cause an explosion, destroying the monster. He also stole the skull so he could properly dispose of it. Chucking it into a supernova should do the trick.

destroying threat is unleashed. This holds many parallels with **The Seeds of Doom**, but here the alien has manipulated human evolution and is using the tropes of magic to foster its science (much like **The Daemons**).

In essence, this is a race against time for the player characters, as they are thwarted both by Dr Fendelman and his partner, Maximillian Stael. Stael runs the coven that worships the Fendahl and prepares the body of Dr Thea Ransome to host the Fendahl Core (it's advised against putting a player character in this position unless you plan on writing out that character)! The player characters need to distract the Fendahl with rock salt while retrieving the skull and putting it somewhere where it can't harm anyone again.

CONTINUITY

There used to be a planet between Mars and Jupiter; this is where the Fendahl evolved before the Time Lords destroyed the planet and put all information about it in a time loop.

The Doctor believed that the Fendahl affected Mars on its way to Earth, possibly explaining its barren nature.

The Fendahl influenced human evolution; presumably this could account for why Earth humans were less advanced than Mondasians. This opens the intriguing possibility that the Fendahl may have been in competition with the Daemons and Scaroth.

⚙ RUNNING THE ADVENTURE

This adventure is a Pandora's box; a group of scientists unwittingly start a ticking time bomb, fostered by a fanatic with resources until a world-

ANY SUFFICIENTLY ADVANCED TECHNOLOGY...

Arthur C. Clarke once wrote that any sufficiently advanced technology is indistinguishable from magic. HP Lovecraft treated gods and magic as alien beings using sciences that humankind didn't understand and was therefore magic to them. This adventure follows in their footsteps, offering scientific explanations for things long thought magical. The Fendahl is an alien composite being made of thirteen parts. Rock salt can damage it. An old psychic gets her powers from living near a temporal rift.

You can deconstruct old myths and give them a sci-fi spin. Perhaps the Labyrinth of the Minotaur was a giant circuit board, or the dwarves of Norse legend a group of stranded Sontarans. Or maybe a line of 'witches' are really psychics (in the Doctor's universe psychic power is a scientific fact), alien hybrids, or genetically modified. Just remember to create an ultimate purpose for it; that is what your players must resolve!

THERE'S A HOLE IN YOUR MIND

There's a definite correlation between psychic powers and holes in the space-time continuum. Martha Tyler lived close to the Fendahl skull all her life, and saw visions of the creature in her dreams. Gwyneth (see *The Unquiet Dead* in **The Ninth Doctor Sourcebook**) grew up near the Space-Time Rift in Cardiff, and developed similar abilities. Amy Pond spent her childhood next to a Crack in Time, and while she didn't have any overt abilities, she was able to recall the universe in order to reboot it.

While close contact with a dimensional rift isn't a prerequisite for psychic powers – they're latent in the human mind – growing up close to such a breach in reality is a great 'excuse' to give a character psychic abilities. If you want to play a human character with such powers, consider including a rift or other temporal weirdness in your background.

THE FIFTH PLANET

The fifth planet of our solar system once held an advanced civilisation that evolved into the Fendahl. This necessitated the destruction of the world and subsequent time loop by the Time Lords and the asteroid belt may be remnants of the planet. All of this took place about 10-12 million years ago.

Still, it's possible that the player characters could go back in time and interact with members of this civilisation. It's also possible that some members went into space and now can't remember where they once called home. Would the Time Lords leave them be or hunt them down for fear of that final evolution happening again?

The Fendahl skull is an exact match for Homo sapiens; it's likely that the fifth planet's race looked human. Perhaps they were also a gestalt species. It would be very interesting to see a 'human' that controlled several non-human creatures as extensions of her being!

SERVANTS OF THE FENDAHL

Three of the archaeologists fell under the influence of the Fendahl in very different ways.

Dr. Fendelman was a brilliant electronics engineer and inventor, a millionaire many times over, before he became intrigued by the search for the origins of the human race. He developed a sonic time scanner that detected the Fendahl skull buried in Kenya. This time scanner created relative continuum displacements in the Time Vortex – in essence, it functioned by looking back through the vortex. Overuse of such a device causes a breach in the vortex, a continuum explosion that could destroy a whole planet.

This technology is many years ahead of what humanity should have been able to create in this era, as Fendelman's whole life was shaped and guided by the psychic emanations of the Fendahl.

THE FENDAHL

The Fendahl is an evolutionary inversion from the fifth planet of the solar system. It consumed the previous civilisation on the planet, gathering all of their psychic power. The Time Lords intervened, fearing that the Fendahl would consume the universe. They atomised the planet and put all record of its existence into a time loop. Unfortunately, part of the Fendahl Core, a skull with a pentagram circuit, came to Earth.

The Fendahl is a gestalt being; it is made up of thirteen parts. At the core is a being that resembles a golden humanoid with large eyes. The other twelve pieces, the Fendahleen, look like giant snakes with pink protuberances coming from their mouths. The Fendahl needs the proper circumstances to regenerate; towards this end it has manipulated humanity's evolution, primarily through one line: Dr Fendelman's. The Fendahl need thirteen host bodies to regenerate fully.

The alien presence inspired his genius, whispered technological secrets into his mind and brought him into a position to free it from its tomb. Fendelman never knew the purpose of his life until it was too late.

By contrast, Maximilian Stahl was the leader of a coven that worshipped the alien. He was part of an occult tradition that went back for thousands of years – the shadow of the Fendahl lies heavy on the history of the human race. While he lacked Fendelman's understanding of technology, he knew how to prepare victims to become part of the reborn Fendahl.

Finally, Dr. Thea Ransom knew nothing of the Fendahl until the skull became attuned to her and she became the vessel for the creature's revival. She was purely a victim of the creature's life-eating malevolence.

Usually in an adventure, there's one big bad guy who commands a group of servants. Sometimes, there's a powerful lieutenant who commands the servants on behalf of the big bad. Sutekh (see **The Pyramids of Mars**) had his robots and his possessed followers, with Scarman as his lieutenant; the Beast (see **The Impossible Planet**) had the Ood as his slaves. In these cases, all the villains are on the same 'side' – they all know each other and work together.

FENDAHL CORE

AWARENESS	4	PRESENCE	9
COORDINATION	3	RESOLVE	9
INGENUITY	6	STRENGTH	3

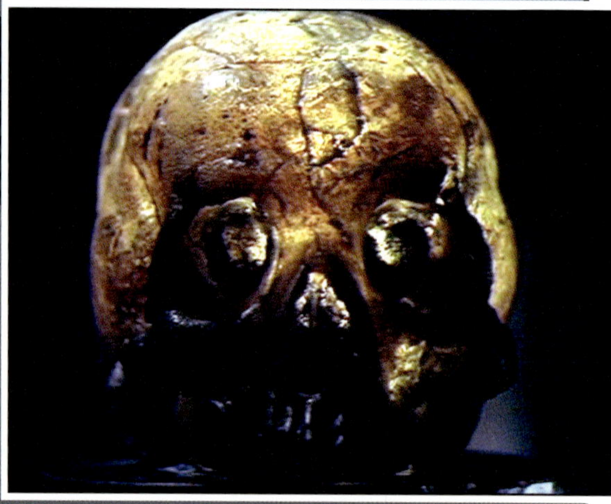

SKILLS
Athletics 2, Convince 4, Fighting 4, Knowledge 5, Medicine 5, Science 6, Subterfuge 2, Survival 4, Technology 5.

TRAITS
Alien
Alien Appearance
Fear Factor 3: Grants a +6 bonus to inspire fear.
Hypnosis (Major): +2 bonus to control another's actions and feelings.
Immunity (Major): The Fendahl takes no damage from physical attacks.
Indomitable: +4 bonus to any rolls to resist psychic control.
Natural Weapon (Major) – Psychic Vampirism: The Fendahl can deliver (4/L/L) damage with a touch, leaving only the victim's dehydrated corpse.
Psychic: +4 against mental attacks and may attempt to read minds. The Fendahl Core may have other psychic powers beyond those listed here.
Shapeshift (Major): The Fendahl Core can assume the shape and abilities of a Fendahleen at will. It can't use any traits that the Fendahleen form doesn't have, although it can shapeshift back to its original form.

Special – Astral Projection: The Fendahl can project an image of itself anywhere within its teleport range. This form has the Immaterial trait.
Special – Psychotelekinesis: The Fendahl can use its mental powers to stop a victim from moving. This requires an Awareness + Resolve +4 test against the victim's Resolve + Strength (defences against psychic traits may also be employed).
Teleport (Major): The Fendahl can shift to another known location with an Awareness + Resolve roll. Failure means she doesn't move.
Weakness (Minor): -2 to rolls for each missing Fendahleen.
Weakness (Major): Rock salt deals 4 levels of damage to the Fendahl.

TECH LEVEL: 5   **STORY POINTS: 10**

However, if you've got a manipulative, cunning villain like the Fendahl (or the Master, for that matter), consider having two or three groups of villains who are all working for the same villainous mastermind, but don't know it. This makes the player characters feel like they're being outwitted when people they trust turn out to be yet more servants of the villain.

FURTHER ADVENTURES

- The player characters arrive on Mars as the Fendahl is destroying the planet. It is too late to stop it, but the characters can help the remaining Martians to escape while they contain the Fendahl (perhaps Varga from **The Ice Warriors** deposits the Fendahl skull on Earth and crashes his ship in the process). Should the Martians survive they adapt to a hard life in space, developing into the Ice Warriors.

- During the Elizabethan Era an alchemist and secret occultist, Dr Johann Fendel, uses sorcery to summon the Fendahl to Earth. While his limited science is not enough to make the Fendahl manifest, it is enough to create one Fendahleen to strike at his enemies, wreaking havoc against Elizabeth's court.

- Asteroid miners in the mid-21st century uncover the remains of an alien city, buried deep inside an asteroid. It is a city of the Fendahl – but before they awaken a Fendahl creature, they trigger an ancient Time Lord booby trap. A vortex bubble pops into existence, locking the asteroid out of time and space and trapping the miners, the player characters and the slumbering Fendahl in a dimensional prison. The only way out may be to harness the power of the sleeping Fendahl – but can the characters tap the power of the death eater without succumbing to its lures?

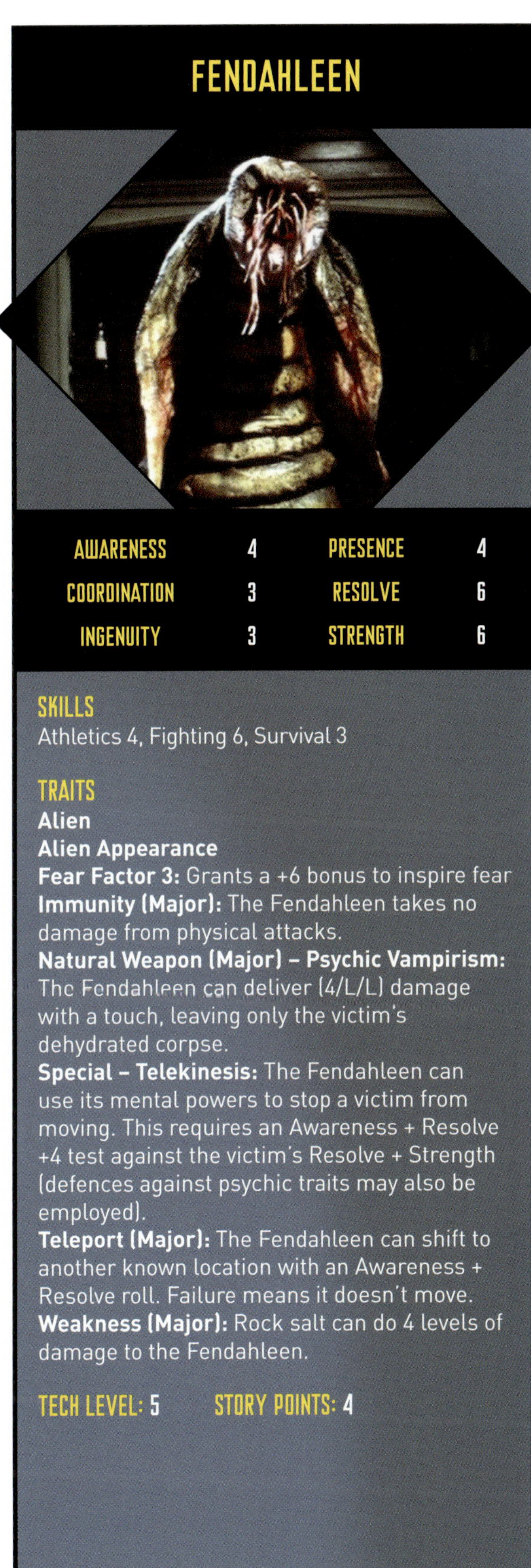

FENDAHLEEN

AWARENESS	4	PRESENCE	4
COORDINATION	3	RESOLVE	6
INGENUITY	3	STRENGTH	6

SKILLS
Athletics 4, Fighting 6, Survival 3

TRAITS
Alien
Alien Appearance
Fear Factor 3: Grants a +6 bonus to inspire fear
Immunity (Major): The Fendahleen takes no damage from physical attacks.
Natural Weapon (Major) – Psychic Vampirism: The Fendahleen can deliver (4/L/L) damage with a touch, leaving only the victim's dehydrated corpse.
Special – Telekinesis: The Fendahleen can use its mental powers to stop a victim from moving. This requires an Awareness + Resolve +4 test against the victim's Resolve + Strength (defences against psychic traits may also be employed).
Teleport (Major): The Fendahleen can shift to another known location with an Awareness + Resolve roll. Failure means it doesn't move.
Weakness (Major): Rock salt can do 4 levels of damage to the Fendahleen.

TECH LEVEL: 5   **STORY POINTS: 4**

THE SUN MAKERS

'Perhaps everyone runs from the tax man?'

⊙ SYNOPSIS

Megropolis 3, Pluto, the Future

The TARDIS materialised in a vast city on Pluto. Soon after landing, the Doctor and Leela saved a man, Cordo, from jumping to his death, as his tax burden was so oppressive he had chosen to die. They learned that the Company taxed every aspect of life on the colony – and that by landing without a licence, they had incurred a significant tax penalty. Pursued by agents of Gatherer Hade, the chief tax collector, the trio fled the time travellers into the undercity in search of a secret underclass of tax evaders.

Mandrel, the leader of the group, took Leela hostage and gave the Doctor and Cordo an opportunity to prove themselves by robbing a bank with a forged card. Unfortunately, the Doctor tripped a security measure and was gassed while Cordo escaped. Cordo returned to the undercity and told them of the Doctor's capture.

The Doctor woke up in the Correction Centre. There he met fellow prisoner Bisham, a former executive that inadvertently discovered that the colony leaders were keeping the population docile through a drug, PCM, which they pumped into the air. At the same time, Hade met with the Controller, an alien investor who owned humanity. The Controller decided to root out the undercity and pass the cost onto the citizens. Leela and Cordo tried to free the Doctor. As they walked through the tunnels, Leela started to feel the

effects of the airborne drug. The Doctor was taken to see Hade. Hade pretended to befriend the Doctor and gave him the money he was stealing from the bank. In truth, he set him free simply so he could track him.

The Doctor returned to Mandrel who couldn't believe the authorities let him go. Cordo returned and informed the Doctor that Leela had been captured on their way back. Cordo also used a blaster to take control of the undercity from Mandrel and began plans for revolution. Meanwhile, the captured Leela was taken to see the Controller. The Controller ordered her death by public steaming.

The Doctor freed Leela but in doing so tipped the Controller off to the revolution. Gatherer Hade met the revolution first-hand as an angry mob threw him off a building to his death. The Doctor confronted the Controller and learned of his alien nature before stopping the villain from gassing the population. The Controller reverted to his true form when he realised that the Doctor had condemned him to bankruptcy by hacking the computer to put a tax on growth – the more money the Collector extracted from Pluto, the more he owed, until his system crashed!

CONTINUITY

Pluto's planetary status is restored and the tenth planet beyond Pluto is named Cassius.
Earth had been depleted of resources, forcing humanity to accept the Usurians' aid in moving to Mars. Once Mars was exhausted, the Usurians moved humanity to Pluto. About 300 million humans live on Pluto.

The Ajacks are humans that run the mines. They aren't allowed to see the light of the artificial sun, but they are not subjected to PCM as much as the city dwellers. The Ajacks have a distinctive form of dress; the Doctor is mistaken for one.

Balarium is a muscle neutraliser that also affects speech.

Dianene is a poisonous gas, potent enough that adding it to the atmosphere could kill all humans in the city within 10 seconds.

PentoCyleinicMethldrane, or PCM, is the gas used by the Usurians to pacify the population. It is pumped through vapour towers and keeps the people submissive.

The Company knows of Gallifrey. They also have a file on the Doctor, noting his long history of violence and economic subversion.

⊗ RUNNING THE ADVENTURE

This adventure is designed around the excesses of capitalism, where a big business utterly exploits a civilisation completely devoted to keeping it profitable. The player characters need to shake the workers free of their complacency for the system and show them that they can be free and keep more of what they earn.

It's notable here that the Usurians overplay their hand. As a fungal species unaccustomed to the humanoid form, the Usurians can't enforce their policies with their own troops; they rely on human employees to police their own. This is coupled with a drug to keep everyone docile. Unfortunately for the Usurians, once the humans are weaned from the drug there is little to stop them from taking control.

While laissez-faire capitalism is the culprit here, it's easy to take any economic system and exaggerate it to an extreme. One could easily visualise a communist system where what is 'necessary' keeps getting downgraded or a green economy that imposes brutal limitations on human existence.

PentoCyleinicMethldrane gas makes its victims more suggestible and submissive. A character exposed to the gas must make a Strength + Resolve roll (Difficulty depends on the gas concentration, but usually 15), or temporarily gain one of the following traits: By The Book, Cowardly, Slow Reflexes or Unadventurous. These temporary bad traits fade once exposure to the gas ends.

HOW MANY PLANETS ARE IN THE SOLAR SYSTEM?

Until recently, it was believed that the Solar System had nine planets. Pluto's downgrade to 'dwarf planet' reduced the number to eight. As the term 'planet' is somewhat arbitrary, one could argue that in the future dwarf planets could get reclassified so that 13 'planets' orbit the sun.

During the Doctor's travels several other planets are known to either exist or have existed within the Solar System. Vulcan, from **Power of the Daleks**, may sit between the Sun and Mercury (as some astronomers once theorised). Earth's twin world Mondas spun away from the solar system at some point in the past. A fifth planet between Mars and Jupiter was home to the Fendahl before the Time Lords obliterated it. In this adventure 'Cassius' is the name given to the tenth planet. Finally, the Cybermen referred to a 'Planet 14' where they met the Doctor.

With astronomers making new discoveries all the time, it's possible that new planets could be discovered or even created (it's possible between now and the time of this adventure that a rogue planet or asteroid is ensnared by the sun and becomes Cassius). It's also fun to create new planets to allow for slower-than-light space adventures and conflicts between species within the solar system.

A FITTING END?

One of the most unsettling parts of this adventure is the rebel crowd's murder of Gatherer Hade. While Hade had been responsible for their crippling taxation and no doubt sent many of them to Correction Centres or death by steaming, he did so under the colour of law. One could argue that he, too, was a

victim, as the PCM merely made him more dedicated to his job. Thus, even though he berated the rebels on the rooftop, it is still unsettling to see a crowd pick up an unarmed man and threw him off a building. Couldn't they simply have confined him until the revolution was over and they could hold court?

While neither the Doctor nor Leela were involved, they've had their share of questionable scenes. Leela has killed where wounding would have

been enough and the Doctor casually flicked a bloodthirsty Horda onto a member of the Sevateem (to say nothing of gunning down an Ogron). When the players do something like this, it's easy for them to slide down the slippery slope of expediency, which is not what **Doctor Who: Adventures in Time and Space** is about.

When this happens (and it seems at least somewhat appropriate to the situation) then you should remind

USURIANS

The Usurians are a fungal race that resembles kelp. They conquer through economics rather than warfare, believing that by taking over a species' economy, quelling its resistance with drugs, and applying crippling taxation then they can profit more than by simply defeating its military forces.

As part of their plan they disguise their true origins. Usurians mask their intent through a Company that makes uses of the native species as its employees. Usurians also change their appearance to look like the race they are conquering, but as a fungus the typical Usurian has problems manipulating more than one or two limbs at a time and lacks the coordination to walk. Thus a Usurian in human form often looks hunched over in his chair and awkwardly moves his arms, hands, and fingers. Usurians have a very distinctive voice.

AWARENESS	3	PRESENCE	5
COORDINATION	2	RESOLVE	4
INGENUITY	4	STRENGTH	2

SKILLS
Convince 4, Knowledge 5 (Business 7), Technology 3, Transport 2

TRAITS
Alien
Alien Organs (Minor Good): The character's organs are not where you might expect. All targeted damage is reduced by 2
Cyborg
Dark Secret: The Usurians feel the need to look human in order to maintain control. Even PCM would not be enough to quell the human population if the true Usurian form was revealed.
Distinctive: -2 penalty to rolls to blend in. Others have a +2 bonus to remember or recognise the character
Immunity (Minor): Usurians do not need to breathe, rendering them immune to poisonous gas.
Obsession (Major): A Usurian is obsessed with profits and productivity.
Shapeshift (Major): A Usurian can shift between its natural and human appearance at will.

Slow (Minor): In human form a Usurian needs a mobile chair that moves at half the Usurian's Speed rate.
Weakness (Major): Loss of business profits put Usurians in an emotional breakdown, causing 4 levels of damage to mental attributes per turn. Once a mental trait hits 0, the Usurian transforms back into its natural state, retreating into the bowl beneath the seat.

EQUIPMENT: Motorised Chair

TECH LEVEL: 6   **STORY POINTS:** 6-8

the players that this is a one-off thing; perhaps the expenditure of a Story Point or three would be appropriate to smooth the rough edges and continue. Should a character continue down this road, then it is probably time for an exit scene.

FURTHER ADVENTURES

- The Company didn't merely come when humanity needed it; it has been secretly manipulating humanity through the centuries to achieve this result. Towards that end, the Company sabotaged humanity's efforts to regenerate the Earth. The PCs could be tasked with preventing any of the Company's more minor schemes, or they could discover that the Company, through shell corporations, has been controlling space exploration so that a permanent off-world solution could never be found.

- The Doctor told the humans that Earth had regenerated itself, but it's likely that it is no longer the planet they left. What if the Silurians awoke and returned the world to a prehistoric state? Would they welcome their human siblings or protect the Earth against them? Even if humanity was allowed to resettle, they may be limited to certain areas of a world now run by Silurians.

- A single Gatherer was defeated, but he wasn't the only governor; there are multiple cities on Pluto. What if the other Gatherers decided to cut their losses when faced with a rebelling population and simply use the artificial suns to incinerate Pluto? Can the player characters stop them?

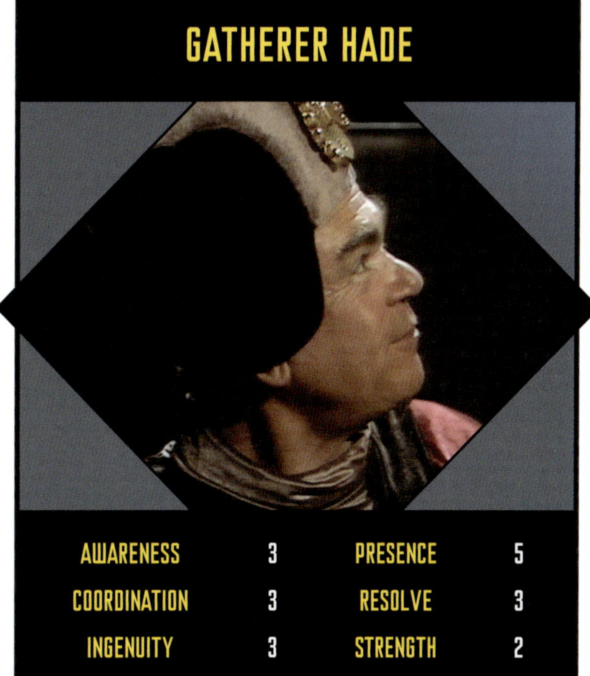

GATHERER HADE

AWARENESS	3	PRESENCE	5
COORDINATION	3	RESOLVE	3
INGENUITY	3	STRENGTH	2

Hade worked as a Gatherer, or tax collector, for Megropolis One, an Earth city on Pluto. While he put on a smiling face, he was ruthless in his collection of taxes. He constantly worried about pleasing the Collector, who held Hade's fate in his hands. Hade's failure to recapture the Doctor and to quell the rebellion led the Collector to dock Hade's pay and refuse him a promotion. This prompted Hade to try and personally stop a group of rebels, who promptly flung him to his death off the side of a building.

SKILLS
Convince 4, Knowledge 4 (tax code 6), Subterfuge 2

TRAITS
Charming: +2 bonus to attempts to use charm.
Distinctive: Hade always wears his tax gatherer robes. He has a -2 penalty to rolls to blend in. Others have a +2 bonus to remember or recognise the character
Impulsive: When there is money to be made Hade doesn't think things through before acting.
Obsession (Major): Hade gleefully collects all the taxes he can apply.
Owes Favour (Major): Hade is obligated to the Collector.
Selfish: Hade puts his own needs first.

TECH LEVEL: 6   **STORY POINTS: 4**

UNDERWORLD

'Ah, myths often have a grain of truth in them, if you know where to look.'

SYNOPSIS

The Edge of the Cosmos, Unknown time

The TARDIS arrived at the edge of the universe and was pulled towards a spiral nebula that was about to form a new galaxy. To avoid being crushed, the Doctor materialised the TARDIS on a nearby spaceship. Once aboard, he recognised some artefacts as Minyan, a race that had destroyed their homeworld 100,000 years ago after receiving help from the Time Lords. The Minyans considered the Time Lords to be gods.

Unfortunately, this ship was also being pulled into the nebula. Captain Jackson accepted the Doctor's help in pulling free from the nebula. Jackson explained that the ship was on a quest to find the P7E, a ship that contained the race banks needed to rebuild the Minyan race.

Jackson noted that he and the other Minyans could regenerate endlessly, although unlike Time Lords they remained the same in each regeneration. Unfortunately their equipment didn't regenerate and their ship systems were failing. While K-9 was able to pilot the ship out of the gravity well, the Minyans

noted that the P7E's signal was coming from a planetoid inside the nebula. The Minyan ship fought its way to the planetoid, where they encountered a band of miners called Trogs. One Trog, Idmom, suggested that the newcomers were from the sky and was arrested for heresy.

The Trog guards tried to attack the Minyan crew with poisonous gas, but the Doctor managed to reverse the flow and knock out the guards. The Doctor and Leela also met Idas, Idmom's son, who fled when the guards took his father. The Doctor learned that there was another ship, the P7E, at the core of the planetoid. The natives called it 'the Citadel,' and it was from here that the Seers ruled the planet. It was surrounded by a zero-G environment that the Doctor used to float the three of them to the Citadel.

Idas freed his father and began a Trog rebellion. The Minyan crew assisted, but one of them, Herrick, was captured. During interrogation, Herrick learned that the Seers were robots. The rest of the crew and the time travellers escaped the guards, but the Doctor wanted to return to the Citadel and find the Oracle, which controlled the Seers. Meanwhile, the Seers decided to simply give the race banks to the Minyans if they would leave. The Doctor, however, realised that the Oracle was a computer program designed to protect the banks; it wouldn't just give them up.

K-9 recognised the 'race banks' given to the Minyans as fission grenades. The Doctor stole the real race banks and swapped them, convincing a guard sent to retrieve them that he had the real race banks. The guard took them back and the Minyan crew convinced the Trogs to come with them. The grenades exploded and destroyed the planetoid, which also propelled the Minyan ship free. With the future of their race secured, the Minyans headed for Minyos II to start a new world.

CONTINUITY

The Time Lords were directly involved in Minyan development, leading to them devastating their world in a nuclear war. It was partly because of this that the Time Lords adopted a non-intervention policy. This happened 100,000 years before this adventure.

The Minyans can rejuvenate themselves with a machine. Unlike Time Lord regeneration, the rejuvenated Minyan simply becomes more youthful in appearance. They've done this at least a thousand times to the point where they are outliving their technological devices.

The Doctor claims that the TARDIS landing sound is the result of the relative dimensional stabiliser; he neglects to mention that it's caused by him riding the brake.

Leela is a seasoned traveller at this point, able to operate some TARDIS controls and involved in unseen adventures.

⚙ RUNNING THE ADVENTURE

As with the Greek myth that inspired it, this adventure is an epic journey. The Minyans have travelled across the universe to find another ship carrying the Minyan race banks. After freeing themselves from a meteor storm the Minyans crash into a new planet, the core of which is the other ship. The Minyans inhabiting it

have forgotten their heritage and the race banks are protected by robotic seers that have gone insane. After causing enough trouble getting to the centre, the player characters and the Minyans cause enough trouble that the Seers hand over the race banks, only for the player characters to discover a bait and switch. The player characters and the Minyans escape as the planet explodes.

While cloaked in science fiction, this adventure has a very 'dungeon crawl' feel to it, where the player characters are expected to descend to the centre of the planet and overcome the obstacles that get in their way.

There is little investigation or mystery beyond why the Seers and the Oracle are acting strangely. So long as the players keep their wits about them, they should be able to overcome the challenges and emerge victorious.

USING MYTHOLOGY

This adventure is modelled on Greek mythology, specifically the Quest for the Golden Fleece. The names of the Minyans echo Greek characters: Herrick (Heracles), Jackson (Jason), Orfe (Orpheus), and Tala (Atalanta). Captain Jackson is the leader, paralleling Jason's role as captain of the Argonauts. Orfe uses a Pacifier, which is an analogue to Orpheus' ability to calm wild animals.

The ship's names parallel the Greek myth as well. 'R' in R1C refers to the Argo. The P7E is named for Persephone, who was trapped in the Underworld. The race banks represent the Golden Fleece and are guarded by a laser beam instead of a dragon. The shield guns echo the shields carried by Greek warriors and the Seers somewhat resemble a Cyclops (wrong myth, but the same ballpark). The Seers and Oracle are located in Hedas, an anagram of Hades, while the Trogs believe their world to be covered with stone (a representation of the Underworld).

When plotting new adventures you can take a story from a different mythology or literary source and re-skin it as a futuristic story. Perhaps the player characters join a group of travellers that have a code necessary to unlock the power of a planet-destroying weapon that sits deep inside the Dalek Empire in a loose retelling of The Lord of the Rings, or perhaps the player characters need to assist a roguish figure get something back that he sold to a dangerous enemy before the colony that relies on it collapses, in a retelling of the Norse tale of the kidnapping of Idunn and her apples, which was facilitated by Loki.

FURTHER ADVENTURES

- What was the Oracle's plan? Was it just a malfunctioning computer that created the whole system of Trogs, Guards and Seers to gather fuel to keep the ship running? If so, why did it plot against the Minyans? Maybe the Oracle had some other scheme in mind, one that was interrupted by the arrival of the R1C. After all, if one wanted to build something in secret, hiding inside an artificial planetoid in a dangerous nebula at the very edge of the universe is a great place to get some privacy. Even the TARDIS had trouble navigating there – was the P7E hiding from the Time Lords?

- Minyan regenerative technology could be a very valuable commodity. What if an enterprising Minyan set up an 'immortality shop' on Earth

---

NEW GADGET: SHIELD GUN/LIEBERMANN LASER

The Shield Gun or Liebermann Laser is a gun set inside a reflective shield. It is held like a shield and can deflect blasts from other energy weapons. The guards on the P7E planet also have these guns, although they lack the shielding.

Traits: Force Field (Minor), Laser (4/L/L),
Cost: 2 Story Points

NEW GADGET: PACIFIER

The Pacifier Gun projects a beam that removes violent impulses. It works like a normal weapon, only instead of inflicting damage, the target must make a Resolve + Convince roll against the operator's Coordination + Marksman + 2; if the attacker succeeds, the target calms down. In effect, it lets you calm people down by shooting them.

Traits: Hypnosis (Minor)
Cost: 1 Story Point

and charged a premium? Earth would soon split into a privileged immortal elite and a mortal lower class. There is a lottery that enables winners to 'upgrade' to the elite, but someone is rigging the system to ensure that only particular people are selected. What is the long game?

- The regenerative Minyan technology is subtly flawed; each generation loses a bit of their 'core' until ultimately amoral Minyans are created.

These bored, amoral creatures see 'lesser races' as playthings and create elaborate and lethal games to run other races through and amuse themselves. Currently, a group of Minyans plan to stoke the powers of late 20th century Earth to see how long it takes them to start a nuclear war.

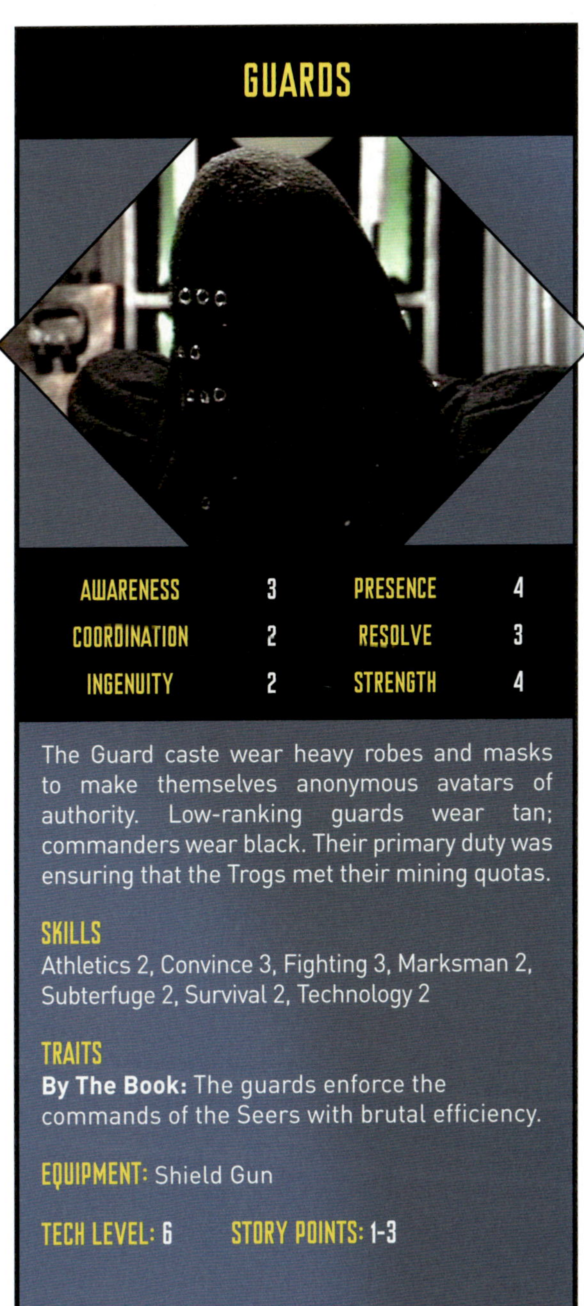

GUARDS

AWARENESS	3	PRESENCE	4
COORDINATION	2	RESOLVE	3
INGENUITY	2	STRENGTH	4

The Guard caste wear heavy robes and masks to make themselves anonymous avatars of authority. Low-ranking guards wear tan; commanders wear black. Their primary duty was ensuring that the Trogs met their mining quotas.

SKILLS
Athletics 2, Convince 3, Fighting 3, Marksman 2, Subterfuge 2, Survival 2, Technology 2

TRAITS
By The Book: The guards enforce the commands of the Seers with brutal efficiency.

EQUIPMENT: Shield Gun

TECH LEVEL: 6   **STORY POINTS:** 1-3

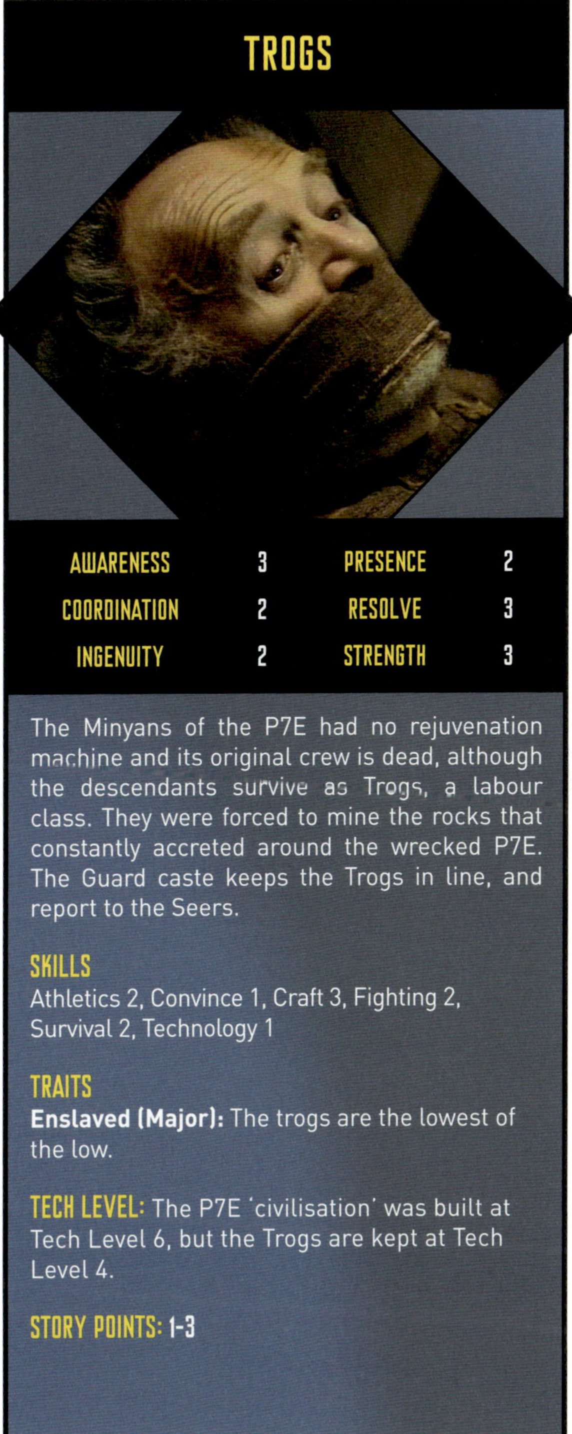

TROGS

AWARENESS	3	PRESENCE	2
COORDINATION	2	RESOLVE	3
INGENUITY	2	STRENGTH	3

The Minyans of the P7E had no rejuvenation machine and its original crew is dead, although the descendants survive as Trogs, a labour class. They were forced to mine the rocks that constantly accreted around the wrecked P7E. The Guard caste keeps the Trogs in line, and report to the Seers.

SKILLS
Athletics 2, Convince 1, Craft 3, Fighting 2, Survival 2, Technology 1

TRAITS
Enslaved (Major): The trogs are the lowest of the low.

TECH LEVEL: The P7E 'civilisation' was built at Tech Level 6, but the Trogs are kept at Tech Level 4.

STORY POINTS: 1-3

MINYAN

AWARENESS	3	PRESENCE	3
COORDINATION	4	RESOLVE	4
INGENUITY	3	STRENGTH	4

The Minyans are a humanoid race that destroyed their home world in a war after receiving advanced technology from the Time Lords. At least two vessels were launched from Minyos before it was completely destroyed. One was the P7E, which contained the race banks, and the other was the R1C.

The Minyans aboard the R1C are the original crewmembers, kept alive by their rejuvenation machine.

SKILLS
Athletics 3, Convince 3, Craft 2, Fighting 3, Knowledge 4, Marksman 4, Medicine 3, Science 3, Survival 3, Technology 4, Transport 3

TRAITS
Immortal (Major): The Minyans are a hundred thousand years old; while they haven't been able to hone their skills as much as their great age suggests, they know a great deal about the universe.

EQUIPMENT: Shield Gun

TECH LEVEL: 6   **STORY POINTS:** 2-4

SEERS

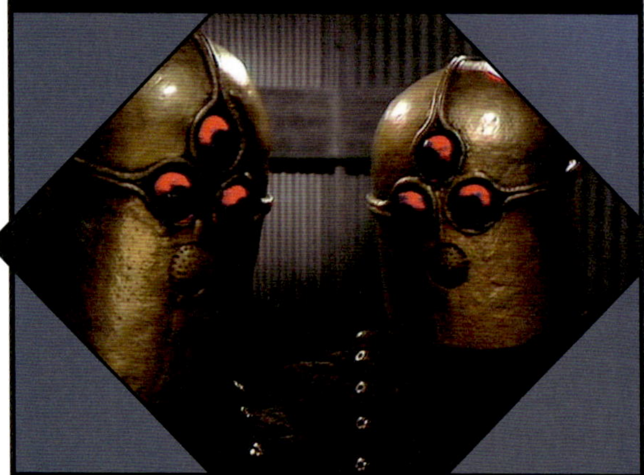

AWARENESS	3	PRESENCE	4
COORDINATION	2	RESOLVE	3
INGENUITY	2	STRENGTH	4

The Oracle, the megalomaniacal computer protecting the memory banks, was protected by Seers. These were three-eyed robot Minyans, upgraded to serve the Oracle computer. The Seers no longer considered themselves Minyan – they believed they had evolved far beyond their base beginnings.

They lived on the P7E starship, or the "Tree at the End of the World" as the Trogs called it. Not even the guards were allowed on the starship; a robotic 'dragon' guarded the entrance to the ship, and the Seers took tribute of fuel ore from the Trogs and used it to keep the Oracle operating.

SKILLS
Athletics 2, Convince 3, Fighting 3, Marksman 2, Technology 2

TRAITS
By the Book: Although the Seers give the guards the orders, they follow the word of the Oracle itself.
Boffin: Able to improvise, say, a fission bomb disguised as the race banks.
Robot
Scan (Minor)

ARMOUR: 10

TECH LEVEL: 6   **STORY POINTS:** 2-5

THE INVASION OF TIME

'Gentlemen, this is no ordinary meeting. I'm privileged to introduce to you your new masters!'

⊙ SYNOPSIS

Gallifrey

The Doctor returned to Gallifrey and claimed the position of Time Lord President as his rival, Chancellor Goth, was dead. He had a lead-lined presidential chamber constructed and connected to the Matrix. He also had Leela banished to the wilderness, on the grounds that she was an alien.

A Vardan invasion force arrived, and the Doctor revealed he was in league with these invaders. He brought down the transduction barrier that protected Gallifrey from the rest of the universe. With the barrier down the Vardans could invade. As President, the Doctor surrendered Gallifrey to the Vardans.

The Doctor met with Chancellor Borusa in his office, where they could speak freely as the Vardans couldn't hear them through the lead shielding. He and Borusa attempted to thwart the Vardans, but Castellan Kelner saw an opportunity to seize power under the new regime. He arrested Borusa and began expelling troublesome Time Lords to the wastelands.

The Doctor enlisted Chancellory Guard Andred to his cause while Leela turned the Time Lord exiles and the outsiders into a resistance force that would storm the Citadel. Confronted by the Vardans, the Doctor 'proved' his loyalty by opening up the Gallifreyan force field so that the entire Vardan force could invade. It also enabled K-9 to target their homeworld and the Doctor used the Matrix to trap the entire Vardan race into a time loop – his plan all along.

Leela led her force into the Panopticon, where the Time Lords were having a victory celebration. The celebration was cut short by the arrival of the Sontarans. The Vardan invasion was actually one of their schemes – by sending the Vardans to conquer Gallifrey, they eliminated the Vardans, weakened the Time Lords and won an opportunity to steal Gallifreyan time travel technology. The Doctor and his allies escaped and the Doctor had Borusa give him the Great Key of Rassilon before they all sought refuge in the TARDIS.

With Kelner's help, the Sontarans gained access to the Doctor's TARDIS. Sontaran Commander Stor wanted the Great Key as well. Leela and the Outsiders managed to overpower most of the Sontarans while the Doctor constructed the Demat gun, an ancient and forbidden Time Lord weapon.

Realising his chance to control Gallifrey was lost, Stor instead decided to destroy the Eye of Harmony. He was prevented by the Doctor, who erased Stor from history with the Demat Gun. The gun also destroyed itself and erased the Doctor's mind of recent events. With the invasion over, Borusa took control and arrested Kelner.

As the Doctor prepared to leave Leela decided to stay behind, having fallen in love with Andred. K-9 decided to remain as well. The Doctor wished them both well as he left on his own, fetching down a box labelled K-9 MII as he departed.

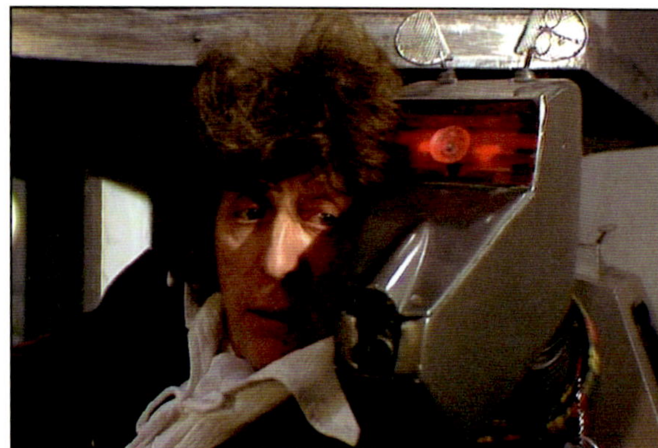

◉ RUNNING THE ADVENTURE

Unlike most adventures, where the player characters arrive in a strange place and have to react to events, this adventure is driven by the Doctor's actions. He seizes control of Gallifrey, sets up a trap, lures the Vardans into it, and defeats them. Player-driven adventures like this can be challenging to run, as the Gamemaster has to follow the players' lead, but are often much more involving and surprising than more conventional investigations or bases under siege. If the players do start plotting to take down a grander foe, run with it! It means they're really engaged in the game. Note that in this case, not even Leela knows what the Doctor is planning. Beware of situations where one player takes complete control of the game. A one-off story where a single player drives the whole plot and has lots of sidebar conferences with the Gamemaster is fine, but it gets frustrating for the other players if one character keeps running off to do their own thing that dominates play.

OMEGA WHO?

In both this adventure and in **The Deadly Assassin** it appears that all of the ceremonial symbols are attributed to Rassilon, who is considered the first Time Lord. Not a single reference is made to Omega. Interestingly, both Time Lords are mentioned as having gone to a black hole, but only Rassilon returned while Omega was sucked into the anti-matter universe. Conspiracy theorists may suggest that the two Time Lords were working together. Was Rassilon simply fortuitous, or was there something more sinister afoot? Certainly Rassilon's behaviour during the Time War suggests the latter as a strong possibility...

THE SONTARAN RUSE

Let's take a moment to appreciate the cunning of the Sontarans here. They manage to outmanoeuvre not one but two extremely powerful civilisations, and come within a hair's breadth of blowing up the Eye of Harmony, mastering time travel, and taking the title of Lords of Time from the Gallifreyans. If the Daleks or the Master did something like this, no one would blink an eye-stalk, but the Sontarans aren't normally seen as a cosmic-scale threat.

In the right circumstances or given the right plan any villain can be 'upgraded'. Try taking a monster that the players aren't scared off, and giving it a chance to really shine. Take the Slitheen, for example – they're small-scale space gangsters, but they're better at blending with humanity than most other invaders. What if a patient group of Slitheen identify the Doctor's human companions, then go to Earth and befriend the companion's family? They insinuate themselves into the companion's life, then start manipulating the companion through her family. What happens when friendly, roly-poly old Mr. Jones – a friend of the family for years, you've known him your whole life, he gave you a life home from school every Wednesday – suddenly peels off his face and hisses *"If you say a word, your parents will die. Now listen – you will help us! Here is a vial of poison – make sure the Doctor drinks it!"*

Try picking a monster that your players might otherwise dismiss, and coming up with a story that makes it terrifying again.

WHAT DOES THE DEMAT GUN DO?

The Demat Gun not only removed Stor and a few of his soldiers from time, it also rearranged the timeline so that Stor (and the other Sontarans that were hit) never existed. As part of this erasure, the Doctor's mind was edited to remove the incident. That said it must be presumed that Stor was behind the whole affair, as the Doctor remembers none of this adventure. Presumably, the memory will fade from the other Time Lords (and Leela and K-9) too.

As it is editing and reknitting time, the Demat Gun should do it in the most unobtrusive way possible. Leela and K-9 may remember coming to Gallifrey but it being uneventful beyond K-9 getting a look inside the Matrix and Leela falling in love with Andred.

Whether used by the player characters or a renegade like the Master, a Demat Gun could have an interesting effect on the player characters, as they were a part of something they no longer remember but someone might. Alternatively, player characters that can Feel the Turn of the Universe may sense that something has changed as you make a few obvious changes to their backstories.

NEW GADGET: PARTIAL ENCEPHALOGRAPHIC SHIELD

This device can be built into a helmet and block psychic attacks (all Vardan traits are considered psychic)

Traits: Delete (psychic effects used against the wearer)
Cost: 2 Story Points

SYMBOLS OF POWER

In addition to the Rod of Rassilon and the Sash of Rassilon, there are two more ceremonial items introduced in this adventure, the Crown of Rassilon and the Great Key.

The Crown of Rassilon

This ornate, gilded and bejewelled crown was primarily a neural link that allowed the President direct access to the APC Net and the vast knowledge stored in the Matrix, including the memories and hidden secrets of all the Time Lord Presidents that went before him. This provided the bearer with a Knowledge Skill of 12 and the Precognition Trait while they wore the crown.

The Crown was only allowed to be worn by the current President of Gallifrey, however, and any other living being donning it would be subjected to mental attack by the 'minds' of the former presidents. This is resolved as a Resolve roll against a Difficulty of 21 and the bearer takes D6 points of damage for each level of Failure.

OUTSIDER

Take everything you know about the average Time Lord and flip it on its head and you have the typical Outsider. They are not primitives, whatever the rest of Gallifreyan society might think of them. Those who leave behind the highly sophisticated trappings of life in the Citadel simply apply all of the intelligence, drive and lifetimes of experience of a Time Lord towards a much more basic, and they would say much purer, goal: the very act of living.

Survival in the harsh wilderness of Gallifrey is not easy, and Outsiders tend to toughen up quickly or die many horrible deaths trying. They are resourceful and more respectful of their environment than the average citizen of Gallifrey, who fears and loathes the idea of living wild. But they can also be just as arrogant and elitist as their Citadel-dwelling counterparts, treating non-Outsider 'weaklings,' especially plebeian Gallifreyans, with a dismissive contempt one typically finds in even the most civilised of Time Lords.

OUTSIDER (SPECIAL GOOD)

This Time Lord rejected the staid lifestyle and effete snobbery of society in the Citadel and exiled themselves into the wilds of Gallifrey, abandoning technology and learning to survive without it.

Effects: The Time Lord is strong, tough and self sufficient, gaining a +1 Strength and Resolve and +1 to both the Craft and Survival skills, but -1 to Technology. They are also assumed to have the Time Traveller Trait for Tech Levels 1 and 2. Their status in Time Lord society, however, adds a +3 Difficulty to any social interaction rolls with other, non-Outsider, Gallifreyans.

Being an Outsider costs 2 Character Points and 1 Story Point.

The Great Key

The Time Lords had a great fondness for the imagery associated with keys. No other symbol so perfectly identified the Time Lords as powerful gatekeepers holding access to the secrets of the universe. This is reflected in their greatest artefact, The Great Key, whose location was known only to the Chancellor. With this key, a Time Lord could access the infinite and unadulterated power of the Eye of Harmony directly and use it to create the most deadly of temporal weapons or lock off entire sectors of space and time from the rest of the universe. In effect, the Great Key has an infinite number of Story Points. These points can be used to power any gadget for as long as Gallifrey and the Eye of Harmony existed; more importantly, they allow for the construction of the Demat Gun.

FURTHER ADVENTURES

- So, how did the Doctor become aware of the Vardan threat in the first place? Presumably

NEW GADGET – DEMAT GUN

This weapon was considered forbidden technology on Gallifrey from the moment it was created and the plans for it could only be found in the deepest recesses of the Matrix. The use of it was tantamount to a high crime in all but the most extreme circumstances, such as the invasion of Gallifrey itself. If an acting President somehow managed to find the information about its construction (a Difficulty 27 Awareness + Technology roll) and actually managed to build the thing (a Difficulty 30 Jiggery Pokery roll), it could only be powered by the Great Key, an object hidden from the Presidents of Gallifrey since time immemorial to prevent such catastrophic abuses of power.

When fired, the Demat Gun completely and totally removes a single target from time and space. The target never existed and never will exist for all intents and purposes. Even if someone attempted to go back and ensure the target did, in fact, come into being, they would find the Blinovitch Limitation Field surrounding the intervention attempt to be so strong that all their efforts would be practically doomed to failure from the outset.

The temporal shockwave from the weapon is so intense that it typically causes unconsciousness and memory loss for everyone in the vicinity of the target, including the bearer of the weapon itself if they are within range. The larger the object the larger the area of effect. Every being within the area of effect must make a Strength + Resolve roll against a Difficulty of 18. On a Success, they are knocked over, but otherwise unharmed. On a Failure they are knocked unconscious for D6 hours. On a Bad Failure they are knocked out for D6 hours and lose all memories from the last D6 days. On a Disastrous Failure, they go unconscious for D6 days and suffer from full blown and total Amnesia for as long as the Gamemaster thinks it appropriate. The Demat Gun is ineffective against any target larger that a large building and its range is limited by the scattering of the Zed Neutrino beam that carries the temporal inversion wave to the target. In effect, you can't 'demat' a planet and there is a +3 Difficulty to hit for every full 90' of range to the target. Misses have to go somewhere, of course, so collateral damage should always be of concern to the user lest they accidentally eradicate an innocent but temporarily significant bystander.

Basically, the only way that your average player character should be allowed access to a Demat Gun is in the most crucial and extraordinary circumstance and only as a weapon of last resort. A single well-placed (or badly flubbed) shot from this weapon can totally eradicate whole timelines and send ripples through the Vortex that can build into great tsunamis of temporal chaos. The Doctor's elimination of the Sontaran Commander Stor, for instance, also removed all of his soldiers from Gallifrey and his ship from orbit, as he never existed to lead those soldiers on that ship to Gallifrey in the first place.

the Sontarans are involved somehow – did they somehow engineer an encounter between the Doctor and the Vardan fleet?

- Andred is not likely to want to live with the Outsiders; Leela will have to adjust to life inside the Citadel. What if she can't? What if she leaves Andred and, like her mentor, steals a TARDIS and travels the universe? The player characters may have to undo the damage she does to the time stream as her direct approach wreaks havoc.

- The Sontarans want the secret of time travel; they try again in *The Two Doctors*. But why? They had time travel of a sort in *The Time Warrior*; how did they lose it? If they merely wanted to eliminate a rival then the Demat Gun may have erased their ability to travel through time. This opens the possibility for the Sontarans to try and steal other time travel experiments; will the player characters be there to stop them this time?

VARDANS

The Vardans are a race of energy beings, although they have the ability to shift into a solid humanoid form in order to interact with the physical world. When they materialise, they can choose to possess and absorb a humanoid host, or form a new body out of spontaneously conjured matter. By transmuting themselves into energy, Vardans move at the speed of light, or travel through communications systems. However, they cannot travel through the Vortex or hyperspace as energy, so they still need spaceships to travel from world to world safely. Culturally, the Vardan prize bureaucracy, military discipline and order. They despise weakness and cowardice. Despite their aggressive, hegemonic culture and array of alien powers, the Vardans fall prey to the Doctor's trap. He wrapped them in a time loop, removing them from the universe.

AWARENESS	3	PRESENCE	2
COORDINATION	2	RESOLVE	4
INGENUITY	3	STRENGTH	2

SKILLS
Athletics 1, Convince 3, Fighting 2, Knowledge 4, Marksman 3, Science 3, Subterfuge 4, Survival 1, Technology 3, Transport 3

TRAITS
Alien
Alien Appearance (Minor): Only when immaterial.
Weakness (Minor): Vardans can't use their powers against lead.
By The Book: Vardans are a highly disciplined and militaristic race.
Immaterial: Character cannot interact with physical objects unless it uses telekinesis. Takes and does no physical damage but energy attacks may still be lethal.
Natural Weapons (Major): A Vardan can release an electrical discharge that does (4/L/L) or (S/S/S) damage
Networked (Major): A Vardan has complete telepathic contact with nearby Vardans.
Psychic: +4 against mental attacks and may attempt to read minds.

Shapeshift (Major): A Vardan can assume a humanoid form at will; he only does this when he doesn't feel threatened.
Special – Energy Reflection: Any beam of energy fired at a Vardan is immediately reflected back against the shooter.
Teleport (Major): A Vardan can shift to another known location with an Awareness + Resolve roll. They can also follow communications signals to travel to locations they are not familiar with.

TECH LEVEL: 9   **STORY POINTS: 6**

RODAN

AWARENESS	4	PRESENCE	4
COORDINATION	3	RESOLVE	5
INGENUITY	6	STRENGTH	2

Rodan is a controller; she maintains the transduction barrier around Gallifrey and monitors threats. She was exiled with Leela into the wastes of Gallifrey, where she found it hard living. She returned to the Citadel and helped K-9 repair the transduction barrier, keeping out the Sontaran battle fleet.

SKILLS

Athletics 2, Convince 3, Craft 3, Fighting 1, Knowledge 4, Marksman 1, Medicine 2, Science 5, Technology 5, Transport 2

TRAITS

Attractive : +2 bonus to any rolls that involve the character's looks.
Boffin: Allows Rodan to create Gadgets.
Code of Conduct (Major): Rodan must follow the Laws of Time.
Feel the Turn of the Universe: +2 bonus to Awareness and Ingenuity to detect something wrong with time or space.
Run for your Life!: +1 bonus to your Speed when escaping pursuit.
Technically Adept: +2 to any Technology roll to fix a broken or faulty device.
Time Lord
Time Traveller (Minor)
Vortex: Rodan may pilot time craft through the Vortex, and gains +2 when doing so.

TECH LEVEL: 10   **STORY POINTS:** 6

COMMANDER ANDRED

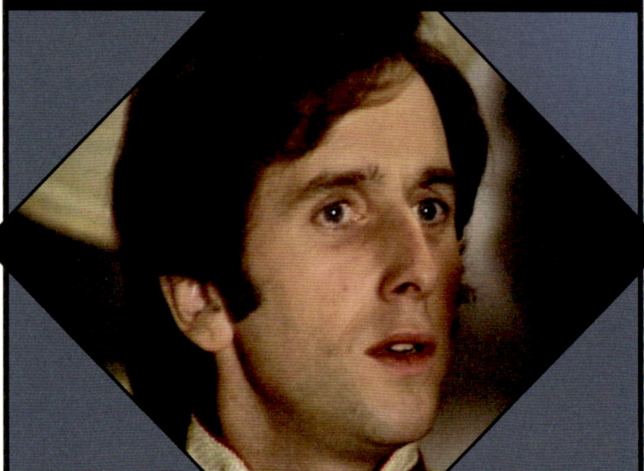

AWARENESS	3	PRESENCE	5
COORDINATION	4	RESOLVE	4
INGENUITY	4	STRENGTH	3

Commander Andred is the head of the Chancellery Guard. He is dedicated to his duty and attempted to kill the Doctor when he thought the renegade Time Lord had betrayed Gallifrey, but changed sides when the truth became apparent. During this adventure he fell in love with Leela and she remained on Gallifrey to be with him.

SKILLS

Athletics 3, Convince 4, Fighting 3, Knowledge 3, Marksman 4, Medicine 1, Science 2, Subterfuge 3, Survival 2, Technology 3, Transport 1

TRAITS

Attractive: +2 bonus to any rolls that involve the character's looks.
By the Book: Andred must be convinced to act against procedure.
Charming: +2 bonus to attempts to use charm.
Code of Conduct (Major): Andred follows Gallifreyan Law.
Psychic: +4 against mental attacks and he may attempt to read minds.
Voice of Authority: +2 bonus to Presence and Convince rolls.

EQUIPMENT: Staser

TECH LEVEL: 10   **STORY POINTS:** 8

THE KEY TO TIME

"I'm so sorry K-9, the holiday's off."

During an attempt to have a holiday, the TARDIS was pulled off course into the domain of the White Guardian. The urbane Guardian tasked the Doctor with a search for the six segments of the powerful and mythical Key to Time. When assembled, this cube-shaped device would allow the Guardian to reset the universe and rebalance the forces of light and darkness. The Doctor was less than keen, but was convinced when the Guardian promised that if the Doctor refused, nothing would happen to him. Ever again!

The Doctor was also told he would be assigned an assistant (something else he had no choice about) and warned that as there is a White Guardian there is also a Black Guardian who would also seek the power of the key.

The new assistant turned out to be a newly qualified Time Lady called Romanadvoratrelundar who graduated top of her class. Romana showed the Doctor the 'tracer' – the core to the Key to Time, which would help locate the segments. Much to the Doctor's dismay she had also put a put a connection port for the tracer in the TARDIS console so it could feed co-ordinates directly into the controls. Together, the Doctor and Romana set off to find the segments of the Key to Time, a search that took their next six adventures.

RUNNING THE ADVENTURE

If your players have proved trustworthy, or at least lucky, they may be sent after an artefact like the Key to Time. Even though the Doctor located the six segments, the cycle can begin again and the Guardians might need to reset the universe once more. You need not use the same adventures the Doctor did, as the segments could now be anywhere in the universe. Conversely, each of the adventures detailed below is easily run without the added factor of the search. The segment may not be an absolutely essential part of the adventure, although it often takes a central role. If you do decide to run the adventures as the search for the Key to Time, you may also decide to change the disguise each segment wears to keep your players on their toes. Here is a brief list of the segment's disguises, and some alternate items and objects that might be the segment instead:

THE RIBOS OPERATION (JETHRIK ORE)

- The staff of the Palace guard captain. It has some odd powers for such a primitive planet. Getting this ceremonial symbol of office will be tricky.
- A Shrivenzale. One of these dangerous beasts might be the segment, but only one, and the last thing you want to do is get close enough to touch it with the tracer and be wrong!
- The Crown Jewels. One of the Ribos Crown Jewels is the segment, which might mean an alliance with Garron and Unstoffe as they have the skills to run this sort of heist caper.

THE PIRATE PLANET (PLANET CALUFRAX)

- The Engines of Zanak. They can move a planet across space, which might easily be due to their power as a segment.
- The Body of Xanxia. Her bid for immortality might only be possible as she is actually a segment. Xanxia might know this, and do her best to avoid being 'reclaimed'.
- The Mentiads. The power of the group might actually come from the segment, which they keep in their sanctuary. Will they allow someone to take it if they discover it is actually the source of their power?

THE STONES OF BLOOD (SEAL OF DIPLOS)

- The Nine Maidens. Somewhat obvious, but one of the stones could be the segment. To make it harder to find, perhaps it is on the hyperspace craft and forms a link to allow Vivian to move in and out of hyperspace.
- Professor Rumford. The good professor might not only be the segment, but aware of being so, being an intelligent and canny woman. The stone circle somehow hides her power, and she will avoid being found by the player characters as much as possible. It is her involvement with the circle that allows Vivian to travel to hyperspace.
- The Megara. One of the coldly logical justice machines might be the key. However, would changing one into a segment be considered contempt of court?

THE ANDROIDS OF TARA (DRAGON STATUE)

- The Crown of Tara. This ancient piece of jewellery is one of Tara's greatest treasures. More importantly, a king cannot be crowned without it.
- Castle Gracht. This great fortress might not just be the family home of Count Grendal, but possibly the source of his power. Whoever controls the castle might be able to shift corridors around on intruders, and observe anyone inside it.
- The Archimandrite. This kindly old soul haunts the background of the story, but maybe he is more powerful than anyone realises.

THE POWER OF KROLL (KROLL)

- The Symbol of Kroll. Maybe Kroll didn't manage to consume the original form of the 5th segment and it still remains hidden in the old temple. The tribesmen would love to have it back, but won't be so keen to let a 'dryfoot' take it.
- Delta Magna III. As it was originally uninhabited, perhaps the moon itself is the segment, in the same way as Calufrax. The problem is what to do with all the people now living on it?
- The Refinery Bedrock. The reason the refinery is finding so much methane is because they have built it on top of the 5th segment. It is providing what they most desire. However, removing the segment will require destroying the bedrock the refinery rests on, as well as stopping the supply of methane.

THE ARMAGEDDON FACTOR (PRINCESS ASTRA)

- The Shadow. Maybe he is aware he is the final part and waiting to sacrifice himself for his master. It might also be possible he is fighting to avoid his fate. Finally, he might not know what he is, but feels a desperate need to possess the key that he doesn't understand.
- The Shadow's Base. With its mind-bending properties, perhaps the base itself is what gives the Shadow his power. The final segment might not fit into the key but surround it, protecting those inside from its effects. In which case possessing five segments might be enough to meddle with the universe, but not protect the wielder from such power.
- The Symbol of Peace. Atrios and Zeos got on rather well before the Shadow came alone. So maybe they had a symbol of peace they shared custody of as a symbol of their unity. The theft of this symbol might be what provoked war, especially if as a segment it had some sort of power. The question then remains, where is the symbol now? Did the Shadow steal it or is he still looking for it? If so, who did steal it?

THE GUARDIANS

The White Guardian, and his counterpart the Black Guardian, are two of the most cryptic entities ever encountered by the Doctor in his travels. The Guardians appear to be the incarnations of universal forces instead of individuals in their own right – they are Chaos and Order, Darkness and Light made flesh, and one cannot exist without the other. The White Guardian, at least, is on good terms with the Time Lords of Gallifrey.

The Guardians are discussed further in **The Fifth Doctor Sourcebook**.

THE RIBOS OPERATION

'I'm not anticipating any trouble, but it's as well to be prepared for these things.'

⊙ SYNOPSIS

Ribos, The Future

On the icy planet of Ribos, two men called Garron and Unstoffe set up a con trick against the deposed warlord the Graff Vynda-K. They planned to sell him the planet Ribos, after convincing him it possessed a plentiful supply of the valuable mineral 'Jethrik'. When the Graff arrived on Ribos, he brought his Marshall Sholakh and a full unit of guards. Garron advised him that they should keep a low profile as the planet of Ribos was a primitive world, making it a place travellers must not interfere with under galactic law.

Having been given a series of false mining reports and a genuine rock of Jethrik, the Graff was convinced that buying Ribos would make him rich. With the wealth that mining Ribos would bring he would be able to build a battlefleet to reclaim his homeworld Livithia. Not entirely trusting Garron and Unstoffe he put his money and the Jethrik in a vault, which was exactly where the con artists intended to

steal it from. They planned to be long gone before the Graff notices his wealth was missing.

Unfortunately, the Doctor and Romana got in the way of the con and the Graff discovered his wealth missing far too early. He became enraged and hunted both the con men and the Doctor and Romana (believing them to be accomplices) forcing them to take shelter in the dangerous catacombs. Deep in the monster-filled catacombs, the Doctor realised Garron and Unstoffe's rock of Jethrik must be the segment they were looking for.

Having suffered the loss of several guards and his loyal Marshall Sholakh, the Graff lost his mind and embarked on a killing spree. He gave a powerful explosive to his last guard, with the intent of sealing the catacombs off for good, trapping Romana, Garron and Unstoffe. However, the guard turned out to be the Doctor in disguise who secretly planted the explosives on the Graff. As he charged off, dreaming of glory and madness, the Graff was killed by his own explosives.

With the Graff and his men disposed of, the Doctor, Romana, Garron and Unstoffe escaped the catacombs. While he hadn't sold a planet, Garron still had the Graff's money. The Doctor used sleight of hand to relieve Garron of his precious lump of Jethrik. Back aboard the TARDIS the Doctor and Romana used the tracer to convert the Jethrik into its true form – the first segment of the Key to Time.

CONTINUITY

Romana reveals the Doctor's age is 759 (although the Doctor insists it is only 756) implying he is certainly more than 'middle aged' and past his prime. Romana herself is a mere 140. While both the Doctor and Romana graduated from the Time Lord Academy, she achieved a 'triple first' while he only managed to scrape through with 51% on the second attempt.

The White and Black Guardians will return to haunt the Doctor, especially in his fifth incarnation. They represent extremely powerful universal forces, but are bound by clear rules of engagement in their conflicts. Exploiting these rules is often the only way to defeat them.

In the brief time after she arrives on the TARDIS and the Doctor returns from the meeting with the White Guardian, Romana has remodelled the console with a socket for the Tracer. This implies that changes to the 'desktop theme' are a matter of programming rather than craftwork.

We also learn something of 'local galactic law'. The peace is kept by a large conglomeration of planets called the Alliance. They manage disputes over sovereign territory but also command a combined war fleet and have an expansionist agenda. Ribos itself is a Grade 3 planet and as such no alliance member may interfere with its development. When it achieves spaceflight it will become Grade 2, allowing other planets of the Alliance to trade with it.

This series of adventures was also the first plot arc that linked several of the Doctor's adventures together. This device, similar to creating a campaign, will be used again most notably for the E-space trilogy and the Sixth Doctor's ***Trial of the Time Lord***.

☉ RUNNING THE ADVENTURE

This adventure is a caper that the player characters find themselves in the middle of. The plan is simple: convince a greedy noble that the planet is rich in minerals and offer to sell it to them, then steal the money the mark brings from a vault you already know how to get into. Your players might be the con artists or find themselves getting in the middle of the con and making a mess of things. They could even be the intended victims.

Generally, this adventure is very freeform, with the events depending on how the player characters end up in the middle of it. This makes it very easy to adapt. What if they run into the Graff first, or get caught by the guards trying to open the jewel vault? One failed roll and they are on a different track. However, the Gamemaster might also switch the morality of the NPCs to really change things around. Garron and Unstoffe, while apparently charming, might be ruthless criminals, willing to stop at nothing to secure the wealth they are after. The Graff might be a caring ruler who seeks to free his people from a terrible despot. His wealth might even come from charitable donations from people who have sold everything to help their only hope for a free Livithia.

RIBOS

The planet Ribos is a small, primitive world, but well placed only three light centuries from the Magellanic clouds. It has an odd orbit that means it spends over thirty years in the grip of a continual winter, before enjoying a similar period of summertime. Its technology level is a little ahead of medieval and the people have no knowledge of the universe outside their world. In fact, the very idea that the stars are not ice crystals hanging in the sky is considered heresy.

Ribos has one capital city, Shur, a fortified city of stone ruled by the palace guard. Most of the other habitations on the planet are small settlements that lie to the north of Shur. As there is little communication between settlements, visitors are advised to simply claim they are 'from the north' to avoid suspicion.

KEY LOCATIONS IN SHUR

- **The Palace Vault:** The Crown Jewels of Ribos are held in a very secure vault in the palace. By day, the palace guards stand watch over the glass cabinet that holds the wealth of Ribos. This cabinet is protected by a very complicated lock that uses multi-levered interlocks, enough to slow down even a Sonic Screwdriver. By night they release a vicious beast, the Shrivenzale, into the room to devour any interlopers.

- **Guest Quarters:** Privileged guests can take rooms in the palace, for a price. These guest quarters are a little primitive for those used to a high tech level but very well appointed.

- **The Poor Quarter:** While there is wealth in Ribos, there is also poverty. Low-quality housing, little more than a small shed, is put aside here for those with little or no money. These hovels surround a square that provides a well for fresh water. The square also functions as a marketplace and can be very busy during the day. Those who live in the poor quarter are lost and forgotten. Luckily crime isn't especially rife here as few of the inhabitants have the energy to brave the cold and seek victims.

- **The Catacombs:** This series of natural caves has been made into a necropolis for the dead of Ribos. Alcoves in the walls store the remains of the dead, and mourners can leave offerings here for those who have passed. The place is a maze though and it is very easy to get lost here. As it is the realm of the dead, few people wander the maze without good reason, fearing it populated with ghosts and spirits. What makes it dangerous is that the catacombs lead into the deeper caves where the Shrivenzale live, in numbers. While a few roam into the catacombs, most prefer the deeps.

FURTHER ADVENTURES

- **Freedom for Livithia:** While the Graff may be dead, he may have several supporters on Livithia looking to take the throne from his nephew. However the nephew may be just as much of a despot as Vynda-K. Can the player characters see to it that the right person sits on the throne?

- **The Legacy of Binro:** The theocracy of Ribos still insists they are alone in the universe. While interference is punishable under galactic law, the player characters might decide to bring the truth to Ribos.

- **Grifting the Galaxy:** This might not be the only time the player characters encounter Garron and Unstoffe. They might choose to assist

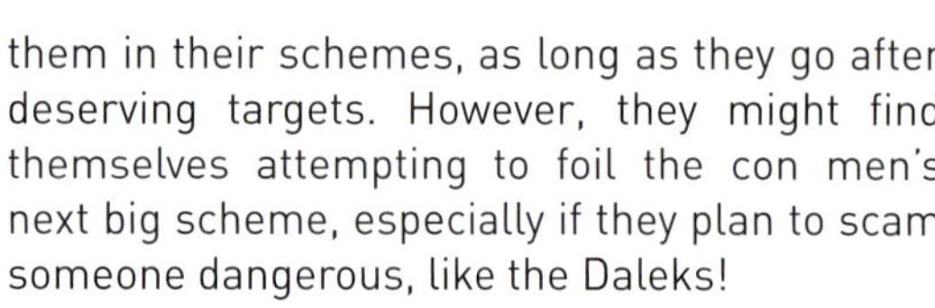

them in their schemes, as long as they go after deserving targets. However, they might find themselves attempting to foil the con men's next big scheme, especially if they plan to scam someone dangerous, like the Daleks!

- **Menace from the North:** While most of Ribos civilisation is in Shur, it isn't the only place you might adventure on the planet. Out in the wild cold of the northlands might lurk any manner of dangers. The tribes might seek to invade the capital to steal its treasures, or they might be on the verge of war between each other over the limited resources. Strange and powerful creatures might lurk in the snowy wastes. It is a land ripe for Norse adventure. The story of Grendel might prove inspiring when the player characters lose their TARDIS in a snowstorm and need a place to stay.

MARSHALL SHOLAKH

AWARENESS	3	PRESENCE	2
COORDINATION	3	RESOLVE	5
INGENUITY	2	STRENGTH	5

Sholakh is the Graff's right-hand man, and the only person who has remained by his side. He is not only the only man the Graff trusts, but the closest thing he has to a friend. Sholakh has been rewarded for his dedication and honestly believes the Graff will one day return to his rightful place, where he will offer rich rewards to those who served him loyally. However, what Sholakh really wants is a war. He lives for combat and fighting and knows the Graff will lead him in never-ending battle across the cosmos.

SKILLS
Athletics 3, Fighting 5, Knowledge 2, Marksman 3, Subterfuge 2, Survival 4, Technology 2, Transport 2

TRAITS
Keen Senses (Major): +2 to Awareness rolls.
Quick Reflexes: Always goes first in their Action Round unless taken by surprise.
Obligation (Major): Serve the Graff until death.
Unattractive: -2 penalty to any rolls that involve the character's looks. May provide +2 to intimidate rolls at GMs discretion.

EQUIPMENT: Mercenary Armour (3 points), Sword (Strength +2 damage) and Laser Wand (4/L/L)

TECH LEVEL: 6   STORY POINTS: 3

GRAFF VYNDA-K

AWARENESS	2	PRESENCE	2
COORDINATION	4	RESOLVE	5
INGENUITY	2	STRENGTH	3

The Graff is a deluded, psychotic madman with the barest of manners. Born to privilege he is utterly selfish and full of his own self importance, seeing even his most loyal companions as tools and slaves. He is unable to see his own shortcomings and failures, always blaming others when things don't go his way. He has no problem with ordering the deaths of others when it suits him. He was once the despotic ruler of the planet of Livithia, until his nephew led a rebellion against him and forced him into exile. However, the Graff is so deluded he firmly believes his people will rise up against the usurper on his glorious return and welcome him with open arms.

SKILLS
Athletics 3, Fighting 4, Marksman 4, Technology 2

TRAITS
Quick Reflexes: The Graff always goes first in his Action Round unless taken by surprise.
Voice of Authority: +2 bonus to Presence and Convince rolls.
Eccentric (Major): Arrogant megalomaniac.
Impulsive: He doesn't think things through before acting.
Obsession (Major): Reclaim the crown of Livithia at all costs!
Outcast: -2 to social rolls with Livithians when recognised.
Selfish: Vynda-K puts his own needs first.

EQUIPMENT: Royal Armour (3 points), Sword (Strength +2 damage) and Laser Wand (4/L/L)

TECH LEVEL: 6   STORY POINTS: 9

THE SHRIVENZALE

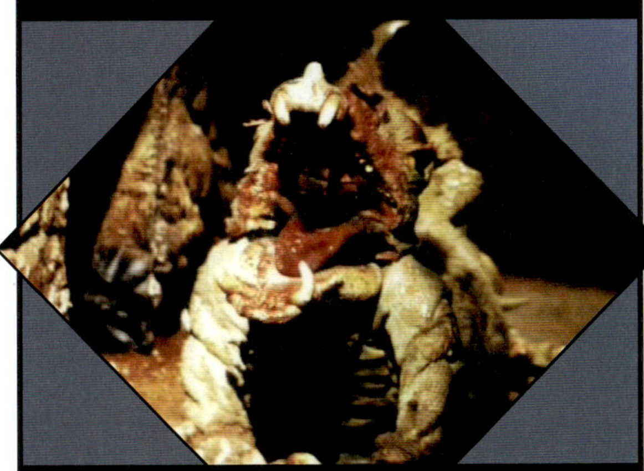

AWARENESS	3	PRESENCE	3
COORDINATION	3	RESOLVE	2
INGENUITY	1	STRENGTH	5

The Shrivenzale are found in the caverns of Ribos, and rarely venture out into the light. However, one is kept in the palace to guard the Crown Jewels over night. Shrivenzale are quite slow, and being nocturnal shy away from light. They are about the size of a large pig, but with powerful teeth and claws they are easily capable of consuming whatever prey crosses their path.

Shrivenzale generally hunt alone, although groups of two or three are not unknown. With food scarce, they tend to attack and eat anything they find, and live off a layer of fat when they cannot find anything.

SKILLS
Fighting 4, Survival 3

TRAITS
Fear Factor 1: Grants a +2 bonus to inspire fear.
Natural Weapons (Minor): Shivenzale have powerful teeth and claws that do Strength +2 damage.
Tough: Reduce total damage by 2.
Slow Reflexes: Always acts last in their Action Round.

STORY POINTS: 4

UNSTOFFE

AWARENESS	3	PRESENCE	3
COORDINATION	3	RESOLVE	3
INGENUITY	3	STRENGTH	3

While he has been part of Garron's con games for some time, Unstoffe is still uncomfortable with doing wrong. He sees himself as more of a Robin Hood figure, only stealing from those that can afford it. However, deep down he knows the truth, which is that he will never make as much money doing anything else.

While he recognises Garron has more experience, he is beginning to tire of being 'mentored'. He seems to always get the rubbish jobs and his opinion is rarely listened to. He often feels as if Garron is running some sort of scam on him, even though they are partners. Otherwise he considers Garron a friend, although that might be because he doesn't have any others.

SKILLS
Athletics 3, Convince 3, Fighting 1, Subterfuge 3, Technology 3, Transport 2

TRAITS
Charming: +2 bonus to attempts to use charm.
Quick Reflexes: Always goes first in his Action Round unless taken by surprise.
Cowardly: -2 penalty to any fear roll.

TECH LEVEL: 6   STORY POINTS: 6

THE SEEKER

AWARENESS	4	PRESENCE	3
COORDINATION	2	RESOLVE	3
INGENUITY	3	STRENGTH	2

Seekers are part of an old order on Ribos that use bones and charms to hunt down criminals. Part soothsayer, part priest and part hunter, these relics of a more primitive age have surprisingly good results. It takes many years to learn how to read the auguries of the bones the seeker's use, but those who can are able to track a target accurately to their hiding place.

SKILLS

Convince 2, Craft 2, Knowledge 2, Medicine 3, Survival 2

TRAITS

Clairvoyance: The Seeker can see other locations, range limited by her Resolve.
Keen Senses (Major): +2 to all Awareness rolls.
Precognition: Gets glimpses of the future, which she may force by spending a Story Point.
Psychic: +4 against mental attacks and may attempt to read minds.
Sense of Direction: +2 bonus to any navigation roll.
Distinctive: -2 penalty to rolls to blend in. Others have a +2 bonus to remember or recognise the character.

EQUIPMENT: Ceremonial robes, augury bones

TECH LEVEL: 2   **STORY POINTS:** 6

GARRON

AWARENESS	3	PRESENCE	5
COORDINATION	4	RESOLVE	3
INGENUITY	4	STRENGTH	2

Garron has worked as a con man for most of his life. He has run hundreds of scams on hundreds of planets and rarely done any jail time. He prefers to steal from the rich, but only because they have more money. Garron doesn't like to get people hurt, as it tends to complicate the plan. What he enjoys most about running a scam (apart from the payoff) is proving himself cleverer than the mark. As he is getting older, Garron avoids the heavy lifting, but is also looking for a big score he can retire on.

SKILLS

Convince 5, Fighting 1, Knowledge 2, Science 3, Subterfuge 4, Technology 3, Transport 2

TRAITS

Charming: +2 bonus to attempts to use charm.
Empathic: +2 bonus on rolls to 'read' another person.
Quick Reflexes: Always goes first in their Action Round unless taken by surprise.
Cowardly: -2 penalty to any fear roll.
Obsession (Minor): Always looking to get rich.
Selfish: Puts his own needs first.

TECH LEVEL: 6   **STORY POINTS:** 6

THE PIRATE PLANET

'Extraordinary. The place is littered with them; diamonds, Andromedan bloodstones, gravel, more diamonds. Don't they have street sweepers here?'

⊘ SYNOPSIS

The coordinates of Calufrax, the Future

After declaring how simple locating the first segment was, the Doctor managed to land the TARDIS badly on the wrong planet when they set off for the second segment. Strangely, they were at the right coordinates for Calufrax – the planet where they intended to go – so they set out to investigate. Romana found the tracer was giving wild readings, so Doctor tried to interview some of the locals for more information, and learned that it was a new 'Golden Age' on Zanak. These Golden Ages appeared to be happening with alarming regularity; each time, the 'Captain' made an announcement and then there were lights and omens in the sky, and the points of light in the night sky changed. Then the mines filled up again with gemstones, and everyone was rich. There was so much wealth even rare minerals like Oolian were found lying around on the street.

The Time Lords were interrupted by screams from the nearby home of elderly Balaton. Balaton's grandson Pralix was ill, and there was nothing

Balaton, his granddaughter Mula or their friend Kimus could do. The Doctor saved Pralix from the city guard who came to execute him in case the sickness took hold and he joined the Mentiads. However, the Doctor failed to save Pralix from the Mentiads themselves when they arrived. Meanwhile, Romana continued looking for the segment but ran afoul of a guard and was taken by air car to the great citadel high above the city called the Bridge. The Doctor set off with Kimus to steal an air car and rescue her, while Mula went with K-9 to find the Mentiads and her brother.

On the Bridge, Romana was brought before the Captain, a cybernetic tyrant who needed a nurse to keep his blood pressure under control. He decided to execute Romana on a whim, but stayed his hand when she insisted she could repair a vital system that the Captain's engineer Mr Fibuli had declared unsalvageable. When the Doctor arrived to rescue Romana he found she had the situation in hand, and the Captain ordered them to be taken to the engine room to see what they could repair. A look around the engine room confirmed what the Doctor suspected, the bridge and engines were actually the remains of a crashed spacecraft. The Doctor and Romana escaped the engine room with Kimus' help and made their way to the mines to investigate a new theory of the Doctor's.

Deep in the mines the Doctor and Romana found the ground was icy and cold, not cavernous. They were not standing on the interior of Zanak, but the surface of Calufrax! It appeared that Zanak was hollow and the Captain used the vast engines to dematerialise Zanak and rematerialise it over other planets so they could envelop them and strip mine their minerals. Whole planets were being stolen to power the Golden Ages of Zanak, murdering billions. Escaping more of the city guard, they joined the Mentiads at their sanctuary. The Mentiads were discovered to be powerful psychics who were growing stronger as they absorbed the life force energies of the murdered planets and their people. They also told the Doctor of Zanak's history and how it was a prosperous planet until the reign of Queen Xanxia. She drained the planet dry of resources trying to wage vast interstellar wars that led to nothing. Zanak was saved from near destruction by the Captain, whose ship, the *Vantarialis*, crashed on Zanak many years ago. He was the only survivor, and even then only due to extensive cybernetic surgery. It was his engineering skills that allowed the Golden Ages to come about and he had ruled Zanak ever since.

On the bridge, the Captain was pleased to hear Mr Fibuli could create a field to nullify the Mentiads' powers, using the gems harvested from Calufrax. He ordered mine production to be increased to maximum and for another planetary jump to be plotted. The new target was a small body in a backward system that the inhabitants referred to as the planet 'Earth'. The Doctor and Kimus were captured attempting to get to the bridge, but Romana, Mula and the Mentiads managed to sneak in by a secret entrance and planned to disrupt the engines before Zanak jumped again.

As a prisoner of the Captain, the Doctor was shown the remains of the planets Zanak had destroyed, held in a delicately balanced stasis of huge compressed matter. The Captain insisted it was more than just an exhibition but his key to power. The Doctor was rescued by Kimus and K-9, who also managed to destroy Polly, the Captain's murderous robotic parrot. They escaped into a hidden room where they found the wizened remains of Queen Xanxia suspended in the last seconds of life by a series of 'Time Dams'. Putting the pieces together, the Doctor returned to the bridge to confront the Captain, and revealed the nurse was actually the true leader of Zanak. She was a living hologram of Queen Xanxia, who was using the Time Dams around her real body to become immortal. Soon, she believed her holographic form would be fully corporeal and she would regenerate forever. She was not pleased when the Doctor informed her she is wrong. The longer the Time Dams remained active, the more energy they would need. Even consuming whole planets would eventually not be enough to give Xanxia the power she needed for immortality.

Unfortunately, Xanxia was happy to destroy the galaxy to gain immortality. She ordered the Captain to continue the next jump and consume the Earth. The Mentiads attempted to stop the engines, but the Captain's psychic damper field blocked their power. The Doctor and Romana used the TARDIS to interfere with Zanak's dematerialisation, bringing the TARDIS to the edge of destruction. Still unable to stop the engines, the Doctor told the Mentiads to instead focus on lifting a spanner in the engine room and smashing the controls. The resulting back-blast shattered the Bridge. In the aftermath the Captain turned on Xanxia, who killed him, but who was in turn destroyed by Kimus whose blaster shot disrupted her holographic body.

To fill the hollow centre of Zanak, the Doctor used the TARDIS to shift the gallery of planets into the centre of Zanak – all but one anyway. The remains of Calufrax were discovered to be the second segment of the Key to Time, which the Doctor and Romana kept for themselves. To deal with the Time Dams the Doctor suggested the more direct approach of blowing up the Bridge forever. As the Mentiads push the plunger and Kimus and Mula consider the new future of Zanak, the Doctor and Romana quietly slip away to continue their search for the third segment.

CONTINUITY

The Doctor 'name drops' that he met Isaac Newton, who failed to pick up his clue about gravity when the Doctor dropped an apple on his head. However, not being especially known for his subtlety, the Doctor explained the principles to Newton over dinner.

Calufrax Minor, which is at least in the same system as Calufrax, is listed as one of the missing planets in the 10th Doctor adventure 'The Stolen Earth'. Given that Zanak ends the adventure in Calufrax's position, the population might have renamed Zanak to Calufrax Minor.

RUNNING THE ADVENTURE

This adventure begins as an investigation, but might quickly turn into a running gun battle if the player characters choose to meet violence with violence. Unfortunately, if they decide to lead a revolution they are unlikely to discover the secret of Zanak and its Golden Ages, and are even less likely to discover the body of Xanxia. As with **The Ribos Operation**, there is a very freeform nature to this adventure and how it plays out will very much depend on the player characters. If they prove themselves useful with their technical ability they can easily ingratiate themselves with the Captain. However, psychic characters might more readily side with the Mentiads and lead a revolution.

There are several ways to adapt the story for a group already familiar with it. Firstly, the Mentiads may not be the good guys. It is they who are moving the planet around to consume others so they might drain the life force to power their abilities. The Captain is simply taking advantage by mining the mineral wealth. Xanxia herself might be the segment and the Time Dams are instead draining her energy to power the planet's piracy. Finally, the nurse may not really be Xanxia herself, but her descendant. The Captain is really in charge and holds her prisoner in the hopes of later taking the crown of Zanak legitimately. Alternatively, the Captain is unaware of the nurse's true identity, and she has worked years to get this close, seeking a chance to kill the Captain and restore her crown.

"THE WHOLE INFRASTRUCTURE OF QUANTUM PHYSICS WAS IN RETREAT"

The Doctor's adventures take place on a broad canvas. They deal with the fate of whole planets, with the rise and fall of vast interstellar empires, with the survival of the whole universe! They're big adventures.

Sometimes, it's worth being absurd. The idea of a hollow planet that runs around the galaxy stealing other planets is one thing – but when you stick a cyber-pirate with a psychotic robot parrot on top, it stops being silly and becomes wonderfully absurd. If you're going to go over the top, don't go a little over the top – strap on your rocket boots and fly!

If you have an idea for an adventure that could be a bit weird, make it very weird. Take **Voyage of the Damned** in **The Tenth Doctor Sourcebook**. A crashing space liner that's basically *The Poseidon Adventure* – in spaaaace! – could be a bit cheesy. Turn it into a scale model of the Titanic, though, and that pushes things from cheesy to brilliantly absurd. Make the players laugh manically at how ridiculous their peril is even as they risk their lives to save the day.

Psychic Abilities

The powerful life force energy on Zanak that gives the Mentiads their power, greatly enhances psychic abilities, including those of psychic player characters. Psychic abilities used on Zanak are very powerful, and the player may double any bonuses gained by spending Story Points.

Upon arrival on the planet, any psychic character will be contacted telepathically by the Mentiads to discern if the character is a threat; if not they will offer an invitation to their order. This allows psychic characters to connect their powers to those of the Mentiads. If they connect their powers to the

Mentiads they must remain close by to benefit, but so long as they do so they gain a constant telepathic connection to the others in the group.

New Psychic Traits

Psychic Shield (Major Good) – prerequisite: Psychic

The character can manifest a powerful shield of mental energy that protects them from physical harm. Manifesting the shield requires no roll, but if the character performs any other action they must make a Resolve + Awareness roll (Difficulty 18) and if they fail it the shield vanishes with their loss of concentration.

The shield can absorb twice the character's Resolve in damage points each round it is maintained. Lethal damage is considered 12 damage points for purposes of shield damage.

Psychic Stun (Major Good) – prerequisite: Psychic

This trait allows a psychic character to blast an opponent with psychic force, overwhelming them into unconsciousness. The character selects a single target and both must make a double Resolve roll. If the psychic character only just succeeds, the target remains conscious but cannot act. They may attempt to stun the target again next round. A Good Success renders the target unconscious, and a Fantastic Success also reduces the target's Resolve by 2 when they awaken.

Should the attack fail the victim's mind has proved too strong and no further attempt can be tried. A Disastrous Failure instead knocks the psychic out, if their target has any form of psychic ability themselves.

ZANAK

The planet Zanak is a place of luxury and wealth, where during the Golden Ages precious stones can be found littering the streets. The cities are built of smooth stone and are open and spacious. The people dress in colourful, layered fabrics, unashamed of their wealth. No one works for a living, with all their needs provided for by trade and automated systems. However, this plenty masks a totalitarian military dictatorship, where wealth and comfort are used to keep the population under control. Those who step out of line or start to ask questions are executed as quickly as possible, often without trial. Some feel they should speak out, but no one wants to bring about the end of the Golden Ages, so long as the authorities aren't coming to arrest their family.

KEY LOCATIONS ON ZANAK

- **The Colonnade:** Dotted throughout the city are several courtyards and colonnades. Most people in the city go for walks through the courtyards and they often serve as meeting places.

- **House of Balaton:** Balaton owns a typical house in the city, sharing it with his grandchildren Mula and Pralix. Open and minimalist, the house is decorated in rich tapestries. Doors and windows are simply open arches to keep the house cool, and ensure no citizen can impede the city guard by locking their doors.

- **The Mentiad's Sanctuary:** Outside the city, the Mentiads live in a small series of abandoned chambers. This sanctuary serves as home and temple where they might gather their power and stay away from the city guards.

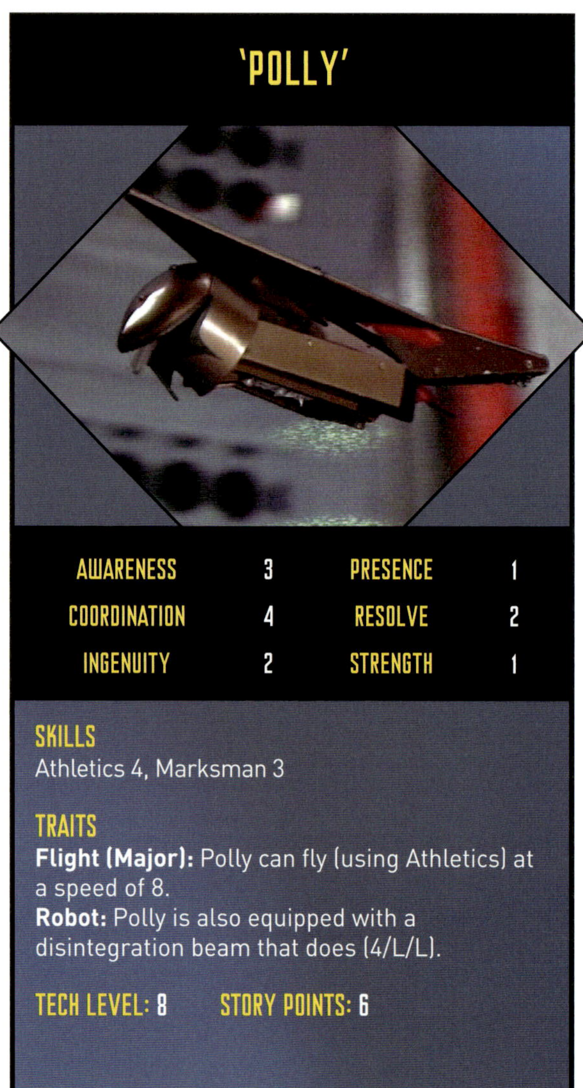

AWARENESS	3	PRESENCE	1
COORDINATION	4	RESOLVE	2
INGENUITY	2	STRENGTH	1

SKILLS
Athletics 4, Marksman 3

TRAITS
Flight (Major): Polly can fly (using Athletics) at a speed of 8.
Robot: Polly is also equipped with a disintegration beam that does (4/L/L).

TECH LEVEL: 8   **STORY POINTS: 6**

THE BRIDGE

Sitting so high on a mountaintop, the Bridge is effectively the royal palace of Zanak. In fact it is a crashed spacecraft, adapted to serve as the control and engine room for moving Zanak across space. An air car is the only official way to reach the Bridge, but a few secret entrances lie at its base for those who like a climb.

KEY LOCATIONS IN THE BRIDGE

- **The Control Room:** At the top of the bridge lies the control room, which also functions as the Captain's throne room. From here the functions of the engines can be controlled as

can the advanced surveillance systems used to watch the populace. An open window leads to an execution platform high above the mountains where prisoners are forced to 'walk the plank' to their death, a spectacle the Captain very much enjoys. At the back of the room is the gallery of planetary remains whose gigantic mass is held in a delicate balance.

- **The Engine Room:** The vast engines of Zanak are located deep in the Bridge. They are capable of moving an entire planet through space and require enormous power. This means that jumps must be carefully planned and managed to avoid any failure leading to an energy backlash. The

THE CAPTAIN

The survivor of a terrible crash, the Captain is half machine now. He is nominally the leader of Zanak and the driving force behind its Golden Ages. While he is a blustering bully he is also a very skilled engineer, having rebuilt his crashed spacecraft's engines so they can move a planet across space. He also created a gallery of the remains of the stolen planets, all billions of tonnes of them balanced precisely to avoid them turning into black holes. In truth, the Captain is a slave to Queen Xanxia. On the verge of death after the crash of his ship, she oversaw his cybernetic resurrection. To ensure his loyalty she retained control of his implants, making him little more than her puppet. However, he refused to bow to his tormentor and has spent his time plotting revenge, with such obsession that he cared little how many planets were destroyed to bring him closer to freedom. For all his power the Captain lives a lonely life, his only friend being Polly, his murderous 'polyphase avatron' robotic parrot, and Mr Fibuli, who he constantly threatens with execution.

AWARENESS	3	PRESENCE	4
COORDINATION	3	RESOLVE	3
INGENUITY	6	STRENGTH	4

SKILLS
Athletics 2, Convince 2, Craft 4, Fighting 3, Knowledge 3, Marksman 4, Science 5, Technology 5, Transport 5

TRAITS
Boffin: He's a hyperspatial genius.
Cyborg (Special): Equipped with several input devices to pull data from the bridge systems and a laser pistol built into his arm (4/L/L).
Technically Adept: +2 to any Technology roll to fix a broken or faulty device.
Voice of Authority: +2 bonus to Presence and Convince rolls.
Distinctive: -2 penalty to rolls to blend in. Others have a +2 bonus to remember or recognise the Captain.

Weakness (Major): Nurse's control pad can do 4 levels of damage to the Captain each round by shutting him down.

TECH LEVEL: 8   STORY POINTS: 10

engines themselves are housed on several levels, with gantries and steps allowing technicians to access the maze of machinery.

- **Xanxia's Chamber:** In this secret room is the wretched body of Queen Xanxia, held in the last moments of life by large screens called Time Dams. The Time Dams require obscene amounts of energy to keep the Queen frozen in time, while her consciousness inhabits the holographic form of the Captain's Nurse. The chamber remains unguarded as Xanxia trusts no one with its location.

FURTHER ADVENTURES

- **Xanxia's Legacy:** In her quest for everlasting life, Xanxia dealt with some very unsavoury and advanced people. Rogue Time Agents, renegade Time Lords and anyone else she could learn what she needed from. Some of these dangerous criminals have heard what she achieved and come to Zanak to discover how far she actually got, and how to construct pirate planets of their own.

- **The New Revolution:** While the people of Zanak are finally free, none of them have any idea how to manage their own government. Used to either tyrants or indolent prosperity they have no skills or any idea of how to make decisions for themselves. Those few who have taken control are facing political rivalry at every turn. The situation is devolving fast. Those in charge are too busy trying to feed the people to properly fight the political battle. Who will they turn to in

---

THE NURSE/QUEEN XANXIA

The most terrible tyrant in Zanak's history was Queen Xanxia. She led wars and hollowed out her own planet in the pursuit of power. When she was gone the people rejoiced, and the Captain's arrival begun a series of Golden Ages. But Xanxia was not gone. Disguising herself as the Captain's nurse, she bided her time as her plan for immortality took on its horrible magnitude. Trapping her body between Time Dams she held it in the last seconds of life. Meanwhile she built a holographic body, channelling such power into it that it gradually became corporeal. Unfortunately, her calculations are wrong, and there is not enough power in the universe to maintain her life forever. Xanxia's arrogance is of universal proportions. She cares nothing for anyone but herself, and is willing to destroy planets to extend her life. The immorality of her actions causes her no concern at all. As far as she is concerned, no one in the universe is more important than her or her needs.

AWARENESS	3	**PRESENCE**	3
COORDINATION	3	**RESOLVE**	5
INGENUITY	5	**STRENGTH**	2

SKILLS
Convince 3, Knowledge 2, Marksman 2, Medicine 4, Science 4, Subterfuge 4, Technology 3

TRAITS
Indomitable: +4 bonus to any rolls to resist psychic control.
Immortal (Major): Xanxia's holographic form can be discorporated for a while but only destroying her true body will kill her.
Voice of Authority: +2 bonus to Presence and Convince rolls.
Dark Secret (Minor): Xanxia hides her true identity with her position as the Captain's nurse.

Obsession (Major): Xanxia will destroy the universe in her quest for true immortality.

TECH LEVEL: 7   **STORY POINTS: 8**

their hour of need, and will those who offer help have truly pure motives?

- **The Captain's Ship:** The *Vantarialis* was the Captain's ship before he crashed, the "greatest raiding cruiser ever built." Just what sort of ship was it that needed engines that can teleport a *whole planet* across hyperspace even *after* it crashed? When that ship was intact, it must have been something truly astonishing. Where was the Captain raiding? Other dimensions? Worlds locked away behind transduction barriers? Other universes?

MR FIBULI

AWARENESS	3	PRESENCE	2
COORDINATION	3	RESOLVE	2
INGENUITY	4	STRENGTH	2

Poor put-upon Mr Fibuli serves as the Captain's taskmaster on the Bridge. He organises the operations of the Bridge, plots the planetary jumps and reports on the wealth they have stolen. In every encounter with the Captain he is threatened with instant execution, to the point that he considers it just another part of the working day. While Mr Fibuli is pleasant and polite, he is really no better than Xanxia and the Captain. He is happy to ignore his moral responsibility by claiming he is 'just following orders'. While the wealth and power is not as important to Mr Fibuli as his colleagues, he is just as invested in the project, being fascinated by the science of moving a planet across space.

SKILLS
Craft 3, Knowledge 2, Science 5, Technology 4

TRAITS
Boffin: Allows the character to create Gadgets.
Face in the Crowd: +2 to any Subterfuge rolls to sneak about.
By the Book: It's a big book. The Captain wrote it. If the book gets thrown at someone, that someone's dead.
Obligation (Major): Serve the Captain well, or be executed.
Unadventurous (Minor): Fibuli avoids adventure and excitement – as much as the first officer of a planet-eating planet that chews up the laws of physics every time it jumps can be said to 'avoid adventure and excitement'.

TECH LEVEL: 6   **STORY POINTS:** 3

MENTIAD

AWARENESS	4	PRESENCE	3
COORDINATION	3	RESOLVE	4
INGENUITY	3	STRENGTH	2

The Mentiads are a community of psychics that draw incredible mental power from their ability to share and enhance their psionic abilities. The destruction of each planet taken by Zanak often releases so much energy that nascent psychics begin to tap into the Mentiad hive mind. They do their best to get to the psychic in question before the city guard obey their standing orders to execute them on sight. Mentiads are not especially powerful alone, which is why they travel as a group. While in close contact they can share their power and coordinate their abilities. In such a state their powers are magnified to the point of almost being invulnerable.

SKILLS
Knowledge 3, Science 2, Survival 2

TRAITS
Clairvoyance: The Mentiads can see other locations, range limited to their Resolve.
Precognition: The Mentiads gets glimpses of the future, which they may force by spending a Story Point.
Psychic: +4 against mental attacks and the Mentiads may attempt to read minds.
Psychic Shield: May create a powerful shield against attacks.
Psychic Stun: Mentiads can blast an opponent with psychic force.
Telekinesis: Mentiads may move objects using Resolve instead of Strength.
Telepathy: May create a mental link to read minds or converse telepathically.

TECH LEVEL: 5   **STORY POINTS:** 8

THE STONES OF BLOOD

'I always knew it was a matter of time before another professional came in and noticed the discrepancies.'

SYNOPSIS

Cornwall, Earth, Present Day

The tracer led the Doctor, Romana and K-9 to Earth. Specifically, to an old stone circle called the Nine Travellers, where they met the aging but stalwart archaeologist Professor Amelia Rumford and her assistant Vivian Fay. The Professor has spent most of her career studying the site and assumed the Time Lords to be fellow academics. She told them no one has yet got an answer for to the mystery of why there are more stones there now than there once was.

When the Doctor came across traces of blood in the circle Vivian told him it was probably the work of the local Druidic cult, led by Leonard De Vries, who she and the professor dismissed as cranks. Leaving Romana with the two scientists, the Doctor set off to visit De Vries at his estate. While initially polite, De Vries knocked the Doctor unconscious and decided he would be the next sacrifice to his goddess, the Cailleach. The Doctor awoke that night tied to a stone altar surrounded by De Vries' sect. Professor Rumford rescued him and broke up the ritual. Together they went looking for Romana, who they found hanging from a cliff. She insisted it was the Doctor who pushed her over. As the third segment of the Key was known for its transformational abilities, it was apparent that someone had learnt to harness its power.

Insisting that when people try to kill you, you're on the right track, the Doctor set off to talk to De Vries again at his house. Romana returned to Vivian's cottage with the Professor, hoping to find some clue in her academic notes. She discovered that all the owners of the stone circle site have been women, dating back to an old convent that once stood where De Vries' house now stands. When Amelia and Romana reached the mansion they discovered the Doctor trying to repair K-9 amidst the ruin of the house. De Vries had been crushed by a creature that also made an attempt on the Doctor's life – it was one of the standing stones, glowing with an unholy energy! K-9 was badly damaged seeing the creature off, but managed to determine the stone was actually a silicon-based life form, an Ogri, that was extremely deficient in globulin, a protein found in blood plasma. The stones fed on blood.

Romana returned to the TARDIS to continue repairs on K-9, while Amelia and the Doctor looked around the mansion. They found three paintings hidden in a basement, all of the same women at different periods of history – a woman who bore a startling resemblance to Vivian Fay. Romana encountered Vivian on her way back, dressed as the Cailleach she has been masquerading as for at least 4000 years. With a smile, Vivian used a crystalline staff to make Romana and herself vanish. The stone circle also functioned as a portal into hyperspace. With a little jiggery pokery, the Doctor built a projector that, like Vivian's staff, let him open the portal and follow Romana. The professor and K-9 remained in the circle to keep the projector working, even though the remaining Ogri were nearby.

The Doctor arrived on a prison spacecraft positioned in hyperspace, where he freed Romana from one of the cells. In their search for Vivian, the time travellers released two beings of light called the Megara. The Megara were coldly logical justice machines, able to function as judge, jury and executioner. While they were waiting to try a specific prisoner, they insisted on trying the Doctor for breaking the seal on their cell, a crime punishable by death.

Vivian, now in her true form of an elegantly dressed silver skinned woman, was amused to discover the Doctor of trial. She was the criminal the Megara sought, Cessair of Diplos, who was accused of murder and the theft of the Seal of Diplos. However, they had no description of her, so they refused to believe Vivian was who they sought. The Doctor's trial became a game of words, as he tried to prove his innocence, and prove Vivian was Cessair. While the Megara were polite and intelligent, they ruthlessly adhered to the letter of the law and would not accept any suggestion of their own fallibility. Even on the witness stand Vivian cleverly sidestepped the truth.

The Doctor was judged guilty, but as the Megara moved to execute him he managed to put Vivian in the way, knowing the Megara cannot harm an 'innocent'. The Doctor insisted the Megara scan Vivian's brain patterns to ensure she is unharmed. The Megara complied, which instantly confirmed Vivian's true identity. Her trial was swift, even though it was 4000 years overdue. She was condemned to be turned to stone, taking her place in the stone circle forever.

Before her sentence was carried out, the Doctor took the necklace Vivian was wearing, the Seal of Diplos – the source of her powers and the third segment of the Key to Time. Unfortunately the Megara had not forgotten the Doctor still needed to be executed, but before they could do so the Doctor used the Seal and some clever adjustments he made to the hyperspace ship to send the Megara back to their own planet.

CONTINUITY

This adventure uses a lot of Celtic imagery, such as crows and the Cailleach, which leads to a few links to King Arthur. Vivian was the name of one of the ladies of the lake, and one of her previous identities was called Morgana, similar to Morgan Le Fay with whom she shares her surname. A Gamemaster looking for an Arthurian feel to their campaign might find this a useful prelude to the Seventh Doctor adventure **Battlefield**.

Among the other (long-dead) prisoners on the hyperspace craft are a Wirrn (see **The Ark in Space**) and a Kraal android (see **The Android Invasion**)

The Doctor claims to have met Einstein (who argued with him about physics) and John Aubrey (who apparently invented Druidry as a 'joke').

Hyperspace itself is a 'theoretical absurdity' to the Doctor and Romana, but as hyperspace ships turn up often in the Doctor's adventures, this means they see it as an oddity of the universe rather than that they don't believe in it. To Romana it is a system of travel so primitive the Gallifreyan academy no longer teaches it.

When the Doctor is asked if he is from outer space he replies he is from 'more what humans might call inner time'.

The Doctor is unable to read the script of the Megara's cell, suggesting the translation abilities of the TARDIS have trouble reaching into hyperspace.

⬡ RUNNING THE ADVENTURE

This adventure relies on a lot of investigation, and if the player characters are not proactive in searching for clues they might find it very slow going. The NPCs that know what is going on will be very reluctant to talk and are intelligent enough not to give themselves away. None of the villains have time-sensitive plans, making their best ploy to wait for the player characters to just go away.

The Gamemaster can keep them occupied with a few red herrings, but too many dead ends will prove frustrating. The villain of the adventure, Vivian Fay, doesn't actually need anything from the player characters, so will only show her hand and act against them if they look like they are getting close to uncovering her identity. In fact, her only goal is to remain undiscovered.

The Gamemaster should use the early parts of the adventure to build atmosphere, offering myths and mysteries about the stones, and letting the Ogri leave a trail of murder in their wake. While there are not many clues to uncover, there are a lot of mysteries to follow.

One way to use this adventure is to make someone other than Vivian Fay the villain. Professor Rumford might easily be the Cailleach herself. De Vries too might be as much of a villain as he appears. While the Cailleach has always been a woman, De Vries could be a disguise created by the power of the Key. Failing that, De Vries's loyal assistant Martha is in a very good position to observe what is going on without making her involvement too obvious, making her a good choice to be Cailleach.

BOSCOMBE MOOR

This small part of Cornwall is an empty, rural place, its nearest town Boscawen some miles away. In the whole adventure the Doctor meets very few people, and no one wanders by the public places they investigate. While the trees and vegetation are lush, the weather is cold, rainy and bleak, making the area feel lonely and unsettling.

KEY LOCATIONS IN BOSCOMBE

- **The Nine Travellers:** This set of ancient standing stones was built 4000 years ago as a marker

THE MEGARA

You might be forgiven for thinking these small, sparkling clouds of light are harmless, but nothing could be further from the truth. Megara usually travel in pairs and are quasi-organic machines designed to try and pass sentence on criminals. They take the law extremely literally and have little regard for mitigating circumstances. If someone did good while breaking the law, they will be very sorry to pass sentence for the crime, but it will give them no pause in delivering justice. Megara sentence most of the guilty to death, although while opening an official seal is a capital crime, murder and theft are punished with a very lengthy imprisonment. Two facts are immutable to the Megara: that the law must be obeyed to the letter, and that they do not make mistakes. Luckily they are programmed to protect the rights of the innocent. They will not use their powers on those not charged with a crime and will do their utmost to avoid harming an innocent. Each Megara has an encyclopaedic knowledge of the law. They can mentally link with a witness or suspect to verify the truth of what is said. When carrying out executions, they use a deadly disintegration beam.

AWARENESS	4	PRESENCE	3
COORDINATION	4	RESOLVE	3
INGENUITY	4	STRENGTH	-

SKILLS
Convince 4, Knowledge (Law) 8, Marksman 2

TRAITS
Detect Truth (Major): +6 bonus to detecting lies.

Immortal (Major): The Megara cannot be killed, but can be injured.
Indomitable: +4 bonus to any rolls to resist psychic control.
Psychic Training: +2 bonus to Resolve rolls when trying to resist psychic attack or deception.
Robot (Special)
Natural Weapons (Major): Disintegration beam (4/L/L) damage.
By The Book: The Law is the Law.

TECH LEVEL: 6   **STORY POINTS: 8**

for Cessair's portal to hyperspace. It is not as grand as Stonehenge, but does have significant archaeological importance as part of the Gorsedd, a series of three stone circles used for augury (the others being Stonehenge and Bryn Gwyddon in Wales). The Nine Travellers is not an especially impressive site, but it does have an air of power to it that unnerves most locals.

- **Vivian Fay's Cottage:** The nearest habitation to the nine travellers is the cottage of Vivian Fey. It is a small and cosy place, decorated in a very rural and feminine style. It looks more suitable to an older woman, a possible clue about Vivian's real age. Professor Rumford's notes are kept here for convenience, and the only other noteworthy fact is that the recipe books have any recipes containing citric acid crossed out.

- **De Vries' Manor:** Built on the site of an old convent, the manor is impressive on the outside but somewhat dilapidated on the inside. De Vries spends his money on his druid sect, rather than home improvement and many rooms are no longer in use. The basement hides a small ritual chamber where De Vries and Martha carry out their ceremonies to the Cailleach.

VIVIAN FAY (CESSAIR OF DIPLOS)

One of the worst criminals of Diplos is the cold and calculating Cessair. She committed murder and theft to get hold of the power of the Great Seal of Diplos, but was finally captured and her trial set. Somehow she escaped her cell and went into hiding on Earth. However, constantly concerned that she might be discovered she kept a close eye on the hyperspace ship that was once her prison. With the power of the Seal at her command, Cessair can shift her appearance as she chooses, although her true form is that of a tall, silver-skinned woman. In her latest incarnation as Vivian Fay she keeps an eye on the work of Professor Rumford, who is investigating the stones. As the stone circle also functions as the portal to the hyperspace ship, it made sense for her to keep an eye on it, so she passes its ownership down to each new identity. Cessair has lived on Earth for 4000 years, and is beginning to think she is in the clear at last. Should a group of time travellers arrive, their temporal vehicle might prove too tempting to her. With such a device even the Megara would never catch up with her.

AWARENESS	3	PRESENCE	4
COORDINATION	3	RESOLVE	3
INGENUITY	4	STRENGTH	3

SKILLS
Athletics 3, Convince 5, Knowledge 5, Medicine 3, Science 4, Subterfuge 6, Survival 4, Technology 3, Transport 2

TRAITS
Alien
Charming: +2 bonus to attempts to use charm.
Immortal (Major): Cessair will never die of natural causes.
Shapeshift (Special): She can shift into several different forms and duplicate other people very well.

Wanted (Major): Known as a criminal on Diplos.
Weakness (Major): Allergic to citric acid, which does 4 levels of damage if ingested.

TECH LEVEL: 7   **STORY POINTS: 10**

THE HYPERSPACE CRAFT

Those who manage to open a portal in the stone circle might slip into hyperspace and find themselves aboard this vessel. There is not a lot to explore here, although it is in very good condition for a ship of 4000-years old. The ship hangs in a multi-coloured void, which it would be extremely inadvisable to walk into, the effects being similar to entering the Vortex unprotected.

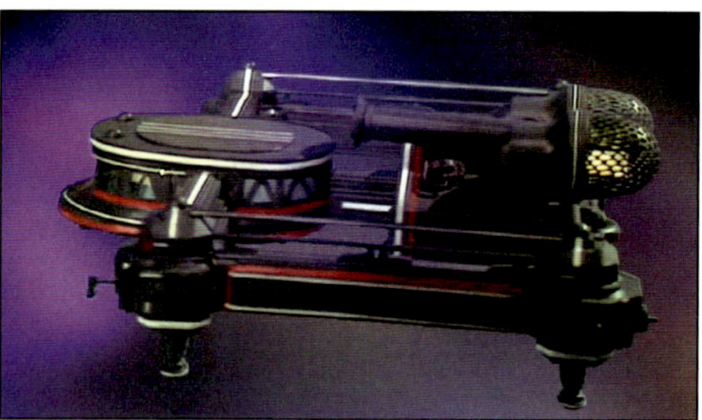

The ship itself is designed as a square. One side houses the engine systems, which are linked to the control room by two parallel corridors. The whole place is open and spacious but plain and white. Cells containing several long-dead inhabitants can be found within the ship, an ideal place for the Gamemaster to let the player characters come across all manner of creatures or clues. In one of these cells, protected by a seal, can be found the Megara. The control room is also large and spacious, with only the flight systems and a pilot's chair failing to fill the space.

FURTHER ADVENTURES

- **Justice will be done:** The Megara return, looking for the Doctor. The idea he might have left when he was awaiting sentence does not enter their minds; it would be illegal after all. Their journey has been a long one and they have not fared well, so remember only sketchy detail about the Doctor. Unfortunately, it is enough for them to potentially believe any Time Lord is actually the Doctor.

- **A Rumford Affair:** Professor Rumford has written a new book, detailing her thoughts about the recent changes in the stone circle. Unfortunately a rogue Time Agent (or similar villain) has read between the lines and realised the circle is Cessair's prison. The Time Agent needs to know more so he can free Cessair, who knows the location of several other treasures she has stolen.

- **The Stone Invasion:** What if Cessair didn't just bring three Ogri? What if all the stone circles have Ogri lying dormant in their midst? If they wake up, they are going to be hungry.

THE OGRI

AWARENESS	3	PRESENCE	1
COORDINATION	2	RESOLVE	4
INGENUITY	1	STRENGTH	6

These silicon-based creatures come from a dark swampy planet Ogros in the Tau Ceti system. On their home planet they absorb proteins from the environment, proteins that on Earth are only found in blood in globulin. Ogri are not especially intelligent creatures, acting mainly on instinct. They can obey simple instructions though, and even be trained for simple tasks. Ogri come in many shapes and sizes, but are generally tall, rectangular standing stones, around six to eight feet high, weighing around three tonnes. As beings of stone they are exceptionally resilient to physical force. Most of their victims are crushed to death, but when they need to feed they suck the life out of anyone who touches them. When they move or feed they glow with a bright light inside that beats to the rhythm of a heartbeat.

SKILLS
Fighting 3, Survival 3

TRAITS
Alien (Special Good)
Immortal (Major): Stone endures.
Impervious (Major): Reduce all damage by one step
Tough (Minor): Reduce total damage by 2
Dependency (Minor): Must feed on blood regularly or suffer -2 to all rolls.

STORY POINTS: 6

PROFESSOR AMELIA RUMFORD

AWARENESS	3	PRESENCE	4
COORDINATION	2	RESOLVE	5
INGENUITY	4	STRENGTH	1

Had she been born a little earlier in history, Amelia Rumford would have been the sort of woman who built the British Empire. Even as an old lady she remains intelligent, forthright and resolute. She has been studying the 'Nine Travellers' for many years, building on the previous work of those who have studied it before her. As these academics were usually men, Amelia rather enjoys it when she proves them wrong. Amelia is fearless, seemingly unable to believe that the application of intellect, old-fashioned decency and hard work might not prevail. She might not be as fit as she once was, but she is still someone you want in your corner. Even if she can't solve the problem, she'll make sure everyone at least has a Thermos of tea.

SKILLS
Convince 2, Craft 2, Fighting 2, Knowledge 4, Medicine 1, Science 3, Technology 1, Transport 2

TRAITS
Brave: +2 bonus to any Resolve roll when the character needs to show courage.
Indomitable: +4 bonus to any rolls to resist psychic control.
Eccentric (Minor): Can be a little dotty at times.
Obsession (Minor): Amelia is dedicated to her work on the stones.

EQUIPMENT: Bicycle, Thermos of tea.

TECH LEVEL: 5   **STORY POINTS: 6**

LEONARD DE VRIES

AWARENESS	3	PRESENCE	3
COORDINATION	3	RESOLVE	2
INGENUITY	2	STRENGTH	2

De Vries is a minor aristocrat who has chosen to build his self importance by leading a local cult. There are around fifteen members of his 'British Institute of Druidic Studies' although none are as dedicated to their patron deity 'The Cailleach' as De Vries and his most ardent follower Martha. De Vries enjoys cultivating an aura of dangerous occultist, mainly to cover the fact he is really a very ordinary little man. However, he does seen to manifest some power over crows and might potentially have other minor abilities from his relationship with his goddess. It is unlikely he knows the true identity of his goddess, but his active collusion with Vivian as Cessair might make him an unexpectedly dangerous opponent. He and Martha are killed by the Ogri, most likely because Cessair decides they are loose ends that might reveal her identity.

SKILLS
Convince 3, Fighting 1, Knowledge 3, Subterfuge 3

TRAITS
Obligation (Major): Serve the will of the Cailleach, no matter the cost.

TECH LEVEL: 5   **STORY POINTS: 6**

THE ANDROIDS OF TARA

'Now look here Zarek, I've got better things to do than meddle in the politics of your piffling little planet.'

⊙ SYNOPSIS

Tara, the Future

Having found three of the six segments of the Key to Time, the Doctor felt he was owed a holiday. So, when Romana insisted they continue with the mission he went fishing instead, leaving Romana to wander the planet Tara in search of the fourth segment. It turned out to be very simple to locate, with the tracer leading her straight to a statue of a warrior defeating a dragon. The dragon statue was the segment, and after transforming it back into its proper form, Romana was set upon by a strange beast. Luckily, help was at hand in the shape of Count Grendel von Gracht, a master swordsman and the supposed ruler of these lands.

Grendel insisted Romana return with him to his castle, but she quickly realised she had become his prisoner. It seemed Romana looked exactly like the Princess Strella, who was also a prisoner in the castle. The Count planned to marry Strella to solidify his claim on the throne, but she was proving most difficult. Now he had Romana, he had two Strellas to choose from.

Meanwhile, the Doctor was interrupted from a pleasant day's fishing by the impetuous swordsman Farrah and his mentor Zarek. While the Doctor was not impressed with their manners, he agreed to come with them when they told him they had an android that needed repair. The knights led him to the home of Prince Reynart, who was preparing for his coronation. As the coronation had to place at a particular time and place, the Prince feared an assassination attempt from his deadly rival, Count Grendel.

They had constructed an android duplicate of the Prince that might foil such an attempt, but it was in dire need of repair. On Tara, nobles considered technical skills beneath them, so none of the knights or their Prince knew what to do. Never one to resist a challenge the Doctor agreed to repair the robot, especially as the Prince was a lot more polite than his knights. His repairs were very successful, so the group celebrated with a glass of wine. Unfortunately, agents of the Count drugged the wine and they all passed out. When they awoke, the Prince was gone, kidnapped by Count Grendel.

While Zarek and Farrah were ready to make a suicidal attempt on the Count's castle to free the prince, the Doctor had another plan. He suggested they let the android Prince attend the imminent coronation, and then rescue the real one once it was all over. The Doctor and the swordsmen set off to sneak into the royal palace through some old tunnels. He dispatched K-9 to find Romana, who he discovered was sharing a cell with the Prince at the castle.

The ceremony went ahead using the android Prince. However, Grendel attempted to use a robot duplicate of Strella (made by his technician Lamia) to assassinate the Prince. The Doctor foiled the attempt, but Grendel managed to buy himself more time by suggesting the ceremony be postponed until the security of the Prince could be ensured. Luckily, with the android Prince malfunctioning, the Doctor needed the extra time to make repairs. One of Count's men told him the Count offered Romana in exchange for safe passage out of the country. It seems the Count had accepted defeat and sought only to leave. It was obviously a trap, but it was still the best chance they had to rescue Romana. Secretly, Lamia has constructed an android duplicate of Romana that the Count planned to use to kill the Doctor.

The exchange at the Pavilion of the Summer Winds didn't go well. The Doctor spotted the false Romana, and when the Count resorted to brute force Lamia was killed in the exchange.

At the Prince's home, where the Doctor meets Zarek and Farrah, the Count arrived under a flag of truce. He attempted to sway the Doctor to his side but his promises of wealth and power fall on deaf ears. Again the Count resorted to brute force to have his way. While he has been searched for weapons, no one noticed the Count had tied his flag of truce to a spear, which he uses to destroy the android Prince. In the chaos he flees back to his castle to form another scheme.

Safe at the castle, the Count told the Prince and Romana he had made plans for their wedding. Once they were married, he could kill the Prince and marry Romana. As the Prince's widow would control the throne, the Count would be able to take the throne himself on the sad demise of his new wife. If either of them refused to comply, he would kill his other prisoner, the real Princess Strella. As wedding preparations were made, the Doctor, K-9 and the knights made a sneak attack on the castle.

The Doctor arrived just in time to stop the wedding but the Count engaged him in a duel to the death. As the Prince's men invaded the castle, Grendel and the Doctor clashed swords throughout the castle. Eventually, the Doctor prevailed, but the Count refused to surrender, jumping from the ramparts into the moat and escaping.

With the Prince and Strella free at last, and ready to take the throne together, Romana and the Doctor quietly recovered the fourth segment from Lamia's workshop and left Tara for the next part of the quest.

RUNNING THE ADVENTURE

This adventure wears its inspiration on its frilly, swashbuckling sleeve – it's drawn from *The Prisoner of Zenda* and other adventure yarns.

When running an adventure like this, charge headlong into clichés. Give the villain a black hat, set the whole thing in a crumbling castle with lots of secret passages, and let no chandelier go unswung-upon. The androids add a science-fiction twist to the basic plot. If you base an adventure on another genre – say, a lost world full of dinosaurs, or a political thriller – then do the same with its own clichés. Fill your political thrillers with meetings in car parks (OK, spaceship parks) and mysterious phone calls; stick rampaging T-rexes and cave girls into your dinosaur romps.

You can even give players Story Points for indulging in appropriate behaviour. First player to swash a buckle, or buckle a swash – have a Story Point! First player to drink the drugged wine – have a Story Point!

TARA

Tara is both the name of the planet and its capital. The place has a distinctly medieval feel in style and attitude, but with several pieces of advanced technology. The nobility fight with electrified swords and the guards are armed with crossbows that fire energy bolts. It is possible that Tara is a lost colony of the Earth empire. The planet itself is lush and green, and while several wild animals are to be found in the hunting grounds it is a very beautiful, safe and pleasant planet.

Two hundred years ago a terrible plague swept through Tara, killing almost nine tenths of the population. Low on manpower the surviving Tarans built androids to do most of the manual labour, a tradition that remains. Android design on Tara is very advanced, with it being difficult to tell an android from a real person. However, there are some telling signs; most particularly they do not move especially fast. For this reason androids are not usually used as guards and warriors.

Taran society is divided into two strata. The nobles rule and make war on each other, with internecine conflict a constant concern. However, all the nobility are brought up with a strong sense of honour and respect for the rules of war, making such conflict deadly, but polite.

The peasantry work the fields but also build and repair technical devices. Nobles are considered above such skills, which they believe only fit for the lower orders. They are far too busy learning how to kill each other properly to learn how to fix an android. This means that a skilled technician can rise quite highly in a noble household.

Tara has an effective Tech Level of 6, as its robotics and weapons technology is very advanced. However, it has no spaceflight, capability or indeed any transport technology above the horse. As nobles eschew an understanding of technology, they have an effective Tech Level of 4.

KEY LOCATIONS IN TARA

- **The Royal Palace:** The Taran throne is found here, as well as the Archimandrite who ministers to the important matters of ritual and protocol. While there is a palace guard, they happily take orders from any ranking noble.

- **The Prince's Hideout:** Looking to keep a low profile the Prince and his retinue maintain a hunting lodge not far from the lands of Count Gracht. It is quite plain for a king, but serves its purpose well and draws little attention.

- **Pavilion of the Summer Winds:** A large single-room pavilion decorated with an oriental theme set in the Count's lands. Its décor suggests there are cultures on Tara who do not follow the European model, or that Tarans are descended from Earth and have records of a variety of Earth cultures and designs.

CASTLE GRACHT

This vast castle is one of the most powerful strongholds on Tara. It has been held by Count Grendel's family for many years and acts as a symbol of his power. The castle has solid stone walls, and a wide moat. While the bridge is the only direct access, a network of canals under the castle, built for receiving supplies, makes another convenient entrance.

KEY LOCATIONS IN CASTLE GRACHT

- **Lamia's workshop:** The Count's favourite technician maintains possibly the most advanced engineering laboratory in Tara. The Count certainly spares no expense when equipping his staff.

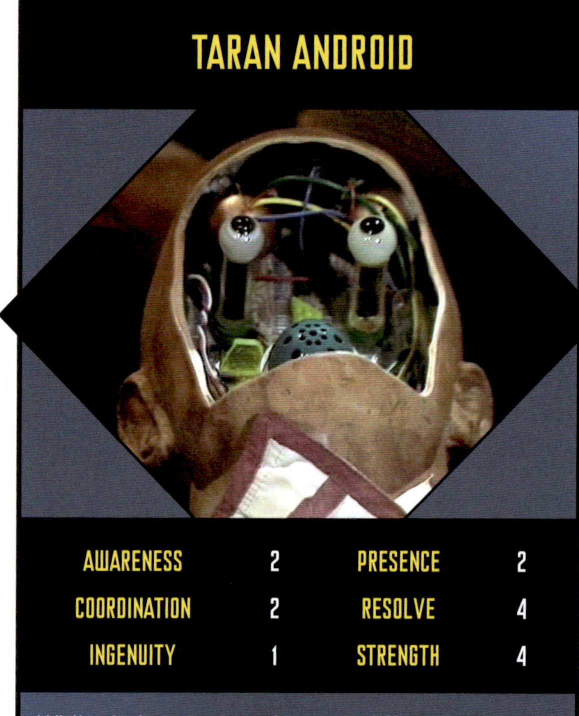

TARAN ANDROID

AWARENESS	2	PRESENCE	2
COORDINATION	2	RESOLVE	4
INGENUITY	1	STRENGTH	4

While their programming may differ, most Taran androids are based on the same design. This basic model can be fabricated quite quickly. The art of bringing it to life is determined by the skill of its programming.

SKILLS
Athletics 2, Fighting 2 (other skills dependant on programming)

TRAITS*
Environmental (Minor): Suffers no ill effects from being unable to breath.
Robot (Special Good)
Clumsy (Minor): When running down or damaged, an android must make additional Awareness and Coordination rolls to avoid knocking vital things over.

*some androids fitted as assassins may have weaponry installed.

TECH LEVEL: 5   **STORY POINTS: 2**

- **Great Hall:** While he'd prefer a throne room, the Count's main audience chamber is spacious and richly decorated. The room is built in grey stone supported with great pillars and decorated with several tapestries.

- **Dungeons:** Castle Gracht has expansive dungeons in the basement. They are very plain stone rooms with straw on the floor and no furniture except for a bed and a chair. They are also very secure with thick oak doors and a constant guard.

- **Lots of corridors:** The castle is full of long stone corridors, some littered with wine casks and weapons racks.

FURTHER ADVENTURES

- **Count Grendel's Revenge:** The Count returns to claim the throne once more. This time he has made some very dangerous deals with alien mercenaries to raise an army he intends to double cross. The aliens want Taran android technology for their own schemes.

- **The Ghosts of Tara:** While visiting Tara, the characters discover that they are not who they think they are. They're actually android duplicates of themselves! Where are the originals, and why were they replaced? And more importantly, can the androids rescue the originals before they run out of battery power?

- **The Black Death:** The plague that killed almost the entire population of Tara returns, but no one can remember how to cure it. Legends tell of an old vault containing technical details deemed too dangerous to be left in the hands of peasants that might offer hope. But even if someone can find these records, will the disease have mutated beyond a cure?

COUNT GRENDEL VON GRACHT

One of the most powerful nobles of Tara is Count Grendel, powerful enough to be a serious challenge to the Prince in the contest for the crown. Grendel thinks of himself as the very archetype of noblesse oblige. He is charming and polite, apparently honourable and carries himself with dignity. However, for all his charm the Count divides everyone he meets into two categories: other nobles, who are rivals, and peasants, who are tools. He uses those who serve him as little more than objects. He is more attached to Lamia than he might ever admit, finding her death distressing, but he certainly doesn't let this pang of feeling interrupt his plans for power.

AWARENESS	3	PRESENCE	5
COORDINATION	4	RESOLVE	3
INGENUITY	3	STRENGTH	4

SKILLS
Athletics 4, Convince 2, Fighting 5, Knowledge 2, Marksman 2, Subterfuge 4, Transport 3

TRAITS
Charming: +2 bonus to attempts to use charm.
Voice of Authority: +2 bonus to Presence and Convince rolls.
Code of Conduct (Minor): Chivalrous, but only when it suits him.
Obsession (Major): Grendel will not rest until he is the King of Tara.
Technically Inept: -2 penalty to any attempt to fix electrical or computer equipment.

EQUIPMENT: Electro-sword (Strength +4 Damage), noble scale armour (2 points).

TECH LEVEL: 4   **STORY POINTS:** 12

SWORDSMAN FARRAH

AWARENESS	2	PRESENCE	2
COORDINATION	4	RESOLVE	3
INGENUITY	2	STRENGTH	3

Farrah is the archetypal impetuous young man. He is a decent kid, who will make a good swordsman when experience gives him a little more wisdom. As part of the Prince's personal guard, it seems clear Farrah is already a very adept swordsman. However, he rarely allows thought to cloud his judgement when his honour goads him to action.

SKILLS

Athletics 4, Fighting 4, Transport 2

TRAITS

Attractive: +2 bonus to any rolls that involve his looks.
Brave: +2 bonus to any Resolve roll when he needs to show courage.
Quick Reflexes: Farrah always goes first in his Action Round unless taken by surprise.
Code of Conduct (Major): Dedicated to the knightly code of honour.
Impulsive: Farrah doesn't think things through before acting.
Technically Inept: -2 penalty to any attempt to fix electrical or computer equipment.

EQUIPMENT: Electro-sword (Strength +4 Damage), noble light armour (1 point).

TECH LEVEL: 4   **STORY POINTS:** 6

MADAME LAMIA

AWARENESS	4	PRESENCE	2
COORDINATION	3	RESOLVE	3
INGENUITY	5	STRENGTH	2

One of the most adept technicians on Tara, Lamia had the misfortune to fall in love with a powerful man who cares little for her. Having proven her skill she was promoted to Count Grendel's 'right-hand woman'. However, much as he might deny it (especially as she is a peasant) there is a bond between them and he trusts no one more than her. This trust is well placed, as Lamia would rather have an eternity of the Count's scorn than live without him.

SKILLS

Convince 2, Craft 4, Fighting 1, Knowledge 3, Marksman 1, Medicine 4, Science 5, Subterfuge 3, Technology 5

TRAITS

Boffin: Allows Lamia to create Gadgets.
Face in the Crowd: +2 to any Subterfuge Skill rolls to sneak about.
Technically Adept: +2 to any Technology roll to fix a broken or faulty device.
Obsession (Major): Lamia will do anything to please Count Grendel.

TECH LEVEL: 6   **STORY POINTS:** 6

PRINCE REYNART

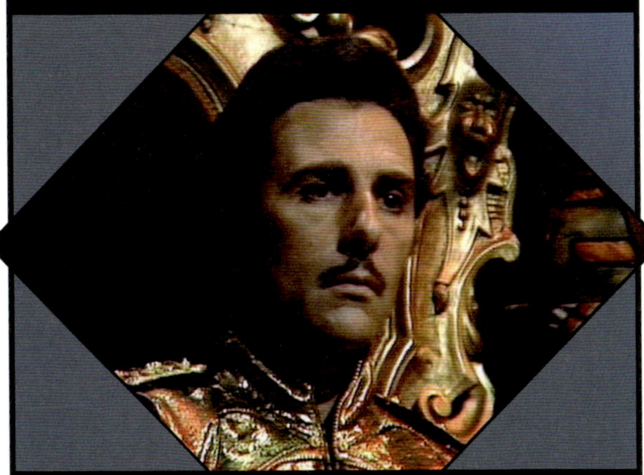

AWARENESS	3	PRESENCE	4
COORDINATION	2	RESOLVE	3
INGENUITY	2	STRENGTH	3

The true heir to Tara is little more than a thoroughly decent man. Prince Reynart is compassionate, honourable and kind, if a little dim and boring. While it is hard not to like the Prince, his rule will probably not leave any great legacy for Tara. He has been brought up to rule, almost by rote. While he does care about his people, he doesn't really understand them or their needs, having met very few of them.

SKILLS
Athletics 2, Convince 4, Fighting 3, Knowledge 2, Subterfuge 2, Transport 2

TRAITS
Attractive: +2 bonus to any rolls that involve the character's looks.
Empathic: +2 bonus on rolls to 'read' another person.
Voice of Authority: +2 bonus to Presence and Convince rolls.
Adversary (Major): Anyone who seeks the throne is plotting against him.
Obligation (Major): Do what is right for the people of Tara.
Technically Inept: -2 penalty to any attempt to fix electrical or computer equipment.

TECH LEVEL: 4   **STORY POINTS:** 8

SWORDMASTER ZADEK

AWARENESS	4	PRESENCE	2
COORDINATION	3	RESOLVE	4
INGENUITY	4	STRENGTH	2

Behind every great king is a loyal retainer doing his best to keep his lord on track. Zadek is dedicated to his Prince and tries his best to offer him the right advice so he can rule well. In a military made up of hotheads, Zadek is remarkably level headed; ready to think before acting and making use of the wisdom of his years. However, he is still as tradition bound as the others, willing to assault Castle Gracht on a suicide mission if honour dictates.

SKILLS
Athletics 3, Convince 3, Fighting 4, Knowledge 2, Marksman 4, Science 1, Subterfuge 3, Transport 2

TRAITS
Brave : +2 bonus to any Resolve roll when the character needs to show courage.
Keen Senses (Major): +2 to all Awareness rolls.
Code of Conduct (Major): Zadek will not act against the knightly code of honour.
Obligation (Minor): Serve the rightful ruler of Tara.
Technically Inept: -2 penalty to any attempt to fix electrical or computer equipment.

EQUIPMENT: Electro-sword (Strength +4 Damage), noble scale armour (2 points).

TECH LEVEL: 4   **STORY POINTS:** 8

THE POWER OF KROLL

'Was it absolutely necessary to land in a quagmire?'

⊙ SYNOPSIS

Delta Magna III, the Future

This time, the tracer led the time travellers to the swampy third moon of the Earth colony Delta Magna. Exploring, the Doctor was arrested by the crew of a nearby methane refinery. They very nearly shot him, believing him to be the notorious gunrunner Rohm-Dutt. Unapologetic, they arrested him as a potential spy. When they reached the refinery, the Doctor impressed the crew with his detailed knowledge (and ideas about improving) their cutting-edge installation.

Romana was captured by Rohm-Dutt himself and a group of the primitive tribesmen who inhabited the moon. Rohm-Dutt was selling arms to the Swampies and assumed Romana was a spy for the authorities on Delta Magna. The tribesmen decided that Romana should be the next blood sacrifice to their god, Kroll. When the Doctor heard the tribesmen had a sacrifice, he realised it might be Romana. However, the refinery crew were almost too eager to help him out. Their commander, Thawn, was looking for an excuse to kill the natives, who were a hindrance to expanding the methane mining operation.

The Doctor slipped away and stole into the village, where he freed Romana. Together they discovered the history of the tribesmen, which talked of Kroll 'awakening' and punishing his people's indolence by destroying their temple and consuming the 'symbol of his power'.

Still eager for a fight, the refinery crew attacked the tribesmen. The battle was short as the tribesmen's guns misfired, but the noise of battle awoke Kroll himself, a gigantic squid-like creature over a mile long. While it killed Swampies and refinery crew alike, its appearance was enough to send them fleeing.

The Doctor and Romana realised the refinery was responsible for waking Kroll, who was in hibernation until they started drilling. Kroll was also the source of the methane they thought they were drilling for in the lakebed. Unfortunately, the tribesmen were even keener on making a sacrifice after having seen their god rise, so the Doctor and Romana were once more sentenced to death by the Swampies, along with Rohm-Dutt, who they considered a traitor for selling them faulty weapons.

While suffering a slow death by tightening creepers, the Doctor and Romana learn from Rohm-Dutt that Thawn actually got him to sell the guns to the natives so he would have an excuse to kill them. As their slow death approached, a massive storm hit the settlement and the refinery, forcing everyone to seek shelter. The rain loosened the creepers that kept the prisoners captive and they escaped execution and run into the swamp.

Once the storm passed, the tribesmen gave chase, but the vibrations of the hunt attracted Kroll's attention and he rose, consuming several tribesmen as well as Rohm-Dutt. He then attacked the settlement, the refinery crew watching with glee. But, just to make sure, they aimed one of their orbital rockets at the settlement to destroy Kroll and the Swampies.

Luckily, the Doctor and Romana managed to get to the refinery before the rocket fired, disabling it. The surviving tribesmen also mounted an attack, saving the Doctor by killing the refinery commander. All this noise and vibrations drew Kroll back to savagely attack the refinery. As Kroll tore it apart, the Doctor decided to test a theory. He used the tracer on Kroll, transforming the monster into the fifth segment. The ancient symbol of Kroll that it swallowed was actually the fifth segment, which made the creature that swallowed it (once no more than a common giant squid) grow to an enormous size.

With the refinery in ruins and most of the crew dead, the natives were free. There was little for the remaining refinery crew to do but help the natives rebuild. Once more, the Doctor and Romana slipped away with the fifth segment.

RUNNING THE ADVENTURE

This adventure present a moral question for the players to answer. The player characters arrive looking for something, and to get to it they will probably have to side with either the tribesmen or the refinery crew. Which side they pick will not only depend on who seems to be the more worthy, but who will get them what they want.

Who is in the right seems quite straightforward. The tribesmen are the good guys, no longer willing to suffer another forcible relocation, and the power hungry refinery crew are the bad guys. The trick to adapting this adventure is to muddy the moral waters a little, leaving the player characters unsure as to who to help.

The refinery crew might be the last, best hope for a dying world. While they regret the persecution of the natives, millions more lives back home might be counting on what they mine, whether vital fossil fuels or protein to save a starving population.

The tribesmen are already capable of blood sacrifice to appease their god, but what if it went a little further? They might be the bloodthirsty savages Thawn believes them to be, looking to kill the refinery crew simply for trespassing. Their relocation might have even saved them. Perhaps there are several moons capable of supporting life around Delta Magna. The indigenous tribes were so warlike; each was settled on a different moon, ending generations of feuding and bloodshed.

If you are a fan of Japanese monster movies, this adventure offers a real opportunity too. How complicated might things be if there is more than one Kroll? Perhaps the fifth segment makes all the giant monsters gigantic! Megasquids take on Gigantocrabs and Crocosauruses! This will be a good way to fool players who insist just touching the tracer to one of them will yield the segment. It might work, but they'll have to be very sure which monster they try this on!

DELTA MAGNA III

The third moon of the Earth colony Delta Magna was initially designed as a tribal reservation. Finding an indigenous population on Delta Magna itself, the advanced Earth colonists forcibly moved them to the swamp moon. After all, they reasoned, it was just the same swamp land they were used to and there was nothing there the colonists wanted. That was until the colonists discovered rich sources of methane on the moon.

Understandably the native are somewhat upset their reservation is being invaded and their homes are in danger once again from the 'dryfoots'. Luckily for them a group of militants, the Sons of Earth want to help. This organisation lobbies for a return to Earth for all humanity, and is not above acts of terrorism to serve their cause. Unfortunately, few people see

Earth as a forgotten paradise, as it is a broken world in desperate need of time to recover from humanity's depredations.

KEY LOCATIONS ON DELTA MAGNA III

- **The Methane Refinery:** This drilling plant is the same size as a large oil rig, and sits quite a distance off shore. It is accessible only by boat or air, and is equipped with both canoes and hovercraft for the crew to reach the mainland. The inside is plain and functional but reasonably pleasant as this is a showcase prototype as much as a working platform.

- **Swamp Tribe Village:** The Swampies live in simple villages made up of mud and reed dwellings. Each dwelling comprises only a single room and each village is quite small. On the edge of the village lies the ritual sacrifice area, where blood sacrifice might be offered to Kroll behind elaborate gates. Some older stone structures and tunnels dating back to early terraforming processes have also been taken over by the tribesmen to serve as ritual chambers or stores.

FURTHER ADVENTURES

- **The Kroll Infestation:** The many giant squid produced by Kroll's destruction grow up big. They begin attacking the inhabitants in large numbers. It seems someone has found a way to control them, but is it a local tribesman or are the colonists making another attempt to destroy them?

- **Trail of Tears:** The colonists discover yet more valuable minerals on Delta Magna III and decide to move the natives again. The natives rebel, so the colonists are thinking about mining the moon with them on it, a process that will turn the atmosphere toxic.

- **Relic Hunters:** A book found by the Swampies suggests there may be a forgotten temple on Delta Magna from the old days, one that may have another symbol of Kroll. They are not allowed to return to the planet, but perhaps the player characters can find it for them? Unfortunately, other treasure hunters have got wind of the discovery, but who will find it first? Perhaps one of these hunters is Rohm-Dutt, who actually escaped Kroll's clutches.

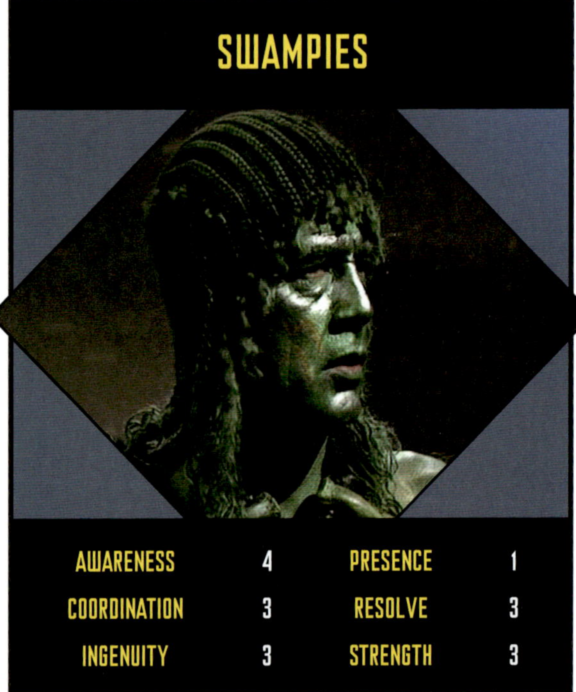

AWARENESS	4	PRESENCE	1
COORDINATION	3	RESOLVE	3
INGENUITY	3	STRENGTH	3

Originally natives of the planet Delta Magna, the Swampies – as the humans derogatively refer to them as – were forcibly relocated to the moon of Delta Magna III. They are green-skinned humanoids, with long, lank green hair. They are a primitive people with little in the way of advanced technology, although they are proficient enough to use technology smuggled to them by Rohm-Dutt. They worship Kroll and venerate him with blood sacrifices.

SKILLS
Athletics 3, Craft 2, Fighting 2, Subterfuge 3, Survival 3, Technology 2, Transport 2

TECH LEVEL: 3*   STORY POINTS: 6

*While Swampies have a low Tech Level, they are aware that other cultures are more advanced and do not see advanced tech as magic or treat it with fear. They may operate (but not repair or build) advanced tech as if their Tech Level is 2 points higher.

ROHM-DUTT

AWARENESS	4	PRESENCE	3
COORDINATION	4	RESOLVE	3
INGENUITY	3	STRENGTH	3

Rohm-Dutt is one of the most renowned gunrunners in the system. He has extensive contacts and is happy to work for anyone so long as they are paying. He isn't evil, however, taking no joy or pleasure in murder and killing. Instead he neatly sidesteps morality by insisting what people do with the weapons he sells is none of his concern. First and foremost, Rohm-Dutt is a businessman, and in defence of his business he can be ruthless. While he isn't especially greedy, he will happily use whatever means are necessary to safeguard his share of the profit.

SKILLS
Athletics 3, Convince 4, Fighting 3, Marksman 3, Medicine 2, Subterfuge 4, Survival 4, Technology 4, Transport 3

TRAITS
Empathic: +2 bonus on rolls to 'read' another person.
Friends (Minor): Rohm has several contacts across the system.
Keen Senses (Major): +2 to all Awareness rolls.

TECH LEVEL: 6   STORY POINTS: 8

MENSCH

AWARENESS	4	PRESENCE	1
COORDINATION	3	RESOLVE	3
INGENUITY	3	STRENGTH	3

Mensch is a captured Swampie who has been 'civilised' and acts as a servant for the crew of the refinery. Mensch does his best to stay out of the way and is generally ignored by the crew as an 'ignorant savage'. However, Mensch is actually spying for the local tribesmen, and signals the settlement with a torch, passing messages in morse code. The refinery crew never figure out that they have a spy in their midst, as Mensch ventures too close to Kroll.

SKILLS
Athletics 3, Craft 2, Fighting 2, Subterfuge 3, Survival 3, Technology 2, Transport 2

TRAITS
Face in the Crowd: +2 to any Subterfuge Skill rolls to sneak about.
Enslaved (Major): Must obey refinery crew, and suffers -2 to attempts to voice opinion.
Obligation (Minor): Warn the settlement of refinery operations.

TECH LEVEL: 3*   STORY POINTS: 6

*While Swampies have a low Tech Level, they are aware that other cultures are more advanced and do not see advanced tech as magic or treat it with fear. They may operate (but not repair or build) advanced tech as if their Tech Level is 2 points higher.

THAWN

AWARENESS	3	PRESENCE	4
COORDINATION	3	RESOLVE	4
INGENUITY	4	STRENGTH	3

The refinery commander is a dedicated and bigoted man. Used to getting what he wants he cares little about the local primitives and only about how he will appear to his bosses on Delta Magna. The more frustrated he gets, the worse he becomes, happy to kill to get what he wants. Initially Thawn is unlikable and something of a bully; by the end of the adventure he is a murderous megalomaniac. What makes him a dangerous villain is that the harder he gets pushed, the harder he pushes back.

SKILLS
Athletics 2, Convince 2, Knowledge 2, Marksman 3, Science 3, Subterfuge 3, Technology 3, Transport 2

TRAITS
Single Minded (Minor): Gains 2 Story Points each time his plans are thwarted.
Voice of Authority: +2 bonus to Presence and Convince rolls.
Eccentric (Major): Bigot, does not consider primitives to be 'real people'.
Obligation (Major): See that the refinery project goes well.

EQUIPMENT: Blaster Pistol (4/8/L)

TECH LEVEL: 6   STORY POINTS: 8

KROLL

AWARENESS	3	PRESENCE	6
COORDINATION	2	RESOLVE	5
INGENUITY	1	STRENGTH	*

*KROLL IS MIGHTY!

Once a humble giant swamp squid, the power of the Key to Time turned Kroll into a titanic monster. Up from the deep, a mile wide and seventy stories tall, he is.... KROOOOOOOOOOLLLLLLLLLLL!

SKILLS
Fighting 3, Survival 3

TRAITS
Alien
Fear Factor 3: Grants a +6 bonus to inspire fear.
Natural Weapons (Major): One of Kroll's tentacles smashes for Lethal damage.
Huge: That's a big monster.
Special – Absolutely, Absurdly Huge: Kroll is the size of a small town. Normal weapons have no affect on Kroll – you need a rocket or a ship-mounted cannon to scratch him. When Kroll attacks a small target, he rolls Coordination + Fighting to hit, not Strength + Fighting.
Special – Kroll is Mighty: Kroll wins any contest involving Strength.

STORY POINTS: 8

THE ARMAGEDDON FACTOR

'Still, nuclear war. It's always difficult walking into these situations. You never know who is fighting who.'

⚙ SYNOPSIS

Atrios, the Future

The sixth segment of the Key to Time was somewhere in the star system containing the two worlds of Atrios and Zeos – two planets locked in a long-running war. While Princess Astra of Atrios was willing to make peace, other members of her government, including the sinister Marshal, considered such diplomatic overtures to be treachery. He lured Astra into a radiation zone to kill her. The Doctor and Romana found her, but before they could free her from her cell, they too were captured by the Marshal.

The Marshal initially assumed that they were Zeon spies, but they convinced him they were from another world. Returning to Astra's cell, they discovered she had vanished. The Doctor agreed to help the Marshal develop a deterrent in the war against Zeon (the Atriosian fleet was mostly wrecked, and the remaining crews inexperienced and ineffective) in exchange for the Marshal's help in finding Astra and the sixth segment of the Key to Time.

The Doctor considered making a force field to block Zeon attacks, but dismissed that idea as being too energy-intensive. Instead, he opted for a psychological barrier, a psychic shield that would stop any Zeons from attacking. To build such a device, however, he needed a Zeon test subject. Meanwhile, Romana discovered that the Marshal was in touch with a third party, who she assumed was on Zeos.

The TARDIS departed for Zeos, but found the world empty apart from a supercomputer called Mentalis. The entire Zeon war effort was operated by the machine, and it was programmed to destroy the whole solar system if defeat was inevitable.

In fact, the Marshal was allied with the Shadow, a servant of the Black Guardian. The Shadow orchestrated the war between the two worlds as a test run for the Guardian's ultimate plan – when the Guardian possessed the Key to Time, the whole universe would be forced into infinite war. The Shadow captured the Doctor and the TARDIS and brought them to his secret world, which orbited between Atrios and Zeos. There, he demanded that the Doctor hand over the five other segments of the Key. The Doctor admitted that the segments were in the TARDIS, but refused to help. The Shadow claimed that the Doctor would be unable to restrain himself,

and that his impatient, meddling nature would give the Shadow a chance to take the key. He permitted the Doctor to leave; the Doctor took the TARDIS to Zeos.

With no more need for the war between Atrios and Zeos, the Shadow informed his pawn, the Marshal, that there would be no more attacks from Zeos. The Marshal launched an attack on Zeos with his few remaining ships – an attack that would, if successful, trigger the mutual-destruction Armageddon mode of Mentalis. To avert this catastrophe, the Doctor and Romana built a temporary sixth segment from chronodyne, then used their ersatz Key and locked the Marshal's ship into a temporary time loop. They then returned to the Shadow's base to find a way to deal with the greater threat.

The Shadow dispatched agents to steal the complete key. First, he used a mind-controlled Princess Astra; later, he lured K-9 to his lair and took control of the robot. The Doctor and Romana continued to search for the sixth segment, which the tracer confirmed was somewhere on Zeos. K-9 captured Romana and brought her to the Shadow.

While exploring, the Doctor encountered a fellow Time Lord and former classmate at the Academy, Drax, a renegade who left Gallifrey long ago. Drax admitted that he had built the Mentalis computer for the Shadow. He persuaded Drax to help him, just as the Shadow sent an ultimatum – hand over the Key to Time or Romana would be killed. Drax repaired K-9, removing the Shadow's influence over his circuits.

Forced to comply with the Shadow's demands, the Doctor opened the TARDIS, whereupon Drax shrank him with a dimensional stabiliser. The two then stowed away inside K-9 until the moment was right to strike. The Shadow identified the final segment of the Key – Princess Astra herself was the sixth segment in living form! Before the Shadow could complete the

Key, the Doctor reverted to normal size and grabbed all six parts. The combined Key blinded the Shadow, giving the travellers a chance to escape...

The time loop ended and the Marshal launched his missiles, but they struck the Shadow's lair instead, destroying it.

The Doctor now possessed the complete Key to Time, which gave unimaginable power and authority over time. The Guardian appeared and asked that the Doctor hand the Key over. The Doctor grew suspicious. The White Guardian was supposed to be an entity of supreme compassion, but showed no pity or regret for Princess Astra's sacrifice. The Doctor realised that this intruder was the Black Guardian in disguise. Unable to fight such a foe, he instead chose to dispersed the Key, scattering the pieces once again through time and space.

The sixth segment became Astra once more, and she returned home to oversee the rebuilding of her world. The other five segments vanished, taking with them the ultimate power.

CONTINUITY

Interestingly, what we learn in this adventure often gives us more questions. The biggest revelation is Drax revealing the Doctor's name as 'Theta Sigma' or 'Theet' for short. This also implies Time Lords can recognise each other even after several regenerations. Mind you, as the Doctor doesn't really recognise Drax, he may simply be pretending to be an old classmate to get Drax's help. Later on, in his seventh incarnation, the Doctor reveals Theta Sigma isn't his real name, but a college nickname.

Drax and the Doctor both graduated from the Prydonian college of the Academy in '92. While they both claim the title Time Lord, Drax never managed to pass the theory part of the tests. This might suggest that there are several layers of Gallifreyan academia. Drax passed the early tests to become a qualified Time Lord, but the Doctor and Romana went on to further 'doctorate level' qualifications as full graduates of the academy.

Romana is quite the entomologist. Not only has she pretended to be a butterfly collector in **The Stones of Blood**, and studied the Gallifreyan flutterwing instead of vintage time capsules at university, but she is also familiar with the social dances of bees.

Having incurred the wrath of the Black Guardian, the Doctor installs a 'randomiser' into the TARDIS console. This device will randomly select a new destination for the travellers, making them difficult to track. The Doctor will get bored of it though and remove it after their adventure on Argolis (see *The Leisure Hive*).

⊙ RUNNING THE ADVENTURE

The first question the Gamemaster needs to ask is 'what does the Shadow want?' If this is to be the final part of a long campaign, the answer is clear; whatever the player characters have been after all this time. However, if not, he needs to be after something important enough to start a protracted war. He might still serve the Black Guardian, and it could all be a test run for a larger universal war, but ideally there should be a little more. This should be something the player characters can provide, so its nature is very much up to the individual campaign.

A lot of this adventure will depend on how perceptive the player characters are. If they notice some of the NPCs are wearing the Shadow's mind-control talismans, they can figure things out reasonably quickly. However, a good way to really confuse them is to make everything to be as it appears to be. The Marshal is a victory-crazed maniac, prepared to burn his own world to destroy Zeos and if so, maybe there are a few Zeons left. They have let a computer take over their weapons, which is why they are doing better than Atrios. However, they are still a broken society. Perhaps they live deep underground, ignoring the war going on above. Many of them might not even know it is even going on at all, explaining why they aren't responding to Astra's attempts to communicate.

Another way to come at this adventure is to put the player characters in Drax's position rather than the Doctor's. They might be engaged to fix the technology of an oppressed world, and slowly discover they are actually part of an aggressive war effort. When they change their mind their employers stop being so kind and welcoming and show their true colours. Now the player characters need to stop a war they have helped start!

ATRIOS

After many years of nuclear war, the remaining population of Atrios live in an underground complex. The surface of the planet is in ruins, and highly irradiated. Life in the complex is far from safe and secure too. After almost constant bombardment, many parts of the complex are weak or irradiated too. People inhabit what space they can find, often turning corridors into makeshift homes and medical centres.

The power systems are all still functioning so machinery is reliable as long as it hasn't been damaged. The television monitors posted throughout the complex offer a constant diet of inspirational programming and propaganda from the Marshal. Most people are too busy trying to feed themselves or keep the complex running to listen to it.

ZEOS

Much like Atrios, the surface of Zeos is no longer fit for human life, so the Zeons also built an underground complex. The corridors under Zeos are beige, not

THE KEY TO TIME

The complete Key to Time was an artefact of unimaginable power, equal to the fabled Eye of Harmony in its capacity to control the Time Vortex. Even an incomplete Key allowed the Doctor to create a time loop big enough to encompass the Marshal's ship.

Trying to assign game rules to the Key is futile – it's much, much too powerful. Assume that anyone in control of it has all the Story Points ever, and can rewrite space and time freely. It's probably for the best that the Key was lost once again.

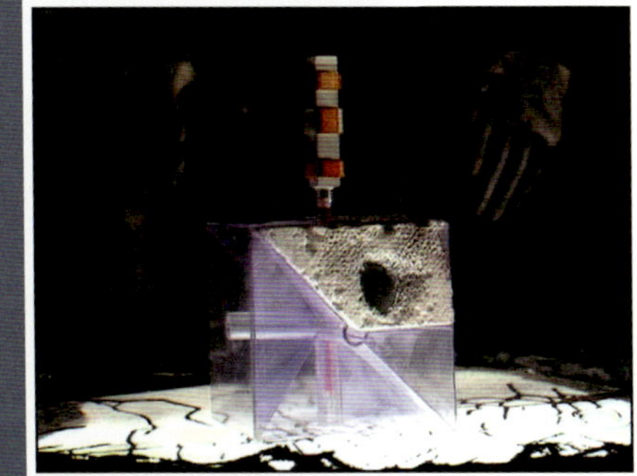

grey and decorated in triangular shapes rather than concrete. However, the place itself is empty, the last Zeons having died many years before.

The only place of interest on Zeos is the command centre run by Mentalis. The door to the command centre is very secure, unless Mentalis can be convinced to let visitors in. Inside, several blaster units protect Mentalis from harm. The room itself is surrounded in computer systems, with the elegant pyramid shape of the main computer set in the centre.

THE PLANET OF EVIL

Set between Atrios and Zeos is an artificial planet, cloaked to escape detection from most sensor systems and serving as the Shadow's base of operations. The inside of this third planet appears more like a cavern than an installation, with the walls appearing to be natural black rock. Holographic

systems throughout the station allow the commander to create illusions to confuse intruders. There are also many hidden cameras to keep an eye on guests. The Shadow uses very little of the station, running most operations from a central cavern. Here he keeps prisoners either chained to the wall or under interrogation in an electrostatic torture chamber. The only other residents of the station are the Mutes who patrol. However, security is reasonably lax as few people can come to the place without the Shadow's knowledge.

FURTHER ADVENTURES

- **New Civil War:** With hostilities over, several Atrions move to Zeos to build new lives, and seek new resources. However, life is still tough for both sides. Rabble-rousers on both Atrios and Zeos begin rumours that the other planet has stockpiles they are not sharing, and tensions

---

THE SHADOW

If anyone is adept at playing 'the long game' it is the Shadow, one of the main henchmen of the Black Guardian. Instead of searching space for the Key to Time he took the simpler route. Locate a single piece and wait for someone with the other five to come looking for it. The Shadow takes his name seriously, and uses technology to cloak both himself and his operations. He serves the will of the Black Guardian completely, looking forward with insane enthusiasm to when they might plunge the universe into total chaos.

AWARENESS	3	**PRESENCE**	3
COORDINATION	3	**RESOLVE**	4
INGENUITY	4	**STRENGTH**	3

SKILLS
Athletics 2, Convince 3, Craft 2, Knowledge 4, Science 5, Subterfuge 5, Technology 4, Transport 2

TRAITS
Hypnosis (Major): +2 bonus to control another's actions and feelings*.
Immortal (Major): The Shadow is thousands of years old.
Indomitable: +4 bonus to any rolls to resist psychic control.
Eccentric (Major): Seeks to turn the universe into chaos.
Obsession (Major): Serve the Black Guardian, find the Key to Time.

Unattractive: -2 penalty to any rolls that involve the Shadow's looks. May provide +2 to intimidate rolls at GMs discretion.
Weakness (Minor): -2 to rolls when in bright light.

TECH LEVEL: 8   **STORY POINTS: 12**

*must place a control chip on the subject's neck to exert control.

are getting stretched. Can the player characters stop another war starting?

- **The Rainmaker:** Drawn to the recovering Atrios, a merchant offers cheap supplies to help the people. However, his price for this help is the planet Zeos. What can he want with the blasted world? Is there something even more valuable buried on Zeos? Do the Atrions really have the right to sell him the planet anyway?

- **The Crown of Atrios:** Princess Astra now rules both planets, with her husband Merak at her side. But another princess claims she is the heir to the throne, and has convincing proof of her lineage. Astra is actually quite happy to step aside, until it becomes clear this new princess does not have the people's welfare at heart. Can the player characters convince Astra to fight for a crown she doesn't want? What if the new princess really is the rightful heir after all?

DRAX

Drax is proof that failing to become a master of time and space need not stand in the way of a decent career. Having no head for academics, but an aptitude for technology, Drax didn't manage to pass the exams required to fully qualify as a graduate of the Time Lord academy. So instead he quietly left Gallifrey and became a galactic 'odd job' man, repairing or building advanced technological systems. As the Time Lords didn't put a stop to his activities, given he was interfering in the affairs of other races, it seems he is also a master of staying away from their notice. His plan is simple: do the job, get paid, move on. (For more detail on Drax see pg. 162 of **The Time Traveller's Companion**)

AWARENESS	4	PRESENCE	4
COORDINATION	4	RESOLVE	4
INGENUITY	5	STRENGTH	3

SKILLS
Athletics 1, Convince 3, Craft 3, Fighting 2, Knowledge 5, Marksman 1, Science 3, Subterfuge 5, Survival 4, Technology 5, Transport 3

TRAITS
Boffin (Major Good): Allows Drax to create Gadgets.
Charming (Minor Good): +2 bonus to attempts to use charm.
Doctorate (Minor Good): +3 when using Engineering.
Face in the Crowd (Minor Good): +2 to any Subterfuge Skill roll to sneak about.
Percussive Maintenance (Minor Good): May re-roll repair attempts.
Reverse the Polarity of the Neutron Flow (Major Good): May reverse a test result once per adventure.
Run for your Life! (Minor Good): +1 bonus to his Speed when escaping pursuit.
Technically Adept (Minor Good): +2 to any Technology roll to fix a broken or faulty device.
Time Lord, Almost (Special Good): As far as the practical stuff goes anyway.
Time Traveller (Minor/Major Good): Familiar with Tech Level 5-7.

Bottom of the Class (Major Bad): -1 Ingenuity and a +2 to the Difficulty on all TARDIS and Temporal Science rolls.
Eccentric (Minor Bad): Spent a little too long in Brixton and got too used to the place.
Wanted Renegade (Special Bad): The Time Lords are looking for Drax, but are not that bothered about finding him.

REGENERATIONS USED: 1

EQUIPMENT: Drax is never without his toolkit.

TECH LEVEL: 10   **STORY POINTS:** 6

THE KEY TO TIME: THE ARMAGEDDON FACTOR

THE MARSHAL OF ATRIOS

AWARENESS	2	PRESENCE	4
COORDINATION	3	RESOLVE	2
INGENUITY	3	STRENGTH	3

It is hard to tell who the Marshal really is anymore, so long has he been under the Shadow's control. Years of being used like a puppet have hollowed him out, leaving little left but the will to win a victory over Zeos. This makes him prone to mood swings when he receives new orders, making his behaviour very erratic as he adapts to fulfil the Shadow's goals.

SKILLS

Athletics 2, Convince 2, Fighting 2, Knowledge 2, Marksman 3, Subterfuge 3, Technology 3, Transport 2

TRAITS

Military Rank (Major): Marshal of Atrios.
Adversary (Major): The planet Zeos.
By the Book: Must be convinced to act against procedure.
Dark Secret (Major): Working for the Shadow.
Obligation (Major): Obey the Shadow.

EQUIPMENT: Hand Blaster (4/L/L)

TECH LEVEL: 6   STORY POINTS: 4

PRINCESS ASTRA

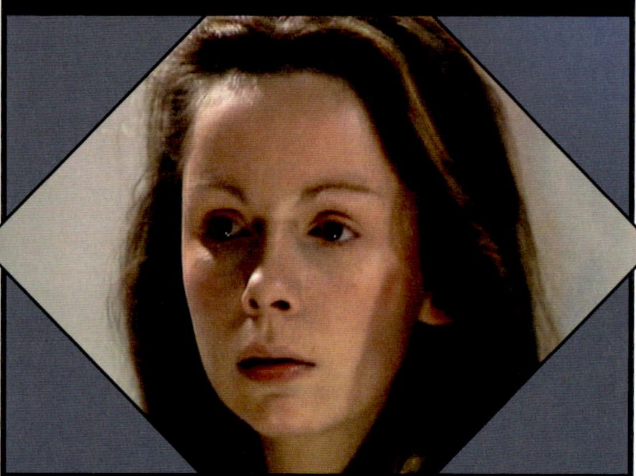

AWARENESS	3	PRESENCE	4
COORDINATION	3	RESOLVE	5
INGENUITY	4	STRENGTH	2

Astra has little to do in the war but be an example for her people and a symbol of hope, but it's a job she takes seriously. While any power she may have once had has been taken over by the Marshal, she still does her best to play her part. Despite appearing to be little more than a figurehead, the Princess is actually a dedicated and clever woman; with the help of Merak she has been trying to find a way to secretly negotiate for peace. All she wants is an end to the war and for her people to be safe. Astra believes this might be the destiny she was born for, but she turns out to be very wrong.

SKILLS

Athletics 2, Convince 3, Knowledge 2, Medicine 1, Science 2, Subterfuge 3, Technology 2

TRAITS

Attractive: +2 bonus to any rolls that involve the character's looks.
Brave: +2 bonus to any Resolve roll when the character needs to show courage.
Empathic: +2 bonus on rolls to 'read' another person.
Inspiring Love: +1 to rolls when with Merak.
Code of Conduct (Minor): Character finds it hard to do bad.
Distinctive: -2 penalty to rolls to blend in. Others have a +2 bonus to remember or recognise the character.

TECH LEVEL: 6   STORY POINTS: 6

DESTINY OF THE DALEKS

'For a place that looked dead, there's a lot going on.'

⊙ SYNOPSIS

Skaro, the Future

Having installed a 'randomiser' to ensure both they and the Black Guardian did not know where they are going, the Doctor and a newly regenerated Romana landed on a seemingly dead world. Exploring, they found a ruined city undergoing excavation by huge digging machines. They also came across a funeral party, made up of weary looking people from across the galaxy. Whoever was digging was also using captured prisoners as slave labour.

Talking to the slaves, Romana learned that their oppressors were Daleks, and they were on the ruined world of Skaro, the planet where the Daleks originated long ago. The city was the same complex that the Doctor visited several times before (notably in **Genesis of the Daleks**). The Daleks were in search of a mysterious buried artefact they needed desperately.

The Daleks were not the only invading force to disturb the dust of Skaro. A second spacecraft arrived, belonging to the Movellans. These newcomers appeared to be humans, and were enemies of the Daleks, so the Doctor agreed to work with them. Sneaking into the Dalek control room, the Doctor got to look at the Dalek's digging plan. Having been to the city before, he recognised the area they were digging towards and remembered a short cut.

The Daleks' objective turned out to be Davros, the Dalek's creator. His life support system had kept him alive in suspended animation since the Daleks attempted to destroy him. Using Davros as leverage, the Doctor managed to negotiate with the Daleks for the slaves' freedom and his own life, but eventually had to hand Davros over to the Daleks to make an escape. Romana returned to the Movellans, but they confirmed the Doctor's suspicion that they were not really their allies; they were actually robots, at war with the Daleks. Their battle fleets had been in stalemate for centuries; their battle computers were so clinically logical that neither could create a vital advantage.

Just as the Daleks had returned for the advice of their creator, the Movellans realised the Doctor might be the illogical mind they required for victory too. The Movellans didn't just want to destroy the Daleks, however; they wanted to rule the galaxy too, so the Doctor refused to cooperate.

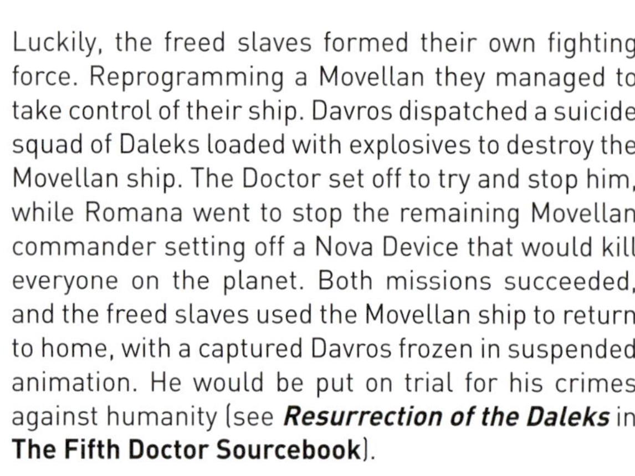

Luckily, the freed slaves formed their own fighting force. Reprogramming a Movellan they managed to take control of their ship. Davros dispatched a suicide squad of Daleks loaded with explosives to destroy the Movellan ship. The Doctor set off to try and stop him, while Romana went to stop the remaining Movellan commander setting off a Nova Device that would kill everyone on the planet. Both missions succeeded, and the freed slaves used the Movellan ship to return to home, with a captured Davros frozen in suspended animation. He would be put on trial for his crimes against humanity (see **Resurrection of the Daleks** in **The Fifth Doctor Sourcebook**).

CONTINUITY

Romana regenerates on a whim, trying on three bodies before settling on a copy of Princess Astra (see **The Armageddon Factor**). This seems to directly contradict the random regeneration the Doctor has suffered over the years, but it is not without precedent. The Doctor's old teacher Cho Je managed to regenerate into a younger version of himself (see **Planet of the Spiders** in **The Third Doctor Sourcebook**) and in his later transformations even the Doctor has proved to have surprisingly adaptive abilities until his regeneration is settled. Perhaps Romana is not 'using up' regenerations, but taking advantage of her body being in flux to shape

it as she pleases. Even this explanation grants her incredible control over her regeneration, but then, she did get a triple first at the academy. Controlled regeneration could easily be just another class she excelled in that the Doctor failed.

The Doctor seems to have met zombies before and he tells Romana you can always tell a zombie from their cold skin.

The Daleks run their operations from command spacecraft, a mobile base being far more secure. Davros doesn't even consider himself safe until he is in space. The Daleks also keep their captives on a prison ship in their fleet. From this, captives are selected for slave duty as operations require. Conditions on the prison ships are so bad even backbreaking work shifting rubble on an irradiated planet is considered a step up.

⊙ RUNNING THE ADVENTURE

The set up for this adventure is quite simple: the Daleks want something and the Movellans want to find out what it is and destroy it. The player characters can very quickly tip the balance of power, able to think outside of the box in a way neither Daleks nor Movellans are capable of. The question then remains, who do they help? Initially this might seem a simple question; given the Daleks are the epitome of absolute evil in the universe.

But what if the Movellans are worse? The Daleks want to enslave the universe, but what if the Movellans want to destroy all non-robotic life? If your player characters are a little more cunning, they might choose to help one side, to ensure both races remain in stalemate. If the Movellans are actually winning the war, helping the Daleks might be a way to return a balance of power. While stopping either force is nigh impossible, ensuring they keep each other occupied for eternity might be the best way to keep the rest of the universe safe.

SKARO

The planet of Skaro is a desolate and barren world. Even centuries after the Dalek/Thal war, the place still has high levels of radiation across the surface. Most of the vegetation has died, taking with it most forms of fauna. This radiation might confuse sensors, which is why the Movellan ship is able to land undetected. The local landscape is stone rather than earth, forcing the slave burial parties to cover bodies in stones rather than bury them. In short, Skaro is a brooding, dead world, still suffering from the legacy of its inhabitants.

KEY LOCATIONS ON SKARO

- **The Ruined City:** The remains of the Dalek complex is little more than a shell. Few of the floors and supports are stable and it is easy to bring the roof down. Dust, rubble and broken equipment litter the place. Explorers should be very careful not to fall through the floor, as they might be carried deep into the undercity.

- **The Underground City:** Under the ruins of the old city are the remains of the command complex of the Kaleds, built to withstand nuclear assault. While it is in no better repair than the city ruins, it has survived quite well. Most lighting systems are active and while many areas have been cut off from each other, those that remain are in good condition, if you don't mind cobwebs.

- **Dalek Central Control:** The Dalek scout party that came to find Davros set up a command centre in the undercity. Like most Dalek installations it is a plain and functional room. It contains the main computer systems, drilling control and an interrogation chamber. As there are comparatively few Daleks here and their slaves are down in the mines, security is quite lax, making it reasonably easy to sneak in when it is unoccupied.

- **The Movellan Ship:** While it is also practical and functional, the Movellan ship is far more comfortable than any Dalek base. Everything is built in white and silver, with space given over for

relaxation as well as work. While the Movellans have little need for 'downtime' or personal space, it is still the sort of ship any human crew would be at home on.

FURTHER ADVENTURES

- The Movellans later win their war with the Daleks by creating a virus that attacks the Dalek mutant (see **Resurrection of the Daleks** in **The Fifth Doctor Sourcebook**). The characters blunder into a secret Movellan research facility where they test early versions of this virus on captured Daleks. If the only way out is to ally with the most evil race in the universe, can the characters escape the Movellan base?

- The Daleks sought out Davros because he was capable of unpredictable insights. Later, that's the role of the Cult of Skaro (see **Doomsday**, in **The Tenth Doctor Sourcebook**). Was the cult behind this plan to consult Davros? Or was it created to deal with the consequences of the Movellan War?

- Davros is accused of crimes against humanity – but humanity isn't the only species that the Daleks attacked. Half the races in the galaxy probably want to put Davros on trial. When the prison ship carrying the most notorious mass murderer in the universe is ambushed by six different fleets simultaneously, the characters are chosen as neutral arbiters to decide which race has the honour of executing Davros. But do some of the prosecutors have their own secret agendas?

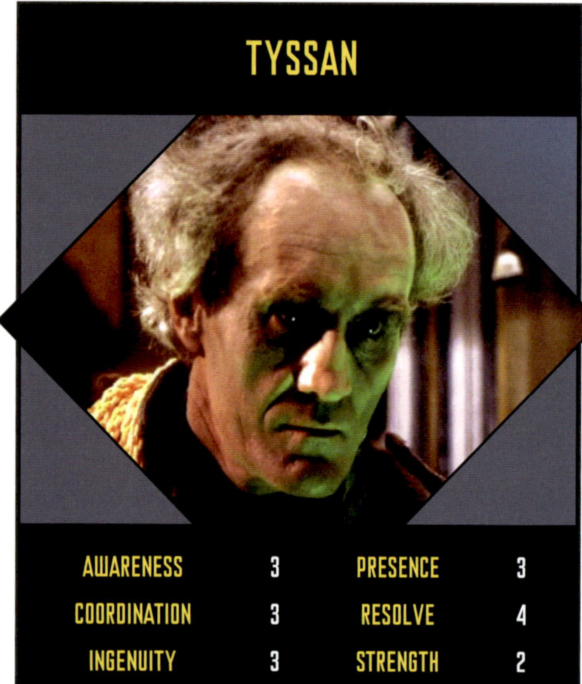

TYSSAN

AWARENESS	3	PRESENCE	3
COORDINATION	3	RESOLVE	4
INGENUITY	3	STRENGTH	2

Apart from Romana, Tyssan, is the only person to escape the Daleks and live, although he might not have survived long on the barren surface without meeting the time travellers. Pale, malnourished and drawn from working in the mines Tyssan nevertheless maintains his resolve. Originally, Tyssan was an engineer on an Earth starship, until his capture by the Daleks. He was one of fifty slaves brought to Skaro for the mining operation. A slave for two years, he passed out on one of the digs and was left for dead, allowing him to escape. When the Doctor frees the other slaves he becomes their leader, organising them into a force able to take the Movellan ship. He returned to human controlled space with the Movellan ship and the captured Davros.

SKILLS

Athletics 4, Craft 3, Fighting 2, Knowledge 2, Marksman 2, Subterfuge 3, Survival 3, Technology 4, Transport 2

TRAITS

Brave: +2 bonus to any Resolve roll when Tyssan needs to show courage.
Technically Adept: +2 to any Technology roll to fix a broken or faulty device.

TECH LEVEL: 6   **STORY POINTS: 4**

MOVELLANS

At first the Movellans appear human, if a little clinical, apart from their silver dreadlocked hair. In fact, they go to great lengths to hide their true nature as advanced self-aware robots. While they are robotic creatures, their designers made each one unique and they respond to different names, such as Sharrel, Agella and Lan. They all dress in the same uniform of white and silver bodysuits. The only outward signs of their true nature are their somewhat stiff attitude and that their skin is cold to the touch. The Movellans are adept at appearing calm and reasonable, but are actually as warmongering as their enemies the Daleks. They remain at war with Davros' creations, each the only obstacle to the other's galactic domination. Their technology is comparable to the Daleks, with intergalactic, time warp capable ships.

Movellans have very little command structure, needing only a single commander to lead any group. The commander is marked by black braids on the tips of his hair. Like Daleks, individual Movellans can work independently towards a goal and obey orders unquestioningly. While both are coldly logical beings, the Movellans are developing in the opposite way to their enemies. The Daleks were human and are developing into cybernetic, even robotic beings, whereas the Movellans are robots who are becoming more human.

There is one weakness all Movellans share: they are powered by battery packs they carry on their belts. When removed the Movellan shuts down in seconds and its Strength and Coordination are reduced to 1 the moment the pack is removed. The battery packs are programmable, allowing a Movellan to be assigned new tasks, skills and data simply by picking up a new pack. However this also means they can be reprogrammed by manipulating the pack they carry, even reassigning their loyalties against their own people. While it is unclear who originally built the Movellans, the battery pack design suggests they were originally built to be multi-purpose robots. They may have become so ubiquitous in a society, able to perform any function with a simple reprogramming, that they eventually outnumbered their creators. They use Disruptor Pistols, which are capable of killing or stunning a target but do not draw power from the Movellan, allowing anyone to use them. While the weapons are very economical with power, they are usually kept in a charging bay on the ship when not in use.

AWARENESS	4	PRESENCE	4
COORDINATION	4	RESOLVE	4
INGENUITY	5	STRENGTH	3

SKILLS
Athletics 3, Craft 2, Fighting 3, Knowledge 2, Marksman 4, Science 2, Subterfuge 3, Technology 3, Transport 2

TRAITS
Armour (Minor): Reduce damage by 5.
Environmental (Major): Movellans are immune to most hostile environments.
Robot (Special Good)
Weakness (Major): Shuts down if battery pack removed*.
Tough (Minor): Reduce total damage by 2.
Adversary (Major) : Greatest enemy of the Daleks.
Eccentric (Major): Movellans cannot act illogically or irrationally.

EQUIPMENT: Disruptor pistol, may be set to Kill (4/L/L) or Stun (-/S/S)

TECH LEVEL: 8   **STORY POINTS: 3**

*Taking a battery pack from a Movellan requires an opposed Coordination + Subterfuge roll. If removed the Movellan's Strength and Coordination are instantly reduced to 1 and it shuts down 2 rounds later. Battery packs can also be loaded with new Skills, allowing a Movellan to gain a higher Skill level instantly on fitting a pre-programmed pack.

CITY OF DEATH

'*Must we go into vulgar threats? Let us just say I shall destroy Paris if that'll help you make up your mind.*'

⊙ SYNOPSIS

Paris, Earth, the Present Day

The Doctor and Romana landed in Paris in the 1970s, so they decided to make a holiday of it and see the sights. While enjoying the ambiance of *la vie Parisian*, they both felt a powerful disturbance in time. The Doctor almost passed out when it happens again during a visit to the Louvre to see the Mona Lisa, and he nearly crushed another visitor, the beautiful Countess Scarlioni. During their encounter the Doctor stole the bracelet the Countess was wearing, a piece of alien technology. The device was a 'micro-meson' bracelet, with which she had been passively scanned the security systems of the gallery.

Upon leaving the Louvre the Doctor and Romana were followed by an investigator called Duggan. He believed them to be complicit in a plot he didn't really understand. Lost masterpieces were appearing on the black market with alarming regularity, and the Countess' husband Count Scarlioni seemed to be at the centre of it. Thugs in the employ of Scarlioni arrived to retrieve the stolen bracelet and take the trio to their master.

Bored with the Doctor's flippant answers to his questions, the Count ordered them all taken to the cellar. After breaking out of their cell they met Professor Kerensky, who was conducting temporal experiments in the basement laboratory. The experiments were very important to the Count who spent a fortune on getting whatever the Professor needed for his work. The Doctor and Kerensky got on very well discussing the project until Duggan knocked the Professor out.

Romana noticed the dimensions of the room were not right, and upon investigating they discovered a secret room. Hidden in a very old cabinet were no less than six versions of the Mona Lisa – they were all originals as well, not copies! The Count's plan became clearer. He intended to steal the Mona Lisa from the Louvre, then sell it to seven black market art collectors. As each collector was buying the painting illegally, they would never be able to tell anyone they own it, so no one would discover there were seven versions. However, the question remained, where did the Count get six Mona Lisas?

Romana and Duggan were sent off to the Louvre to stop the theft taking place, while the Doctor decided to pay a visit to his old friend Leonardo Da Vinci in Florence in 1505. Taking the TARDIS back to Da Vinci's workshop, the Doctor was disappointed to discover Leonardo wasn't around. However, his patron, Captain Tancredi was there, and looked exactly like Count Scarlioni. The Captain and the Count were actually aliens. Actually, they were the same alien. Both were splinters of Scaroth, last of the Jagaroth. The Jagaroth landed on Earth millions of years ago. Their ship was badly damaged, and Scaroth attempted a dangerous take off using its powerful warp engines. The manoeuvre went terribly wrong, destroying the ship and splintering Scaroth across time. His shards had all worked hard to provide his modern incarnation, Count Scarlioni, with the resources and wealth to mount a rescue. His Captain Tancredi incarnation asked Leonardo to paint seven Mona Lisas and then hid the other six where Scarlioni could find them. Other Scaroth-incarnations worked to guide human civilisation to produce the technology needed to build a time machine.

Tancredi captured the Doctor and planned to torture him to learn how he travelled in time. However, the Doctor took advantage of a distraction to escape. But before he did so, he wrote 'this is a fake' in felt tip on the canvases Leonardo was about to use to paint the extra Mona Lisas. Then he left a quick note to the artist to just paint over the words before returning to Paris.

Having failed to stop the theft of the Mona Lisa, Romana and Duggan decided to confront the Count. He convinced Romana he simply wanted to go back in time and prevent the death of his crew. Seeing it as a way to get rid of the Count, Romana adapted Kerensky's work to send him into the distant past. However, she built in a fail-safe that meant the Count would only have two minutes in the past. The Doctor arrived just as she finished adapting the device, but he failed to stop Scaroth going back in time. Unfortunately, Scaroth's mission would not only save his people, but could destroy all life on Earth. The explosion of the ship millions of years ago gave the primordial soup of life the vital spark it needed to begin developing. Without it, life on earth would never have developed.

The Doctor, Romana and Duggan went back in time in the TARDIS to stop the Count. Scaroth cared nothing for the human race, seeing them only as the tool he developed to allow him to save his own people. With the Doctor unable to appeal to his morality, Duggan punched Scaroth and knocked him out. His two minutes up, Scaroth was brought back, unmasked, to his chateau, where his henchman Hermann failed to recognise this green monster as his master.

Hermann threw a piece of equipment at the 'monster' and the machine, causing it to explode, killing Hermann and Scaroth, and setting fire to the château. One of the Mona Lisas was rescued from the fire and returned to the Louvre. However, much to Duggan's dismay, no one was really sure if it was the original or not. The Doctor and Romana left him to keep the secret and set off to enjoy Paris once more.

CONTINUITY

On Gallifrey computers produce the art, much to the Doctor's distaste. While the Louvre remains one of the Doctor's favourite art galleries, Romana finds it less impressive than the Academius Stolaris on Sirius V, the Solarian Pinnacotheque on Strikian and the Braxiatel Collection.

Once more the Doctor claims to be a friend of historical celebrities. He knows Leonardo Da Vinci well enough to leave him a mirror-written message confident he will follow the Doctor's instructions. Also, when shown a manuscript of Hamlet, the Doctor claims to have helped write it.

Scaroth claims to have been responsible for many of humanity's early achievements, including the invention of the wheel and the discovery of fire.

The Doctor is able to disengage the randomiser from the TARDIS controls in order to be able to visit Da Vinci and go back to stop Scaroth in Earth's prehistory. Luckily the Black Guardian doesn't turn up.

SPLINTERED CHARACTERS

If a player is looking for an unconventional character to play, they could take inspiration from Scaroth and play someone who's been splintered across time and space. The character only becomes aware of his splintered status after coming into contact with other time travellers. In each new adventure, the rest of the characters encounter a new incarnation of the splintered character – and after that encounter, that incarnation can psychically communicate with the other 'active' incarnations. Playing a Splintered character like this is a Special Good Trait, costing 3 Character Points. The Gamemaster should assign suitable Traits to each incarnation to reflect their new situation.

⊙ RUNNING THE ADVENTURE

While it may seem this adventure is all about gallivanting around Paris, it could easily become part of a larger campaign. The Doctor and Romana are actually very lucky they arrive in the 1970s at the climax of Scaroth's plot. How different might their adventure have been if they encountered an earlier Scaroth, perhaps one involved in building the pyramids? Discovering something odd they will have to follow the trail of years towards the present day to find out exactly what Scaroth is actually up to. Each time his next incarnation might have planned for the arrival of such interlopers.

The other interesting thing about Scaroth's plans is that while he is interfering in history, he isn't changing it; in fact, he's responsible for it. The achievements he has nudged humanity into making are now a part of Earth's temporal make up. This means he is grossly manipulating human development, but without changing their history. This makes him a difficult enemy to stop. What should he be allowed to get away with and what must be stopped? This offers several moral conundrums as well as temporal ones, and predestination can become a powerful factor. Scaroth's interference ensures humanity becomes as advanced as it should be by the 20th century. Imagine stopping the bad guy to discover you have plunged Earth into a new Dark Ages.

To a certain degree, the Mona Lisa is a red herring in this adventure. It is only important for the wealth selling seven of them will bring the Count. One of the easiest ways to adapt the adventure is to have the player characters stumble over a different theft, possibly even in a different city. Scaroth need not be a thief at all. Money and funding are what is important here. He could make just as much money trading on the stock market. This might be especially lucrative if his present splinter is able to send stock tips back in time to a previous incarnation, who puts the money in a high-interest savings account.

As Scaroth wears a mask, you might also adapt who he pretends to be. As an arrogant warrior race it seems fitting a Jagaroth will insist on being powerful and in charge. However, the Count manages to maintain a relationship with a human woman who never has a clue about his true nature. So, perhaps the Countess is the Jagaroth instead, marrying powerful men throughout history and siphoning off their funds. She would be a subtler villain, and a hard one to track as she could change her identity any time she liked.

THE JAGAROTH

AWARENESS	3	PRESENCE	2
COORDINATION	3	RESOLVE	3
INGENUITY	4	STRENGTH	3

This warlike race is a repugnant species in almost every sense of the word. Humanoid in shape, they have green, mossy skin and a single eye. On the inside they are just as ugly, believing in their own superiority with a 'might makes right' attitude. While they were a highly advanced species before life even began on Earth, they had already warred themselves almost to extinction. Scaroth was convinced his ship was the only one left, and even that was badly damaged. However, he might have been wrong, and another faction might have survived.

SKILLS
Athletics 3, Knowledge 3, Marksman 2, Science 5, Subterfuge 4, Survival 3, Technology 5, Transport 2

TRAITS
Alien
Alien Appearance (Major): The Jagaroths' features are utterly inhuman.
Obsession (Minor): Destroy all enemies, prove the superiority of the Jagaroth.

TECH LEVEL: 7   **STORY POINTS: 6**

FURTHER ADVENTURES

- **Da Vinci's Time Machine:** With Count Scarlioni gone, the remaining splinters of Scaroth concoct a new plan. Captain Tancredi gets Da Vinci to work on a time machine, and the maestro begins to get results. While he will never be able to create an actual time machine, Scaroth hopes that the temporal disturbances the machine is creating will attract the attention of someone with a time machine of their own, which he can then steal.

- **Scaroth's Revenge:** Perhaps Scaroth isn't actually killed when Hermann destroys Kerensky's machine. Instead he is thrown back in time a little further, or even thrown forward. He begins his plan again, this time looking to create a new race of Jagaroth with cloning technology.

SCAROTH, LAST OF THE JAGAROTH

For centuries, Scaroth has borne a terrible burden: he was the pilot of the last remaining Jagaroth spacecraft, who failed to save his race. Not only did he fail to save them, but it was his decision that led to their destruction when he ordered the badly damaged craft to take off. The explosion was so powerful he was fractured into several splinters and scattered across time. Desperate to save his people he tried to advance human technology so he could go back in time to stop his past self bringing an end to his race.

As his true appearance is quite horrible to human eyes, Scaroth uses a mask to pass for a human. With each incarnation working to build the resources of the next he is always fabulously wealthy. As such he has developed a certain sense of noblesse oblige and maintains rather an urbane charm. However, he cares nothing for humanity, viewing them as little more than tools. There is nothing he will not do, no line he will not cross and no one he will not sacrifice to undo his failure and save the Jagaroth.

AWARENESS	3	PRESENCE	5
COORDINATION	3	RESOLVE	4
INGENUITY	5	STRENGTH	3

SKILLS
Athletics 3, Convince 4, Craft 3, Knowledge 6, Marksman 2, Science 5, Subterfuge 4, Survival 3, Technology 5, Transport 3

TRAITS
Alien
Alien Appearance (Major): Without a mask Scaroth is utterly inhuman.
Boffin: Allows Scaroth to create Gadgets.
Charming: +2 bonus to attempts to use charm.
Dark Secret (Minor): Actually an alien.
Last of my Kind (Minor Bad): -2 to any but life threatening rolls when alone.
Obsession (Major): Save the Jagaroth!
Splintered: Scaroth is in contact with his other splinters, granting him a wide selection of knowledge and experience.
Voice of Authority: +2 bonus to Presence and Convince rolls.

TECH LEVEL: 7   **STORY POINTS:** 12

- **Save the Jagaroth:** Scaroth was wrong; his was not the last ship, not by a long chalk. The wars among the Jagaroth have continued for centuries. However, one group seek desperately to escape the eternal battle. Will the player characters believe such horrible creatures can actually be artists and peacemakers? Will they help them when the rest of their race come to destroy these 'lunatics' before they spread the dangerous message of peace?

DUGGAN

AWARENESS	2	PRESENCE	3
COORDINATION	4	RESOLVE	3
INGENUITY	2	STRENGTH	4

Duggan is possibly the least subtle private detective in the world. He charges into every situation like a bull in a china shop, punching first and asking questions later. It is no wonder he cannot get to the bottom of the Count's plans when he'd rather knock people unconscious than talk to them. Duggan isn't quite the thug he might seem; he is loyal to those he trusts and is always looking to do the right thing, he just doesn't often understand what the right thing might be, especially when an opportunity to punch someone or break something presents itself.

SKILLS
Athletics 3, Convince 2, Fighting 3 (Punching 5), Knowledge 2, Marksman 2, Subterfuge 1, Technology 2, Transport 2

TRAITS
Brave: +2 bonus to any Resolve roll when the character needs to show courage.
Quick Reflexes: Duggan's quick to swing his fist. He always goes first in his Action Round unless taken by surprise.
Argumentative: Duggan doesn't know when he's in over his head.
Impulsive: Punch first. Investigate later.

TECH LEVEL: 5   **STORY POINTS: 8**

HERMANN

AWARENESS	2	PRESENCE	2
COORDINATION	3	RESOLVE	3
INGENUITY	2	STRENGTH	4

This broad-shouldered thug is the perfect henchman. Utterly loyal to the Count and Countess, he follows orders without hesitation. While he knows nothing of the Count's true nature he knows all he needs to know; that the Count will make him wealthy and powerful if he does he is told.

SKILLS
Athletics 3, Fighting 4, Marksman 2, Subterfuge 3, Technology 2, Transport 2

TRAITS
Quick Reflexes: Hermann always goes first in his Action Round unless taken by surprise.
Tough: Reduce total damage by 2.

TECH LEVEL: 5   **STORY POINTS: 2**

COUNTESS SCARLIONI

AWARENESS	3	PRESENCE	4
COORDINATION	3	RESOLVE	3
INGENUITY	3	STRENGTH	2

While the Countess was drawn to her husband's charm, she has only ever been interested in money and power. Theirs is nothing more than a marriage of convenience, although the Countess does see her husband as a daring partner in crime. While she adopts the air of a bored noble, the Countess is in fact a thief. She is drawn to power and loves to be on 'the winning side'. It is a shame she discovers the truth about her husband too late, and even more of a shame for her she decides to challenge him on the subject.

SKILLS
Athletics 2, Convince 2, Knowledge 2, Marksman 1, Subterfuge 4, Transport 2

TRAITS
Attractive: +2 bonus to any rolls that involve the character's looks.
Charming: +2 bonus to attempts to use charm.
Obsession (Minor): She wants money and power, and cares little about how she gets them.

TECH LEVEL: 5   STORY POINTS: 4

PROFESSOR KERENSKY

AWARENESS	2	PRESENCE	2
COORDINATION	2	RESOLVE	3
INGENUITY	5	STRENGTH	2

As naïve as he is brilliant, Professor Kerensky is the world's foremost temporal scientist. In a sense he is the pinnacle of human achievement that Scaroth has worked so hard to create. Kerensky believes his work will end world hunger, growing cattle to maturity in seconds to feed the hungry. While the Count is a slavedriver, Kerensky is so dedicated to his work he allows himself to be pushed into sleepless nights and long hours. With no friends and family, Kerensky has little in life but his work, but even after his dedication Scaroth kills him without a second thought, aging him to a skeleton just to prove his ruthlessness to Romana.

SKILLS
Craft 4, Knowledge 2, Medicine 2, Science 5, Technology 5

TRAITS
Boffin: He builds time machines.
Face in the Crowd: +2 to any Subterfuge Skill rolls to sneak about.
By the Book: He's a bit myopic and finds it hard to notice things out of the ordinary.
Insatiable Curiosity (Minor): Once Kerensky's got a puzzle to solve, he obsesses over it.
Obligation (Minor): Do as the count asks as he pays the bills.
Obsession (Minor): Build the machine, and help humanity with it.

TECH LEVEL: 6   STORY POINTS: 6

THE CREATURE FROM THE PIT

'We don't want several hundred cubic feet of angry blob heaving itself around the country crushing people!'

SYNOPSIS

Chloris, the Future

Romana discovered a Mark 3 Emergency Transceiver in the TARDIS' junk room. The Doctor had previously removed it to stop the Time Lords from bothering him. When reactivated, it drew the ship to the jungle world of Chloris. Soon after landing, they found a huge broken metal shell. Before they could investigate more thoroughly, guards sent by the local ruler, Lady Adrasta, came to arrest them for trespassing. Adrasta had a strange interest in the metal shell. K-9 and Romana were captured, while the Doctor jumped into a terrifying pit where a 'creature' lurked to escape the guards.

Romana was taken back to Adrasta's palace, where she prevented Adrasta taking K-9 apart by telling her the data she needed on the shell is in his memory banks. Unfortunately, Adrasta learned that the TARDIS was more than just a blue box, and that she could use it to steal metal, the most rare and valuable commodity on Chloris, from other worlds. Somehow this meant 'the creature' was no longer useful and she set off with Romana, K-9, her henchwoman Karela and her guards to destroy it.

Meanwhile, the Doctor was still in the Pit, but had managed to avoid the creature. He met another resident, the fortuneteller Organon, who had also been cast down here for displeasing Adrasta. The

caverns under the Pit were quite extensive as they were the old exhausted mine where the planet's metal once came from. The Doctor and Organon tracked down the creature, but unfortunately communication with the big green blob proved tricky. The creature drew a symbol on a wall that resembled the seal on the wall behind Adrasta's throne.

Meanwhile, bandits took advantage of Adrasta's absence to raid her palace, which was full of valuable metal. During the raid the bandits took a liking to the seal, which glowed and sparkled strangely. It exerted a hypnotic control over the bandits holding it, and they found themselves taking the seal towards the creature in the pit.

Adrasta's hunting party caught up with the Doctor and Organon. The Doctor was pleased to see Romana again, but less happy that Adrasta insisted her guards destroy the creature. In her rage she let slip that she knows it is a 'Tythonian' and that it could not speak. The bandits arrived with the seal, placing it on the creature. The seal turned out to be a communication device, stolen by Adrasta so no one could learn the secrets of the creature, whose name was Erato. Erato was no ordinary Tythonian, but was their high ambassador. He came to the planet to trade metal for vegetation. His planet had more metal that it needed, but was desperately in need of plant matter as the Tythonians fed on chlorophyll. While the deal would have solved almost all the problems of Chloris, Erato made the mistake of offering the deal to Adrasta. Seeing the threat this posed to her metal monopoly, she trapped Erato in the Pit.

Hearing how she has betrayed her people, Adrasta's guards turned on her. Erato took his revenge as well, killing Adrasta. The Doctor helped Erato out of the pit, but felts the Tythonian was not telling them the whole story. They allowed Erato to repair his ship, the shell, which he could weave back together. When he was ready to leave he told the Doctor that unfortunately his ship had been sending a distress call for the last fifteen years. His people had declared war on Chloris and sent a neutron star to collide with the planet, which would atomise Chloris it on impact. The Doctor convinced Erato to help in a dangerous plan to stop the incoming star, but the photon drive from Erato's ship was missing. It had been stolen by Karela, who attempted to enlist the bandits' help in reclaiming Adrasta's power. Karela was so obsessed with wealth she would rather risk the planet's

destruction than help the Doctor, so he ordered K-9 to destroy the metal the bandits stole. Left with nothing, Karela turned over the photon drive.

Using Erato's ability to weave metal and the TARDIS' power to hold the star, the Doctor, Romana and Erato managed to wrap the star in aluminium and deflect it into space. The plan nearly destroyed the TARDIS, but eventually succeeded. Having saved the planet the Doctor had only one thing left to do: he passed Organon a draft trade agreement from the Tythonians, which ensured the future of both planets.

CONTINUITY

Romana unearths a variety of interesting artefacts while spring cleaning of Hold Number 4, amongst them a ball of string that the Doctor gave Theseus and Ariadne to stop them unravelling his scarf. In fact, mazes and Minotaurs must be a hobby of the Doctor's as he met one in Atlantis (see the T*he Time Monster* in **The Third Doctor Sourcebook**,) and will meet another one again very soon (see **The Horns of Nimon**) and sometime in his future (see the Eleventh Doctor adventure **The God Complex**). Romana also found the jawbone of an ass, possibly the one Samson fought off the Philistines with.

The Mk 3 Emergency Transceiver Romana finds was removed by the Doctor on purpose. While he is not usually one to ignore distress calls, he was getting tired of the Time Lords using it to get in contact.

The Doctor tells Organon he was born under the sign of 'crossed computers' which are the symbol of the Gallifreyan medical unit.

The Doctor cannot read Tibetan, although he could speak it well enough in **Planet of the Spiders** (see **The Third Doctor Sourcebook**)

The Doctor claims his lucky number is 74,384,338, which has changed from 7 (see **The Power of Kroll**).

⊙ RUNNING THE ADVENTURE

The universe doesn't need to hang in the balance every week, and not every villain needs to be a warlord with a legion of killer robots or an ancient horror from beyond time. **The Creature from the Pit** is a nice, small-scale affair with lots of intrigue, treachery and monsters in dungeons, who turn out to be quite reasonable green blobs.

CHLORIS

The planet Chloris is a lush jungle world. The earth here is extremely fertile, making food plentiful, but cultivation and farming a little more difficult.

Unfortunately, the entire planet is woefully lacking in mineral resources. Metal of any kind is extraordinarily rare, stunting its technological advancement. While the people of Chloris use swords and look to soothsayers for advice, they are aware of other planets. Although they have no space-flight capability of their own, they are used to visitors from other planets. Even so, they are a superstitious people and hold hard to their traditions. One of these traditions is a matriarchal society. Women are not so much in charge as the only ones trusted to make important decisions, and if Torvin's bandits are any indication of the men of Chloris it is not surprising. Men are simply not considered clever or resourceful enough to be independent of a woman or act on their own. Until the Doctor proves his usefulness, Adrasta naturally assumes Romana is not only his superior, but his 'commander'.

KEY LOCATIONS ON CHLORIS

- **The Pit:** When it ran out of metal ore, Adastra found a new use for her mine, making it the Pit and trapping Erato here. The Pit has only one public entrance, but the tunnels below are extensive. Adrasta maintains three other secret entrances to the mines, one of which leads to her palace throne room.

- **The Place of Death:** Dominated by the ruins of Erato's shell-like spacecraft, the Place of Death is forbidden to trespassers.

- **Adastra's Palace:** Lady Adrasta maintains a palace not far from the Pit and the Place of Death. While we only see the throne room, the palace has several rooms, living quarters and space for several guards. Metal is everywhere, to display Adrasta's wealth, and her guards are positioned throughout the building.

- **The Bandit Camp:** Hidden in the jungle is the ragged camp of Torvin's group. It is little more than a series of tents, the main one, Torvin's tent, being the place to store their stolen artefacts.

Security is very lax on the camp, but in the thick jungle it is difficult to find. The bandits are most likely to be arguing rather than standing guard.

PLANETOLOGY & CULTURE

Much of Chloris' culture arose as a result of the planet's unusual distribution of resources. Its lack of metal limited its technological development and gives Adastra a stranglehold on power. Conversely, the thick jungle gives bandits plenty of places to hide, so those who oppose the status quo can escape into the green underworld. Other planets can have similar effects on the people who live there. A world where the surface is uninhabitable and everyone lives in tunnels underground might create a culture where everyone has to live in close proximity to each other; there's no such thing as privacy or secrets. A desert world might be one where water is the most precious resource of all, and people kill each other for moisture. Think of two or three big ways that an unusual environment would affect the people of that world.

FURTHER ADVENTURES

- **Jungle Revolt:** The Wolfweeds are not the only plant creatures of Chloris. There are larger creatures that have happily remained dormant amidst the lush jungle. But once the inhabitants start cultivating land and sending large amounts of vegetation to Tythonus, the jungle decides to fight back to protect itself.

- **Steel Pirates:** Even though the trade with Tythonus helps everyone, greed remains. Even

---

WOLFWEEDS

AWARENESS	4	PRESENCE	1
COORDINATION	3	RESOLVE	3
INGENUITY	1	STRENGTH	2

With little animal life on the planet, Wolfweeds are plant creatures used in much the same way as hunting dogs. They are balls of vegetation that roll over their quarry and pin it to the ground. While they do not look especially dangerous, they hunt in packs and can move quicker than you'd expect. When they have captured their prey they excrete a web-like substance that renders it immobile.

SKILLS

Athletics 3, Fighting 3, Subterfuge 3, Survival 3

TRAITS

Alien Appearance (Minor/Major Bad)
Alien (Special Good)
Alien Organs (Minor Good): The plant's organs are not where you might expect. All targeted damage is reduced by 2.
Fast: Wolfweeds move faster than might be expected.
Special - Invisible: Wolfweeds are hard to spot, and gain a +4 bonus to rolls to avoid detection.
Natural Weapon (Minor) – Web: When on top of a creature, the Wolfwood may cover them in web, reducing their Coordination by 1 each round.

STORY POINTS: 4

KARELA

AWARENESS	4	PRESENCE	2
COORDINATION	3	RESOLVE	3
INGENUITY	3	STRENGTH	2

Adrasta's right-hand woman is as bad as she is. A talented knife fighter and a vicious advisor, Karela has served her mistress for no better reason than she loves the power and wealth Adrasta offers. With Adrasta gone, she is quick to try and maintain the status quo, and would rather sacrifice the planet than give up her own wealth. Under a wise, if callous, exterior, Karela is a bitter old woman with nothing in her life but that which Adrasta's wealth can buy.

SKILLS

Athletics 3, Convince 2, Fighting 3 (Knives 5), Knowledge 2, Subterfuge 3, Survival 2

TRAITS

Quick Reflexes: Karela always goes first in the Action Round unless taken by surprise.
Obligation (Minor Bad): Serve Lady Adrasta.

EQUIPMENT: Fighting knife (Strength +2).

TECH LEVEL: 3   STORY POINTS: 6

though metal has become severely devalued, there are still many bandit groups raiding the trade caravans. However, some groups are more organised, well equipped and successful. Could there be someone behind them looking to build a new metal monopoly by controlling the trade route?

- **Eco-Warriors:** Not everyone is happy that the jungle is being cleared to make way for fields.

Groups of eco-warriors calling themselves 'the children of the jungle' are committing terrorist acts to prevent more cultivation. There still seems plenty of jungle left, so how can the group's claims that an ecological disaster is imminent be true? The new cultivation has brought great wealth to the landowners, so might they be hiding the truth? Does the deep jungle hold even more secrets than anyone knows?

ERATO, TYTHONIAN AMBASSADOR

Tythonians are vast green blobs, essentially a huge brain that lives on chlorophyll. Despite the disadvantage of having neither hands nor human senses, Tythonians have developed their own technology and form of spaceflight due to their ability to weave metal. They can create spacecraft by weaving a capsule and a small photon drive around themselves. The shells they build are extremely tough. While Erato is kept in Adrasta's Pit for 15 years, to a Tythonian this is not a long time as they live for some 40,000 years. While they are very different to humans they share many traits, such as greed, revenge and a desire to trade. The Tythonians are a peaceful people and few are warriors. When their planet is threatened they propel neutron stars at their aggressors.

AWARENESS	3	PRESENCE	2
COORDINATION	1	RESOLVE	3
INGENUITY	4	STRENGTH	5

SKILLS
Convince 3, Craft 5, Fighting 3, Knowledge 4, Science 3, Subterfuge 1, Survival 1, Technology 4, Transport 3

TRAITS
Alien
Alien Appearance (Major): Big green blob.
Alien Organs: Erato's organs are not where you might expect. All targeted damage is reduced by 2.
Alien Senses (Minor): While Tythonians have no eyes or ears they are still aware of their surroundings so cannot be blinded or deafened by normal means.
Empathic: +2 bonus on rolls to 'read' another person.
Tough: Reduce total damage by 2.
Natural Weapons (Minor): Crush attack Strength +2 damage.
Special - Weave Metal: Tythonians can weave almost any metal from their bodies rapidly, creating a shell that can withstand space flight or barricade an area.
Dependency (Major): Erato suffers a -4 penalty to all rolls if starved of chlorophyll for several days.

Distinctive (Minor): -2 penalty to rolls to blend in. Others have a +2 bonus to remember or recognise the character. Again, it's a big green blob.
Size (Huge)
Slow (Minor Bad): Erato moves at half its Speed rate.
Slow Reflexes (Minor Bad): Erato always acts last in his Action Phase.
Uncommunicative (Minor): Erato cannot talk to humanoid creatures without a translator device. Presumably, it has no issue talking to other big green blobs.

TECH LEVEL: 6   **STORY POINTS: 8**

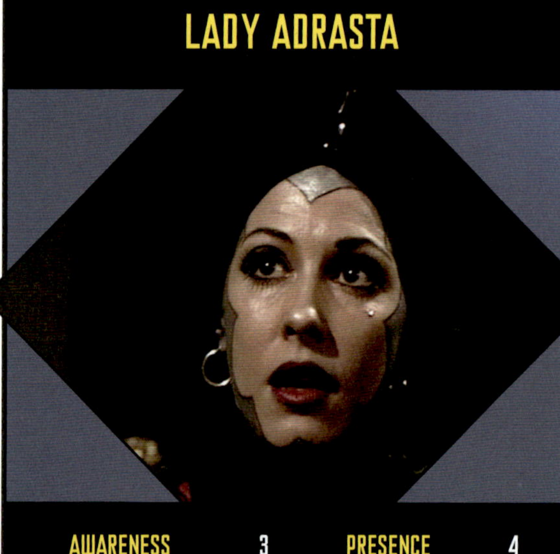

LADY ADRASTA

AWARENESS	3	PRESENCE	4
COORDINATION	3	RESOLVE	3
INGENUITY	3	STRENGTH	2

The most powerful woman on Chloris is neither a queen nor an elected governor, but simply the one who owns the only source of wealth on the planet. Adrasta loves wealth, but more than that the power that comes with it. Unfortunately, her mine, the only source of metal on Chloris, is now empty of its bounty and with the metal so goes her power. The trade deal offered by Erato was simply the thin end of the wedge. Adrasta is unrepentantly evil; she has no concern for anyone but herself and will sacrifice anything to preserve her power, or even make a point. She is so thoroughly rotten that even the Doctor stands by and does nothing when Erato finally takes his revenge on her.

SKILLS

Convince 2, Knowledge 2, Marksman 2, Science 2, Subterfuge 3

TRAITS

Voice of Authority: Adrasta's charisma gives her a +2 bonus to Presence and Convince rolls.
Dark Secret (Major): The creature she imprisoned in the Pit is an ambassador from another planet.
Impulsive: Adrasta is quick to make decisions, but they don't always turn out for the best.
Obsession (Major): Maintain her power base and wealth.

TECH LEVEL: 3   **STORY POINTS: 8**

ORGANON

AWARENESS	4	PRESENCE	4
COORDINATION	2	RESOLVE	3
INGENUITY	3	STRENGTH	1

Many on Chloris hold onto superstition and the job of seer can still be a lucrative one. Organon is more showman than prophet; after all, it is not enough to foretell the future, you need to make people believe you can do it, and adding an air of mysticism always helps. Unfortunately, Organon gave the wrong prophecy to the wrong person: Lady Adrasta. Never one for small punishments, she commanded Organon to be thrown into the Pit. However unlike so many before him, Organon escaped Erato and managed to survive, living off the scraps thrown into the Pit for the creature. While Organon appears to be a dotty old man, he is also a reasonably shrewd survivor. Interestingly, his prophecies have an alarming degree of accuracy, but whether this is coincidence or not, even he would be hard pressed to say.

SKILLS

Convince 4, Craft 2, Knowledge 3, Science 1, Subterfuge 3, Survival 3

TRAITS

Empathic: +2 bonus on rolls to 'read' another person.
Lucky: You may re-roll any 'double 1s'.
Dark Secret (Major): Doesn't have a gift for prophesy.
Obsession (Minor): Loves to work out people's horoscopes.

TECH LEVEL: 3   **STORY POINTS: 4**

NIGHTMARE OF EDEN

'Will you please listen?! Vraxoin is the biggest killer drug in existence and it's on this ship!'

◎ SYNOPSIS

In orbit above Azure, 2116

The Doctor and Romana were drawn to a crash between two spacecraft, a cruise liner called the *Empress* and a small transport ship called *Hecate*. As the *Empress* was materialising from warp space at the time, both ships were merged together, with a strange mist filling the 'null zone' that existed where they met. When the Doctor and Romana arrived on the bridge of the *Empress* they found both Captains in a heated argument. Dymond of the *Hecate* blamed Captain Rigg of the *Empress* for being off course. Rigg, aware that his navigator Secker seemed to be unusually distracted, insisted the *Hecate* shouldn't have been anywhere near this area of space anyway.

The Doctor claimed to be an agent of Galactic Salvage and Insurance and managed to defuse the situation by suggesting all they needed to do was reverse the circumstances of the accident to free the two ships. The only problem was that the Empress' power systems were inaccessible behind the null zone where the ships meet. The Doctor went with Secker to find an alternate route and discovered the navigator's ambivalent attitude was due to him being under the influence of a powerful narcotic, Vraxoin.

Romana went to visit the upper class passengers and met the zoologist Tryst and his assistant Della. Tryst proudly showed her his CEI (Continual Event Transmuter) machine. The machine could capture areas of land, complete with their flora and fauna, and store them in data crystals. The image it projected was no mere recording but a window into a living ecosystem. Romana found it a little primitive, and was somewhat concerned about the effect the local space distortions from the crash might have on the machine.

Now more worried about the Vraxoin than the accident, the Doctor questioned Rigg about how the drug has got on board. Unfortunately, the liner only went back and forth bringing holidaymakers to Azure, the planet they are orbiting. The only person at all well travelled was Tryst. When the Doctor questioned Tryst he discovered Tryst hasn't been near a known source of Vraxoin. However, Tryst did feel there was something odd about one of his crew who was killed on the recent Eden expedition. A local creature called a Mandrel killed this crewman, Stott. These same creatures, Mandrels, appeared on the ship, as they had escaped the Eden projection on the CET machine.

With Dymond ranting that he needed to leave quickly or he would lose his contract, the Doctor returned to trying to separate the ships. Unfortunately, a mysterious assailant spiked Captain Rigg's drink with Vraxoin, which was partly to blame for the failure to free the ships. However, in the attempt, the null zones cleared for a moment allowing K-9 to get to the power systems. Before another attempt could be made the customs police from Azure arrived, and with the Doctor's credentials somewhat vague he became their prime suspect. Reasoning that if creatures were escaping the CET projection, they could get in, the Doctor and Romana made a run for it and hid inside the Eden projection.

Inside the Eden projection they were surprised to meet crewman Stott, who they discovered was actually a Major in the Space Corps investigating Tryst. He was caught in the field when this part of Eden was captured for the CET machine, and only since the crash has it been unstable enough for him to leave. He was convinced Tryst was part of a Vraxoin smuggling ring as the CET machine was the perfect way to smuggle the drug, as it was undetectable while stored as data on a crystal.

With Mandrels running riot on the ship, the Doctor developed another ploy to separate the ships and stabilise the projection. As they tried to carry out the plan, the Doctor was attacked by a Mandrel who he electrocuted. It dissolved into a pile of Vraxoin – the Mandrels a source of the drug! The Doctor's plan worked and the ships separated, but he was pulled through the null zone and onto the *Hecate*. In the *Hecate's* hold he discovered another CET machine and an Enchooka laser, a device for beaming data

between spacecraft. Dymond's mission was to receive the Vraxoin when the Eden projection was transmitted as data to his own device.

With the ships stabilised, the police and crew herded the Mandrels back into the projection where they were caged. Returning to the *Empress*, the Doctor told Romana the best way to find the smugglers was to catch them red handed. As Dymond received the Eden projection in a transmission, the Doctor reversed the system and collected the *Hecate* bridge in a new projection. Tryst himself turned out to be the accomplice, insisting it was all for his research.

CONTINUITY

The Doctor once more proves the utility of Time Lords being able to slow their metabolism when he finds himself in Dymond's shuttle without a spacesuit. He goes into a short trance to reduce his need for air during the short journey from the *Hecate* to the *Empress*.

Drugs are still a problem in the future, but a concerted attempt to wipe out Vraxoin has been made, its only known source having been destroyed. The Doctor insists whole planets have been destroyed because of the drug.

RUNNING THE ADVENTURE

Nightmare of Eden takes a real-world problem and turns it into a Doctor Who adventure by adding science-fiction elements. Let's rewrite it without the sci-fi to see where it started.

A cruise liner and a small boat collide at sea. One of the passengers on the cruise liner is a biologist, returning from a research expedition in South America with a collection of botanic samples. It turns out that he's smuggling drugs hidden inside these samples, and the boat that hit the liner was supposed to collect the drugs from him in the dead of night.

Each element of this story gets replaced by a science-fiction idea that fulfils the same purpose in the narrative. Swap out the ships for spaceships, the samples for the CET machine, and add some extra complications for the player characters to overcome.

You can turn any real-world headline into an adventure in the same way. For example, taking today's headlines, we've got:

Two neighbouring countries – one a technologically advanced democracy, and the other a backward and brutal regime – are on the verge of war. The two countries were once one until they were divided in a war. The brutal regime has weapons of mass destruction aimed at the capital of the other nation. A third country, an international superpower, sends diplomats to try to avert the war.

Countries become planets. Instead of having them divided by a war, maybe they're both the same planet, but in different dimensions. Somehow, time became forked and you've got one alternative reality planning war with another version of itself. On that scale, the 'international superpower' has to be the Time Lords, who send the characters in to deal with this paradoxical conflict.

Or how about a more mundane headline like: *Half of pet owners prefer hugging pet to partner.*

Instead of replacing elements in this case, try giving a science-fiction explanation behind the headline. People prefer hugging their pets – is that because they love their pets, or are common Earth pets being replaced by mind-controlling aliens that feed on emotion? And when the characters discover this plot, will they be chased through London by an army of cute kittens and adorable laser-wielding puppies? Yes. Yes, they will.

THE *EMPRESS*

The cruise liner *Empress* is a huge spacecraft. It has several decks, packing in holiday-makers of all shapes and sizes. Once the sort of ship that might

have been the pride of the fleet, it is now relegated to shuttling passengers from Station 9 to the holiday planet Azure. Despite the gigantic size of the vessel, it only requires a pilot and a navigator to fly. There is a large crew, but they are mostly security guards and passenger stewards.

The passengers are divided up into first class and economy class. Economy-class passengers are packed into a series of cabins, each containing seats for 20–30 passengers. The *Empress* can take around 300 or so passengers in economy class. The shielding around these areas is not very good, making it important the economy class passengers wear protective silver coveralls and dark protective glasses.

Economy-class passengers must remain in their seats for the entire journey, although they are provided with magazines and other entertainments to keep them occupied.

First-class passengers (such as Tryst) get a small suite of rooms and are allowed to move around the ship as they please. They don't need to wear the protective garb as their rooms have better shielding. The *Empress* has a warp drive, travelling in hyperspace and rematerialising into real space at the end of the journey. While it doesn't take long to rematerialise it is possible for the ship to phase with anything in the same position. For this reason the space lanes are kept very clear by Azure control.

THE *HECATE*

This ship is significantly smaller than the *Empress*, and designed for a single pilot to fly. It is unclear if the *Hecate* has warp drive capability, but it is certainly capable of interstellar flight. There is little space on the *Hecate*, having only a control room, cargo hold and quarters for the crew. There is also a small shuttle bay containing a one-man shuttle for travelling ship to ship. The shuttle isn't pressurised and has only room for a pilot and a single passenger.

AZURE

The holiday planet of Azure is a very popular holiday destination. It is very similar to Earth offering ocean views and blue skies, much as its name suggests. The Azure authorities operate their own customs police, who have jurisdiction over anything in orbit. The Azure customs police are extremely bureaucratic and have a lot of autonomy when investigating ships in orbit. This authority includes the power to decide to open fire on suspects.

VRAXOIN

Vraxoin, or XYP, is one of the most dangerous drugs in the galaxy. In its pure form it is a white power, which is processed into a liquid. Each dose is only a few drops and has a powerful soporific effect. Users initially feel very relaxed and euphoric, and then become completely detached from what is going on around them. They perform tasks very sloppily, and eventually give up doing even that. They also become hysterical and find almost anything funny. As the

CAPTAIN RIGG

Rigg is a career pilot who has worked for the line for many years. He is not especially ambitious, having realised he is not a young man any more and no rising star within the company. Even so, he has worked hard and become the Captain of a very large interstellar cruise liner. It may not be very exciting work but he does command his own ship, even if its faded glory matches his own.

Rigg is not especially talented, but he is both conscientious and good at his job. He doesn't necessarily care about each individual passenger, but he appreciates they are his responsibility to get to their destination safely. If he hadn't been given Vraxoin he would have continued to be a valuable asset to the Doctor and curbed the actions of the customs police. The Captain is assisted in his duties by a navigator, Secker, who has similar attributes when he isn't smashed out of his skull on Vraxoin. Secker is completely useless whilst on the drug.

AWARENESS	3	PRESENCE	3
COORDINATION	3	RESOLVE	3
INGENUITY	4	STRENGTH	3

SKILLS
Athletics 2, Convince 3, Fighting 1, Knowledge 2, Marksman 2, Science 3, Subterfuge 2, Technology 3, Transport 3

TRAITS
Voice of Authority: +2 bonus to Presence and Convince rolls.
Obligation (Minor): Ensure the safety of the passengers and crew.

TECH LEVEL: 6　　**STORY POINTS: 4**

drug wears off they become increasingly paranoid and upset. As the euphoria fades they are left with a desire for more that will lead them to violence if denied.

A dose of Vraxoin reduces the user's Intellect and Coordination by 1 point every half an hour until both reach 1. They remain at this level for two hours, at which point they return to half their original score. During this time the user gains the Trait Obsessed (Major Bad) – Getting Another Fix of Vraxoin. After an hour they return to normal, but still retain a desire to take another dose.

The original source of Vraxoin was a fungus. To destroy the drug trade, the planet where this fungus originated was destroyed. Desiccated Mandrel tissue was discovered to possess the same chemical properties as the drug.

FURTHER ADVENTURES

- **Holiday in Eden:** A holiday company builds a new resort on Eden, offering hunting holidays among the dangerous flora and fauna. Unfortunately, the resort is a cover. Someone has discovered the link between Vraxoin and the Mandrels and is looking to create another smuggling ring. At the moment they are looking for buyers and distributors, so when they visit on holiday the player characters will be surprised to discover they are surrounded by gangsters and criminals, not all of whom are on the same side.

- **The Azure Connection:** Tryst and Dymond don't have the contacts to sell Vraxoin, so they were going into partnership with some extremely nasty people instead (possibly the Foamasi, see *The Leisure Hive*). These nasty people are not especially happy they didn't get the drugs as they have lost money and been made to look fools. They come after the player characters after dealing with Tryst and Dymond for their failure. Initially they might be very pleasant to the player characters, offering the player characters the opportunity to become part of their operation and procure them some more Vraxoin. A refusal will upset them, and they will hunt the player characters down to make an example of them. The only option may be to take on the gang and destroy the large Mafia empire they're a small part of.

- **The Empty Spaces:** Months after the accident, there are reports of ships going missing, and of a higher number of accidents occurring

PILOT DYMOND

AWARENESS	3	PRESENCE	2
COORDINATION	3	RESOLVE	3
INGENUITY	3	STRENGTH	3

Dymond is a small-time crook with a big time plan. The plan is to arrive with the Hecate close enough for Tryst to beam the drugs onto his ship using his Enchooka laser, but when Secker misplots the jump he finds he is too close and the ships merge together. Dymond is greedy and something of a bully, but he isn't a complete fool. When things go wrong, Dymond copes badly, ranting at and bullying anyone he can to get things back on track.

SKILLS
Athletics 3, Convince 2, Fighting 2, Marksman 2, Subterfuge 3, Technology 3, Transport 3

TRAITS
Friends (Minor): Knows far too many criminals for his own good.
Argumentative: He'll argue his point of view no matter what the circumstances are.
Dark Secret (Minor): Actually a smuggler, not a trader.
Impulsive: Dymond flies and acts by the seat of his spacesuit.
Selfish: Dymond's out for himself.

TECH LEVEL: 6   **STORY POINTS: 4**

around Azure. Navigation is tricky and ships are constantly arriving off course. It seems the collision between the *Empress* and *Hecate* did more damage to this layer of space than previously expected and the fabric of reality in the area is breaking down. The problem might even be spreading. Can the breach be healed before it gets worse? To make matters worse, some pilots have talked of strange beings appearing on their ships. Maybe the hole won't close because someone on the other side is forcing it wider.

TRYST

AWARENESS	2	PRESENCE	3
COORDINATION	3	RESOLVE	2
INGENUITY	4	STRENGTH	2

An eminent zoologist, Tryst is looking to catalogue and conserve every species in the galaxy. However, his passion has a lot to do with the fame it will garner in academic circles. While he appears polite and personable, he is utterly obsessed with his work. He will happily trample over anyone who gets in his way, and make deals with anyone who can fund his research. He tries to justify this as 'making a sacrifice for the work' but such 'sacrifices' are always the easy way out.

SKILLS

Convince 3, Craft 2, Knowledge 4, Medicine 2, Science 3, Subterfuge 3, Survival 2, Technology 4

TRAITS

Charming: +2 bonus to attempts to use charm.
Empathic: +2 bonus on rolls to 'read' another person
Cowardly: -2 penalty to any fear roll
Obsession (Major): Complete the work!

TECH LEVEL: 6   **STORY POINTS: 6**

MANDRELS

AWARENESS	2	PRESENCE	2
COORDINATION	3	RESOLVE	4
INGENUITY	1	STRENGTH	7

One of the many dangerous creatures on the planet Eden, Mandrels are humanoid beasts with large fishlike eyes and massive clawed hands. They attack pretty much anything they come across, as everything on Eden is dangerous. When subjected to extremely high voltage electric charge they dissolve into a pure white substance that is actually the dangerous narcotic Vraxoin.

SKILLS

Athletics 2, Fighting 3

TRAITS

Alien (Special Good)
Armour (Minor): Reduce damage by 5.
Natural Weapons (Minor): Close combat weapons (claws, teeth) that do Strength +2 damage.
Slow (Minor): They move slowly.
Slow Reflexes: Mandrels always acts last in their Action Phase.

STORY POINTS: 4

THE HORNS OF NIMON

'You know K-9, sometimes I think I'm wasted just rushing around the universe saving planets from destruction. With a talent like mine I might have been a great slow bowler.'

⊘ SYNOPSIS

Skonnos, Unspecified Time

Thrown off course by a singularity, the TARDIS crashed into an ancient and half-crippled Skonnan battleship. Of the flight crew, only the co-pilot was still alive. Waving a gun around he demanded the Time Lords repair his ship, as it was vital he reach his home planet of Skonnos so he could deliver tribute to 'the Nimon'. The tribute was a captured group of peaceful people from the nearby planet of Aneth and a few large crystals of hymetusite, a rare radioactive mineral that stores great power. Using

some parts from the TARDIS, and a couple of the hymetusite crystals, the Doctor and Romana got the old battleship working again. However, the co-pilot resumes his course, leaving Romana still on board and the Doctor stranded on the temporarily immobilised TARDIS.

Held at gunpoint, Romana confronted the Skonnan leader Soldeed when they arrived. Soldeed was more concerned with appeasing the Nimon with tribute; in return, the Nimon had promised to rebuild their decaying empire. Romana and the Anethans were sent into the labyrinthine power complex as the final tribute. When the Doctor arrived, he followed them into the complex.

The inside of the power complex was a maze where the corridors shifted and changed. Romana and the Anethans reached the central control area where they discovered the intended fate of the tribute. The hymetusite crystals were used to power the massive furnace that energised the facility. The Anethans themselves were to be placed in suspended animation in a 'larder' until the Nimon fed on their life energy.

Running from the Nimon, the fugitives discovered an operations room that contained a transmat capsule. The massive power being generated here created the singularity that had initially trapped the TARDIS. This black hole was the opening of a wormhole through which the transmat capsule could reach another planet across the galaxy in . Finding a place to hide, the fugitives watched as the Nimon activated the controls and used the transmat to bring more Nimons to Skonnos.

When the Nimons left, the Doctor started investigating the equipment again, but accidentally sent Romana across space in the transmat capsule. She arrived on the planet Crinoth, a world the Nimons had already laid waste to. They had sucked the life out of the world, leaving only one survivor, Sezom. The Nimons were like locusts, moving from planet to planet and draining everything from it before moving on to another. Sezom gave his life to help Romana escape so she could warn Skonnos and end the horrible cycle of the Nimons' Great Journey of Life.

Dodging the growing number of Nimons, Romana found Soldeed and explains the truth to him. Unable to accept the dream of a new Skonnan empire was a lie he went mad, setting the power furnace to overload. When the furnace detonated it destroyed the power complex and the Nimons. With nowhere to go the remaining Nimons on Crinoth were destroyed when they blew up the planet in an attempt to get the power they needed to escape. The Great Journey of Life had finally come to an end.

CONTINUITY

The Doctor also references Theseus and the Minotaur again, unsurprisingly, mentioning how he forgot to remind the Greek hero to use a white sail when he returned home. As the white sail was a sign for his father to see he had survived the quest, Theseus' father committed suicide when the crew rigged a black sail instead.

The shields that protect the TARDIS are in two layers: one set protects the ship itself, and another protects the doors. These shields can be manipulated and projected into space to create corridors that are safe to walk down (so long as the other end is sealed!).

K-9 proves able to follow the Doctor and Romana's 'psychospoors'. It is unclear whether it's just Time Lords who leave such a trail, or whether K-9 is only equipped to follow theirs.

⚙ RUNNING THE ADVENTURE

If the previous adventure was an adaptation of modern-day events, this one is based on mythology. It's the story of the Minotaur, with the Anethans as the sacrifices from Greece and Skonnos as Crete. There are differences, of course – instead of being the son of the Cretan king, the Nimon is an invading alien, and the Greek myth makes very little mention of atomic power crystals (maybe they got lost in translation). Similarly, **Underworld** is a retelling of the story of Jason and the Golden Fleece, while **Battlefield** (see **The Seventh Doctor Sourcebook**) draws on the stories of King Arthur and the Knights of the Round Table.

Any myth can inspire an adventure, but don't retell the myths directly – the players likely already know the story. For example, if the solution to **The Horns of Nimon** was to use a ball of string to thread the labyrinth and then chop the monster's head off, that wouldn't be surprising to the players. Even replacing the ball of thread with a cosmic string arachnavigator gadget and the sword with a blaster doesn't really change the story – it's just cosmetic. **The Horns of Nimon** works because the Nimon isn't just a space Minotaur.

For example, take the story of Robin Hood. Everyone knows it – Robin, Little John, the Sheriff of Nottingham and so forth. If your player characters run into a gang of merry asteroid pirates (who hide out in an impenetrable asteroid belt), then spotting the correspondences can be great fun. However, you can't then make the fact that the asteroid pirates are secretly giving their ill-gotten gains to the poor into a shocking surprise. You need to twist or subvert the legend.

Maybe Space Robin Hood is actually funding a revolution against the Star Lord of Nottingham, or maybe they're hiding all their stolen goods in Nottingham's dungeons, so that one day they can frame the Sheriff for all their crimes and have him removed.

Just be careful of twisting the legend too much by making heroes into villains; it can feel like tricking the players.

SKONNOS

The planet Skonnos was once the centre of a mighty empire that commanded over 100 star systems, but now it is a shadow if its former self. Power led to infighting, and these squabbles led to full civil war. The empire fell apart, with only the soldiers of the prevailing side surviving the destruction. However the Skonnans have not forgotten their heritage, and believe they are born to lead. The empire was not something they lost but a birthright they will one day reclaim.

The Nimon has been the answer to their prayers. The ruling council of Skonnos appointed their only remaining scientist, Soldeed, to see to the Nimon's needs, and he has quickly used this connection to take control of the council.

Despite its faded glory, Skonnos itself is still a grand and well-ordered society. The buildings are well maintained and feature great archways and large, open chambers. The army runs the entire planet, and military order is evident everywhere. However, they are badly under equipped. Most of the guards are ceremonial, and while their uniforms are grand (with huge shoulder pads and feathered helms) their weapons are old and outdated.

THE POWER COMPLEX

The power complex is a large installation built by the Skonnans so the Nimon might develop the technology to bring them a new empire. There is only one entrance, in the main chamber of the Skonnan capital. This archway contains a field that transports the entrant to the power complex itself, located some way from the capital.

The layout of the power complex resembles a positronic circuit, which is exactly what it is on a grand scale. This means the corridors inside move and change as they form the gates and switches that power the system. This makes it extremely difficult to navigate the maze unless you can calculate and predict the movements of the corridors. Doing so requires an Ingenuity + Technology or Ingenuity + Survival roll at Difficulty 15.

The complex itself is powered by a huge furnace designed to draw energy from hymetusite crystals. The positronic circuit system then projects this energy across space to create a wormhole so that more Nimon can be brought to Skonnos. When active, the complex lights up in a variety of bright, cycling colours.

KEY LOCATIONS IN THE POWER COMPLEX

- **Main Control Room:** The Nimon spends most of his time in this area, where both his food supply and the furnace control are located. The furnace has a portal for adding hymetusite crystals and some basic controls. The area also contains dials and readouts for monitoring the system. The room then opens out into the storage area where several Anethans are kept in suspended animation until the Nimon gets hungry. Those consumed are taken to a table in an anteroom where their energy is drained until all that remains is dust.

- **Transmat Room:** While a lot smaller, the transmat room is more important than the main control room. Banks of computers are connected here to direct energy and calculate coordinates. In the centre of this cramped room are the transmat controls, which can bring a capsule across space by resetting a large lever. The transmat capsule resides in a nearby bay, just large enough to contain it. The unit can take two to three passengers, and while it is a cramped journey it is a short one.

SKONNAN BATTLESHIP

The remaining tatters of the Skonnan battlefleet are a sorry sight indeed. The ships themselves are barely able to make a simple journey and the stress of combat would probably destroy one even if it didn't get hit. To keep them flying at all, they have been augmented with Nimon technology. This technology is more advanced and very different from Skonnan technology, which will be obvious to anyone who makes any repairs on the ship. There are only two real rooms of note on the ship, the prisoners' room and the control room, which are linked by a corridor containing several door seals. The prisoners' room was once used for troop transport, and everything about it is plain and functional. There may be other rooms that are currently unsafe for occupation.

ANETH

This peaceful planet once knew the awesome power of the Skonnan Empire. Grandparents remember a time the battlefleet blotted out the sun. It was a show of power so terrible that no one on Aneth questions the might of Skonnos, even though there has been no invasion for years. Aneth is a pleasant planet with a peaceful people. Even though it was conquered by Skonnos is has had little to do with them apart from offering frequent tribute.

CRINOTH

The most recent victim of the Nimons, Crinoth is a dead world. Only one of the original inhabitants survived, Sezom, his 'reward' for bringing the Nimons to his world. The surface of the planet is barren and empty, but does still contain rocks of Jasonite, a powerful mineral able to intensify and focus energy. Crinoth's power complex remains, and this is where the Nimons live, waiting to continue the next step of the Great Journey of Life. It is a dark place, consisting of metal gantries and corridors. Its only purpose now is to house the transmat capsules that will bring the rest of the Nimons to Skonnos.

FURTHER ADVENTURES

- **The New Skonnan Empire:** Not everything of the Nimons' technology has been destroyed. Among

THE NIMONS

This race of bull-headed creatures are a plague of locusts on the galaxy. The Nimons move from planet to planet, consuming everything in their path, in a process they refer to as the Great Journey of Life. They are not looking to conquer or control, just to consume and move on. They care nothing for the lives they destroy, seeing anything outside their race as no more than food. Luckily for the universe, the Nimons only move as one. They first send a scout ahead to create a base on a new planet, then, when they have laid waste to their current home, the scout facilitates a mass transport to the new world. Each scout keenly feels the responsibility they are given for the welfare of their race, and will do anything to ensure the Great Journey of Life continues. Having destroyed many civilisations, the Nimons have acquired a high level of technological ability. They are a highly advanced race, although they make a point of only attacking less advanced worlds, where their technology will impress the greedy natives. Even without their technology the Nimons are dangerous opponents. As well as being physically imposing, their horns can fire energy beams that can kill or stun prey. They feed on energy (reducing their prey to a grey husk) so are almost immune to most energy weapons fire.

AWARENESS	2	PRESENCE	4
COORDINATION	3	RESOLVE	3
INGENUITY	4	STRENGTH	6

SKILLS

Athletics 2, Convince 3, Craft 4, Fighting 2, Knowledge 3, Marksman 3, Science 3, Subterfuge 3, Technology 3, Transport 2

TRAITS

Alien
Alien Appearance (Major)
Armour (Major): Reduce damage by 10.
Fear Factor 1: Grants a +2 bonus to inspire fear.
Immunity (Major Good): Low-power energy weapons (not enhanced by Jasonite).
Natural Weapons (Minor): Claws inflict Strength +2 damage.
Natural Weapons (Major): Horn energy blast (4/8/L) damage, may opt to do stun damage instead.
Obligation (Major): Continue the Great Journey of Life.
Slow (Minor): The Nimon is slow but steady.
Slow Reflexes: The Nimon always acts last in its Action Phase.

Voice of Authority: +2 bonus to Presence and Convince rolls.

TECH LEVEL: 7   **STORY POINTS: 8**

the ruins of the power complex the Skonnans discover pieces of advanced technology and dream once more of a new empire. Lacking scientists among their own people they secretly kidnap them from other worlds. They are close to unlocking the power of the Nimons and a new superweapon, unless they can be stopped, and the scientists freed.

- **The New Anethan Empire:** Not everyone on Aneth is as peaceful as they appear. When Seth and Teka tell their story the people are happy to be free of Skonnos, but they also feel like fools for handing so much tribute to a defunct empire. Anger turns to hate and the Anethans begin to build weapons, at first to protect themselves, and then to avenge themselves on a hostile galaxy. Can they be stopped before they become as warlike as the Skonnans?

- **Greek Tragedy:** When Crinoth explodes, two Nimon were in a transmat capsule. The power surge and collapse of the wormhole throws them across time and space, landing them in ancient Crete. They crash into a city under construction, and while one escapes the crash the other is driven mad by the journey. The locals are unable to destroy the mad Nimon and instead trap it in the half complete city, which becomes a labyrinth. The player characters might be tasked to destroy the beast in the labyrinth. However, the other Nimon has already insinuated himself into the king's good graces and has offered him powerful technology in return for tribute...

SOLDEED

The de facto leader of Skonnos is its last remaining scientist, Soldeed. However, he is far more of a politician than he is a researcher. He is very much an example of how, in the kingdom of the blind, the one eyed man is king. The idea of a new Skonnan empire has become not just a dream but an obsession. Having inspired the ruling council of Skonnos with the same dream, they follow his every command in the hope their world will return to glory, but also in the fear they might raise the ire of the Nimon, who speaks only through Soldeed. Too used to being the cleverest person in the room, Soldeed believes he is more intelligent than the Nimon. He thinks the creature seeks the same fame and notoriety he does, and that as long as it receives tribute and is treated like a god it can be controlled. To this end he plays the role of grand prophet, making every announcement with grand religious theatricality. This conceit will eventually cost Soldeed his life and dreams.

AWARENESS	3	PRESENCE	4
COORDINATION	3	RESOLVE	4
INGENUITY	4	STRENGTH	2

SKILLS
Convince 4, Craft 2, Fighting 1, Knowledge 3, Marksman 1, Science 3, Subterfuge 3, Technology 3, Transport 2

TRAITS
Boffin: Allows Soldeed to create Gadgets.
Quick Reflexes: Soldeed always goes first in the Action Round unless taken by surprise.
Voice of Authority: +2 bonus to Presence and Convince rolls.
Distinctive: -2 penalty to rolls to blend in. Others have a +2 bonus to remember or recognise Soldeed.
Obsession (Major): Restore the Skonnan Empire.

Eccentric: Soldeed does everything with a great amount of flamboyant theatricality.

EQUIPMENT: Soldeed carries a ceremonial staff, a gift from the Nimon and symbol of his authority. It can also function as an energy weapon (4/8/L)*.

*with Jasonite to focus the beam, the staff can affect Nimons.

TECH LEVEL: 6   **STORY POINTS: 8**

THE LEISURE HIVE

'I'm sick of being old; there must be some way of reversing the process.'

SYNOPSIS

Argolis, 2290

The travellers arrived on the leisure planet of Argolis, home of the fabled Leisure Hive. It was built after a war between the human-like Argolins and their enemies the reptilian Foamasi as a place for different species to interact peacefully. Unfortunately, the Leisure Hive as not doing well, having been supplanted by newer attractions on other worlds. Many of its more impressive entertainments were based on tachyonic technology, which could create and manipulate solid images. Despite being the leaders in the field, the Argolins had not made any advances for over 40 years. Nevertheless, the Doctor and Romana were rather impressed with the demonstration they saw, if only from a nostalgic point of view.

Meanwhile, two visitors from off-world, Brock and Klout, negotiated with Mena, the chairwoman of the Leisure Hive, to purchase the complex on behalf of the Foamasi. Mena was reticent to sell what remained of Argolis to their old enemies, which would be a final defeat for this once proud people. However, one of the Argolin scientists, Hardin, developed a new application of tachyonics – he could, he believed, renew the youth and health of lifeforms to the planet. The Argolins were sterile after the war with the Foamasi; Hardin's process could restore their ability to reproduce and save the Leisure Hive from bankruptcy. The Doctor and Romana helped Hardin perfect his technology, although the Doctor was briefly aged by several hundred years in an accident.

The Doctor and Romana worked with Hardin to try and find out what went wrong. The only conclusion they could come to was that the Tachyon Recreation Generator did not have the specifications they were told it had. Mena's son Pangol was the main authority on the device, making him the prime suspect for adapting it, especially as he insisted Hardin's experiments must end as they were endangering the Leisure Hive's systems. While investigating Pangol, Romana discovered there were two factions of

Foamasi on Argolis: Brock and Klout were members of the West Lodge organised crime syndicate, who planned to bankrupt the Leisure Hive and seize the planet. They were opposed by the Foamasi government, whose agents infiltrated the Leisure Hive to expose Brock.

Pangol had his own agenda too. He declared himself the leader of Argolis, and planned to create an army of clones to usher in a new age of conquest. He locked down the facility and destroyed the Foamasi shuttle when they tried to leave. In moments his new army emerged from the Recreation Generator. However, the Doctor had adapted the machine. The copies were all unstable versions of the Doctor and when they disappeared the only one left was a newly restored Doctor.

Meanwhile, Hardin brought Mena to the Recreation Generator to restore her, Pangol forced his way in too so he can rebuild his army. The device started up once more, but this time a rejuvenated Mena steps out, with Pangol regressed into a baby in her arms. Mena took control again, and everything returned to normal. The Foamasi were actually unharmed, as only Brock had been on the shuttle that was destroyed. They agreed with Mena that the two peoples should forge a new peace together.

CONTINUITY

K-9 spends the adventure in repair after he takes Romana's absent-minded order to fetch a ball too literally and chases it into the sea at Brighton. However, it is not entirely Romana's fault as his 'sea water defences' failed. Possibly due to the Doctor's latest upgrade.

The Doctor decides he has had enough of using the randomiser and not only removes it from the TARDIS but leaves it behind on Argolis.

Assisting Hardin build a tachyonic regenerator isn't really in line with the Time Lord's non-intervention policy. It seems Romana has been spending too long with the Doctor!

◯ RUNNING THE ADVENTURE

There is a lot going on in this adventure, which is essentially a series of sub plots collected together. How they interact and resolve will depend very much on how the player characters run into them.

The first plot is that the Leisure Hive is failing and looking for new investment, and how young Pangol has his own aims for it.

The second is Hardin's attempt to master tachyonic regeneration, and the plot by his backers to sell it to the Argolins, even when it doesn't work.

Thirdly, the Foamasi have their own internecine struggles, and one faction is trying to devalue the Leisure Hive to make it a new base, even while government Foamasi agents are hot on their tail.

Finally, the Argolins themselves are trying to find a way to survive and save their culture with Pangol's experiments in duplication.

ARGOLIN DEATH CYCLE

Argolins suffer from a degenerative effect caused by the mass radiation poisoning they were subjected to during the war. Even protected by the Leisure Hive, any Argolin living on their home planet eventually succumb to the death cycle.

The cycle starts suddenly and cannot be stopped by anything short of tachyonic regeneration. When it begins the Argolin loses a point of Strength, Coordination or Resolve each hour. These points are deducted at random, but are only reduced to 0 if all three attributes are at 1 or less. Once one attribute falls to 0 the end is near, and when all three are at 0 the Argolin dies. With each attribute loss they look older, their skin wrinkles and goes grey and they become frailer and weaker. No one knows when the death cycle will begin; there are no warning signs or tests, although most Argolins live anywhere between 40 and 60.

There are plenty of ways the player characters might come to the Leisure Hive, and each one might give the adventure a different slant. Like the Doctor and Romana, they may just come here on holiday. However, they might come looking to invest in the place, or to secretly investigate reports of sabotage or West Lodge activity. They might even come here to try and help the dying Argolins or sell them their own tachyonic regeneration process.

If the Gamemaster broadens the scope of West Lodge operations, she might create a whole campaign where the player characters try to uncover their operations. We never discover who is behind the drug trafficking in **Nightmare of Eden**, so why not make it the West Lodge? If you want to make things really complicated, maybe there are several Foamasi Mafia families. There might be a North, South and East Lodge as well, all jockeying for control of the crime in this sector. Perhaps they all have a particular speciality, but secretly seek to undermine each other. If this clandestine conflict breaks into open gang warfare, things are going to get very messy indeed for anyone stuck in the middle.

It is not only the Foamasi that are secretive. While Mena is shocked by Pangol's actions, she is complicit in the experiment to create him, and fully aware of who he is. Maybe Pangol is not the only Argolin who thinks his people should go out in a blaze of glory; Mena herself is prone to grand gestures, after all. And who exactly made Pangol in the first place – are they long dead or simply conspicuous by their absence?

ARGOLIS

Argolis is a beautiful but deadly world. Its only real feature is the Leisure Hive, but the views from the place are staggering.

Light patterns ripple across the sky as the sun rises and sets across the red landscape. Sadly, this beauty is due to radioactive fallout from the war with the Foamasi, a war that lasted 20 minutes but has rendered the surface uninhabitable for at least three centuries. The radiation has also taken its toll on the people of Argolis. They are all sterile, and remain reasonably young and vital until they enter a death cycle, when they rapidly age and die.

Argolis is essentially a world in decline. The population is shrinking and all that remains of Argolin culture is housed in the Leisure Hive. However, the Argolins remain a proud people, doing their best to endure and retain their dignity until the end.

THE LEISURE HIVE

The most famous feature on Argolis is the pleasure habitat called the Leisure Hive. It was built after the war with the Foamasi as a symbol of peace. The Argolins hoped that people of different species would come here and find commonality and fraternity as they enjoyed the entertainments on offer. The Leisure Hive is not just an entertainment centre, as far as the Argolins are concerned, it is perhaps their last, best hope for peace...

The building itself is laid out in a star pattern. A large central building sits at the centre, connected by passageways to several smaller buildings arranged around it in a circle. Most places offer a view of the outside, as both a spectacle and a reminder of the destruction of the environment.

The facility has a shuttle pad where it regularly receives space vehicles to transport guests.

The once-glamorous Leisure Hive is something of a faded celebrity. While it does what it does very well, it hasn't changed for over 40 years, and many of its entertainments are somewhat dated. It still attracts visitors, but these days a good day doesn't bring as many guests as the worst days of long ago. Even so, the place is very well maintained, the corridors clean and the suites well-appointed. The Argolins take pride in the facility and do their best to look after it.

KEY LOCATIONS IN THE LEISURE HIVE

- **Grand Atrium:** This great hall is the most popular place in the Leisure Hive as it houses its most impressive entertainment, the Tachyon Recreation Generator. Demonstrations of tachyonics are given daily (by Pangol) and always draw a good crowd. The Recreation Generator itself is a small booth topped with a spherical screen, with a discreet control array nearby. The grand atrium also has wide panoramic windows, offering a spectacular view across Argolis.

- **Council Chamber:** This smaller hall is not open to the public and is rarely used. Formal gatherings of the Argolins take place here, as do trials, but the council chamber sees little use. A reminder of their warlike past is embodied in Theron's Helmet, which hangs in the chamber. This is the helmet worn by the Argolin leader who united Argolis but then led them into the interstellar war that destroyed them.

- **Board Room:** The Leisure Hive is run from the Chairperson's office that also functions as an operations room and meeting area. It is a plain, formal room, more functional than grand. A large table dominates the room, with space for several people to hold meetings. There is also a view screen that can run demonstrations or link to the security cameras around the facility.

- **Guest Quarters:** While guests are no longer treated to premier accommodations, the guest suites at the Leisure Hive are spacious and well maintained. They are quite minimal and plain, but offer everything a guest will need for their stay.

FURTHER ADVENTURES

- **The Hidden Foamasi:** Stopped in their attempt to buy the Leisure Hive, the West Lodge decides to use Argolis as a base anyway. They land on the other side of the planet and construct a secret base. The hostile environment ensures they are left alone, even though it doesn't bother them. Tracking the operations of the West Lodge to Argolis, the Foamasi government believes the Leisure Hive has been infiltrated, and they begin their own investigation. However, if the Argolins discover Foamasi spies in their midst, will it be considered an act of war?

FOAMASI

The ancient enemies of the Argolins are quite a reserved and civilised species, despite their reptilian exterior. The Foamasi resemble a cross between a lizard and a praying mantis. They are inhumanly strong and have powerful claws, but still have the dexterity to operate controls. Their technology is equal to that of the Argolins. They communicate with a series of chirps and whistles, making diplomacy quite difficult. However, they have developed translation devices that allow them to speak with humanoid species. These devices are not usually given to government agents though, which may be because they are expensive or that the West Lodge controls the technology.

When they do speak, the Foamasi are quite urbane and civilised. They have no desire for war, but are willing to stand up to any aggressor. After the war with Argolis they suffer an increase in organised crime which occupies much of the government's time, making them quite insular.

AWARENESS	3	PRESENCE	3
COORDINATION	3	RESOLVE	3
INGENUITY	3	STRENGTH	5

SKILLS
Athletics 3, Convince 2, Fighting 3, Subterfuge 3, Survival 3, Technology 3, Transport 2

TRAITS
Alien Appearance (Major)
Natural Weapons (Minor): Close combat weapons (claws) that do Strength +2 damage.
Uncommunicative (Minor): Foamasi cannot talk to humanoid creatures without a translator device.

TECH LEVEL: 6   **STORY POINTS: 3**

- **The Greatest Show in the Galaxy:** While the regeneration technology has brought a new lease of life to Argolis, the Leisure Hive is still a failing business. Having been isolated for so long, the Argolins ask the player characters to find them a new attraction. Plenty of people are lining up, but plenty of them are crackpots and conmen. Can the player characters find a solid draw from the prospective acts, or will they have to provide an entertainment of their own?

- **Wasteland of the Daleks:** Not every species avoids irradiated environments. The Daleks find Argolis very much to their taste and build a secret base to create more mutant children of Skaro. However, when their agents discover the Recreation Generator and its power to create whole armies they set their plans on acquiring it.

BROCK

The real Brock was an Earth businessman who simply refuses to invest in the Leisure Hive. The one that arrives on Argolis is a Foamasi agent of the criminal organisation the West Lodge in disguise. His plan is to continue negotiations, but at the same time make it appear as if the facility is failing. The more worn out the Leisure Hive appears, the better the price he will get for it. Unfortunately he does not bargain on Mena's dedication to her people. She is a tough sell as she would rather see the Argolins perish than sell what little they have left to their enemies.

Brock wears a rubber suit to disguise himself. Despite his pleasant businessman-like disguise, Brock is a career criminal. He will kill anyone he needs to so he can make the sale. As far as he is concerned, its not murder, its just business.

AWARENESS	3	PRESENCE	3
COORDINATION	2	RESOLVE	3
INGENUITY	2	STRENGTH	4

SKILLS
Convince 3, Fighting 1, Subterfuge 4, Survival 2, Technology 3, Transport 2

TRAITS
Alien Appearance (Major Bad)
Dark Secret (Major Bad): Actually a Foamasi.
Empathic (Minor Good): +2 bonus on rolls to 'read' another person.
Friends (Major Good): Connected to Foamasi organised crime.
Natural Weapons (Minor Good): Close combat weapons (claws) that do Strength +2 damage.

Shapeshift (Minor Good): Able to appear to be Brock the businessman with a 'skinsuit'.

EQUIPMENT: Human disguise, Foamasi translator.

TECH LEVEL: 6   **STORY POINTS: 6**

TACHYONICS

Tachyons are particles that travel faster than light, and hence can go backwards in time from certain frames of reference. On most worlds, they are a mere scientific curiosity or used as a means of communication, but experiments – first on Earth, and later on Argolis – showed they could be used to reverse or hasten the aging process or to create solid illusions. Tachyons could also be used to create duplicates of living beings.

With all these astounding properties – it's a fountain of youth and a cloning machine – it's surprising that tachyonics are not more widely used. Even the Time Lords, who have a vastly greater understanding of the underlying physics, made little use of them. It's likely that there is some unseen drawback to tachyonics that limits their utility.

Sometimes, when you introduce a new technology into the background of a planet, the players find some creative way to abuse it. You describe how one alien swamp lizard emits a natural bioelectric field that disrupts antigravity, because you want the players to have to fight their way through the swamp instead of flying over it with their spaceship, and suddenly the players start loading lizards into missiles and exploiting this property to paralyse Dalek invasion fleets.

As a one-off, this is wonderful – when players come up with a creative solution to a problem, run with it. It's only when the players keep repeating the same exploitative tactic that you need to change things. Fortunately, alien super-science lets you overrule almost any problem. Maybe the lizards modulate the natural electromagnetic field of their planet, so that trick only works on planets with exactly the same mass and composition.

Maybe tachyonics can reverse aging and create clones – but any advanced civilisation can whip up an anti-tachyon inverse pulse oscillator that dispels the effects of tachyons.

MENA

AWARENESS	3	PRESENCE	4
COORDINATION	3	RESOLVE	2
INGENUITY	3	STRENGTH	2

Mena was promoted to the chair of the Leisure Hive by the death of her predecessor Morix during negotiations with Brock. She is a little matriarchal, but a good leader. Unfortunately she is nearing death herself, and soon after taking up the chair begins her death cycle. She is not looking to save Argolis, she only wants to be able to ensure that it dies with dignity. She has a relationship with the scientist Hardin. While she admonishes him that her new position will not allow her to grant him any special favour, they do share a bond that will ultimately drive Hardin to save her life.

SKILLS

Convince 3, Knowledge 3, Subterfuge 2, Technology 2

TRAITS

Alien Appearance (Minor)
By the Book: She must be convinced to act against procedure.
Code of Conduct (Minor): Mena is dedicated to upholding the laws of Argolis.
Empathic: +2 bonus on rolls to 'read' another person.
Obligation (Minor): See to the dignity of Argolis.
Tough: Reduce total damage by 2.

TECH LEVEL: 6   **STORY POINTS: 4**

PANGOL

AWARENESS	3	PRESENCE	3
COORDINATION	3	RESOLVE	3
INGENUITY	5	STRENGTH	3

The ranking expert on tachyonics is a man of secrets. Pangol is one of Argolis' best kept secrets, a 'child of the generator'. Years ago the Argolins used a mixture of tachyonics and cloning technology to create a child, hoping to overcome their race's sterility with science. The experiment was a success, but ever careful the Argolins wanted to see Pangol grow to maturity before they considered the experiment complete. Told he was special and the key to saving his people throughout his childhood, Pangol has developed something of a messiah complex. He dedicated himself to the experiments that created him, and began to consider ways he could improve on the plan. He decided that it was not enough to be the start of a new race of Argolins if that wasn't going to mean greater glory for the species, so he spent many years developing tachyonic technology to allow him to create an army of super-soldiers based on his own 'perfected' form.

SKILLS
Athletics 2, Convince 2, Craft 3, Knowledge 2, Science 5, Subterfuge 3, Technology 4

TRAITS
Boffin: Pangol is a technical genius.
Alien Appearance (Minor)
Dark Secret (Major): First 'child of the generator'.
Obsession (Major): "I am the new age of Argolis!".

TECH LEVEL: 6   **STORY POINTS: 8**

HARDIN

AWARENESS	2	PRESENCE	2
COORDINATION	2	RESOLVE	3
INGENUITY	4	STRENGTH	3

Hardin is a good man in a bad position. Like many scientists he begun his research into tachyonics because he foresaw the results being of great benefit to society. When his work gained funding from powerful businessmen he thought he would be able to realise his dreams. However, it has become clearer and clearer that the businessmen have no concern for their fellow man. They see his experiments as a marketable commodity and nothing more than a way to get rich. By the time he understood what he was getting into, Hardin was in too deep. He faked the regeneration demonstration in the hopes someone would see through it, but when the Argolins are convinced their hopes have been answered he once more realises he has dug himself deeper into a hole. Hardin is a good man though, just a misguided one. He is too easily walked over, as long as he gets to continue his work. Even so, he has his limits and once Romana joins him he gains new confidence. He is able to stand up to the con men surrounding him and ultimately prove his work can be used for the purpose he intended.

SKILLS
Craft 3, Fighting 1, Knowledge 2, Science 4, Technology 4

TRAITS
Cowardly: -2 penalty to any fear roll.
Dark Secret (Minor): 'In with the wrong people'.

TECH LEVEL: 6   **STORY POINTS: 4**

MEGLOS

'You'll have to do better than that Doctor. I think you're a fraud and a liar!'
'Well, that makes even less sense.'
'Oh? Why?'
'Well, I just don't do that sort of thing.'

⊙ SYNOPSIS

The Prion System, Present Day

The Doctor received a message from an old friend, Zastor from the planet Tigella. The people of Tigella lived in a vast underground city, as the plant-life on the surface was extremely dangerous. The complex was powered by the Dodecahedron a polyhedral device that was worshipped by a Tigellan faction called the Deons. The Deons, led by their priestess Lexa, refused to allow the Savants, a faction of technicians, to study their holy artefact. This was a problem because something was going wrong and if the Dodecahedron stopped providing power the whole city would fail. Zastor was trying desperately to

mediate the argument between the Savants and the Deons, neither of whom were prepared to negotiate. He needed the Doctor to help find a solution before all of Tigella suffered.

Unfortunately for Tigella, the only remaining inhabitant of the neighbouring planet Zolfa-Thura had designs on the Dodecahedron. This creature was Meglos, an intelligent plant creature who had enlisted the help of a group of mercenaries called Gaztaks, led by General Grugger and his Lieutenant Brotadac. Meglos had been living for centuries in a hidden facility under the Screens of Zolfa-Thura, huge pentagonal plates arranged in a circle in the desolate waste, the only feature on a dead world.

Grugger and Brotadac brought Meglos an Earthling they had captured and who Meglos possessed. Using his technology, Meglos then turned his stolen body into a duplicate of the Doctor! He intended to answer Zastor's call for help himself and use the Doctor's identity to steal the Dodecahedron. Meglos understood the Dodecahedron far better than the Tigellans and planned to unleash its full potential.

Needing to get the real Doctor out of the way, he locked the TARDIS into a state of chronic hysteresis – a time loop. By the time they broke free and arrived on Tigella, Meglos had already ingratiated himself with the Tigellans and stolen the Dodecahedron. When the real Doctor arrived he was arrested for Meglos' crime as the complex's power systems began to catastrophically fail. With the complex in disarray, Meglos was still unable to escape. The Earthling he had possessed was fighting back, making it hard for him to maintain his disguise. Romana unwittingly helped him escape, but on discovering her mistake, realised there was an imposter.

Meglos, the Gaztaks and the Dodecahedron returned to Zolfa-Thura and prepared to turn the Dodecahedron into a terrifying weapon. Using the Screens of Zolfa-Thura to enhance its power, they could destroy anything in the universe. When asked to pick a test target, General Grugger picked Tigella. Meglos was happy to oblige, but before firing the weapon decided to check the alignment of the screens. Having followed Meglos to Zolfa-Thura in the TARDIS, the Doctor used the opportunity to change places with Meglos, and reversed the settings on the weapon controls. When Meglos returned, Grugger and Brotadac double crossed him and took control of the system, believing they could control the power themselves. Unable to undo the Doctor's work, Meglos could only watch as the Dodecahedron vaporised Zolfa-Thura, the screens, Meglos and itself in a blaze of energy.

CONTINUITY

K-9 turns out to have a manual, with a set of special test questions to help with repairs. Has the Doctor written a manual for the dog? This seems unlikely

as he is so contemptuous about the TARDIS manual. Perhaps Professor Marius didn't build K-9 from scratch; he might be a kit you can buy.

Meglos has been waiting underground for 10,000 years for a chance to steal the Dodecahedron. Seems a little odd the opportunity hasn't presented itself sooner, so perhaps something else was stopping him.

This adventure takes place during contemporary Earth time, judging by the clothes the captured 'Earthling' is wearing.

When the Doctor and Meglos are held prisoner together, the Doctor is finally able to ask a question that's been bugging him about his enemies. He asks Meglos why he wants to rule the universe, as it seems a lot of work. Sadly, Meglos doesn't really have an answer.

RUNNING THE ADVENTURE

As usual, the player characters find themselves in the middle of someone else's problem, but at least this time they've been invited. It need not be Zastor that invites them to Tigella either. The adventure can be very effective if the player characters are called back to somewhere they have already been by someone they know who has a vital piece of technology fail. Using someone the player characters already know lets them return to the scene of an old adventure and see how things have progressed after they left. Did everything work out or have things gotten worse?

Whether you use a previous adventure or invent an old friend, it is important that the player characters have some sort of access to the 'object of desire' that most people do not. This is the reason Meglos will be trying to steal one of their identities after all. If your players enjoyed having a double in **The Androids of Tara** this is another opportunity for more of the same fun. However, it is not essential to

have a shape-shifting villain. Meglos might actually employ the player characters instead of the Gaztaks to steal the Dodecahedron from a group of religious zealots (as Meglos will describe them) who are about to abuse its power and destroy themselves. If your player characters don't trust the talking cactus, the Gamemaster might decide that this time Meglos is telling the truth.

We also have to wonder what might have happened if Meglos had hired decent help. If the Gaznaks successfully double cross Meglos he might have become their prisoner, using his knowledge to build them a terrible weapon. The player characters might need to rescue Meglos to save Tigella.

TIGELLA

The planet Tigella lies in the Prion system. It is a lush green world you might easily mistake for a paradise. Unfortunately the plant-life is both carnivorous and aggressive, making life on the surface quite dangerous. The people of Tigella live in a huge underground city complex. This makes the doorway to the complex the only real feature of note on the surface of Tigella. With the plant-life constantly growing, it masks any other features under a canopy of leaves.

Travellers on the surface of Tigella need to keep their wits about them. Few of the plants can move, but plenty can reach out with vines or thorns to catch unwary prey. The Gamemaster should call for frequent Awareness checks if the player characters insist on exploring. The plants won't exactly attack, but should a player character fail an Awareness + Athletics roll to dodge the vines or thorns they will be caught by something hungry. If so they will have to cut themselves free or fight the Strength of the plant (usually ranging from 2-5). Those who fail will be trapped, and take damage from the fluids

in the plant every hour that they cannot get free. Some plants may also use poison to render victims unconscious before dragging them into their maws. The Gamemaster should indulge herself with as many triffid-creatures as she sees fit!

THE TIGELLAN CITY

The Tigellans themselves live in a huge underground complex. Much of the complex is dug out of rock, and in many areas the metal walkways run through rock passageways and caverns. The place is very empty, as it can house more Tigellans than actually live here, another sign of their gradual decline.

KEY LOCATIONS IN THE TIGELLAN CITY

- **The Control Room:** The nerve centre of the complex is the home of the Savants. This large room is packed with so much technology it appears smaller than it is. The systems here monitor and control the entire complex, and many need constant maintenance and attention. While the council chamber is reserved for big decisions, the day to day running of the complex is handled from here.

- **The Council Chamber:** This large room decorated in red and purple is used for formal discussions, if only because it is the only room the main factions of the city can all fit into, and because it is neutral territory for all of them. Several chairs are arranged around a circular area where those who are putting a case can stand and offer their case. Several ornaments in glass cases stand against the wall behind the speaker, containing relics and symbols of Tigellan history.

- **The Power Room:** One of the deepest and plainest parts of the complex is the domain of the Deons. The rooms in this area are open

and spacious but unadorned, made up of plain grey angular walls. The chamber containing the Dodecahedron is forbidden to any but Deons to enter. It sits on a platform in the centre of the room, its amber light filling the space. However, the room is designed so even from the antechamber next door only the glow of the Dodecahedron can be seen.

ZOLFA-THURA

Zolfa-Thura is the only other inhabitable planet in the Prion system, and Tigella's only neighbour. Unlike Tigella it is a hot, dead world. After a war that took place centuries ago the place is a barren desert. Given Meglos is a plant creature it is likely that once Zolfa-Thura was as verdant as Tigella. The only feature on the whole planet are the Screens of

MEGLOS

The only survivor of the civil wars that laid waste to Zolfa-Thura describes himself as the last of the Xerophytes. Meglos is an intelligent plant, little more than a three-foot high cactus, but what he lacks in physical ability he makes up for in mental acuity. He easily outsmarts the Gaztaks when they first try to double cross him, but he underestimates their greed and stupidity, ultimately leading to his destruction. While Meglos doesn't especially enjoy causing chaos and killing his enemies, he does want to rule the universe. He is a subtle creature though and works using deception and intelligence rather than brute force.

Meglos is able to use his extensive technology to take possession of a host body by transferring his consciousness to them and dominating the original occupant. The process is not perfect though and particularly resilient or dedicated hosts can break the control for short moments, making Meglos revert a little to his plantlike form. If cast out of a host (or if he chooses to leave) he can become a fast-moving slug-like creature. He can maintain this form until returning to his original body or a new host.

Meglos' ability to possess a host is purely technological, and without using the booths in his base he cannot take a new host. He might also have access to other forms of advanced technology – further artefacts of Zolfa-Thura.

AWARENESS	4	PRESENCE	4
COORDINATION	0*	RESOLVE	4*
INGENUITY	7	STRENGTH	0*

SKILLS
Convince 4, Craft 4, Knowledge 3, Science 4, Subterfuge 6, Survival 3, Technology 6

TRAITS
Alien
Alien Appearance (Major)
Boffin: Meglos is an evil genius.
Eccentric (Major): Meglos is a complete megalomaniac. He's a Meglos-a-maniac!
Environmental (Minor): Highly resistant to heat and dry deserts.
Selfish: Power! More power for Meglos!
Shapeshift (Special): Meglos can alter his form at will.
Special - Possess: Meglos may attempt possession with a +4 bonus (see p57 **Gamemaster's Guide**).

Voice of Authority: +2 bonus to Presence and Convince rolls.

TECH LEVEL: 7   **STORY POINTS: 10**

*In his natural form Meglos has no physical attributes. When possessing a host he uses their physical attributes.

Zolfa-Thura. These massive pentagonal plates are arranged in a circle, a last monument to the people who once lived here.

However, the world is not entirely dead. Under the screens, Meglos, the last survivor of the war hides in a secret bunker facility. The bunker has an entranceway that can rise to the surface for access, but only at Meglos' command.

FURTHER ADVENTURES

- **The Master of Meglos:** It may seem odd that Meglos' base seems built for humans rather than planets. Perhaps Meglos was created, not born, by a humanoid Zolfa-Thuran scientist. Returning home to discover his planet gone and his plant creatures destroyed, he vows vengeance on Tigella. He unleashes more plant creatures (walking and hungry ones) on the new Tigellan surface settlements.

- **Parliament of Trees:** If there are intelligent plants on Zolfa-Thura, why not on Tigella too? As the Tigellans begin to settle the surface they find themselves under attack from the local plant life. After the Tigellans clear land for fields the plants are in no mood to negotiate. Can the player characters help them find the rumoured Parliament of Trees, the rulers of the plant kingdom, and broker a truce?

- **Seeking the Twelve:** While the blast from the Dodecahedron destroyed Zolfa-Thura, Meglos and the Gaztaks, it didn't utterly destroy itself. Instead, it was broken into twelve fragments, each one a powerful artefact capable of generating vast amounts of energy. These fragments have scattered across space, and perhaps even time. Can the player characters collect them before someone else puts the artefact together and wields its power once more?

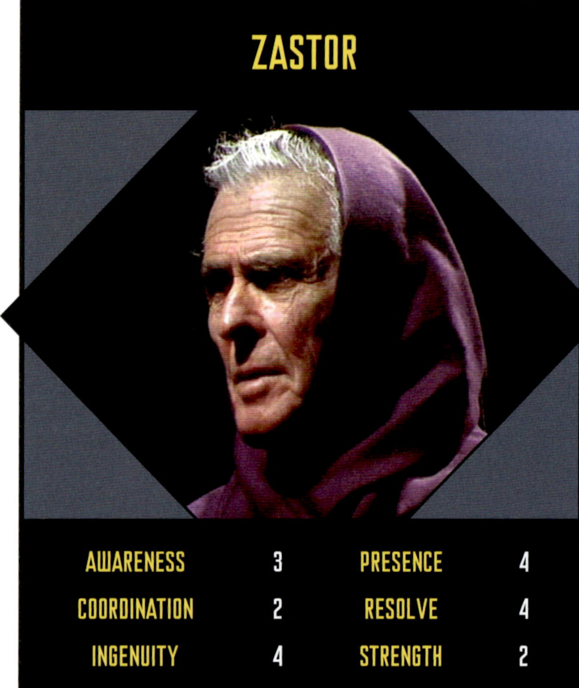

ZASTOR

AWARENESS	3	PRESENCE	4
COORDINATION	2	RESOLVE	4
INGENUITY	4	STRENGTH	2

The leader of the Tigellans met the Doctor in his youth, and can recognise him in his new incarnation. He is a kindly old man, only seeking to do the best for his people. However he is not a strong enough leader to dominate and control the two factions, the Savants and the Deons. A skilled compromiser, he really cannot understand why everyone cannot just get along. While he isn't a strong leader, he has built up a lot of respect from everyone in the city for his wisdom and kindness.

SKILLS

Convince 3, Knowledge 3, Medicine 2, Science 2, Survival 1, Technology 2

TRAITS

Brave: +2 bonus to any Resolve roll when he needs to show courage.
Charming: +2 bonus to attempts to use charm.
Code of Conduct (Minor): Zastor always tries to reach a harmonious compromise, which limits his ability to act in a crisis.
Obligation (Major): Keep the people of Tigella safe and harmonious.
Slow Reflexes: Zastor always acts last no matter what he's doing.
Unadventurous (Minor): Zastor avoids adventure and excitement.

TECH LEVEL: 5   **STORY POINTS: 6**

GENERAL GRUGGER

AWARENESS	3	PRESENCE	3
COORDINATION	3	RESOLVE	4
INGENUITY	3	STRENGTH	4

The leader of the Gaztaks is something of a petty warlord rather than the commander of an elite (or even competent) unit. Grugger is a simple creature, for him it is all about the money. There is no one he wouldn't double cross to steal from, as long as he thought he could get away with it. While he is the cleverest and most competent of the Gaztaks, that isn't much of a compliment. Like the others he is a bully and a coward, only fighting those he knows he can beat. While he is capable of making a decent plan, he only ever considers the short term gains. He'd rather grab a pile of credits nearby than take part in a plot to clear out a bank vault.

SKILLS

Athletics 2, Fighting 3, Knowledge 1, Marksman 3, Subterfuge 1, Survival 2, Technology 3, Transport 2

TRAITS

Impulsive: The General is focused on the short term.
Obsession (Minor): Get rich or die trying.
Run for your Life!: +1 bonus to his Speed when escaping pursuit.
Selfish: The General's out for himself.
Tough: Reduce total damage by 2.

EQUIPMENT: Laser Pistol (4/8/L)

TECH LEVEL: 6   **STORY POINTS: 8**

GAZTAKS

AWARENESS	2	PRESENCE	2
COORDINATION	3	RESOLVE	3
INGENUITY	2	STRENGTH	3

Grugger's mercenary team are the Gaztaks. They are not so much mercenary soldiers as a loose collection of thugs and pirates. They have little or no real loyalty to Grugger, following him only because he leads them to better jobs than they could each get on their own.

Having said that, they rarely retreat and they follow orders without question. However, this might be because they believe the General would never send them against a force they couldn't easily crush.

SKILLS

Athletics 3, Fighting 3, Marksman 3, Science 1, Subterfuge 2, Survival 2, Technology 1, Transport 2

TRAITS

Tough: Reduce total damage by 2.

EQUIPMENT: Laser Pistol (4/8/L), armour vest (2 points)

TECH LEVEL: 6   **STORY POINTS: 2-3**

FULL CIRCLE

'Why can't people be nice to one other, just for a change? I mean, I'm an alien and you don't want to drag me into a swamp do you? Oh, you do.'

⊙ SYNOPSIS

Alzarius, E-Space

The Time Lords summoned the TARDIS back to Gallifrey to recall Romana. She had no desire to go home now she had seen the universe outside the cloistered halls of the Citadel, but the Doctor reminded her they have no choice. However, before they reached Gallifrey the TARDIS passed through a powerful anomaly. They found themselves on a planet called Alzarius instead of Gallifrey, even though the viewscreen and coordinates showed Gallifrey.

The locals were having problems of their own. The Deciders, the ruling trio of elders who ran an idyllic rural society, were seeing signs that Mistfall might be on its way. They ordered the people to make their way to the Starliner, their sanctuary, as they believed that the air would soon turn poisonous. However, not everyone did what the Deciders tell them to.

A small group of teenage rebels calling themselves the Outlers had formed under the leadership of Varsh. One of their prospective members, Varsh's brother Adric, found his way into the TARDIS by accident trying to shelter from Mistfall. He led the other Outlers there and they attempted to take Romana prisoner. She was not impressed with their teenage antics, but let them stay nevertheless.

Exploring, the Doctor and K-9 encountered the Marshmen emerging from the rivers. Avoiding the creatures, he broke into the Starliner (well, no one answered the door) but left the door open, allowing in a curious juvenile Marshman. While the Alzarians worked towards making the Starliner ready to return to their ancestor's home planet of Terradon, the Doctor wandered around. However, he and the curious Marshman were taken prisoner and brought before the Deciders. He told them the air was actually fine and they admitted they knew this, but deceived their followers to get them all into the Starliner, away from the increasingly dangerous local creatures.

Meanwhile, Romana and the Outlers were unable to leave the TARDIS as it was surrounded by Marshmen, who disabled K-9 by beheading him! Romana was injured by a Alzarian Spider, and in the ensuing panic, Adric pressed the wrong button and the TARDIS dematerialised to land in the Starliner. The Deciders offered amnesty to the Outlers if they joined the repair crews working towards 'the embarkation'.

The Deciders also gave their scientist Dexeter permission to conduct vivisection experiments on the captured Marshman, the first of which woke Romana who had been infected with a psychic link to the Marshmen. Before the Doctor could stop the experiments, the Marshman broke free, killing Dexeter and itself when it was electrocuted as it smashed up the laboratory. The Doctor was disgusted with the Deciders and accused them of grand fraud. He had noticed the repair crews were swapping out perfectly good components; the Starliner was ready for take off immediately, not in generations' time as the Deciders have been saying. The Deciders were forced to tell the Doctor the truth: the System Files in the ship told them how to rebuild the whole ship, but none of the files told them how to fly it!

Meanwhile, Romana's bite continued to affect her mind and made her join the Marshmen. She opened the Starliner's hold to let them in. The Marshmen caused chaos in the Starliner, and no one could organise a defence as the Deciders were (somewhat ironically) paralysed by indecision. Nefred, the First Decider was fatally injured, and begged the other Deciders to make sure the Starliner takes off. However, as he died he cryptically told them they could not return to Terradon as they had never been there. Decider Login took control, ordering the doors sealed, and organised a defence of the ship.

The Doctor continued his research in the laboratory and discovered that the Alzarians, Marshmen and Alzarian Spiders all shared the same form of cells. He managed to find a cure for Romana, which he was able to give her when she attacked the laboratory with the other Marshmen. The Doctor and the Outlers discover the Marshmen had not quite adapted to an oxygen rich atmosphere, and managed to use oxygen cylinders to force them back. Escaping the laboratory they found Login (and K-9's head, which was being used as a club by a Marshman) and told him to flood the ship with more oxygen. The plan worked and the Marshmen were driven back.

With the Starliner secure the Doctor and Romana taught the remaining Deciders how to fly the ship. However, they could not return to Terradon. They were not descended from the crashed Starliner's crew, but from the Marshmen who discovered it and adapted to make use of it. The adaptive powers of the Marshmen meant the Alzarians adapted and evolved at a greatly accelerated rate. However, they had a universe to choose from to find a new home, and the Starliner finally lifted off – but not before Adric stowed away on the TARDIS.

The Doctor also discovered why the TARDIS view screen shows Gallifrey when they are clearly on Alzarius. They had passed through a Charged Vacuum Emboitement (CVE) into Exo-space, a smaller universe that sat alongside the prime universe, N-Space. They were in the area of E-Space that corresponded to Gallifrey, which the view screen showed as it lacked the ability to work from 'negative coordinates'. Neither Time Lord knew how they might find a way out of E-Space. They could be trapped here forever.

CONTINUITY

For the next three adventures, the Doctor and Romana are in E-Space, another, smaller, universe layered near to our own. E-Space is linked to normal N-Space by CVEs. These dimensional tunnels are extremely difficult to detect and enter, and act as stable wormholes into other universes. The problem is that because they are so difficult to find it is very hard to find a way back.

In E-Space, all coordinates become negative. So, as the viewscreen only deals in absolute values it keeps showing Gallifrey when they are actually on Alzarius as they share the same coordinates, albeit ones with 'reversed polarity'.

This time, the Time Lords are a little more polite when they recall the Doctor, sending a message rather than dragging the TARDIS back to Gallifrey or knocking everyone out and transporting them into a holding cell. This may have something to do with the way the Doctor seems resigned to doing as he is told. When Romana suggests they challenge their authority, as the Doctor has before, he tells her he has only fought and lost.

After the many repairs he has undergone in recent adventures, K-9 seems to be somewhat upgraded as he can pilot the TARDIS by remotely controlling the console.

Adric proves non-Time Lords can pilot the TARDIS, but he is probably only setting it in flight as Romana has already set the coordinates. She may well be a far better TARDIS pilot than the Doctor. The course she sets allows Adric to take the TARDIS on a short trip, which the Doctor tells him are actually more difficulty and precise. He does manage to reverse the course rather easily though.

The TARDIS is equipped with small homing devices to help the crew locate it on unfamiliar planets. When Varsh is killed, Keara offers Adric Varsh's reed belt, making him one of the Outlers at last.

Romana proves to have little fear of spiders. This is somewhat unfortunate as the Alzarian ones are quite dangerous.

RUNNING THE ADVENTURE

The first thing you need to decide with this adventure is which universe it is going to be set in. E-Space offers some great possibilities, but the universe is a pretty strange place already, so there is little you can do in E-Space that you can't do in normal space. However, it does mean you can mess with any laws of physics or rules you might have set up in previous games. Gravity, energy, space and time might all work in slightly different ways in E-Space. If you enjoy pulling the rug from under your player character's feet, E-Space allows you to do so on a spectacular scale.

An E-Space campaign is usually driven by the search to get home again. However, it will initially be driven by the need to get all the player character's technology working properly. How badly E-Space affects their tech is up to you. The Doctor only had a dodgy viewscreen, what if the TARDIS could no longer calculate coordinates without some sort of base reference? Maybe energy works differently, making equipment run out of power in moments. They may face all the same problems the Tenth Doctor faces in the adventure **Rise of the Cybermen** and **The Age of Steel**.

However, an E-Space campaign might not be accidental. If places like Alzarius are 'twinned' with places like Gallifrey, there may be all manner of ways to use this to a villain's advantage. You might launch attacks from E-Space, passing all manner of defences. Even if you can't take an army, the viewscreen problem could become an incredible tool for spying on other worlds. If someone developed the technology to make use of this effect, someone would have to try and stop them.

While E-Space is an excellent device, to use **Full Circle** as an adventure you need not set it there. The planet Alzarius could be anywhere. Much of the player character's involvement will depend on when they arrive and what they need when they get there. The Doctor and Romana arrive just as Mistfall is starting to happen. Your player characters might begin the adventure earlier. In trading with some peaceful locals they notice the ruling elite and scientists are conducting secret tests. What are they up to and what do they fear? If the player characters arrive after Mistfall, they find a deserted and hostile planet. The Starliner is sealed so they will have to break in to get answers, especially if an Alzarian spider has bitten one of them.

Given the lies the Deciders tell the public, the Gamemaster is somewhat spoilt for choice about how to adapt the adventure. You just need to pick which lies are really lies, and which secrets are actually true. They might be telling the truth, that the mists are poisonous and they are repairing the ship so they might return home.

Maybe one of the Deciders does know how to fly the ship (but then destroyed the flight manual) but is concerned they might lose political power if they return to Terradon and is doing everything to stop

launch. Maybe the people are repairing the ship, but the Outlers decide to start sabotaging the Starliner.

The Gamemaster should also decide on the origins of the Alzarians. Maybe they really are the descendants of Terradonians. Perhaps there is actually a mixture of Marshmen and Terradon descendants, and the discovery of 'pure breeds' might be cause for internal conflict. Perhaps evolution is running in a slightly different direction. Maybe the Terradonians became the Marshmen, and the Alzarians are moving towards becoming Marshmen rather than evolving away from it. Old friends might become Marshmen as the mists adapt and change those caught in them.

ALZARIUS

The planet Alzarius is a lush green world, an idyllic rural place apparently inhabited by the descendants of a crashed Terradon Starliner. The people live a pastoral existence as hunter/gatherers as the lush vegetation needs little cultivation to produce food.

MARSHMEN

The Marshmen are humanoid creatures that emerge from the rivers on Alzarius during Mistfall. They are brown, reptilian creatures and move in packs. While they are quite strong they are not especially dextrous and move quite slowly. They adapt extremely quickly to changes in their environment. Marshmen have a low intelligence but their mental capacity can improve significantly given the need.

AWARENESS	3	PRESENCE	2
COORDINATION	2	RESOLVE	3
INGENUITY	1	STRENGTH	4

SKILLS
Athletics 3, Craft 1, Fighting 3, Subterfuge 2, Survival 2

TRAITS
Alien
Alien Appearance (Major)
Environmental (Minor): Marshmen can adapt to any environment, but quite slowly, taking about a day to adapt to minor toxic changes, and much longer for major changes. They are also amphibious and can survive for long periods in water.
Fast Healing (Major): Attribute Points lost due to injury are regained at 1 point per hour.
Slow Reflexes: Marshmen always act last in their Action Phase.

Weakness (Major): Concentrated oxygen injures Marshmen, inflicting four levels of damage on them.

TECH LEVEL: 1   **STORY POINTS: 6**

The main habitation is by the rivers near the Starliner, where the Alzarians harvest the watermelon-like riverfruit. The ground beyond the river valley becomes more rocky and hilly with several caves set into the mountains. It is in one of these caves the Outlers live.

Every fifty years, Alzarius experiences Mistfall where the planet's atmosphere changes under the influence of another nearby planet. Mist rises from the ground and the rivers, and several hostile creatures that have been in hibernation move out onto land and begin to adapt to the changes in climate. Some species (like the Alzarian Spiders) have a life cycle linked to this planetary event. The eggs naturally found in riverfruit begin to hatch into spiders.

FURTHER ADVENTURES

- **The Ghost Liner:** The player characters come across the Starliner travelling through space on course for an inhabited world. However, the ship is devoid of Alzarians. Have they evolved into something new, and is it friendly, or even human? With a large ship to hide in, trying to find the remaining crew could be difficult, as will

ALZARIAN SPIDERS

During Mistfall the spiders complete their life cycle and hatch from the riverfruit. Until this time their eggs lie dormant. Just before Mistfall the eggs grow, becoming easily noticeable in the open fruit, and are one of the initial signs of Mistfall. These eggs grow over the course of a day and fully grown spiders hatch from the fruit.

The spiders are very big, around the same size as large rats, and move quite quickly. They are quite groggy just after hatching and are not especially aggressive, but they soon recover and seek out larger animals to bite. This bite does little damage but can render human sized prey unconscious. The bite is infectious, contaminating the victim with Alzarian DNA.

AWARENESS	2	PRESENCE	1
COORDINATION	4	RESOLVE	2
INGENUITY	1	STRENGTH	1

SKILLS
Athletics 3, Fighting 2, Subterfuge 3, Survival 2

TRAITS
Alien
Alien Appearance (Major)
Fear Factor 1: Grants a +1 bonus to inspire fear.
Natural Weapons (Minor): Bite, Strength +2 damage.
Special – Climbing: Spiders gain a +4 bonus to climbing rolls, and may climb sheer and smooth surfaces.
Special - Infection: If the spider damages an opponent they are infected with Marshman DNA

-this does initial Stun damage. The victim then counts as being hypnotised, making them predisposed to cooperating and aiding with the Marshmen. A protein serum will cure the victim Ingenuity + Medicine roll (Difficulty 12).
Size (Tiny)

reversing the process. The controls have been destroyed and the ship is on course to crash into another planet. Can the player characters stop the collision, and if it lands, can they stop the evolved Alzarians wreaking more havoc?

- **Kiss of the Spider:** A ship lands on Alzarius during Mistfall and unknowingly picks up a few spiders. They escape when the ship gets home, infecting some of the population. These new proto-Marshmen begin causing chaos. They want to get back to Alzarius at any cost, but Alzarius might be the only place to find a cure.

- **Mission to Mistfall:** Having heard of the amazing healing ability of the Alzarians, a medical research team travels to the planet to try and understand the process. They hope to be able to use what they learn to increase the healing speed of patients. However, another team is also dispatched in secret looking to steal what they discover so it might be used to breed a new type of fast-healing super-soldier. Can the player characters keep the medical team safe, and how far are the medical team willing to go to learn the secrets of Alzarius?

THE DECIDERS

The Alzarians are ruled by a tripartite of elders called 'Deciders'. These three men make all the decisions for the small society and serve in office until they die or retire. When a Decider passes away, the remaining Deciders choose a candidate to offer the vacant position to. There is no voting procedure, but most Deciders realise that choosing a candidate popular with the Alzarians is the best way to remain in power. One of the Deciders takes the role of First Decider, whose decisions carry more weight as they alone are privy to the System Files which contain the secret of the Alzarian's true ancestors.

When the Doctor and Romana arrive, the First Decider is Draith, who is lost while chasing Adric. The other two Deciders are Nefred and Garif. Nefred is promoted to First Decider, and Login fills the vacant position. While the council of Deciders have only the good of the Alzarians people at heart, they often choose to lie or manipulate the people 'for their own good'. When faced with a real crisis, they are often paralysed with self-doubt, preferring to talk over a problem in council rather than make a decision they are unsure of. When the Marshmen attack the Star liner they decide that doing nothing is the only course as "hasty action would only add to the general sense of panic."

AWARENESS	2	PRESENCE	3
COORDINATION	2	RESOLVE	3
INGENUITY	3	STRENGTH	2

SKILLS
Convince 4, Knowledge 4, Science 2, Subterfuge 3, Technology 2

TRAITS
By the Book (Minor Bad): Precedence is everything.
Dark Secret (Major): The truth about their ancestors and the Starliner.
Fast Healing (Major): Attribute Points lost due to injury are regained at a rate of 1 point per hour.
Obligation (Major): Lead the people of Alzarius towards embarkation.
Unadventurous (Major): The Deciders decide. Other people do.

Weakness (Minor) – Procrastinator: The Deciders suffer a -2 penalty to rolls when in a rushed or panicked situation.

TECH LEVEL: 5   **STORY POINTS: 6**

STATE OF DECAY

'The lords rule in the tower, the peasants toil in the fields. Nothing has changed in a thousand years.'

⚙ SYNOPSIS

An unnamed planet, E-Space, 2929

While searching for a way out of E-Space, the travellers landed on a desolate planet that had only one settlement, a village next to a great tower. When investigating the village, the Doctor and Romana met Ivo, an innkeeper, who told them that strangers were not just rare but unheard of. He suggested they speak to the 'lords in the tower' who rule here. While the village was no more advanced than the medieval age, when the time travellers left, Ivo used an advanced communicator he had hidden away to pass on news of the stranger's arrival to a group of rebel dissidents.

On their way to the tower, the Doctor and Romana were met by the rebels, who took them to their cave hideout. The cave was full of old broken technology, under the care of Kalmar. This old scientist was glad to meet them as he needed help understanding the equipment. The rebels explained that the rulers in the tower – King Zargo, Queen Camilla and Chancellor Aukon – forbade science, knowledge and even reading.

The whole society had stultified, living in a 'state of decay' with no advancement. The Doctor helped Kalmar get an old computer working which turned out to contain the crew records of a ship called the Hydrax that crashed here many centuries ago. Interestingly the pictures of the three command crew were remarkably similar to the three rulers in the tower. The Doctor decided it was time they met them and he and Romana set off for the tower again.

Meanwhile, K-9 discovered that Adric had stowed away on the TARDIS. Adric was also of a mind to explore and wandered down into the village. He met Ivo and his wife Marta who took him in as night was falling. Unfortunately, Aukon made a surprise visit to make another 'choosing' and chose Adric. Those who were chosen sometimes joined the tower guard, but most were never heard from again.

In the tower, Zargo and Camilla, who were very polite but a little odd, met the Doctor and Romana. The King and Queen saw no problem with living in decadent luxury while the peasants starved, and they became coldly excited when Romana cut her finger. Zargo and Camilla left the Doctor and Romana under guard in the throne room, where the Doctor confided his theories to Romana. He believed the tower is actually the crashed remains of the Hydrax, and the three rulers were not just descendants of the old crew, but the actual crew themselves. They found an inspection hatch and escaped the throne room to investigate the rest of the tower, which was indeed actually an ancient spacecraft.

At the top of the tower they found the turrets were actually scout ships, old, but in working order. Working their way down they found a storeroom with several desiccated bodies drained of blood. The blood was stored by the gallon in the ship's massive fuel tanks. They followed pipes leading from the area into a series of underground caves where a great heartbeat could be heard. Something was buried in the cave, feeding on the blood being pumped into its lair.

Before the Doctor and Romana could investigate further, Aukon caught them. Instead of attacking them he suggested they join his side. Soon the Great One would rise and need more followers to lead a new plague of Vampires into N-space. The Doctor and Romana refused, telling Aukon he'll have to do better to corrupt a Time Lord. However, Aukon recognised the title as the enemies of the Great One. He ordered them both taken prisoner, to become fitting sacrifices upon the Great One's awakening.

In a prison cell, the Doctor tells Romana an old legend of Great Vampires that were fought in ages past by the Time Lords. She replied that when she used to work in the records archive on Gallifrey she heard that TARDIS models as old as the Doctor's were installed with some emergency guidelines in case the Great Vampires should rise again. They managed to break out and returned to the TARDIS to locate the old records, but discovered Adric had been captured by Aukon. Romana stayed in the tower to find him while the Doctor returned to the TARDIS to find the records. Romana found Adric but was recaptured in the process.

Back at the TARDIS, the Doctor found the old records and discovered the Time Lords did indeed face a race of Vampires. These creatures were so powerful the only way to destroy them was by using a steel stake fired from a Bowship to destroy their heart. Realising he would need help the Doctor went to the rebel camp and inspired both the rebels and villagers to make an assault on the castle. He needed the distraction to put his plan into action to destroy the Vampire.

The assault began, while deep under the tower the ceremony to release the Great Vampire commenced. Aukon, Zargo and Camilla were unconcerned about the battle in the tower, knowing that when their master rises he will consume anyone who was left. As the battle raged, the Doctor frantically tried to get just one of the three scout ships to work. The last one had enough power for a short flight and he sent it on an automatic course. The scout ship crashed into the

CURSE OF THE VAMPIRE!

While the Great Vampires were destroyed, or at least exiled, they were able to corrupt other sentient life forms to vampirism. While the Three Who Rule die the instant the Great Vampire does, others may have been able to survive the death of their master. The myths of Vampires endure throughout the universe, after all. It may be that Vampires who have not passed their natural lifespan when their master dies are able to live, and the strongest can maintain their existence by drinking blood. If they are not wholly reliant on their master to maintain their immortally, they can survive. In time, older Vampires gain more power, until they can finally offer some of their essence to create new Vampires. Newly created Vampires who rely on their master to sustain their unnatural life span cannot survive without him and will give their lives to defend him.

In general, the Gamemaster is free to create whatever version of the Vampire myth they prefer. There are certainly enough different versions of the creatures to justify pretty much any interpretation. Even if they are all descended from the Great Vampires, over so many years they might have evolved and adapted in any number of ways.

Vampire's heart as the creature broke the surface. The last of the Great Vampires died, and his followers aged and perished with him.

CONTINUITY

In this adventure, we learn the origins of the Vampire myth, a myth that appears on planets across the universe due to a great battle the ancient Time Lords once fought against a race of gigantic space Vampires. However, Vampires are not the only blood-drinking creatures, and not every form of Vampire is necessarily linked to the great Vampires (see *The Curse* of Fenris in **The Seventh Doctor Sourcebook**). The Great Vampires were terrifying creatures, able to destroy entire planets by draining them of life. The war they fought with the Time Lords was bitter, as the Gallifreyans were not yet Lords of Time. However, they were an extremely advanced people, who already felt it was their responsibility to police the universe. The Great Vampires were an enemy that would remain unmatched until the Last Great Time War. Energy weapons were no use against them and they healed physical damage rapidly. The only way to destroy them was to utterly destroy their heart. To this end the Gallifreyans built Bowships, which fired massive steel arrows at the Vampires.

This incredible battle is now forgotten by most Time Lords. Romana only heard a similar tale while cataloguing archives on Gallifrey. The Record of Rassilon was also only installed in old model TARDISes. When later models were constructed it was believed no longer necessary to include this warning. While the legend said the leader of the Vampires escaped (apparently to E-space) he'd not been heard of for millennia. The record itself is an interesting addition to your player character's TARDIS. It may include details on several other powerful enemies of the ancient Time Lords that they have since forgotten. There may be many other creatures that, like the Great Vampire, may yet remain in hibernation.

Apart from Vampires, we do also learn a couple of other things in this adventure. K-9 can scan further than the TARDIS sensors as he detects the planet before the TARDIS does.

We also learn something about the nature of E-Space: that compared to our own universe it is extremely small. Romana isn't even sure it will have that many inhabited planets. This size does have an advantage though, as it makes short jumps with the TARDIS a lot more accurate. And since locations in E-Space map to locations in N-Space, like Alzarius to Gallifrey, E-Space is a great way to take short cuts across the universe.

VAMPIRES

All Vampires have the following Traits:

Hypnosis (Major): +2 bonus to control another's actions and feelings.

Immortal (Major): Vampires are eternal.

Indomitable: +4 bonus to any rolls to resist psychic control.

Psychic: +4 against mental attacks and may attempt to read minds.

Psychic Training: +2 bonus to Resolve rolls when trying to resist psychic attack or deception.

Telepathy: May create a mental link to read minds or converse telepathically.

Tough (Minor): Reduce total damage by 2.

Dependency (Major): Suffers a -4 penalty to all rolls if denied blood for a specific period.

Distinctive (Minor): -2 penalty to rolls to blend in. Others have a +2 bonus to remember or recognise the Vampire.

Enslaved (Major): Must obey the will of the Vampire who made them, and suffers a -2 penalty to attempts to voice opinion. If the elder Vampire dies, so do its progeny.

Frenzy: The Vampire must roll to resist frenzy when hungry. Rolls Resolve + Strength against a Difficulty of 12. In a frenzy, the Vampire attacks anything nearby.

Obsession (Minor): Hungry for the blood of the living.

Weakness (Minor): -2 penalty to rolls when in the presence of holy objects and certain herbs.

VAMPIRE PLAYER CHARACTERS

You *really* shouldn't let players be Vampires, but if they insist:

- Vampires gain +3 to their Strength.
- Vampires get all those nice Vampire traits, with the exception of Enslaved – a player character Vampire is assumed to have broken free of the control of its master. They instead gain Adversary (Major) instead.
- Being a Vampire costs 6 Character Points and 4 Story Points.

⊙ RUNNING THE ADVENTURE

This adventure is all about Gothic horror, so the atmosphere is almost more important than the actual Vampires. It shouldn't be a big mystery that the Three Who Rule are some sort of Gothic creature, allowing the Gamemaster to skip a lot of the investigation and get to 'how can we defeat them?' a lot quicker. Obvious clichés are great for skipping boring investigations. If the nature and identity of the monsters is the point of the adventure, that's when you want a detailed investigation sequence with clues and people to talk to. Here, the Three Who Rule might as well be wearing T-shirts with "I'm A Vampire, Ask Me How" written on them.

THE TOWER

The great spire of the tower dominates the area. It is not only a residence, but a symbol of the authority of the Three Who Rule. The tower is a huge maroon spire that was once a spacecraft called the Hydrax. It landed on the resting place of the Great Vampire and hasn't moved for nearly a thousand years. While it appears to be a building to anyone approaching or entering it, there are a few inspection hatches that lead into the maintenance corridors. In these secret corridors, all metal and gantry rather than stone pillars, it becomes obvious the tower is more than it appears.

KEY LOCATIONS IN THE TOWER

- **The Throne Room:** The main audience chamber where Zargo and Camilla hold court was once the control room of the ship. Now its command chairs have become thrones and the whole place is decorated in red baroque velvet hangings. A hatch in one of the thrones leads into the maintenance gantries.

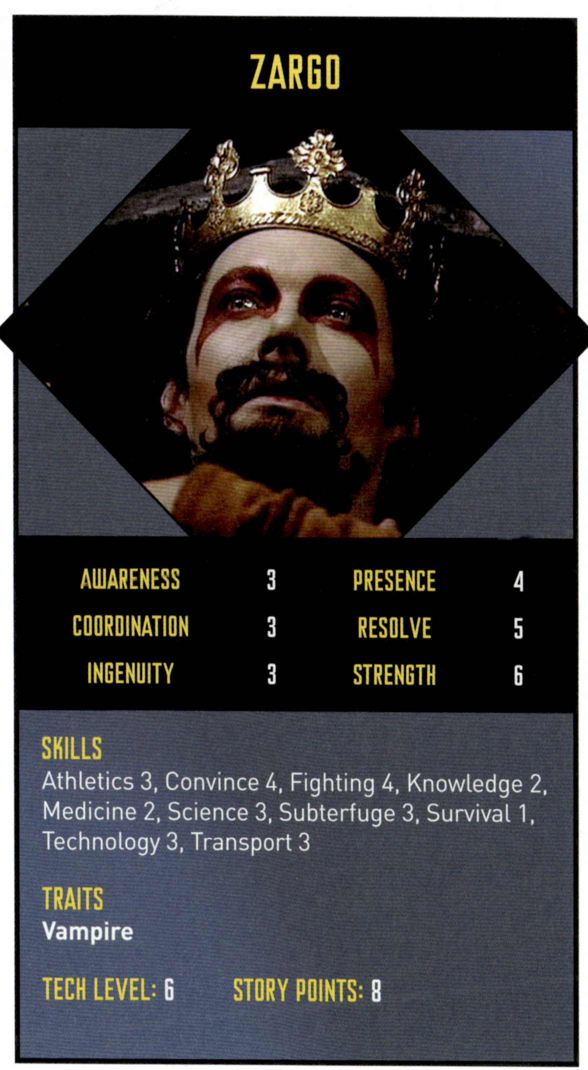

ZARGO

AWARENESS	3	PRESENCE	4
COORDINATION	3	RESOLVE	5
INGENUITY	3	STRENGTH	6

SKILLS
Athletics 3, Convince 4, Fighting 4, Knowledge 2, Medicine 2, Science 3, Subterfuge 3, Survival 1, Technology 3, Transport 3

TRAITS
Vampire

TECH LEVEL: 6   **STORY POINTS: 8**

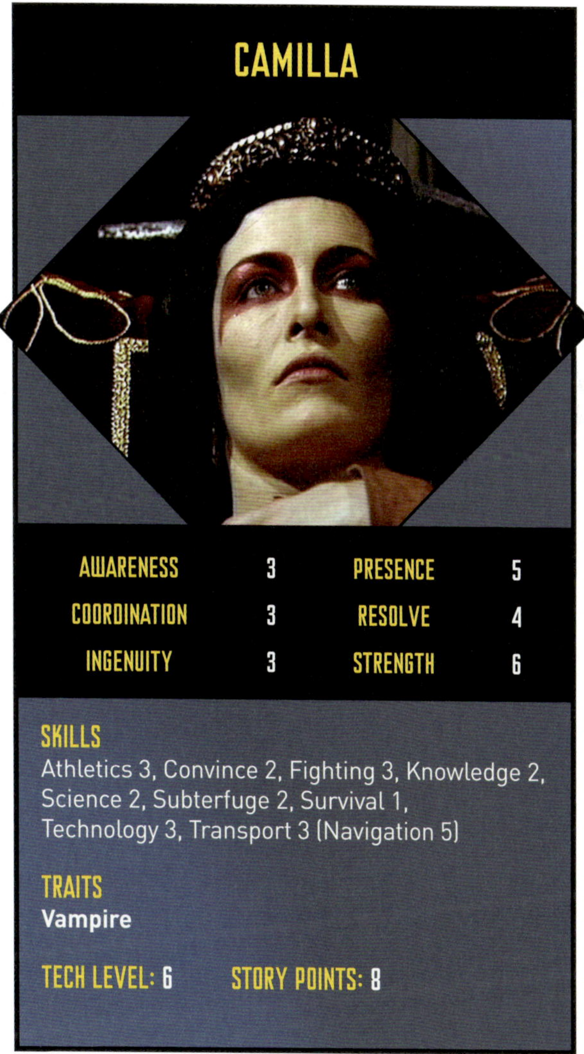

CAMILLA

AWARENESS	3	PRESENCE	5
COORDINATION	3	RESOLVE	4
INGENUITY	3	STRENGTH	6

SKILLS
Athletics 3, Convince 2, Fighting 3, Knowledge 2, Science 2, Subterfuge 2, Survival 1, Technology 3, Transport 3 (Navigation 5)

TRAITS
Vampire

TECH LEVEL: 6   **STORY POINTS: 8**

- **The Inner Sanctum:** Zargo and Camilla sleep in what may once have been their private quarters. The sanctum is a large bedroom deep in the tower, accessed only by a card key locked door. Only the guard on duty outside has the correct card key and the thick door is extremely difficult to break through without it.

- **Prison Cells:** The tower isn't really equipped to handle prisoners, as most criminals are fed to the tender mercies of the Vampires. However, there is one prison cell remaining, little more than a lockable, bare storeroom

- **The Fuel Tanks:** At the bottom of the ship are the fuel tanks, now filled with blood from many years of sacrificing the peasantry. The area used to serve as crew bunks as well and victims are racked in one of the bunks to be drained, where their desiccated remains are left to wither away. Pipes lead from the fuel tanks into the caverns under the tower to feed the blood to the Great Vampire.

- **Cavern of the Great One:** Under the tower lies a vast cave where the Great Vampire rests under the earth. Pipes from the fuel tanks constantly pump blood into the creature's lair so it might rejuvenate. The cavern itself is bare, but to the servants of the Great One it is a holy place.

THE THREE WHO RULE

King Zargo and Queen Camilla rule the village and the tower, with the assistance of Chancellor Aukon, as far as the villagers are concerned at any rate. In truth, all three serve the Great Vampire who has granted them immortality as Vampires in return for their service. They are also far from equal. Aukon is the only one actually in contact with the Great Vampire, a power he guards jealously.

Zargo, Camilla and Aukon were once Captain Sharky, Navigation Officer Lauren MacMillan and Science Officer Anthony O'Connor, the command crew of the ship Hydrax. O'Connor was contacted by the Great Vampire who lured him and the other members of the crew into E-Space with promises of power and eternal life. All three of them were utterly seduced and have worked for centuries to see the Great Vampire is well fed so he can heal and restore himself.

The Three Who Rule have pale, almost grey skin with an amber cast around their eyes. They move with an unearthly grace and seem distracted and far away when spoken to. As Vampires, they are extremely strong and highly resistant to physical damage. Aukon also manifests powerful psychic abilities. All three have a craving for blood, which they prefer fresh from a living victim. They prefer the night and slumber during the day, but suffer no actual ill effects from sunlight.

FURTHER ADVENTURES

- **The Spire:** On a remote planet, there is an ancient steel spire that has stood for centuries on a hilltop. The government wants to knock it down, but a group of protesters insist the spire must remain or 'terrible darkness will fall'. The government is refusing to listen to this

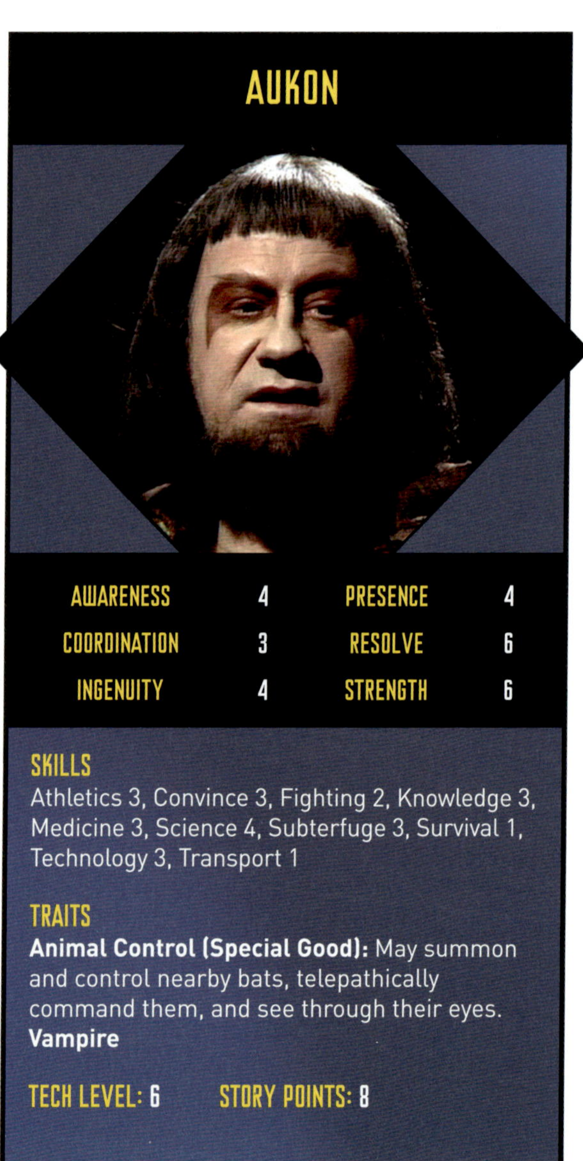

AWARENESS	4	PRESENCE	4
COORDINATION	3	RESOLVE	6
INGENUITY	4	STRENGTH	6

SKILLS
Athletics 3, Convince 3, Fighting 2, Knowledge 3, Medicine 3, Science 4, Subterfuge 3, Survival 1, Technology 3, Transport 1

TRAITS
Animal Control (Special Good): May summon and control nearby bats, telepathically command them, and see through their eyes.
Vampire

TECH LEVEL: 6   **STORY POINTS: 8**

local superstition but the protest has slowed down work. Unfortunately the protesters are right; the spire is the remains of a shaft from a Bowship that nailed a Great Vampire to the earth centuries ago. Unsure if it was destroyed, they left it buried in the earth but warned the inhabitants never to move the spire. If they do, the Great Vampire might heal its wounds and rise again...

- **The Calling:** The player characters find themselves on the Hydrax, before it entered into E-Space and the command crew are behaving a little strangely. One of them is under the influence of a powerful psychic force, but who? Can the player characters stop the ship being taken into E-Space? What if the mysterious force starts making them promises of power and immortality too?

- **Blood of the Vampire:** Unbeknownst to anyone in the village, the remains of the Great Vampire under the tower retain their potency. One of the locals drinks the blood of the creature and discovers he has gained incredible powers. He creates a new cult, the members of which are eager to share the power he offers. Can the player characters unmask the secret leader of this dangerous new cult, and did the scout ship penetrate the Great Vampire's heart well enough that it has not spent this time recovering? Worse yet, perhaps its spirit is being transferred by the blood into the new cult members, who will form a new gestalt body!

THE GREAT VAMPIRES

These beings are so powerful, direct conflict with one can only end badly. They are gigantic bat-like creatures several feet tall, with huge clawed hands and great wings that allow them to fly, possibly at interstellar speeds. It is unclear if they required physical contact to drain blood, but their ability to cause destruction on a planetary scale suggests they can easily drain the life from anything nearby. As the Time Lords discovered, these creatures can only be killed by destroying their heart. To do this, a stake the size of at least a knight's lance is required, as well as a good aim. We provide statistics for these monstrosities more to put your players off a direct assault (and these statistics are for a newly-awoken Great Vampire, not one at full strength). These creatures can only be defeated by guile and resourcefulness.

AWARENESS	4	PRESENCE	5
COORDINATION	3	RESOLVE	12
INGENUITY	4	STRENGTH	12

SKILLS
Athletics 4, Fighting 4, Knowledge 4, Science 2, Subterfuge 3, Survival 2, Technology 3

TRAITS
Armour (Major): Reduce damage by 10.
Special - Drain Life: Can suck the life from up to ten people each Action Round as a free action.

Fast Healing (Special): Attribute Points are recovered at 1 point per minute.
Fear Factor 3: Grants a +6 bonus to inspire fear.
Flight (Major): The Vampire can fly at a Speed of 3x Coordination.
Huge
Hypnosis (Major): +2 bonus to control another's actions and feelings.
Immortal (Special): Millions of years old and still going strong.
Immunity (Major): The Vampire takes no damage from energy weapons.
Vampire

TECH LEVEL: 11   **STORY POINTS:** 10

WARRIOR'S GATE

'We faced the time winds and we lived!'

⊛ SYNOPSIS

Zero coordinates, unknown time

The Doctor and Romana attempted to force the TARDIS out of E-Space, but failed. However, their attempts were noticed by the enslaved navigator of another ship, a leonine Tharil called Biroc. This ship had been trapped for days in a void and while the crew is apathetic, Captain Rorvik was still determined to break free. During another failed attempt by the ship's crew to escape their predicament, Biroc escaped and crossed the void between the ship and the TARDIS. As Biroc opened the TARDIS doors, he exposed the console room to the 'time winds', which badly damaged K-9, and he took control of the TARDIS, landing it near the trapped ship he had escaped from. Before leaving he warned the TARDIS crew that others would follow him, and they were not to be trusted.

Romana noticed the ship had landed on 'zero coordinates'. Given E-Space was negative and N-Space positive, zero must be a point between the two universes. The Doctor chased Biroc out into the void to get answers, and was led through a white fog to a ruined cathedral. Inside the cathedral was a great hall, covered in dust and cobwebs. The only feature of the place was a large mirror that Biroc passed through. Left to investigate the great hall, the Doctor discovered that not everything in the place is as dead as it appeared, and two of the 'suits of armour' turned out to be robot warriors who attacked him.

Captain Rorvik was furious at the loss of his navigator. Without Biroc to 'visualise' the time striations they could not use their warp drive. He ordered more Tharils held in suspended animation below to be woken up, even though doing so might kill them with the equipment they had to hand. When another of the crew detected the TARDIS nearby, the Captain decided to investigate.

The crew could not get into the TARDIS, but Romana suspected they might have the spare parts she needed to fix K-9, so she stepped out to talk to them, warning Adric to stay inside. When Romana demonstrated she understood warp engine design, Rorvik captured her and took her to the ship. Believing Romana to be 'time sensitive' like the Tharils, Rorvik ordered her clamped into the navigator's chair. Under duress she visualised the ruined cathedral. Rorvik ordered his men to investigate the place, hoping it might lead to a way out.

In the great hall, the Doctor managed to defeat the robots and upon taking one apart found the vital spares he needs for K-9. He also found a history file that explained the robots are Gundan warriors built by the slaves of a brutal empire. The rulers of the empire could cross time, and took slaves and spoils from hundreds of worlds. Unable to survive the time winds, the slaves built the Gundan to destroy their masters. The Gundan followed the masters to their citadel and destroyed those who couldn't flee through 'the Gateway'. The Doctor needed more power to learn the secret of this Gateway and luckily K-9 arrived to provide it. Unfortunately, so did Rorvik, who threatened the Doctor into revealing the secret. Predictably unimpressed with Rorvik's bully tactics, the Doctor made a run for it, slipping through the mirror where he found Biroc waiting for him. Rorvik was unable to follow and became even more annoyed. He demanded the crew bring the MZ laser, a powerful cannon that he believed could blast through the mirror.

Back on the ship, the crew believed their attempt to wake a new Tharil navigator was horribly unsuccessful. However, they were wrong, and while badly burned the Tharil survived. He freed Romana from the navigator's chair and she hid under the tarpaulin covering the MZ, where she found Adric who had chosen the same hiding place Taken outside with the MZ, Romana and Adric got a chance to investigate the ship, which had a gaping hole in its outer hull. Romana noticed the warp engines were three times the size they need to be for the ship, but this was because it was made of 'dwarf star alloy' a super-dense metal. This metal was the only material that could hold a time sensitive captive. Rorvik was not just a trader, but a slave trader treating the Tharils as nothing but commodities. Unfortunately, there was also another problem; the mass of the ship was so great that it was actually causing the void to collapse!

Adric sets off to the cathedral to find the Doctor. Romana was found by the ship's crew, but she was rescued by the Tharil who took her beyond the mirror. She found the Doctor here with Biroc and learned the

history of the Tharils. They were the 'masters' who controlled the oppressive empire the Gundan robots brought to an end. The Doctor admonished him for the Tharil's arrogance and the way they treated and oppressed those they conquered. Biroc replied that the slavery his people now suffered as warp navigators had surely paid their debt.

Suddenly, the Doctor and Romana found themselves back on the other side of the mirror, surrounded by Rorvik and his crew. Adric threatened to use the MZ to destroy everyone and the three of them escaped. Rorvik was incensed and used the MZ on the mirror, to no effect. Desperate, he decided the only thing to do was use more force, despite the fact any force was reflected back. He ordered the crew to use the warp engines of the ship to blast the whole ruined cathedral. The Doctor and Romana tried to stop the engines, infiltrating the ship while it manoeuvred into position.

The Doctor fought with Rorvik as Romana short circuited the engines. However, Biroc appeared and transported the two Time Lords back to the TARDIS, telling them that everything had been planned, and the best thing they could do was nothing. Rorvik activated the engines and the reflected energy utterly destroyed his ship.

The Tharils aboard had secretly been woken by the burned Tharil, and quietly slipped across the time striations to the other side of the mirror, unharmed by the explosion.

As the Doctor prepares to leave, Romana told him she had decided not to go with him. The Tharils would need the help of a Time Lord to free the rest of their people from slavery, and she volunteered. The Doctor leaves her K-9 to help with the work ahead, and he and Adric use the Gateway to finally escape E-Space.

CONTINUITY

We learn here is that there are not only other universes like E-Space, but there also places between those universes.

Unsurprisingly we discover the TARDIS stores are not only very sparse but badly organised, according to Romana. It is easy to imagine the Doctor insisting he has a definite order to the chaotic state he has left the maintenance stores.

In this adventure we lose both Romana and K-9, who leave to help the Tharils rebuild their broken culture. We discover that K-9 has enough technical details to build a TARDIS, so Romana might not remain with the Tharils forever.

⚙ RUNNING THE ADVENTURE

The Doctor's experiences during **Warriors' Gate** make for a somewhat unengaging adventure. The Doctor doesn't actually do anything of consequence – everything happens according to Biroc's schemes and manipulations. Other than providing an initial distraction for the crew of the slave ship, the Doctor's influence on events is minimal. Even when he tries to interfere, Biroc pops in to warn him to do nothing. In a roleplaying game, the players' actions should always have some effect on what happens. The player characters don't always have to be at the centre of events, but the game should be all be about their adventures, not the tale of some mysterious alien... unless, of course, you make that reality-shifting alien into a player character. If you want to run **Warriors' Gate** as an adventure, consider making Biroc a player character.

Concerns about player character 'agency' (i.e. their ability to affect the plot) aside, **Warriors' Gate** is beautifully strange and surreal. The void between universes is a place of crumbling ruins floating in infinite whiteness, where alien slaves move like the Cheshire Cat and talk like warrior poets. The universe of the Doctor is forever bizarre and wonderful, and allows for fascinating juxtapositions and surreal concepts. Why shouldn't a gap between universes look like a ruined cathedral? Why can't a medieval tower be a spaceship, or a battered blue police box be a time machine?

THE VOID

The void that surrounds the Gateway and trapped ships is a white fog of nothing. It is eerily silent and still, with no landmarks, creatures or inhabitants. It is easy to get lost in as well, and once out of sight of any feature (such as their ship) anyone walking the void will get hopelessly lost without a supernaturally good sense of direction. Visibility is limited to about twenty yards, but the fog appears thin, making it easy to underestimate how quickly you will lose sight of any landmarks.

The best way to navigate is to use a sensor to detect mass. As you would only walk the void to get to something, you essentially need a way to detect that something and steer yourself towards it. Even if you are just exploring you need a way to return as well, as scarves and balls of string only last for so long. Luckily, the void is finite. The fog does not do on forever and those lost within it often find themselves returning to their point of origin again, even if they have never changed direction.

RORVIK'S SHIP

The slaver ship is not an especially sleek or stylish spacecraft. It is essentially a set of engines with a bridge and a small hold. It is designed specifically to transport time-sensitive slaves as cargo. This cargo is so valuable that only a few need to be captured to make a voyage profitable. 12-15 slaves are held in the storage bunks at any one time. They are kept unconscious during transportation, in such a way they can only be woken with special equipment not available in anything but its most basic form on the ship.

The ship is divided into only a few areas: the bridge, slave hold, storage areas, engines and crew quarters. The ship is double hulled, with everything but the engines inside the inner hull. The outer hull surrounds the whole ship and is made of dwarf star alloy, a rare and expensive super-dense metal. This metal makes it extremely difficult for time sensitive beings to escape the hull, even when out of phase. Only when a time rift puts a hole in the ship can Biroc escape.

Inside, the ship is basic and functional, plain metal gantries link steel corridors. Little or no effort has been spared to make it a pleasant work environment; it is simply a tool to transport a valuable cargo. Not even its Captain loves this ship.

THE GATEWAY

The ruin is the only feature in the void, apart from trapped spacecraft. From the outside it is little more than a solid oak door set in a stone arch, with the remains of a window rising above it. However, passing through the door takes you into a great hall, even though you might walk around the ruin and find nothing. The great hall was once the feasting hall of the Tharils and was the first place attacked by the Gundan warriors. Among the cobwebs and dust lie the bodies of the Tharils who were taken by surprise and killed, nothing more than bone remains now. Surrounding the hall is a small colonnaded balcony, accessed by some stairs.

The balcony is in the same state as the hall, but grants a good view of the whole area. The only other real feature in the hall is the gateway mirror that faces the door. At least two Gundan warriors stand among the cobwebs in hibernation mode.

BEYOND THE MIRROR

Those who can pass through the mirror can enter the Tharil's domain. Passing through the mirror is extremely difficult. Tharils can do so with ease, as can those who can understand and follow the paths of time. There is a 'secret of the gateway' though; something programmed into the Gundan warriors, who can pass through the Gateway as easily as the Tharils. Passing through the Gateway 'resets the temporal state' of any individual. This means they heal any recent wounds, and even any mechanical damage.

The Tharil's domain is layered with 'time striations' allowing a traveller to move through time as easily as space by crossing to the layer of time they desire. It is a similar process to moving between the grooves of a record, much like 'time tracks'. This also means that should you skip a groove you can suddenly find yourself dumped back in a different layer of the past or future.

The land beyond the mirror is a series of stately monochromatic gardens and mazes. The remaining Tharils exist layered in different parts of both time and space here, giving the whole place an eerie silence.

FURTHER ADVENTURES

- **A Dish Served Cold:** A group of Tharils need the player character's help to stop a renegade Tharil faction committing horrible crimes against the humans that have been keeping them captive. While all the Tharils are dedicated to feeing their people, the rebel faction is looking for revenge. If

they pursue their agenda, other races will unite against the Tharils once again. However, can the Tharils be trusted, or are they looking to use the player characters and their time technology as cat's-paws for an attack of their own.

- **Midnight Murders:** A museum has suffered several unexplained deaths recently and the player characters are sent to investigate. The murders have actually been committed by a Gundan warrior who was unearthed years ago and is on display as a suit of armour. How had no one noticed it is actually a robot? Is it simply random chance it is animating to attack lone victims or is someone controlling it? What other

artefacts might have been unearthed with it and are now exhibits in the museum?

- **Graveyard of the TARDISes:** The Tharils need certain parts to build new Gateways, parts only available from a TARDIS. They have heard of a graveyard of broken TARDISes, but they cannot get there alone. It will take the player characters and the Tharils working together to find the place. Certainly the player characters could do with restocking their TARDIS spares, but what else might they find in such a place? Is there even a graveyard, or are the Tharils actually looking to take what they need from the player characters' TARDIS?

GUNDAN WARRIOR ROBOTS

These armoured warrior robots were built with only one task in mind, to destroy the Tharils. They are single-minded killing machines, created by slaves looking to avenge themselves on their oppressors. Gundan appear to be armoured knights, and it is easy to mistake a dormant one for a suit of armour. They have the ability to follow the paths the Tharils make when they move through time, but cannot move through time as they please.

While Gundan have no need to talk, their memories contain detailed history files so those who find them will know how the Tharils oppressed so many worlds. Those who run out of prey settle into a hibernation mode that might last centuries. While they are programmed attack only Tharils, those coming out of hibernation might attack any living thing they find.

AWARENESS	3	PRESENCE	1
COORDINATION	3	RESOLVE	3
INGENUITY	2	STRENGTH	6

SKILLS
Athletics 3, Fighting 4, Knowledge 2, Science 2, Subterfuge 2

TRAITS
Armour (Major): Reduce damage by 10.
Environmental (Major): Robots don't breathe. Or eat. Or sleep. Or go to the bathroom. At least, not while anyone's watching.
Impulsive: They have relatively simple programming.
Obsession (Major): Kill all Tharils.
Robot (Special Good)
Vortex: Gundan robots can follow established paths through time.

EQUIPMENT: Axe or Sword (Strength +2 damage)

TECH LEVEL: 8   STORY POINTS: 4

Older models who have hibernated for many years will have lost points from their attributes and skills, and gained the 'Slow' trait, at least until they have properly 'woken up'.

THARILS

The Tharils are a race of lion-like humanoids with the ability to move through time at will, phasing themselves out of the normal space/time continuum. Instead of using their powers carefully like the more enlightened Time Lords, they used their ability to build an empire. They became temporal raiders, walking across the universe as they liked and taking what they wanted. They took chattel and slaves from dozens of worlds and lived like kings on the plunder, considering this lifestyle their divine right.

However, the Tharils were not as indomitable as they believed. While their prey was unable to follow them across time, they managed to build robot warriors who could. These Gundan robots slaughtered many Tharils, forcing the survivors to flee. Scattered among the worlds they had enslaved, the Tharils found few willing to help them, and plenty prepared to exploit and enslave them. Their ability to see the layers in time and space proved invaluable for warp drive navigation, making them highly sought after 'commodities'.

Biroc is the first of his people to free himself and return to the Gateway his people first used to walk the universe. With Romana to help them rebuild and the rest of Rorvik's 'cargo' released by Lazlo (healed of his burns by the Gateway) the Tharils may make their mark on the universe once more, but hopefully in a more enlightened way.

AWARENESS	3	PRESENCE	4
COORDINATION	3	RESOLVE	4
INGENUITY	4	STRENGTH	5

SKILLS
Athletics 2, Convince 2, Fighting 2, Knowledge 3, Science 2, Subterfuge 3, Survival 2, Technology 3, Transport 2

TRAITS
Alien

Alien Appearance (Minor)

Alien Senses (Minor): +4 to Awareness when looking into time.

Attractive: +2 bonus to any rolls that benefit from the Tharil's eerie charisma.

Empathic: +2 bonus on rolls to 'read' another person.

Environmental (Minor): Tharils suffer no ill effects from the Time Vortex or time winds.

Feel the Turn of the Universe: Tharils have a close affinity with the time-stream.

Immaterial (Special): May move 'out of phase' at will. In this state they cannot interact with physical objects unless they use telekinesis. Takes and does no physical damage but energy attacks may still be lethal.

Keen Senses (Major): +2 to all Awareness rolls.

Networked (Minor): Tharils can sense others of their kind and know if they are in trouble.

Psychic: +4 against mental attacks and may attempt to read minds.

Selfish: The Tharils were once slavers and marauders, and still consider humans beneath them.

Vortex (Special): Tharils may pilot time craft through the vortex, and gain +2 when doing so. They may also walk into the vortex without a capsule if circumstances are right.

TECH LEVEL: 8   **STORY POINTS: 8**

CAPTAIN RORVIK

AWARENESS	2	PRESENCE	3
COORDINATION	3	RESOLVE	4
INGENUITY	3	STRENGTH	3

The captain of the slaver ship is a small man, equally obsessed with making the most profit and proving he is in charge. He has little idea how to motivate his crew, who are only with him because of the money they will make. Rorvik is a doer not a thinker. He would rather act dangerously than sit and do nothing, making him bullish and impetuous. If force doesn't work, he simply applies more force. He enjoys the feeling of being in charge, and wishes dearly his men felt the same as he does about the beauty of procedure and smart uniforms.

SKILLS
Athletics 2, Convince 3, Fighting 3, Knowledge 2, Marksman 2, Science 2, Subterfuge 3, Technology 3, Transport 2

TRAITS
Indomitable: +4 bonus to any rolls to resist psychic control.
Tough: Reduce total damage by 2.
By the Book: Rorvik must be convinced to act against procedure.
Impulsive: Rorvik doesn't think things through before acting.
Obsession (Major): Prove his strength by defeating every problem.

EQUIPMENT: Blaster Pistol (4/8/L)

TECH LEVEL: 7   **STORY POINTS:** 6

THE SLAVER CREW

AWARENESS	2	PRESENCE	2
COORDINATION	3	RESOLVE	2
INGENUITY	3	STRENGTH	3

The crew of Rorvik's ship are the most apathetic group of men to ever pilot a ship. Sagan and Packard are responsible for ship's operations, piloting the ship along the time lines established by the time sensitive navigator. Lane is the engineer, responsible for taking care of the engines and general maintenance.

Finally there are Aldo and Royce, who work as general technicians. They have a tendency to shirk off as often as possible, which is unsurprising as the other members of the crew do their best to delegate all their work to them.

SKILLS
Athletics 2, Convince 2, Craft 2, Fighting 2, Knowledge 2, Marksman 2, Medicine 2, Science 2, Subterfuge 2, Technology 3, Transport 2

TRAITS
Selfish: They're in this for the money.
Unadventurous (Minor): They're not adventurers. They want to stay away from trouble.

EQUIPMENT: Blaster Pistol (4/8/L)

TECH LEVEL: 7   **STORY POINTS:** 2

THE KEEPER OF TRAKEN

'Yes, Traken, Traken Union, famous for its universal harmony. A whole empire held together by, well, by people just being terribly nice to one another.'
'Well, that makes a change.'
'Yes, I don't think I've actually been there.'

⊙ SYNOPSIS

Traken, Present Day

There were few things powerful enough to enter a TARDIS without a key, and one of these was the Keeper of Traken who for a thousand years had used the power of the Source to watch over the peaceful union of Traken. However, as he neared the end of his life, he was gravely concerned about the future of the planet and asked the Doctor to investigate the growing evil the Keeper believed had taken root there.

There was indeed evil on Traken, in the form of a Melkur, an evil spirit commonly drawn to Traken. Such things usually calcify and die in the benevolent atmosphere of Traken. One particular Melkur had endured, and was tended to (as was the tradition) by a girl called Kassia, who had grown to become a Consul of Traken. Kassia had also recently married another Consul, Tremas. As the Keeper was dying, the five Consuls who formed the governing body of Traken must choose one of themselves to succeed him. When Tremas was nominated, Kassia was consumed with despair, as she would lose her husband when he became the Keeper and merged with the Source. She confided in the Melkur, but much to her surprise, the Melkur spoke, and told her it had a plan to help her.

When the Doctor and Adric arrived, Traken was in a state of growing unrest. The Fosters, who acted as a police force when required, had been armed due to a recent murder. As strangers, the Doctor and Adric quickly became suspects. Luckily, Tremas recognised the Doctor's scientific ability as an asset in their investigations and vouched for him.

The next day, the Doctor and Adric were introduced to Tremas' daughter Nyssa, and discussed the Source, an immense power source of bioelectrical energy collected from the combined population of the Traken Union and used by the Keeper to maintain order and equilibrium. The Doctor and Tremas investigated the Grove where the Melkur resided. Adric and Nyssa followed as Adric detected the energy readings of a TARDIS, but one far more advanced than the Doctor's own. Before they could investigate these readings the Melkur revealed it had been manipulating Kassia and attempted to kill the Doctor, forcing them all to flee the grove.

Meanwhile Kassia politicked with the other Consuls, trying to convince them Tremas' protection of the criminal known as the Doctor proved he was not fit to be Keeper. Someone else should be chosen. The Consuls decided Tremas should take Rapport with the Source, an extremely dangerous process where his motivations would be made clear. Another

Consul, Seron, claimed he was privy to Tremas' plans, as they had been investigating together and insisted on undergoing Rapport in his place.

Her plans frustrated, Kassia went to the Melkur for advice. He gave her a collar, which would allow him to see through her eyes, and told her everything was going to plan. However, the collar had the ability to control Kassia's actions and she began to realise the Melkur was only using her as a tool. Under the influence of the Melkur, Kassia joined Seron as he underwent Rapport. He was found innocent, but as they were alone, the Melkur used Kassia to murder him. Returning to the other Consuls, Kassia proclaimed Seron's death to be proof of his guilt, and therefore also the Doctor's. The Doctor and Adric were arrested, as was Tremas for supporting them. Kassia took control of the council, but had also become the only viable successor to the dying Keeper, now that Tremas was in prison.

Nyssa broke Tremas, Adric and the Doctor out of prison, but the alarm was soon raised and they had to flee. They hid in Tremas' apartments, as these had already been searched. Realising the Melkur must be trying to take control of the Source, Tremas showed the plans for the Source manipulator, the heart of the system, to Adric and the Doctor.

Source was not yet complete, and it needed time to rest and complete the transition.

Adric and Nyssa escaped to the TARDIS and worked on a plan of their own. Adric had understood enough of the Source manipulator plans to construct a device to sabotage it. However, using it would destroy both the new Keeper and the Source itself. After building it in the TARDIS they crept into the Source control room and installed the device.

Meanwhile, the Doctor and Tremas uncovered a series of codes that would sever the Keeper's connection without destroying the Source, but before they could input the last three digits into the controls the Melkur appeared and used his power to take control of them like puppets. The Melkur planned to use the Source to turn Traken into his empire. He intended to build and equip an army here with the power at his disposal and conquer the universe. The Doctor was taken inside the Keeper's summoning booth and found himself inside the Melkur! It was actually a TARDIS controlled by the decaying form of his old enemy, the Master. The Master could not resist gloating while the Doctor was in his power. Not only would he use the power of the Source for evil, but he also planned to take the Doctor's body and with it his remaining regenerations.

Unfortunately, the Keeper's life was failing and the weather on Traken became more violent as he lost control. Kassia was summoned to take his place, and before the Doctor and Tremas could stop her, she was invested as the new Keeper. As soon as the connection activated, she died horribly and the Melkur appeared in her place, having used her as a conduit to take control of the Keepership. As the new ruler of Traken, the Melkur ordered the Doctor to be executed. However, before the sentence could be carried out the Melkur vanished. Its power over the

However, as the Master used his new power, Adric and Nyssa's device tore the Melkur apart. The Doctor escaped in time to give the last three numbers of the code to Adric. When they were keyed in, the Melkur's connection was severed, saving the Source from destruction. Consul Luvic was hastily appointed as the new Keeper and peace was restored. The Doctor and Adric bid farewell to Tremas and Nyssa and left Traken in the TARDIS. But the Master was not entirely defeated. An old clock Tremas decided to adjust turned out to be another TARDIS, which the

Master had used to escape the Melkur. Paralysing Tremas, the Master stole his body, rejuvenating it in the process. With renewed vigour the Master returned to his TARDIS, intent on further plans to destroy the Doctor.

CONTINUITY

This adventure is actually the beginning of a trilogy, renewing the Master and leading to the regeneration of the Doctor into his fifth incarnation. As such it sows the seeds that will lead to a climax in **Logopolis**, the after-effects of which will still be felt in the Fifth Doctor adventure **Castrovalva**. Nyssa will eventually become a companion of the Doctor's, but she remains on Traken for now.

The Master's TARDIS has been adapted with a functional chameleon circuit to resemble a Melkur. However, it differs from other TARDISes in several ways: it materialises in a red light and it is also able to walk. In **Logopolis** when the Doctor realises the Master has escaped he tells Adric "he must have had a second TARDIS". So it appears the Master has one TARDIS docked inside another ready to act as a lifeboat when the Melkur is destroyed.

⊙ RUNNING THE ADVENTURE

For all the powerful entities and epic plots, this adventure is a political drama and an investigation. The Keeper asks the player characters to visit Traken and investigate a growing evil. A murder (the first in living memory) has been committed. Investigating this crime leads the player characters towards a greater evil at the heart of it all. However this evil need not be the Melkur or the Master, and Kassia need not be in league with it. All you need is for there to be something evil seeking to take control of the Source. It might be another villain known for working

behind the scenes (perhaps even the Daleks) or a Traken who has gone mad. Given the main villain will remain behind the curtain for a long time; it is a great opportunity to bring back an old enemy of the player characters. This villain still wants the Source, but if he can get even with the player characters too, so much the better. Like the Master they will take great pleasure in revealing their involvement, but be careful to remain hidden until the right time, when they believe their plot cannot be stopped.

TRAKEN

The Traken Union is a place of peace and tranquillity. For thousands of years the people of the place have lived together in harmony. The land is fertile and all their needs are met. It is said that evil simply withers and dies on Traken. While that might seem like a fairy tale, something is certainly working.

Traken is ruled by a council of five noble Consuls. One of them is selected to serve as the next Keeper when the current incumbent dies. The Keeper is able to harness the combined mental energy of the Traken people to moderate the state of the planet and protect it. Even though each citizen contributes very little, the collected power is vast.

CONTROL COLLARS

The control collars issued by the Master to Kassia and Proctor Neman are deceptively powerful pieces of technology. Once round the neck of a subject, the controller of the collar is connected to the subject. This link allows them to see through their eyes, and even channel energy through them.

To a certain extent they can control their actions, and they can punish the subject with pain at will. The control collars must be put around the neck to be effective. This might be forced, but the Master prefers to talk his victims into putting on the collar themselves of their own free will.

The Traken people have an Elizabethan sense of style, living in grand spacious buildings. Clothing is also in a very Elizabethan style with velvet robes popular among the nobility. Ladies accent these heavy fabrics with underskirts of thin fabric in a petal design.

The Trakens are a very advanced people, but their technology is kept in the background. They understand spaceflight but have no need to leave their home to seek something better. Energy weapons are available to the government but the police, the Fosters, are usually unarmed, as are the civilians.

KEY LOCATIONS ON TRAKEN

- **The Keeper's Audience Chamber:** The main government building on Traken is effectively a throne room. At one end is a glass booth on a dais where the Keeper appears when summoned. In the dais are several controls for maintaining the Source. The Council meet here too, but gather informally on a circle of chairs in front of the Keeper's dais.

- **The Source Control Room:** Under the audience chamber is the actual Source Manipulator itself, a glowing sphere surrounded by complicated technology. The chamber can only be entered by a Consul as their rings act as a key. A short tunnel from this chamber leads to the Grove.

- **The Grove:** All evil that arrives on Traken is drawn to the Grove. Here, Melkur appear and are tended by young girls until they calcify and pass into the soil. The Fosters can also be found here, working as gardeners. The Grove is a lush park, where tall bushes and trees make each section quite secluded. The Grove is surrounded by a high wall,

and the only gate is kept locked by the Proctor. No one but the Consuls know of the hidden tunnel that leads to the Grove from the Source control room.

MELKUR

Melkur are evil spirits drawn to the goodness of Traken like moths to a flame. As soon as they land in the Grove they are paralysed and gradually turn to stone. This stone then withers and crumbles into the earth where it dissipates. The more evil the spirit, the more quickly it is paralysed. Some have been known to move a little but this is very rare. The Traken people, ever sympathetic to these poor creatures (despite their evil) assign children to watch over them and keep them company. Few Melkur last more than a few years.

The Melkur in this adventure is very different; in fact it is the Master's TARDIS (see above). This Melkur can move and blast energy bolts at anyone who meets its gaze and even speak to those nearby. The energy bolts do (4/8/L) damage, and while it can only target those who meet its gaze, those who do are hit automatically. The Melkur is too slow to attempt physical combat, but is nearly impervious to damage. If you choose not to make it a TARDIS, the Melkur might be more similar to a Teselecta (see the Eleventh Doctor adventure **Let's Kill Hitler**).

THE KEEPER OF TRAKEN

While each Keeper was once a Traken Consul, the power they are invested with upon becoming the Keeper makes them an extremely powerful entity. They control an energy force drawn from the ambient mental energy of an entire planetary union. This power is localised to the surrounding galaxy, but that still gives the Keeper a lot of range to extend their power.

draws the bioelectric energy which is controlled by systems in the summoning booth on Traken and fed to the Keeper. Usually the Keeper exists outside time and space, allowing them to keep watch over many aspects of the planetary union simultaneously. When the Keeper wishes to speak to the council they appear in the summoning booth or wherever they wish. Not even a TARDIS can keep them out if they wish to enter one.

There are no statistics that can fully reflect a Keeper. They will vanish before any attack can damage them, and are immune to most weapons fire. However, they never use their power to harm others, simply vanishing when the situation becomes dangerous – in game terms, they've got all the Story Points. If the Source should fall into the wrong hands it could be used as a weapon and possibly a way to move armies across the galaxy, so it is well not to make an enemy of the Keeper. There is little that escapes the notice of an old Keeper who has kept watch for hundreds of years.

Keepers serve until their death, and the power they have prolongs their life for over a thousand years. A new Keeper is chosen from among the serving Consuls, who is selected for their wisdom and dedication to Traken. Even so, any Traken can become Keeper if need be.

The Keeper appears sitting on a chair that links him or her to the Source Manipulator. This device

CONSUL KASSIA

Born into the nobility, Kassia is used to being in charge and getting what she wants although she isn't a selfish person. She was assigned to watch over the Melkur and over time found talking to it a good way to talk about her life and worries. She never knew the Melkur was really listening. When she met Tremas and fell in love she felt she had a whole new life ahead of her, but the nomination of Tremas as the new Keeper put an end to all her dreams of a happy life with the man she loved.

Kassia is a dedicated and driven woman. She is clever, but not as shrewd and manipulative as she thinks she is. When her plans go wrong she panics and doesn't quite know what to do. Desperate to save her husband from the Keepership she doesn't question the Melkur's plans until it is too late. But even when she realises the Melkur is plotting against Traken she is willing to sacrifice herself if that is the price to save her husband.

AWARENESS	3	PRESENCE	3
COORDINATION	3	RESOLVE	2
INGENUITY	3	STRENGTH	2

SKILLS
Athletics 2, Convince 2, Knowledge 2, Science 2, Subterfuge 3, Technology 2

TRAITS
Attractive: +2 bonus to any rolls that involve the character's looks.
Noble: +2 bonus in high society.
Passionate Love (Major): -2 to all rolls without Tremas.

TECH LEVEL: 7   **STORY POINTS: 8**

FURTHER ADVENTURES

- **Scavenger Hunt:** The new Keeper (Luvic) asks the player characters for help once again. The Source Manipulator was badly damaged by Adric's device and now barely functions. He needs the player characters to track down the parts required to fix it, and find someone who knows the design now the plans have been destroyed. Unfortunately, with the system not entirely under control a new cult has appeared on Traken who believe the end times are coming. They believe the Keepers have had their time and Traken must fall at last. When this doomsday cult discovers the player characters' quest it sets out to stop them.

- **Stolen Property:** A Time Agent (or similarly technologically advanced person) arrives on Traken to reclaim their property. They insist the technology for the Source Manipulator was stolen from their ship when they visited Traken many years ago and can even provide technical drawing and evidence that this is the case. He initially wants it back, but is prepared to work out a hire deal as the Traken people seem decent folk. Is it a scam or did the ancient Trakens actually steal the technology? How can the player characters prove it either way?

- **Tourist Trap:** A visitor to Traken has been horribly murdered. The victim's family are demanding justice. However the Traken authorities refuse to believe a Traken could be responsible. They firmly believe the murderer must be one of the visitors and insist they all leave before Traken is further polluted by the evil. Both sides turn to the player characters as neutral adjudicators, but secretly make it clear to them they won't accept a decision in the opposing faction's favour. Who is responsible, and why? Is there a murderer among the tourists, or has a Traken gone crazy? Perhaps it is a more insidious plan to sow decent in the peaceful planet. More to the point, if the murderer can't be found, will he kill again?

CONSUL TREMAS

Tremas is a rising star among the Traken Council. He is their most skilled scientist and considered one of the most honourable and decent people on Traken. He has a daughter, Nyssa, who follows very much in his footsteps. The only hint of sadness in his life is that his first wife, Nyssa's mother, died during childbirth. However, Tremas subsequently fell in love with Kassia, another Consul, and their wedding was blessed by the Keeper. Tremas constantly puts others before himself, making him a prime candidate for the honour of becoming the next Keeper. Unfortunately, his wife's despair at losing him to his work will have grave consequences.

AWARENESS	3	PRESENCE	4
COORDINATION	3	RESOLVE	4
INGENUITY	4	STRENGTH	3

SKILLS
Athletics 1, Convince 4, Craft 3, Knowledge 3, Medicine 2, Science 5, Subterfuge 1, Technology 4

TRAITS
Brave: +2 bonus to any Resolve roll when he needs to show courage.
Charming: +2 bonus to attempts to use charm.
Code of Conduct (Major): Tremas follows a strict code of honour and decency.
Empathic: +2 bonus on rolls to 'read' another person.
Noble: +2 bonus in high society.

Technically Adept: +2 to any Technology roll to fix a broken or faulty device.
Obligation (Major): Serve the needs of Traken.

TECH LEVEL: 7   **STORY POINTS: 6**

LOGOPOLIS

'The Master is at work on Logopolis. I'm going to stop him if it's the last thing I do.'

⊘ SYNOPSIS

Earth and Logopolis, the Present Day

The Doctor decided it was high time he fix the Chameleon Circuit so the TARDIS could appear as something other than a police box. They materialised the TARDIS over a police box on the side of a motorway, so it appeared in the control room. Nearby, Tegan Jovanka and her Aunt Vanessa were trying in vain to fix their car so Tegan could get to her first day of work as an air stewardess. From across the road a strange figure in white watched them silently.

The Doctor explained to Adric they needed to measure the police box precisely so they can take the data to the planet Logopolis. The people there were experts in a mathematical form called Block Transfer Computations. These calculations were so detailed they could manipulate physical objects. The TARDIS itself was a form of mathematical construct, and the right calculations could fix the broken Chameleon Circuit.

Unfortunately, they had not materialised over a normal police box. The Master lured them into a trap by disguising his own TARDIS as a police box to draw the Doctor closer. The control room wrapped around itself creating layers of copies inside copies. The Doctor and Adric travelled through these layers hoping to find an end. Meanwhile, the Master moved his TARDIS deeper inside the Doctor's.

Unable to fix the car, Tegan decided to use the nearby police box to make a call and blundered into the TARDIS. She got hopelessly lost inside. The Doctor and Adric escaped the nested loop to find themselves outside the TARDIS. They were nearly arrested by a police detective who had found the body of Aunt Vanessa, who the Master killed her with his Tissue Compression Eliminator.

Returning to the TARDIS, the Doctor decided to flush the Master out of his ship by landing underwater and opening the doors. Instead he managed to land on a pier, but once more saw the white-clad Watcher beckoning him over. When he returned to Adric he would only say he has 'dipped into the future'.

The Doctor set off for Logopolis, just as Tegan found her way back to the control room, much to the Doctor and Adric's surprise. When they arrived on Logopolis they were welcomed by the Monitor, and found Nyssa of Traken there too, who the Watcher had brought her to Logopolis. The Logopolitans began working on calculations for the Doctor's TARDIS, but the Master had followed them here too. He quietly assassinated some of the lone

Logopolitans to disrupt their calculations, so when the Doctor input the data into his TARDIS, it instead shrank to a fraction of its size, trapping the Doctor inside.

The TARDIS was taken to the Central Register, an incongruous building modelled on the Pharos Project radio antenna on Earth. Adric and the Monitor investigated the mistakes in the equations and discovered the murdered Logopolitans. The Monitor was deeply concerned this may have wider implications, but they managed to recalculate the equations and restored the TARDIS.

While the Doctor took stock of the situation, the Master snuck into the Central Registry and killed more Logopolitans, placing sonic dampers to silence their spoken calculations. When Nyssa noticed the planet has fallen silent the Master revealed he was now in control of Logopolis. He would only allow the calculations to continue if the Monitor reveals the 'secret of Logopolis'. This secret turned out to be that the universe was already worn out.

The spoken calculations of Logopolis had been responsible for holding open the Charged Vacuum Emboitements or CVEs that led into E-Space and other universes. These CVEs drained away the natural entropy that would have destroyed the universe centuries ago. By silencing Logopolis the Master had doomed the universe. Logopolis itself began to fall apart as entropy engulfed it and its people turned to dust.

The Doctor and the Master were forced into an alliance to save the universe. The Monitor told them they had been working on a plan to stabilise the CVEs, but it was incomplete. However, if the calculations were broadcast using the radio array

of the Central Registry, then they might be able to stabilise one of the CVEs. Unfortunately, the antenna and the Monitor were crumbling and the Doctor and Master had to leave. All was not lost though, as the real Pharos Project on Earth might be able to broadcast the signal with the help of some Time Lord jiggery pokery.

Sneaking into the control room of the Pharos Project, the Doctor and Master adapted the systems to broadcast the equations. However, they needed to align the radio antenna, which was guarded. Tegan, Nyssa and Adric distracted the guards so the Time Lords could get to the antenna control. The Master got there ahead of the Doctor, and configured the equipment for the broadcast. When the Doctor arrived they broadcast the equations and stabilised the CVE.

The Master always had a plan. He rigged the equipment to allow him to close the CVE with similar equations. He then sent a message to the universe, demanding that everyone everywhere to bow down before him or he would destroy them all. The Doctor attempted to disconnect the cable that would allow the Master to close the CVE and they fought on the gantry of the antenna.

The Doctor managed to pull out the cable, but as he did so he fell to the ground far below. With security guards about to arrive the Master fled. While his plan had been foiled he had at least seen the end of the Doctor.

Nyssa, Tegan and Adric gathered round the dying form of the Doctor, but all was not lost. The moment had been prepared for. The Watcher was to be a shadow of the Doctor's future and they merged to allow him to regenerate into a new incarnation.

CONTINUITY

This is the last adventure of the Fourth Doctor, and the first for Tegan. We are also reintroduced to Nyssa who joins the Doctor on his travels as well. The Doctor regenerates into his fifth incarnation with the help of the Watcher a future version of himself (see pg.186 of the **The Time Traveller's Companion**)

In this adventure we learn a lot about the TARDIS. The Doctor tells Adric about the Cloister Bell, and that it sounds at times of great disaster. We see a new room in the TARDIS, the Cloister, where the Doctor likes to pace while he's thinking. The Cloister is akin to a gazebo, and even has plants growing among the columns and benches. The Doctor also shows Adric how the Chameleon Circuit works, revealing a new control panel that rises out of the console. In other adventures the Chameleon Circuit appears to work automatically, so we can infer from this a functional system automatically disguises the TARDIS but might be overridden by the operator. There is also another new system, the Architectural Configuration Circuit, which the Doctor uses to eject Romana's old room.

The Master is kind enough to demonstrate what happens when a TARDIS materialises over another TARDIS. However, this isn't the first time this has happened (see **The Time Monster** in **The Third Doctor Sourcebook**). Before the Doctor has ensured both TARDISes are trapped together in a stalemate, but this time he is caught off guard. The Master is able to create a gravity bubble inside the TARDIS that creates a potentially infinite loop of layers of interiors. The Doctor and Adric have to find their way to the end of the layers while the Master's TARDIS is free to roam around inside the Doctor's. The extra 'weight' of the gravity bubble prevents the Doctor's TARDIS taking off, and it is only when he ejects Romana's old room that the Doctor and Adric free to escape.

The Doctor is in contact with Traken, possibly through the Keeper, and he receives a message telling him Tremas has vanished. Unfortunately, this connection doesn't last long as Traken is destroyed by the encroaching entropy, along with many other planets. The Watcher takes Adric and Nyssa outside time and space to protect them from the entropy. This void outside existence seems a lot easier to enter and leave than E-Space or a CVE (see **Warriors' Gate**) and appears to be nothing more than a black emptiness. The Doctor also introduces Block Transfer Computations (BTCs), a higher form of mathematics enabling adepts to create physical objects. This ability to remould reality with pure mathematics is extraordinarily powerful, so no wonder the Master seeks its secrets. BTCs can only be calculated with a living mind, as a computer would be changed by the process. The Logopolitans use a language of maths to input these complicated equations in a more condensed form. Interestingly this ability to use a language to manipulate reality is very similar to the Carrionite's power to use language as magic (see the Tenth Doctor's adventure **The Shakespeare Code**, while the Krillitane plot in **School Reunion** to crack the Skasis Paradigm likely involved Block Transfer. They needed living minds for that, too).

The Doctor mentions that he and the Master, being Time Lords, "in many ways have the same mind".

We might also wonder what the Time Lords are doing during this time of universal Armageddon. It is possible they don't know about Logopolis, but it is more likely they are responsible for the idea in the first place. Given their stance of non-intervention and somewhat selfish attitude it is possible they decided there was nothing to be done to stop the entropy, and moved Gallifrey itself outside time and space so they could watch from a distance.

⊘ RUNNING THE ADVENTURE

This can be a tricky adventure to run because despite revelations about the structure of the universe and its very existence caught in the balance there isn't much of an actual adventure going on. Essentially, the Master hitches a lift to get to Logopolis. There he tries to hold the place to ransom and accidentally screws up the safeguards protecting the universe from entropy. So he helps the Doctor fix things. This adventure is actually a heist caper by the Master that goes badly wrong, if anything, he is the player character rather than the Doctor!

So this adventure runs best as a climactic middle part of a continuing battle against a recurring enemy. This villain can be fought in the previous adventure; where unknown to the player characters he somehow survives and hides aboard their TARDIS. The player characters are then drawn to an important secret that their enemy tries to take control of. If they defeat him a second time he attempts a more personal revenge in the final part, as the Master does in the Fifth Doctor's adventure **Castrovalva**.

Logopolis might also work well as the final encounter of a long quest. In a sense, the plot of Logopolis began when the TARDIS falls through a

USING BLOCK TRANSFER COMPUTATIONS

Making a BTC calculation requires immensely lengthy and difficult calculations that can only be done by a living mind. The Difficulty for the Ingenuity + Science roll is at least 24, even if you're just trying to mathematically describe a spherical cow or something equally simple. Doing something more complicated, like conjuring a duplicate of an individual or making a whole city from nothing (as in **Castrovalva**) increases the Difficulty to 27 or more. Only a character with a Science score of at least 4 who has great expertise in mathematics can even attempt a BTC. Getting a really, really good result on the roll can reduce the Story Point cost – a Fantastic Success reduces the number of points needed by 50%. In addition to the calculation, the character needs to spend Story Points to 'fuel' the computation. Also he'll need a transmitter of some kind (like a radio telescope or a Hadron Web) if the computation is going to manifest beyond the character's immediate vicinity.

The Story Point cost depends on the size *and* complexity of the computation, but as a guideline:

1-3 points: A small, simple object like a spanner.
4-6 points: A large simple object, like a small building, or a small complex object like a Gadget.
7-9 points: A living being.

The Story Point cost can be paid over time, representing the character working on the set of calculations in advance, or paid by an external

'battery' of Story Points like a suitable gadget. For example, the Master was able to use Adric to create a whole false city in **Castrovalva** – that would have cost at least 50 Story Points, paid for by draining Adric, the Story Points from the Hadron Web, and the Master's own supply.

The conjured objects last for as long as the calculation is maintained. A character can maintain multiple BTCs at once, but each one increases the Difficulty for future BTCs by +3. For example, the Monitor uses Block Transfer Computation to conjure a cute kitten. This kitten lasts as long as he continues calculating the mathematical phase-space of the kitten, but it does increase the Difficulty of his BTC calculation to save the universe from total collapse by +3. On the bright side, it is a very cute kitten.

CVE into E-Space. The Doctor is more interested in escaping E-Space, but if instead he started investigating the nature and purpose of the CVEs he would also have been led to Logopolis by another route. The important thing here is that Logopolis holds an important secret, and dark forces in the universe want to know and control it. The player characters might even be sent to search out the place by the White Guardian, given how important it is to the universe.

Whatever you decide the secret of Logopolis to be, it should be big. Big enough that when the player characters' old enemy destabilises it they must make an alliance to save the universe. This is why you need to have a villain the player characters have fought several times before, someone they know and have dedicated themselves to defeating. This will turn the alliance into not just an offer of help but a dangerous game of cat and mouse. The player characters know their enemy will eventually betray them, but when and how?

LOGOPOLIS

The planet of Logopolis is located in a quiet backwater of the galaxy. Given it is populated by old men and women it is more like a monastery than a civilisation. The ascetics of Logopolis spend their lives in quiet contemplation of mathematical issues. It is a peaceful place, apart from the low murmur of muttered equations and the clattering of abacuses.

As the Master needs to hide in the Doctor's TARDIS, we can assume the Logopolitans are not without defences. Visitors need permission to land, but are made welcome by the Monitor, who leads the community. There are few visitors though as Logopolis is a dry desolate world, with little but sandy streets and arid landscape to distract the inhabitants from their studies.

KEY LOCATIONS ON LOGOPOLIS

- **The Streets:** The main living area of Logopolis is divided into a series of narrow streets cut into the sandstone that might resemble the outside of a brain from above. Each inhabitant has a small nook where they live and work, which are all arranged in lines along the edges of the streets.

- **The Central Registry:** The most incongruous landmark on Logopolis if the Central Registry, as it is modelled on the Pharos Project, an Earth installation that seeks signs of intelligent life. The great antenna dish dominates the streets. Inside the Central Registry are banks of late 20th century computers. In corridors behind the main control room, rows of Logopolitans sit at benches working on more equations.

LOGOPOLITANS

The people of Logopolis are a very dedicated group. They spend their days lost in their calculations; to the point they have very little idea what is going on around them. Violence and aggression are utterly unknown to them. As they will not resist any use of force, and rarely speak to anyone, their statistics are unimportant. Each is a willing cog in a mathematical machine that to an outsider (such as Tegan) might look like a sweatshop. In truth, their minds are travelling whole universes of numbers.

While Block Transfer Computation is immensely – indeed, infinitely – powerful, it's also limited. You need a mathematical mind equal to that of a Time Lord to even read the equations, they take time to calculate and the slightest error can have unexpected repercussions. It's not magic and it's not easy.

Still, with knowledge of BTC equations and time to prepare *and* a really good Ingenuity + Science roll *and* spending the appropriate number of Story Points, you can work wonders.

FURTHER ADVENTURES

- **Servant of Entropy:** Someone has broken into the Pharos Project and stolen several computer parts, the same ones that held the Logopolitan equations. From a secret base the villain plans to hold the universe to ransom, threatening to use the equations to close the only remaining CVE. Can the player characters find him and stop him?

- **Logopolis Reborn:** Several prominent mathematicians have vanished. They have actually been kidnapped in a plan to rebuild a new Logopolis. This new version will be a 'sweat shop' where the inmates are forced to rewrite reality one equation at a time. But there may be a larger plan at work. The villain in question seeks to use Logopolitan equations to break into the Time War, perhaps to rescue or destroy the Time Lords, or even just to steal their secrets?

- **The Broken Equation:** There is something very wrong with the universe; the essential equations that hold reality together are actually flawed. This bad calculation is creating a cascade failure in the universe itself, possibly manifesting as a crack across time and space. The problem is, with the Time Lords and Logopolitans gone, there is no one who knows how to fix the problem. Is there a universal mathematician, and how can he be found? Perhaps someone out there still understands Block Transfer Computations, but has hidden for years as too many villains seek the power for themselves.

- **The E-Space Invasion:** A new threat is using the remaining CVE to invade N-Space. Normally the best plan would be to destroy the portal to their universe, but if that happens N-Space will be doomed to destruction by entropy. Can the player characters form an alliance large enough to fight off the invaders? Maybe the invaders are only attacking as entropy is destroying their universe, making N- Space the aggressor...

THE MONITOR

AWARENESS	3	PRESENCE	3
COORDINATION	2	RESOLVE	4
INGENUITY	7	STRENGTH	2

The leader of the Logopolis community is referred to only as the Monitor. His job is to manage the mathematical workload rather than rule. As equations are recited, he monitors the results to make sure everything is working properly. Even with only one person checking the calculations, the Logopolitans pride themselves on never making a mistake. The Monitor is a very personable man, happy to converse with visitors and eager to welcome people to his world that he can share his love of mathematics with someone new.

SKILLS

Convince 2, Knowledge 4, Science 5 (Speciality: Mathematics), Technology 3

TRAITS

Block Transfer Specialist (Major): +3 to any Mathematics roll and +1 to all Jiggery Pokery rolls.
Charming: +2 bonus to attempts to use charm.
Code of Conduct (Major): Follows a strict code of peace and logic.
Feel the Turn of the Universe: +2 bonus to Awareness and Ingenuity to detect something wrong with time or space.
Obligation (Major): Protect the secrets of Logopolis.
Unadventurous (Major): Character avoids adventure and excitement.

TECH LEVEL: 8   STORY POINTS: 8

APPENDIX

SHADA

"Well Mr Skagra, or whatever it is you call yourself, you killed a Time Lord, and a very old friend of mine. It's time you and I had a little chat."

DESIGNER'S NOTE

Shada is one of the great unaired masterpieces of Doctor Who, due to be the climax of the 17th series but left unfinished following industrial action. It was intended to follow on from **The Horns of Nimon** and out of a sense of completeness, we've presented the adventure here in the appendix.

SYNOPSIS

Cambridge, England, 1979

The Doctor took Romana to Cambridge, introducing her to an old friend, Professor Chronotis. However, it is not just a casual visit; the Professor is actually a retired Time Lord and has called for the Doctor's help. When he left Gallifrey he took away an important and dangerous book called 'The Ancient and Worshipful Law of Gallifrey'. The book is one of the artefacts from the age of Rassilon so he wants the Doctor to return it to Gallifrey. There is only one problem: he can't find it.

The Doctor is not the only one looking for the book. A scientist called Skagra has come to Earth seeking it too. The book is actually in the hands of a student called Chris Parsons. The Professor remembered who might have the book and the Doctor set off to collect it. Chronotis is visited by Skagra, who used a silver sphere to drain the Professor's mind. When Romana found him he gave her a message before he died: "Beware Skagra, Beware the Sphere, Beware Shada".

The Doctor collected the book, but when Skagra sent the sphere after him he dropped it. Skagra collected the book and returned to his ship. K-9 found a way to track the sphere, which led the Doctor, Chris and Romana to the ship. Skagra captured them, holding Chris and Romana hostage to force the Doctor to reveal the secrets of the book. The Doctor refused and his mind was drained by the sphere. Skagra discovered turning the book's pages could take him to the place he seeks: Shada, the prison of the Time Lords.

Clare went to the Professor's rooms but found everyone gone. Looking for clues she found a strange console. The whole room dematerialised and took her outside time and space. The Professor appeared, brought back by an odd temporal anomaly. He told Clare the room was actually an old TARDIS he stole, and that they must stop Skagra finding Shada.

The Doctor recovered, having ensured the sphere took a copy of his mind rather than stealing it. With Skagra gone in his TARDIS, the Doctor took control of the ship and set off to Skagra's most recent destination. The trail led them to the Institute for Advanced Scientific Studies (IASS), a derelict space station populated by brainless old men. The Doctor managed to restore one of the old men enough to discover they were all eminent scientists conned into joining Skagra, but he tricked them and stole their minds. The old scientist told the Doctor that only one piece of Skagra's plan remains: he needs to find the old Time Lord criminal Salyavin, who is imprisoned on Shada.

Using the book and the Doctor's TARDIS, Skagra arrived at Shada with Romana. He located Salyavin's cell but it was empty. The Doctor arrived, as did the Professor and Clare. The Professor revealed that he was Salyavin, imprisoned by the Time Lords for his ability to project his mind into others. This was why Skagra wanted to find him; he wished to steal Salyavin's mind and power, which would allow him to use the sphere to both steal minds and project his own mind into others. He wanted to create a universal hive mind with himself at the centre. Skagra didn't want to just control the universe; he wants to *become* the universe.

Skagra used the sphere on the Professor, but K-9 blasted it. Unfortunately the sphere broke into smaller spheres, each one latching onto someone and stealing their mind. Romana reminded the Doctor that a copy of his mind was still in the sphere, which allows the Doctor to mentally challenge Skagra for control of the gestalt. Skagra was imprisoned in his own ship and the Doctor returned the stolen minds

to their rightful owners. The Doctor, Romana, Chris, Clare and the Professor then return to Cambridge for a well-earned cup of tea.

CONTINUITY

Shada is an ancient Time Lord prison. The inhabitants might be some of the worst renegades in Time Lord history, who might easily become great allies or terrible enemies of the characters.

The Professor began his retirement 300 years ago. Retired Time Lords are not allowed to own a TARDIS. The Doctor earned an honorary degree from Cambridge in 1960.

Romana finds a Gallifreyan children's book that she once read as a 'Time Tot' that teaches how Rassilon laid down five great principles. She and the Doctor are also reminded of the Time Lord oath: "I swear to protect the ancient law of Gallifrey with all my might and brain. I will to the end of my days, with justice and with honour temper my actions and my thoughts".

The Professor is old enough that he remembers Type 40 TARDISes coming out when he was a boy. He also knows they were designed with the kitchen very far away from the control room.

Despite being on his last regeneration, the Professor is brought back to life by Clare taking his TARDIS into the Vortex by accident. While the Professor doesn't explain why ("think of me as a paradox within an anomaly, and get on with your tea") it offers another potential way that a Time Lord can cheat death.

⊘ RUNNING THE ADVENTURE

Instead of being about old enemies, this adventure is about old friends. Almost any adventure might come from meeting up with an old retired Time Lord.

When running the adventure, the Gamemaster should decide what has actually happened to Salyavin. Perhaps Professor Chronotis isn't Salyavin after all; instead, any of the NPCs might be Salyavin in disguise, perhaps even one of the characters. Perhaps even the Doctor!

CAMBRIDGE

Cambridge is best known as a university city, with a collection of renowned colleges making up its university, and remains in constant rivalry with Oxford as England's most prestigious academic centre. The pace of the town reflects the academic atmosphere: slow and peaceful, but dedicated. Many of the buildings in Cambridge date from hundreds of years ago, the original settlement being founded in 1209. It is said the founders were breakaway scholars from Oxford who left after a dispute, a rivalry that continues to this day with the annual boat (rowing) race on the Thames in London.

KEY LOCATIONS IN CAMBRIDGE

- **St Cedd's College:** One of the smaller colleges, far less famous than Kings College or Trinity College. St Cedd's is a quiet place with an old faculty that is happy to admit visitors as long as they are polite to the porter. The gatehouse leads into a small central garden courtyard that the buildings of the college are arranged around in an idyllic maze of colonnades and paths.

THE INSTITUTE FOR ADVANCED SCIENTIFIC STUDIES (IASS)

This space station was to be a marvel of scientific endeavour, but was in fact nothing more than a trap. The idea was to use technology to join the minds of several eminent scientists, allowing them to become greater than the sum of their parts. Doctor Skagra created the project, and only offered places to the most renowned experts in their fields. In reality, the IASS was designed to steal minds, delivering the genius of the scientists to Skagra himself. When he had what he wanted, Skagra left the station and the scientists to rot there.

SHADA

The prison of the Time Lords is a large complex built on a small planetoid in deep space. No maps point the way to Shada and it actively cloaks itself to prevent anyone coming across it by accident. It is even possible the place exists slightly outside time and space to make it even more secure. The only way to find Shada is by already knowing where it is, or using a Gallifreyan artefact to take you there.

Access to the complex is by a docking area that leads to a records room. This room details where each prisoner is being held, by 'cabinet' and 'chamber'. The rest of the complex holds prisoners, racked up in suspended animation. These prisoners are those who have crossed the Time Lords, not necessarily criminals. While it is a prison, the purpose of Shada is not to reform or punish. Instead it is a facility designed to remove dangerous elements from time and space.

THE WORSHIPFUL AND ANCIENT LAW OF GALLIFREY

In this adventure the book is only important for what it might lead to, as this red book is the key to finding Shada. However, it is a powerful artefact in its own right. Physically it has some amazing properties. It absorbs radiation, has no discernible atomic structure and refuses to be spectrographically analysed. It is also impervious to damage and even time 'runs backwards over it'. Written in ancient

Gallifreyan it can control a TARDIS just by turning the pages. As the 'law' of Gallifrey it might hold greater power over the laws of time and space. But it might also be the 'lore' of Gallifrey and contain detailed secrets of the Time Lord's history, perhaps even a way to break them out of the Time War.

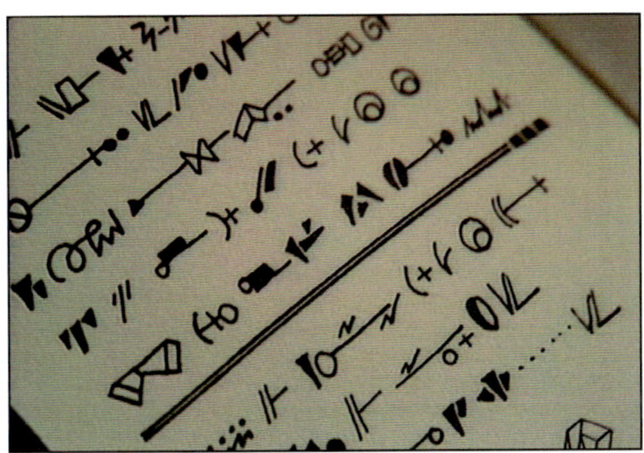

FURTHER ADVENTURES

- **Cambridge Retirement:** What if Chronotis is not the only Time Lord hiding out in academia. Perhaps Cambridge and Oxford are full of eccentric immortals. What secrets might they be keeping, and who might be seeking those secrets? Perhaps the rivalry between Oxford and Cambridge is more than it seems. Ancient foes might be waging a secret battle over the stewardship of the most powerful secrets in the universe.

- **The Accused:** The player characters are arrested and tried for crimes against the Time Lords, and sentenced to Shada. Are they actually innocent, in which case how can they prove it? Is it a simple miscarriage of justice or is someone out to get them? Their biggest problem is how to survive life in Shada among the worst criminals of the universe.

DOCTOR SKAGRA

Skagra is one of the most brilliant minds of his generation, but unfortunately he knows it. His monumental arrogance is not entirely displaced though, as he is a renowned authority in several fields of academic expertise, including science, technology and philosophy. He treats everyone around him as if they were ants, insignificant and unworthy of his genius. Skagra's plan is to possess every mind in the universe with his own. Once his great hive mind is complete the universe will think as he does and be better for it.

AWARENESS	3	PRESENCE	3
COORDINATION	3	RESOLVE	5
INGENUITY	7	STRENGTH	3

SKILLS
Athletics 3, Convince 2, Craft 4, Fighting 2, Knowledge 4, Marksman 2, Medicine 4, Science 5, Subterfuge 3, Survival 2, Technology 5, Transport 3

TRAITS
Arrogant (Minor Good): -2 to Fear rolls, -1 to social rolls with inferiors.
Indomitable (Major Good): +4 bonus to any rolls to resist psychic control.
Quick Reflexes (Minor Good): Skagra always goes first in his Action Round unless taken by surprise.
Technically Adept (Minor Good): +2 to any Technology roll to fix a broken or faulty device.
Voice of Authority (Minor Good Trait): +2 bonus to Presence and Convince rolls.

Distinctive (Minor Bad): -2 penalty to rolls to blend in. Others have a +2 bonus to remember or recognise Skagra.
Obsession (Major Bad): Control the universe.
Selfish (Minor Bad): Skagra puts his own needs first.
Silver Spoon (Minor Bad): -2 penalty to low-class interactions.

EQUIPMENT: Sphere (see page 253), Invisible Ship (Cloak – Major)

TECH LEVEL: 7   **STORY POINTS:** 12

PROFESSOR CHRONOTIS

While he appears to be an elderly retired Time Lord reaching the end of his last regeneration Chronotis is actually one of the most renowned criminals of Gallifrey. In his younger days he was Salyavin, a Time Lord with the ability to project his mind into others. As a boy, the Doctor was something of a fan of Salyavin's exploits, although by that time he was a figure of history and myth.

When he was caught, Salyavin was incarcerated in Shada in perpetuity. However he managed to escape from the facility. Older and wiser he decided to leave his life of crime behind him and retire settling in Cambridge to catch up on his reading.

AWARENESS	2	PRESENCE	4
COORDINATION	2	RESOLVE	4
INGENUITY	8	STRENGTH	2

SKILLS

Athletics 2, Convince 4, Craft 3, Fighting 2, Knowledge 7, Marksman 2, Medicine 4, Science 5, Subterfuge 4, Survival 2, Technology 5, Transport 3

TRAITS

Boffin (Major Good): Allows Chronotis to create Gadgets.
Charming (Minor Good): +2 bonus to attempts to use charm.
Face in the Crowd (Minor Good): +2 to any Subterfuge Skill roll to sneak about.
Feel the Turn of the Universe (Special Good): +2 bonus to Awareness and Ingenuity to detect something wrong with time or space.
Hypnosis (Minor Good): +2 bonus to control another's emotional state.
Possess (Special Good): Chronotis may attempt possession with a +4 bonus (see p57 Gamemaster's Guide)*.
Psychic (Special Good): +4 against mental attacks and he may attempt to read minds.
Time Lord, Experienced (Special Good)

Time Traveller (Major Good): Familiar with all tech levels.
Vortex (Special Good): Chronotis may pilot time craft through the Vortex, and gains +2 when doing so.
Code of Conduct (Minor Bad): Having put his criminal past behind him, Chronotis finds it hard to do bad.
Dark Secret (Major Bad): Actually the Time Lord criminal Salyavin.
Eccentric (Minor Bad): Chronotis is terribly absent minded.
Forgetful (Minor Bad): -2 penalty to any Ingenuity and Resolve roll to remember something vital.
Wanted Renegade (Special Bad): Salyavin is an escaped criminal from the Time Lords' most secure prison.

REGENERATIONS USED: 12

TECH LEVEL: 10   STORY POINTS: 12

*On a successful possession Chronotis can give the target the same level of skill as he has in any area. The target can choose to allow the possession, in which case no roll is required.

SKAGRA'S SPHERE

The sphere Skagra uses is able to steal the minds of those it touches. Once the floating device makes contact with a victim's forehead they are paralysed and forced to engage in a mental battle to keep their mind intact.

The minds stored in the sphere can be viewed with technology on Skagra's ship. However, Skagra himself can use his own connection to the sphere to control those who have lost their minds to it.

TRAITS

Control (Major): The sphere can control those whose minds have been stolen.

Resilient (Major): If it suffers lethal damage it breaks into several smaller spheres, each with the same power. Otherwise energy weapons have no effect.

Robot

Propulsion (Major): The sphere can float and act with a Coordination of 4. It has a Fighting skill of 3 for the purposes of attempting to dodge its attack.

Steal Mind: The sphere can steal the mind of any intelligent being if it manages to touch their forehead. The target is allowed an Ingenuity + Resolve test but at a Difficulty of 30. Success allows the target to give the sphere a copy of their mind rather than be left mindless.

KRARGS

AWARENESS	3	PRESENCE	2
COORDINATION	3	RESOLVE	3
INGENUITY	2	STRENGTH	6

The Krargs are a servitor race, designed by Skagra as crew for his command ship. They are intelligent beings but utterly loyal to their commander. Krargs are around six feet tall and made of molten minerals. This makes them immune to most energy and able to burn with a touch.

Krargs are made rather than bred, Skagra having constructed vats that can create a new Krarg in a matter of seconds. Krargs are adept at using most technology and make competent pilots and crew as well as guards and soldiers. Some are armed with close range electroshock devices, although their physical abilities are quite formidable.

SKILLS

Athletics 2, Fighting 3, Knowledge 2, Marksman 2, Subterfuge 2, Technology 3, Transport 3

TRAITS

Alien (Special Good)

Armour (Major Good): Reduce damage by 10 due to the Krarg's stone-like form.

Environmental (Minor Good): Krargs suffer no ill effects from extreme heat.

Immunity (Major Good): Krargs take no damage from energy weapons, although they might hold them at bay.

Natural Weapons (Minor Good): Powerful burning fists that do Strength +2 damage and ignite inflammable substances on contact.

Alien Appearance (Major Bad)

Obligation (Major Bad): Obey Skagra.

Slow Reflexes (Minor Bad): Krargs always acts last in their Action Phase.

EQUIPMENT: Electroprod (4/4/8)

TECH LEVEL: 6   STORY POINTS: 6

INDEX